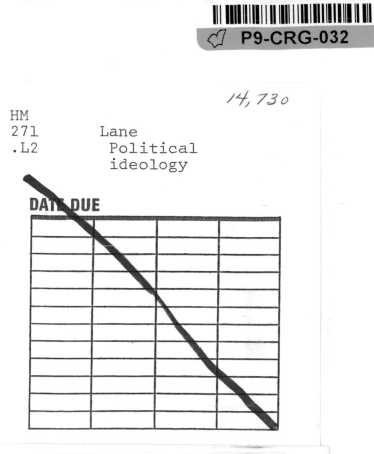

Political Ideology

ROBERT E. LANE

Political Ideology

Why the American Common Man
Believes What He Does

THE FREE PRESS, *New York*
COLLIER-MACMILLAN LIMITED, *London*

Library of Congress Catalog Card Number: 62-15344

FIRST FREE PRESS PAPERBACK EDITION 1967

printing number
4   5   6   7   8   9   10

To *Larry* and *Tommy*

Acknowledgments

But for the willingness of fifteen men to talk freely and frankly about their beliefs and themselves, there would be no book. I am grateful to them and wish them well. I am also grateful to two friends, James D. Barber and Fred I. Greenstein, for their insightful and constructive comments on a draft of the manuscript. As a consequence of their remarks, I have revised some chapters and regrouped others, discovering in the process a way of giving the work a unity it would not otherwise have achieved. In addition, Mr. Barber conducted a separate study of political discussion with six of these fifteen men, a study that shed light upon their behavior in the absence of an interviewer and upon their modes of adjusting to one another. David Sears helped to devise and to score the objective tests and gave counsel on some early drafts of two of the chapters. The burden of transcribing the tapes fell upon Mrs. Claire N. Julianelle, a wonderfully sensitive and accurate person. Mrs. Elizabeth D. MacIntosh gave excellent editorial and secretarial assistance.

About nine years ago I studied the strategy and tactics of psychotherapy with John Dollard; under his supervision I learned and practiced the art of "listening with the third ear" as I tried to help a patient survive the misfortunes that then encumbered his life. Mr. Dollard's counsel and ideas at that time gave impetus to the project here reported.

I want to say something about foundation help. I have received financial assistance from the Social Science Research Council, the Ford Foundation Behavioral Sciences Division, the Center for Advanced Study in the Behavioral Sciences, and the Carnegie Foundation. If this book has merit, it is because I had the time to give to it that the money from these sources bought for me. More than that, because the money has been given in a spirit of trust, it has not been confining; rather it has permitted me to take time for a larger view of my subject, to follow leads unthought of at the moment of conception, to rethink this project and a related one now only emerging from this one. Foundation funds give scholars freedom, a freedom in which I am grateful to have shared.

The questions employed in the interviews were not all original with me. I borrowed some from the Survey Research Center, others from M. Brewster Smith, and still others from David Riesman. These questions greatly improved certain portions of the discussion.

The *American Political Science Review* has kindly granted permission to reprint the material in Chapter 4. *The American Sociological Review* has similarly granted permission to reprint material in Chapter 17. Most of the substance of these two chapters first appeared as articles in these journals.

As always, my dear wife, Helen, has helped with ideas, with her proofreader's skills, with patience toward a preoccupied husband.

ROBERT E. LANE

Contents

PART THREE *The Political Consequences of an Ideology*

Political Ideology

INTRODUCTION

Exploring the Political Mind

If we are to talk about the human mind, let us start with human beings. Rapuano is a big, somewhat clumsy man with a worried look that breaks into fleeting smile and a somewhat high-pitched laugh when he finds something funny in the otherwise seriously burdensome business of life. He is a checker in a meat-and-provision company, and worries after hours about the records he keeps and the high rate of spoilage in his trade. One of seven children of an immigrant and illiterate street cleaner, he has shaped his life to fit the requirements of success in working-class America. Rapuano is the head of a small household; at forty he earns slightly more than his neighbors, his wife does not have to work, and he can afford to send his three girls to parochial school. He does not drink; he keeps out of trouble with the law; he has never been on relief; he is a veteran and a patriot; indeed, no one could be more patriotic than Rapuano.

As we settled down for an evening's talk, I asked him about the main problems facing America today. He said: "Well, it seems to me that the major problem is defense, right now, and, well, I wouldn't mind paying extra taxes to accomplish this missile program and get it going as fast as possible. I mean, the few dollars

here or there doesn't matter to me. I think if they would increase
the taxes a bit, I think that people like me would agree to it. And
I don't mind paying, you know, a few more dollars just to—to safe-
guard my life, and my children's way of life more so, because, as
I said before—two dollars or three dollars or four or five dollars
—whatever it means—doesn't mean as much as my girl's life, see.
I've lived my life. . . ."

Johnson, at age thirty-seven, is developing that little bulge
just below the navel, so that one is uncertain whether he should
wear his belt above it or below it—mostly it slips below. He is not
fat; he is vigorous, full of energy and enthusiasm, friendly, a man
such as might be found with his foot on a brass rail in a thousand
bars throughout the nation. Of Danish-American descent, he
works as a mechanic in a large utility plant, supplementing this
with a little private repair work when he can find it. Father of a
family of three boys and a girl, for whom he has great affection
and pride and a steady flow of advice based upon his own worldly
experiences, he professes a cynicism about man's eternal search for
"a fast buck" that largely reflects his own anxious wish to have
more money—money needed to keep up with his spendthrift
nature.

About a week after I first talked to Rapuano, I asked Johnson
what _he_ thought were the major problems facing America today.
Eager to please, and a little nervous, he said: "Well, I think a race
problem—more so—is coming up more so. . . . I think—I think
that's a serious [problem], and will be quite serious as time goes
on, I believe. Myself, if you want my opinion of it . . . ["Yes, I do."]
I have nothing against the colored race. . . . For instance, this
project I live in—I'll bring it out as an example. I mean the—I
don't feel I'm any better than the colored man, but I still don't—
I feel he's colored, and I'm the white race. I don't believe that they
should—for instance, one thing—put them in the same building
to live together. I don't believe that's right. But [pause] and I feel
that the majority of them I know—that I've met, being in Eastport—there's quite a few colored people in the Eastport area—
once they start getting into one thing they start getting into others.
And, I don't know, it seems they like to force themselves. I think
that is a serious problem—one of them which could be very serious. I believe it will become very serious, as it is starting to become
all over the country."

Asked what the government should do about it, Johnson is

puzzled and, frowning at his shoes, says: "I really—if I was in a position, I don't think I would know what to do about it, to tell you the truth. I mean, it's a very touchy thing."

About three weeks later, I asked Sokolsky what he thought were the major problems in America today. Sokolsky is short of stature and solidly built, a Jewish factory operative who for fourteen years has been turning out bicycle pedals, and is sick of his job. In February of 1958, the factory had cut back its work force and he was on short time, filling out his truncated income with a janitorial job he loathed even more than the factory job. Worried about a lung infection, speaking quickly but sometimes with a catarrhal cough, jealous of his more successful brother, filled with prurient interests about delinquent girls—but, withal, a lively, likable, and warm man, Sokolsky turned to "America's problems" and, so to speak, found that they were closely related to his own.

"Well, right now," he said, his sharp, expressive face alert and serious, "I think it's jobs. I mean the unemployment, and I think they're going at it in the wrong way—the government. Instead of giving jobs here, they're sending most of them over—the—what do you call it?—foreign aid. I think they're sending too much of the foreign aid over. They're not concentrating on this—on the present. They say things are going to pick up—and Eisenhower said in March, but it's not going to pick up in March. I think it's going to pick up in June. At present I think that's the [problem] —the unemployment."

Three Aspects of Ideology

The material providing the core of evidence for this book is a set of extended conversations with fifteen men like Rapuano, Johnson, and Sokolsky. It is a book about three aspects of political ideology. First, it undertakes to discover the latent political ideology of the American urban common man. Second, it attempts to explain the sources of this ideology in the culture and experiences this common man knows. In doing so, the book develops some ideas about the origins and maintenance of ideologies generally. And, third, it deals (more briefly) with the way in which the American common man's ideology—or any ideology—supports or weakens the institutions of democracy. Although I use this set of interviews with working- and lower-middle-class men as a core of evidence, I often go beyond this material to formulate some modest theoretical constructs to help explain what is happening. In this work of mixed ideas and illustrative evidence, I can suggest but, alas, I cannot prove.

Fifteen Political Authors

The conversations with these fifteen men were recorded and transcribed so as to form fifteen political books, varying in size from one that is 154 pages, "written" by Dempsey, a drill-press operator of limited education and intelligence and small political interest, to one 322 pages long, "written" by Flynn, a railroad supply clerk with a high-school education, unusual intelligence, and a reflective cast of mind. The authors of these autobiographical works were citizens of Eastport, U.S.A., a city of over 100,000 population in the Atlantic seaboard area. Physically it is an old city, with old buildings, rather narrower streets than are built today, yet its center square, its old churches, and outlying parks rimmed by hills and cliffs that seem to contain the city lend it a distinctive charm. While not so much of a depressed area as, say, Providence or Fall River, Eastport has had a standard of wages lower than the national average and a rate of unemployment that, in 1957–1958, was higher than the national average. Ethnically, the population is about a third of Italian extraction, about an eighth of Irish extraction; close to an eighth of the population is Jewish, and about a tenth is Negro, many of whom came to Eastport from the South during World War II to man its defense industries. Old Anglo-Saxon families are few but, of course, socially dominant; their money comes from investments, land, and banking. Many of the major industrial plants are branches of nationally owned and operated firms, but several are locally owned, not by old families, but by migrants of Anglo-Saxon stock and American backgrounds who settled in Eastport two or three generations back. The "newer races," as the Boston Irish say of themselves and other non-Anglo-Saxon groups, while mostly wage earners, are moving into middle-class positions; the Jewish community now established in commerce and the professions, the Irish established in politics and moving into law and business, the Italians tending to concentrate in construction and service trades. In short, Eastport is like dozens of other cities in America, particularly in the East.

Our Eastport "authors" are residents of Hilltop, a government-subsidized "middle-income" housing development of about 240 units in apartment blocks of eight.[1] Without much variety of architecture, Hilltop nevertheless manages to have an attractive suburban look about it, with curving roads, ample parking space, green (or sometimes green) areas between the apartment blocks, and a view of fields and hills edging the community. Its separateness from the rest of the city gives it some of the community spirit that, just perceptibly, supports the morale of the people living there. Down the road, beyond Hilltop and within sight in the winter when the trees are bare, lies Stern Terrace, a public housing project that is looked down upon by the people in Hilltop. According to them, the residents of Stern Terrace, whose income level is markedly lower than their own, lack moral fiber, live loose lives, go on relief when they can, and drink and roister with disturbing frequency. There is, in fact, a relatively higher proportion of individuals on relief and of broken homes in Stern Terrace. The reputation serves to set off the moral, industrious, and conservative lives of Hilltop, including the lives of our fifteen authors.

I selected these fifteen white Hilltop-Eastport men from the list of voters on the basis of a table of random numbers. In return for a modest cash consideration, the first fifteen selected agreed to enter into conversations on "what people are thinking about these days." Some were flattered and eager to participate; many

1. Choosing our men from Hilltop's selected population establishes certain social boundaries for the group. They had to be married, and at the time of admission to the housing development a preference was given to those with children. The family income allowed had certain lower and upper limits, with variations permitted according to the number of children; generally the lower limits were about $4,000, and the upper limits around $6,500. Because there was a waiting list, the management could give weight to the steadiness of a family income in recent years; thus there was a tendency to admit men with a record of stability and industry. Almost all the residents of Hilltop were, as they say in Eastport, "made voters" as soon as the residence laws permitted. (There was, in fact, very little difference between the city-directory lists for the area and the lists of voters.) Yet the fact that we selected our men from the lists of voters left out of account the marginal men who are truly apathetic, withdrawn, sick. Because Hilltop has been operating less than ten years, our sample is younger than would be a similar sample drawn from the general population in Eastport. Because it is a rental development, it tends to attract men on wages and salaries more than small entrepreneurs in the same income bracket but with a stronger penchant for owning their own homes. Because it has a waiting list, the sample has fewer transients than other neighborhoods in Eastport. Because it includes Negroes, the level of interracial tolerance is higher. Yet, I think, these are somewhat marginal considerations. The people of Hilltop absorb the general attitudes of their families living in other sections of the city; there is a constant movement in and out: two of the fifteen moved out of Hilltop during the seven-month period of interviewing. Four years later eight had moved to another neighborhood. Hilltop is an integral part of the city.

were moved primarily by the cash consideration, which they and I both formally treated as irrelevant to our study; two were markedly reluctant, and would agree only after many efforts at persuasion and after it was settled that I would talk to them in their own kitchens and not in my office, where I interviewed the others. These two men, Dempsey, a drill-press operator, and Kuchinsky, a roofer, were sufficiently different from the others so that the policy of not relying on volunteers and of making every effort to include exactly those selected by a randomization process was, I think, amply rewarded.

The characteristics of these fifteen authors are, then, as follows:

1. They are all men, white, married, fathers, urban, Eastern seaboard.

2. The incomes of all but one range from $2,400 (supplemented by wife's wages) to $6,300. (The one man whose income was higher was just moving from the development partly because his income in 1957 had been $10,000.)

3. Ten have working-class (blue-collar) occupations such as roofer, plumber, mechanic, truck driver, machine operator.

4. Five have white-collar occupations such as salesman, bookkeeper, supply clerk.

5. Their ages range from twenty-five to fifty-four; most are in their thirties.

6. Eleven are Catholic (including one former Protestant); two are Protestant (including one whose father was Catholic); two are Jewish.

7. All are native-born; their nationality backgrounds are: six Italian (two with non-Italian mothers); five Irish (one with non-Irish mother); one Polish; one Danish (with Yankee mother); one Russian, one Yankee.

8. Those with foreign nationality backgrounds are divided about equally between those whose parents were immigrants and those whose grandparents were immigrants.

9. All were employed at the time of the interviews, but many were on short time, in one case permitting supplementary payment by unemployment insurance.

10. Their education distribution was: three had only grammar-school education; eight had some high school; two finished high school; one had some (mediocre) college experience; one had completed graduate training.[2]

2. The presence of this "overeducated" man, Farrel, in our sample is, on balance, unfortunate. He was included in line with a complete randomization process on the

11. On Hollingshead's class scale, the group ranked as follows: one II, five III's and nine IV's.[3]

The Conversations

At their convenience, usually in the evening, I drove over to Hilltop, called for the men, who were always ready, and drove with them to a special office I used for these interviews, about seven miles away. There, in quiet professional surroundings, over coffee and, if they wanted, cigars, relaxed and comfortable, we talked about the nature of man and society. The tape recorder, concealed, and used by permission of the men, but with a visible microphone on the table, seemed to impose no obstacle to confidence; nothing was said in the car, for example, that was not said with the tape recorder going. We would talk for perhaps two or three hours and then adjourn for another time. The laconic men seemed to finish what they had to say in four sessions; the talkative men took six or seven. My problem was twofold: to learn about the social ideology of the men, and to learn about the men themselves and their life experiences. In the conversations we were to build a record for future analysis; but part of the record could not be taped but stored only in the memory, and of course part of what happened could not be captured at all.

With an assurance of anonymity in the report to follow from these conversations—an assurance honored by changing names and other inessential details, substituting equivalent occupations for those that might betray a man, and creating some doubt about the exact locale—these men talked freely about the following features of their world. First, because it was easiest, we turned to policy matters dealing with unions, foreign policy, subversion, atomic bombing, big business, and much more. We spoke of the causes and probable future of war and of poverty. Then, on more strictly political topics, we dealt with the men's views of the Democrats and the Republicans, their concept of the way political decisions were made, their feelings about elections. Political leaders were

---

basis of residence and income. In this sense the sample properly includes the underpaid professional—here, an apprentice social worker. His father was a laborer; his home background is similar to that of the other men, but, of course, he has a somewhat different perspective on the world. Since the focus of this study is on the "common man," the upper working class and lower middle class (by occupation), I have tended to give less weight to his views, sometimes employing them, only for purposes of contrast.

3. See August B. Hollingshead, *Elmtown's Youth* (New York: Wiley, 1949), pp. 27–45.

treated in some detail, particularly Franklin D. Roosevelt and
Dwight D. Eisenhower. Group memberships were explored to
ascertain the inner, latent meaning of various identifications and
antipathies. We examined the nature and significance of various
political roles, such as citizen and patriot. Turning to the large
ideological questions that form the core of political theory, we
discussed at some length the meaning of freedom, equality, democracy, and the uses and abuses of government. I sought to find
out the range and meaning of various kinds of participation and
exposure to these men. I tested their political information. And
then, when we were well acquainted, I asked them about themselves, their early years, their families, their careers, the nature
of their work, their health and sexual views and habits, their attitudes toward themselves and their friends.[4] There were some
standardized tests, but the bulk of the information about the men
came from what they said in these discussions—the meanings they
intended to convey and those they intended to conceal. (The
specific topics covered, the main questions asked, the scales developed in the analysis, and the various tests employed are listed
in Appendix A.)

"Listening with the Third Ear"

Theodore Reik calls the sensitive listening of the psychoanalyst searching for materials to reconstruct a half-concealed and
thoroughly distorted story into a reasonable whole—"listening
with the third ear." [5] The ability to see things as the patient sees
them is the basis of the physician's capacity to cure. Drawing upon
his experience in Indian villages, Robert Redfield cautions the
social scientist that he must understand the outlook of the man
he studies, see things as they see them, before he can profitably
employ the apparatus and objectivity of science.[6] In this spirit I

4. I am grateful to David Riesman for certain questions on emotional responses
to the news and on the causes and future of war and poverty, as well as for some
very useful criticisms and suggestions in the earlier stages of the planning of this
study. I used a number of questions from the Survey Research Center 1952 and
1956 electoral studies, as well as some of their standardized scales. M. Brewster Smith
was kind enough to let me have a number of the questions and interview guides
used in *Opinions and Personality* (New York: Wiley, 1956), by Smith, Jerome Bruner,
and Robert White. These dealt largely with life history and "emotion in concrete
situations," and contributed greatly to the biographical portions of my analysis. For
all this, I am most grateful.

5. Theodore Reik, *Listening with the Third Ear: The Inner Experience of a
Psychoanalyst* (New York: Farrar, Straus, 1949).

6. Robert Redfield, *The Little Community* (Chicago: University of Chicago Press,
1956), p. 81.

have sought in these interviews to understand these men as men, to understand the private import of what they say, to penetrate the latent meaning of their remarks, and then to see the social implications of what they have said. In this I am aided by certain features of a clinical, relaxed, conversational situation.[7]

The interviews were *discursive;* the responses of the men rambled, followed their own trains of thought, gave scope to anecdote and argument, moral comment and rationalization. This had several advantages: it offered insight into connotative meanings of words and phrases; it permitted one to follow the course of associative thinking (something relied upon for clinical insights); it illuminated the mechanisms of argument and evasion employed in dealing with sensitive political material. Because we had plenty of time, this was possible within the framework of a set schedule.

The interviews were *dialectical,* that is, conversational. There was opportunity for extended probing, for pushing further into the personal meanings of clichés and conventional phrases, for testing whether or not the first impression gained was the correct one, for reflecting back the sense of what was said to clarify the men's own thinking. More than that, there was opportunity for developing some transference in the sense that the men could be observed in a difficult but close social relationship, often revealing feelings of hostility, inferiority, and sensitivity that shed further light upon their social outlooks.

By the use of a tape recorder the interviews provided a *textual* account of everything said. The choice of words employed, the hesitations between words, the style and language of discourse were all revealed in the transcript. The New Critics have urged us to give a close textual reading to what we seek to analyze. Here this is genuinely possible.

Extended conversational interviews of this character provide an opportunity for *contextual* analysis. An opinion, belief, or attitude is best understood in the context of other opinions, beliefs, and attitudes, for they illuminate its meaning, mark its boundaries, modify and qualify its force. Even more important, by grouping opinions the observer often can discover latent ideo-

7. About four years prior to undertaking these interviews, I associated myself with the Yale Institute of Human Relations, where I had the good fortune to take a course on the strategy and tactics of psychotherapy with John Dollard. Under his guidance, and after studying and observing psychotherapeutic methods, I was assigned a patient for whom I served as therapist for twenty-two sessions. It was this experience and Professor Dollard's tolerant help that launched me upon this study of the political mind and that shaped the character of my conversations with these fifteen men.

logical themes; he can see the structure of thought: premise, inference, application. There is no other satisfactory way to map a
political ideology.

Our interviews were *biographical,* and hence we were able to
relate life experience to social thought, to show how events made
men defensive, bitter, passive, defeated, and how these qualities
were then used to shape a congenial political ideology. By tracing
attitudes back to experience, and by searching for common experiences among these men, we were able to discover something of
the social institutions that lie at the roots of much social thought.
We are able to do so because social institutions channel and
sometimes determine the nature of man's experience.

Not individual experience but group experience, not case his-
tories but social history, not the unique but the common, the
shared, the institutional—these are our objectives. By taking
fifteen men with similar backgrounds we have *socialized* our
material and made it possible to discover how common premises
lead to common ideological patterns, common life experiences
give emphasis to common social themes.

The third ear is a poor tabulator. The fifteen men produced
roughly 3,750 pages of verbatim transcript. This material had to
be sorted, coded, classified, related to the objective tests, sifted
for the latent and the repressed. Where the text of the following
discussion makes an apparently casual judgment about "most"
of the men, or where some inference of a casual nature is easily
put forward, there is likely to be a large number of unreported
tallies of themes and statements to support these views. And for
every theme reported, there are many more discarded after investigation.

The Plan of the Book

In Part One I outline what seem to me to be the most important themes in the ideology of the common man. The first section
deals with certain central ideals in our political culture: freedom,
equality, democracy; the second section extracts from the discussion of a variety of topics the central ideas about the use and
abuse of power in the American society; and the third section
attempts to explicate some more general ideas about man's relationship to government both in this real world and in some imagined utopian society. Of course, this is more expository than

the later sections, but I have tried to search out some of the specific sources of these more or less latent themes as I went along.

Part Two is more technical. The underlying idea here is that an ideology is shaped by the nature of life in a society, by the generalizations made from everyday experience, by the cultural premises, the widely shared personal qualities of the population, and by society's current and historic social conflicts. It is in an effort to discover some of these specific elements of the Eastport culture and experience, and then to relate them to the ideology of the Eastport common man, that these chapters struggle first with description and then with theory.

Finally, in Part Three I search for the implications of both the ideology and its underlying components for the working of a democratic system. This is, of course, not a value-free study; the values are those of a rational, open society governed through democratic institutions.

PART ONE

Ideology in Eastport

The Meanings of Ideology

The science of ideas.
—*Webster's New International Dictionary*, 2nd ed. (1948).

The integrated assertions, theories, and aims constituting a politico-social program, often with an implication of factitious propagandizing; as, Fascism was altered in Germany to fit the Nazi *ideology*.
—*Webster's New International Dictionary*, 2nd ed. (1948).
(additional definition in "New Words" section)

During the Napoleonic Era . . . "ideology" came to mean virtually any belief of a republican or revolutionary sort, that is to say, any belief hostile to Napoleon himself.
—HENRY D. AIKEN, *The Age of Ideology*, pp. 16–17

What [Marx and Engels] . . . call "ideology" includes not only the theory of knowledge and politics, but also metaphysics, ethics, religion, and indeed any "form of consciousness" which expresses the basic attitudes or commitments of a social class.
—HENRY D. AIKEN, *The Age of Ideology*, p. 17

We speak of a *particular* and of a *total* conception of ideology. Under the first we include all those utterances the "falsity" of which is due to an intentional or unintentional, conscious, semiconscious, or unconscious, deluding of one's self or of others, taking place on a psychological level and structurally resembling lies. . . . Since suspicion of falsification is not included in the

total conception of ideology, the use of the term "ideology" in the sociology of knowledge has no moral or denunciatory intent. It points rather to a research interest which leads to the raising of the question when and where social structures come to express themselves in the structure of assertions, and in what sense the former concretely determine the latter.
　　　　—KARL MANNHEIM, *Ideology and Utopia*, pp. 238–239

They [ideologies] are compounds of projective systems, in the interest of which empirical evidence is mobilized, and have therefore the same structure as rationalizations.
　　　　—ABRAM KARDINER and associates, *The Psychological Frontiers of Society*, p. 34

Ideology is the conversion of ideas into social levers. . . . For the ideologue, truth arises in action, and meaning is given to experience by the "transforming moment."
　　　　—DANIEL BELL, *The End of Ideology*, pp. 370–371

Ideology refers to a more or less institutionalized set of beliefs— "the views someone picks up." Belief-disbelief systems contain these too but, in addition, they contain highly personalized pre-ideological beliefs.
　　　　—MILTON ROKEACH and associates, *The Open and Closed Mind*, p. 35

The term ideology is used in this book, in the way that is common in current literature, to stand for an organization of opinions, attitudes, and values—a way of thinking about man and society. We may speak of an individual's total ideology or of his ideology with respect to different areas of social life; politics, economics, religion, minority groups, and so forth. Ideologies have an existence independent of any single individual; and those which exist at a particular time are results of both historical processes and of contemporary social events.
　　　　—T. W. ADORNO and associates, *The Authoritarian Personality*, p. 2

　　　　I have set forth above a number of interpretations of the meaning of "ideology." Even if we limit our interest to political ideology, the range and variety are formidable. I shall use the term "political ideology" to mean a body of concepts with these characteristics:

　　　　1. They deal with the questions: Who will be the rulers? How will the rulers be selected? By what principles will they govern?

　　　　2. They constitute an *argument;* that is, they are intended to persuade and to counter opposing views.

3. They integrally affect some of the major values of life.

4. They embrace a program for the defense or reform or abolition of important social institutions.

5. They are, in part, rationalizations of group interests—but not necessarily the interests of all groups espousing them.

6. They are normative, ethical, moral in tone and content.

7. They are (inevitably) torn from their context in a broader belief system, and share the structural and stylistic properties of that system.

Most ideologies also have these qualities:

1. They are group beliefs that individuals borrow; most people acquire an ideology by identifying (or disidentifying) with a social group.

2. They have a body of sacred documents (constitutions, bills of rights, manifestos, declarations), and heroes (founding fathers, seers and sages, originators and great interpreters).

And all ideologies, like all other beliefs, imply an empirical theory of cause and effect in the world, and a theory of the nature of man.

In some of the current literature, there is a suggestion that ideology is not so important as it once was. This is neatly reflected in two book titles, one, a volume on nineteenth-century philosophy edited by Henry Aiken, called *The Age of Ideology*,[1] the other, a book of essays by Daniel Bell, called *The End of Ideology*.[2] What is implied in this contrast is, first, that analysis is taking the place of ideology (the comparable volume for the twentieth-century philosophers is called *The Age of Analysis*);[3] second, that at midcentury there is a kind of exhaustion of political ideas in the West, and hence, third, that the transformation of broadly conceived political ideas into social action is no longer the center of an exciting struggle. There is some confirmation of this point in what follows. But lest one be deceived by a phrase, there should be no doubt that in Eastport the common man *has* a set of emotionally charged political beliefs, a critique of alternative proposals, and some modest programs of reform. These beliefs embrace central values and institutions; they are rationalizations

1. Henry D. Aiken, *The Age of Ideology: The Nineteenth Century Philosophers* (New York: Mentor, 1956).

2. Daniel Bell, *The End of Ideology: On the Exhaustion of Political Ideas in the Fifties* (New York: The Free Press of Glencoe, 1960).

3. Morton White, *The Age of Analysis: The Twentieth Century Philosophers* (New York: Mentor, 1956).

of interests (sometimes not his own); and they serve as moral justifications for daily acts and beliefs.

Of course, there is a difference between the articulated, differentiated, well-developed political arguments put forward by informed and conscious Marxists or Fascists or liberal democrats on the one hand, and the loosely structured, unreflective statements of the common men of Eastport. In general, of course, what I have to say has to do with the ideologies of just such common men; but occasionally it is useful to distinguish between these two varieties. In those few cases I distinguish between the "forensic" ideologies of the conscious ideologist and the "latent" ideologies of the common man.

In what follows I shall first deal with the political ideals of the Eastport common man, then with his interpretation of the nature and location of social power, and finally with his views on the more general relationship of a man to his government. In this discussion I intertwine the discussion of social outlook and social character, since they often seem uniquely closely linked.

□ □ □ □ □ □ □ □ □ □ □ □ □ □ □

Political Ideals

1

The Idea of Freedom

The most elusive word in the political vocabulary, "freedom" is also one of the most important in the American consciousness. It is the first image the American invokes when he counts the blessings of his state. The inheritor of the English and French revolutions, as well as of his own, he has gazed so long into the pool of freedom that he has fallen half in love with his own reflection in it.

—MAX LERNER, *America as a Civilization*, p. 452

It was McNamara, the gentle poker-playing bookkeeper, who said, when asked what the word "freedom" made him think of, "Well, it's kind of an overworked word, I guess." In the language of politics none is worked harder. Many have interpreted its special meaning to Americans, and most have stressed three themes: (1) the emphasis upon freedom of opportunity, an emphasis that permits the marriage of freedom and equality; (2) the conformist and rigid nature of American uses of freedom, and (3) the American concept of freedom as a set of rights against the government—negative rather than positive freedom. We briefly explore each of these themes in Eastport.

A

THE AMERICAN IDEA OF FREEDOM:
EASTPORT VERSION

Freedom as Opportunity

Freedom, in the sense that "no barriers denied the citizen's right to move forward," has been, says Laski, the very "essence of American individualism."[1] Gorer holds that freedom represents primarily the opportunity "to make more and better things."[2] Potter believes that the American interpretation of equality depends upon a special sense of liberty, "keeping the scale open," offering to all the opportunity to rise in the world.[3]

Is it easy to go from one class to another—from the working class to the middle class? The Eastport common man thinks not. Asked how they feel about the social class they say they are in, they tend to say that it doesn't "bother" them and that there is nothing to be done about it. Do they think they are cut out for the work they are doing? Only a few say, with Johnson, that they think they are made for better things; the rest take a little pride in saying yes, they are well matched with their jobs. Rapuano says, early in the interview, "I've lived my life." Perhaps he is morbid when the others are not. Many of the men who see themselves as "better off" in five years think of this in terms of an advancing economy, not individual promotion. These are the reasons why Eastport does not think of freedom in terms of opportunity.

Freedom and the Nature of Conformity

Today we know that we are "other-directed," that we are "organization men," that we are conformist, subservient to the opinions of others, no longer individualists. There have been dissenting voices, but there has been more agreement. Tocqueville said we were individualists; but he conceived of the idea as a drawing apart from society, ignoring it, a quality that he disliked

1. Harold Laski, *The American Democracy* (New York: Viking, 1948), p. 718.
2. Geoffrey Gorer, *The American People: A Study in National Character* (New York: Norton, 1948), p. 158.
3. David M. Potter, *People of Plenty: Economic Abundance and the American Character* (Chicago: University of Chicago Press, 1954), p. 92.

and that he said was declining in America even then.[4] On the other hand, he is quite clear that Americans defer to public opinion in an uncommon way.[5] Santayana, too, felt that "even what is best in American life is compulsory"; men felt constrained to believe and act as others did.[6] And though Laski says that "Americanism is . . . at its very roots, nonconformist," [7] David Ricsman says that the modern American style is "radar" directed—conforming in anticipation of other people's reactions.[8]

I shall argue below that, in Eastport, the common man asserts his independence, asserts that he would not, even to relieve his ignorance, consult anyone in particular about the issues and candidates in an election—but would rather make up his own mind (or possibly go to anonymous man-in-the-street sources—as Tocqueville said he would). Independence is prized; men say they would rather be known for their independence than for their capacity to get along in a discussion; they value leaders who give the impression of independence—like McCarthy and Kefauver. They think it improper for unions to advise them on how to vote. There are a few, like Costa, an assembly-machine operator, who interpret freedom as the absence of social pressures and demands: what he wants is "freedom to pursue the things you want to do, without interference from your friends or your family or your higher-ups, whoever they may be, politically or socially."

But the fact is that Costa is one of the most conventional of all the men. As for the others, they rarely made it appear that their interpretation of the concept of freedom included casting off the bonds of public opinion or the pressures to conform that their friends and neighbors impose upon them. Rather, I believe, these pressures are interpreted in an unconscious way as supports, like buttresses on a wall that cannot bear the stress without them. They do not want to be "told"—that produces a strong negative reaction—but they want to be cued, they want to be "filled in," they want to receive the right sign at the right time, so they won't look foolish. And this, as they see it, is no more a restriction on

4. Alexis de Tocqueville, *Democracy in America,* Phillips Bradley, ed. (New York: Knopf, 1945), II, 98–101.
5. *Ibid.,* 10–11.
6. George Santayana, *Character and Opinion in the United States* (Garden City, N.Y.: Doubleday, 1956), p. 130.
7. Laski, *op. cit.,* p. 719.
8. David Riesman, *The Lonely Crowd* (New Haven: Yale University Press, 1950), p. 26.

their freedom than is a libretto a restriction on the freedom of the opera star.

Freedom from Restraint

It is self-evident that "all men are created equal, that they are endowed by their Creator with certain unalienable Rights, that among these are Life, Liberty and the pursuit of Happiness." "Freedom as the American conceives it," says Lerner, is "the right of an individual against hostile forces outside—usually the government." [9] Laski criticizes our "excessive love of the rhetoric of rights." [10] But I think it is the case that Lerner and Laski and, indeed, many contemporary observers, misread the content of the common man's idea of freedom. Not completely, of course: De-Angelo remarks, "I can go to any part of the country I want; don't need no passes or anything." Kuchinsky, the roofer, who most nearly fits the Lerner-Laski model, says, "When they [immigrants] come here, they're free of everything; they're free of fear; nobody's jumping at 'em or knocking on the door." And Flynn, a supply clerk, who is one of the few to mention the freedom to vote among those freedoms he thinks important, refers to the fact that "anybody . . . can express themselves on politics, without fear of reprisals, I would think, legal reprisals." But, except for Kuchinsky who has friends in Poland and who contrasts America with "the old country" on several occasions, the references to freedom from legal barriers are expressed with less emotion, come later in the discussion, and seem more remote from experience than other aspects of the discussion. They have to "reach" for these ideas. In general, these men of Eastport are not afraid that government will trespass upon them; they hardly give it a thought. Partly, it is because they do not feel the bite of the law; it confines them to doing what they feel they should do. Partly, they feel protected because they have political "connections." Partly, they live in a community where due process is taken seriously, at least for those who are white and are not vagrants.

In a broad sense it is the industrial discipline and not the political discipline that confines them. In a narrower and more meaningful sense, it is the managers of factories and businesses,

9. Max Lerner, *America as a Civilization: Life and Thought in the United States Today* (New York: Simon and Schuster, 1957), p. 463.
10. Laski, *op. cit.*, p. 720.

reinforced by social conventions fitted to their needs, who direct them. When they say "boss," they mean foreman, not ward leader. Johnson speaks of his boss in this way: "Not that I dislike my boss, but it's—he, he himself seems to make these moods in me . . . compliments me on my work occasionally . . . but [pause] he depresses me the way he goes about things, you know? But I mean it's nothing strong. I mean it may only last for a short while, you know. I don't know how else I could explain it." Johnson has a rival for a promotion at the shop, and he speaks of his boss's attitude toward this rival: "At times he leans to this man an awful lot and . . . when this fellow isn't around he leans to me. I don't like that action." Freedom for Johnson would be deliverance from this supervision, this anxiety, this sense of being watched and judged. Geoffrey Gorer says, "Respect and awe are the usual emotional responses to personified authority, and are therefore among the most painful emotions that the Americans recognize, and are as carefully avoided by them as the feeling of shame-facedness is by the Japanese." [11]

Costa, with a different perspective but the same interpretation of what is valuable in freedom, contrasts the freedom in America with the lack of it in the Soviet Union. His opening remarks are: "Well, to get away from your direct question again, I read in Russia where you're liable to be fined a month's pay for being fifteen minutes late for work. That does not constitute freedom. . . . I like to feel that I can get up in the morning and go to work, and be late if I get a flat tire on the way to work without having to spend a year in jail, and I like to feel that I do the best I can, and when the day is over, I come home to my family and if we want to go somewhere in the car, we can go . . . in the ordinary pursuit of happiness, I just like the system we have."

Freedom to be accidentally late to work without being punished! There has never been a "Scottsboro case" on this freedom; there is nothing like Holmes's ringing dissent in the Gitlow case to serve as a standard to which men in doubt can repair to receive vigor and clarity when their freedom is imperiled. But for millions, like Costa, there is no effective pursuit of happiness without such freedom in the industrial system. Is it a negative freedom, a freedom from restraint? Perhaps it is. But for the man who seeks it, it is linked in many subtle ways with the positive freedom to be themselves.

11. Gorer, *op. cit.*, p. 41.

B

AN OUTLINE OF POSITIVE FREEDOM

Freedom has, for these men of Eastport, a positive frame of meaning. O'Hara, a factory maintenance man, says freedom means to him "being able to do what you want, within the law"; Woodside, a railroad guard, says "to be able to do what you feel like doing, . . . to express your feelings, being able to express your feelings any way you want without fear of obstruction of anybody else." What are these feelings? What is it that they want to do?

The concept that is most closely associated with the idea of freedom, mentioned first and most frequently, is the *freedom of religion*. It is salient for these men, most of whom are Roman Catholic, partly, I think, because their religion and national origins are, in their own minds, a shadow upon their Americanism, a barrier to complete integration into the American society. Freedom of religion means for them not simply, as Costa says, "We like to go to church on Sunday; we go—we go to any church we please"; it also implies, in Sullivan's words, "Freedom of religion means that a person can choose his own religion, and *nobody's got a right to say anything about it.*" "People don't look down on you—because you're in one [church] or the other," says O'Hara. Sokolsky, a product of the Eastport ghetto, quick to express anger and assert his dignity within the capacity of his short solid frame, says of freedom: "Freedom is doing—to do what you want, what you want to worship, what you want to be." I ask him, "Anything else?" and he says, after a pause, "To worship, to—I said that— to think the way I want to think." But it was hardly three sentences back when he said, speaking of the social mixing of people of different races and religions: "That's the trouble with this country— there's a lot of people that think that one is better than the other. . . . Because you get right back to religion now, and like they say, 'love thy neighbor.' " He wants, as everyone does, freedom of religion where no one thinks one religion is better than another, and where he, a Jew, feels loved by all. Those who have read Handlin's sympathetic treatment of immigrant life in America will understand how cold and barren of satisfaction the legal right to worship in one's own way can be.

There is one feature of this discussion of freedom of worship that is, I think, peculiarly American. Sullivan's phrase "A person can choose his own religion" is significant; and Costa's comment, "We go to any church we please," illustrates the same point. Whereas in other parts of the world one might expect an equally fervent demand for freedom to worship according to one's faith, it would be unusual to emphasize the aspect of *choice*. This is so like the matter of national identity for immigrants, and religion and natural origin are so closely connected in any event, that once the idea of choice in one of these traditional aspects of life has been admitted, perhaps the idea that the other is open to conscious decision follows. "Americans," says Gorer, "differ from the rest of the world in their belief that nationality is an act of will, rather than the result of . . . destiny." [12] Thus there is a special urgency in the emphasis placed upon freedom of religion—not because people actually choose their religion as they might choose an article of dress, but because they are held accountable for having elected to be Catholics, Jews, or Jehovah's Witnesses. The question "Should I be what I am?" is constantly encouraged by this and other aspects of American society.

While freedom of worship, qualified in this special way, is by all odds the most frequently mentioned "meaning" of freedom, *freedom of movement,* not speech, is second. As noted above, DeAngelo, a machine operator, says, "Well, freedom, you know— I can go to any part of the country I want." And Kuchinsky, the roofer: "I mean we can go anywhere we want, and nobody stops us. I mean within reason." And Dempsey, older than the others, and infinitely sober, gives the idea of free movement a curiously frivolous twist. After mentioning freedom of worship, he says:

> You can go out on the street corner and holler and sing, if you want to, as long as you don't get too noisy or boisterous and have someone complain about you. Otherwise you have that freedom. You can go into any store, or place of business, that you want. You have your choice.

Perhaps for the less well educated, the freedom to come and go, somatic freedom, so to speak, has an immediacy that freedom of speech has not. The restrictions on movement in the totalitarian countries, which they are dimly aware of, seem more punishing, somehow, than the restrictions on saying heterodox, or unconventional, things.

Few, then, mentioned *freedom of speech*, although surely all

12. *Ibid.,* p. 188.

value it in some sense. Rapuano, a packinghouse checker, gives a moving testament revealing these priorities:

> My God, I work where I want to work, I spend my money where I want to spend it. I buy what I want to buy. I go where I want to go. I read what I want to read. My kids go to the school that they want to go to, or where I want to send them. We bring them up in the religion that we want to bring them up in. What else—what else could you have?

Thus he can do what *he* wants to do. He does not want to advocate another social system, to talk about the virtues of Soviet Russia or Chinese Communism, or preach pacifism to draftees. He criticizes the government, but he does not associate this with a fundamental freedom. Perhaps it is so fundamental he does not easily imagine it being taken away, or perhaps he would rather not examine this phase of his freedom. In this he is like the others —few of the fifteen mentioned the right to criticize the government. Yet all of them did criticize it—but within more or less conventional bounds. Thus, Costa says: "Boy, I really believe in exercising free speech, when I get the opportunity"; and O'Hara, his blue Irish eyes snapping, says, ". . . if you don't like the President of the United States, you can say you don't like him. Like I said many a time I didn't like Truman, and I didn't. And Eisenhower's a good man, but I don't like Dulles and Nixon; and I can say it, and who's going to do anything to me for saying it?" In short, the right to criticize the government has a value for many of the men that they prize, but they do not immediately think about this right as part of the concept of "freedom."

"Besides the right to do what one likes, when one likes, without the interference of authority, Freedom means, over and above everything else, Freedom to make more and better things, without external interference from government or sentimental do-gooders." [13] In saying this about the American people, Gorer is missing the frame of mind of Eastport's common man. For one thing, the workingmen we are concerned with were fully as interested in *freedom of consumption* as they were in making things. For another, the emphasis would be much better placed on *freedom to choose your job* than on the "creative" aspects Gorer mentions. They have a sense of workmanship, but "making more and better things" does not describe their attitude at all closely. Still, the attention focused upon the importance of economic functions in

13. *Ibid.*, p. 158.

defining freedom is correct, particularly as it takes such a high priority in the thinking of these men. Rapuano and Dempsey earlier spoke of "going into a shop" or "buying what I want to" to illustrate what freedom meant to them. The lives of men of Eastport, like most Americans' lives, are much more concerned with the business of buying and selling, earning and disposing of things, than they are with the "idle" talk of politics. Gorer's countryman described it better: "Getting and spending, we lay waste our powers." Aside from carping at the government, another freedom of speech that counts, as Sullivan says, is freedom of speech in a union to protect your interests. And freedom of movement is illustrated with examples taken from commercial acts. One could caricature this position by the expression, "I don't care what I am allowed to say, so long as I can buy what I want, work where I want, and go where I want."

There is some evidence that the great historic quarrels in which freedom has figured have, in part, masqueraded as struggles for free institutions, for freedom of speech, or for religious freedom. The desire for free expression, such as it was, was sometimes a self-deception by men who were really talking about something else, namely, economic opportunity. If this is true, it would be possible to carry out a modern economic revolution dedicated to a higher per capita income, without feeling embarrassed by the knowledge that speech was stifled at the source. The Soviet Union and the underdeveloped countries may well offer to their citizens occupational mobility and consumer choice within a very limited framework of free expression and political freedom, and find that they have the complete loyalty of their common men, eager citizens of the local GUM, Macy's, Bon Marché. The ordinary man wants to be a supermarket statistic, in his own way.

2

The Burden of Freedom

It may be said . . . that liberty is to be found at the summit of civilization, and that those who have the resources of civilization at their command are the only ones who are free. But the resources of civilization are capital; and so it follows that capitalists are free, or, to avoid the ambiguities in the word capitalist, that the rich are free. Popular language, which speaks of the rich as independent, has long carried an affirmation on this point.
—WILLIAM GRAHAM SUMNER, quoted in CHARLES and MARY BEARD, *The American Spirit,* p. 345

The American more or less open society provides Eastport with the freedoms it is looking for; but perhaps it offers too much. Perhaps the choices of occupation, religion, association, consumption, movement are too demanding, and there is a secret longing to escape from this freedom. In Eastport, at least, it is the case that in most areas of life the irritations and confusions of freedom find sources for relief or find reasons for acceptance. Actually, the circumstances of life are often such as to minimize the sense that life offers too much choice; rather it seems to offer unchosen obligations without end.

A

FREEDOM AND THE "MANY TINY MESSAGES"

Big, moody Ferrera, a wholesale shoe salesman, turns his large frame toward me to say what the word "freedom" means to him. The bony structure of his jaw and nose is massive; his large head is set solidly on a pair of huge shoulders. He says:

> What it makes me think of is a pastoral scene—I don't know why—being soothed by a nice balmy breeze, green pastures, and a girl and a boy romping through the fields. That's what freedom means to me. . . . It would suggest to me a closeness to God. . . . There are times, I'll say that "what the heck" to my existence, rather that or crying. You're bombarded by so much—ah, pressure in the present day, pressures of business, pressures of actual day-to-day living—cost of living—the pressures of whether you are bringing your children up right, or whether you said the right thing to your child. . . . There are so many things that you are constantly bombarded with—tiny messages the people are trying to get across to you in their effort to sell you. It's a tough life. I think the recluse has probably got something. And every so often you get a little bit tired; you sort of wish you could get some place and just lead that kind of existence.

These translucent lines introduce a problem intimately related to the nature and durability of the open society. The problem is, simply, the capacity of the mind to receive and deal with a wide variety of stimuli, most of which require some kind of response. As Freud says, "Protection against stimuli is an almost more important function for the living organism than *reception* of stimuli." [1] He goes on to point out that the receptive cortical layer of the brain "has long been withdrawn into the depths of the interior" where it may be properly protected, leaving sense organs near the surface to communicate with it.

The bearing of these observations on the problem of the nature of freedom in a society is a direct one. It is no secret that the transformation of this or any nation from a rural to a metropolitan society increases the number and variety of interpersonal contacts; that the industrial revolution, the commercial revolution, and the technological revolution have burdened people with de-

1. Sigmund Freud, *Beyond the Pleasure Principle*, translated by James Strachey (New York: Bantam Books, 1959), p. 53. For the complementary problem, *lack* of stimulus, see Philip Solomon and others, *Sensory Deprivation* (Cambridge, Mass.: Harvard University Press, 1961).

mands for clock watching, machine watching, television watching, and hideously increased the cacophonous sounds to which the ear is exposed. The number of voices heard in a day, the number of messages aimed at a person in a day, the number of responses he is called upon to make during a day have increased exponentially.[2]

Ferrera yearned for the peace of a recluse, where no one would try to sell him anything, an escape from freedom others, too, might seek. Is there a genuine, if archaic, demand for the simpler life? Consider what DeAngelo would like to see different in this country:

> Everything is too fast in this country, everything is too hopped up. Shops is all production—there's too much rush, rush, and—I don't know. That's why everybody's got so much heart trouble; everybody is always rushing, running around crazy, making cars faster—everything is faster, y'know? Planes are faster, cars are faster, trains are faster, and everyone is going at a terrific pace. I don't know, maybe we ought to slow down a little bit, take it easy, know what I mean? . . . Somebody has got to do something about it, know what I mean? Settle the country down a little bit. What the hell are we going like this for? We're not at war or anything—I mean—I don't know.

The advocate of a return to the good old days, the simple life, the homely virtues, would seem to have raw material here that he might fashion to his taste. He might. But Ferrera has never been to a Roman Catholic retreat, and DeAngelo has two jobs and maintains his union stewardship. I think, probably, that this nostalgia is not an actionable emotion. Although the love of simplicity and quiet produces irritation with our times, it does not, at least here among these men, produce even a latent movement for the simplified life.

How, then, do these men deal with the "many tiny messages" that are sent to them every day. In some ways the new knowledge made available in our society may help men to cope with these flooding stimuli, but in other ways it just makes matters worse. Knowledge of the consequences of his actions often makes the

2. Richard Hoggart describes the problem for the British workingman in moving phrases: "Today he is so bespattered by the ceaseless exoteric voices, is invited so frequently to feel this, this and this, to react to this, to do that, to believe this—that in recoil he often decides to feel none of these things, neither the glories nor the horrors. He goes dead to it all. He develops a strong patina of resistance, a thick solid skin for not taking notice. When the voices, especially those of the Press, really have something important to speak to him about, he gives the old smile and continues to read the funny bits. They have cried 'wolf' too often." *The Uses of Literacy* (Boston: Beacon, 1961), p. 227.

anxious parent worse, and his response to advice more uncertain.[3] Knowledge of the many subtle poisons in food (cholesterol, albumen, caffeine) makes the choice of diet more worrisome. The educated are as overstimulated as the ignorant. The overloaded electric circuit cuts out, blows a fuse, and protects itself in this way. It is a fact that Ferrera, whose poetry set this theme in motion, has just emerged from a period of melancholia and low morale that served as a kind of screen against some of the "tiny messages." But there is no evidence of a widespread escape from freedom into apathy or of a withdrawal or neurosis of this kind in Eastport or American society generally.

It is a paradox, in a way, but the most common and most significant protection against the demands of important messages, particularly human interchange, is found in flooding the system with banal, trivial, unimportant messages. Beyond all question the chief narcosis against these tiny messages is the television. This may seem strange, since it, after all, is a singularly important source of tiny messages—and they take their toll. But rather than helping to overload the nervous system, the television, and probably the newspaper too, serves an opposite function. Although these men watch television for a very substantial part of their non-working hours—even while attempting to read a book (as Rapuano reports), they watch it as a way of relaxing and avoiding situations that are or may be burdensome. The television demands almost nothing of them—and those who argue for a superior program must face the fact that "art" (at least unfamiliar art) is demanding; "Kitsch" is not. One cannot say, of course, what this background of synthetic excitement does to a person—tightening the throat, swelling the sinus membranes, producing tension in the sphincter—but for these men at their stage of life it seems modestly catabolic, a draining off of emotion produced during the day; in its own way, an avenue of escape from the many voices of freedom.

B

TOLERANCE TOWARD CONFLICT AND CONFUSION

Politically speaking, freedom of speech brings in its train two especially troublesome aspects of life: conflict and confusion. Men

3. See Bruno Bettelheim, *The Informed Heart* (New York: The Free Press of Glencoe, 1960), p. 74.

are exposed to conflicting opinions on political and other matters, and are told that they must choose. They are given scraps of information, vague indications of where their interests lie, ambiguous advice, and are told that it is their duty to keep themselves informed, to understand. Perhaps too much is expected of them.

If it were true that the men of Eastport sought to avoid the conflict and confusion inherent in the role of citizen of a free city, they might well agree to the question I put to them: "Do you sometimes feel that listening to all the different points of view on a subject is too confusing and that you would like to hear just one point of view from somebody who really knows?" Most of them did not. To this question, they said "No"; they prefer to hear more than one side of an issue. Part of this is a little self-conscious pride in open-mindedness. But when it is placed in the context of familiar experience, it is convincing.

O'Hara says, "I think too much [advice] is no good but I don't think you should have only one." He talks about the usefulness of getting confirming medical advice where there is a sickness, and then moves more easily into a world he knows: "Two heads are better than one, no matter how you look at it. . . . You can go up on any job in the shop and no matter how many times you do it, you can get somebody new coming in on the job—he might have an idea that may make it 100 per cent easier. You didn't think of it because you were doing it all the time." The reader will see later how furious O'Hara got when a crane driver told him he had done something wrong, and, remembering these phrases, may smile. Nevertheless, O'Hara thinks concretely of situations where he believes it is valuable to have conflicting advice—not in terms of some glossed-over and somewhat empty notion of democracy and free speech. And this is generally true of even the angry men in the group; they are patient enough to want to hear more than one side.

Still, at some partially unconscious level for all the men, and manifestly for a few, there is a grave struggle against confusion, disorder, disorientation. Many of the strongest advocates of free discussion recognize the problem. O'Hara, referring to the presentation of a variety of points of view, says, "Too much is no good." Farrel acknowledges the difficulty of dealing with "a babble of voices." Johnson says: "I like to hear all points of view. Sometimes it is confusing, but I'd rather like that." There is, then, a tolerance of confusion, ambiguity, and conflict among these men—a recognition of the cost and an acceptance of it.

Some of the reasons for this acceptance and capacity are on the surface. Costa derives some slight distinction among his friends by being better informed than they, and so seeks political argument. Ruggiero says, "I like to debate on different subjects, rouse people"; it serves his needs to have a variety of views current. The retailers of opinion, the grass-roots opinion leaders, are advocates of an open society because they are its interpreters.

Behind it all there is some sense that expertness is not value-free; the experts may be "biased"; or, as Sullivan says, "You can never be sure that he's giving you the right picture," even though "he might be as far as he's concerned." Then, too, there is the question of how you distinguish an expert. "How can you say somebody *really* knows? You know what I mean?" asks DeAngelo. There is something of the idea that every man is his own expert, an echo of Tocqueville's views on opinion in democracy. And probably, too, there is a partial belief in the view that so infuriates social scientists—anybody's opinion is as good as anybody else's.

But there is also a fairly clear understanding of the reason why, as O'Hara said, "two heads are better than one"—most of the Eastport men see that one can check the other, make him more responsible in his statements, and give "the other" point of view. This suggestion of "the" other point of view comes up often, as though, like the American party system, the truth system had a kind of dualism built into it.

It seems to me, however, that there are several additional causes of this toughness, this readiness to bear the pain of conflict and confusion, that are features of the culture and the social system in which these men live. One of them is the sense of "givenness" of things that Boorstin finds in our political cosmos, a quality expressed in "the belief that values in America are in some way or other automatically defined; given by certain facts of geography or history peculiar to us." [4] For other reasons Santayana holds that in America "every man finds that what most matters has been settled for him beforehand." [5] Perhaps so. At

4. Daniel J. Boorstin, *The Genius of American Politics* (Chicago: University of Chicago Press, 1953), p. 9.
5. George Santayana, *Character and Opinion in the United States* (Garden City, N.Y.: Doubleday, 1956), p. 131.

least the men of Eastport felt no problems of choice among competing and organized world views, say, Communist, Monarchist, Fascist, Christian, and Social Democratic.

But more important and less noticed is what might be called *conflict dissonance,* a term that refers to the relation of (1) role conflict and (2) group conflict to ideological conflict. It would be harder to bear the internal conflict occasioned by competing advice if these verbal conflicts were consonant with some systematic personal conflicts of the individuals. But they are not. Aside from psychic conflicts, the main sources of tension, the most difficult choices the men must make are created by role conflicts, of which the central one is that between the role of husband and father (the domestic role), on the one hand, and the role of workman, employee, factory colleague (the producer role) on the other. It arises, for example, in the decision on whether or not to take a second job, and, if one does, how to find the time to listen to and care about matters at home. Another such conflict is posed in the problem of how to be a good son to an aged parent living in the confines of a small apartment, or how to be a good husband to a wife with limited sympathy for a difficult oldster about the home. A third role conflict emerges outside the home: How to get ahead in the shop, how to demonstrate skill and initiative, and still not violate the code of "brothers" that forbids ostentatious excellence. If political conflicts reinforced these personal role conflicts, as might be the case if ideologies were more comprehensive or codes of personal behavior and political outlook were culturally linked, then conflict-producing freedoms would be harder to bear. Totalitarian parties, of course, do make this linkage, and seek a consonance of personal role behavior and political behavior.

A third reason why these Eastportians can bear the conflicts of a free society is one that has been noticed more in connection with European than with American politics. In Europe, political conflicts are more meaningful because they coincide with strong group loyalties—church, union, ethnic group, region. But, aside from the South, these loyalties are systematically discouraged in the United States; they are obscured, repressed, driven underground. Of course, we can discover them with hardly any trouble, but because of the atomistic state of the American individual, pried loose from ancestry and community, there is much less consonance here between political conflict and group identification than in most other places—making for an effective tolerance of ambiguity in political affairs.

A fourth reason why Eastport embraces conflicting opinion is that the conflict, although it is within each man as well as between groups of men, has a low salience. On the one hand, it seems a curious and discouraging thing that when these men are asked how government affects their lives they respond with trivial answers ("It cleans the streets") or perhaps deny that it affects their lives at all ("The government doesn't bother me any"). But the social reward for this sense of disengagement from government is the capacity to bear an internalized *political* conflict without excessive pain. Perhaps it should be said that the price of freedom is eternal vigilance for some and a modest disengagement for others.

Four Men Suffering from Freedom's Confusion

But for a few, the price in confusion may be too dear for the satisfactions they gain from hearing more than one side. Perhaps they didn't want to hear even one side to begin with—thus the attention problem, discussed earlier in this chapter, and the conflict problem tend to merge. Consider, then, the comments of four men as illuminating the matter, first, of what seems to be stimulus fatigue, and, second, conflict and confusion. For Dempsey, a slow and restrained machine tender endowed with more "character" than intelligence, the pace of debate is too swift. "Too much of that stuff is confusing," he says. "Sometimes you would rather sit down and listen to one person who will state his case, and then give the other fellow a chance to talk." He says he wants two points of view, but when pressed seems really to favor someone whose word he can accept without too much concern. Indeed, the inference is fairly clear: he would really prefer to have the expert take over and not bother him.

Ferrera, a shoe salesman, is really not at all like Dempsey, yet in this respect they seem to express a common idea. Ferrera says, "I like to hear different points of view—up to a certain point, that is; [when] it reaches the saturation point, it begins to get boring and meaningless." I ask him, "At that point perhaps you'd like to have some expert opinions to help you out?" But Ferrera will not accept that. He says: "Nay. I think that—[pause] of course, everybody's saturation point is different. Perhaps I'm limited and that's why I tire of the thing so easily. And after all it is kind of selfish of me to have [these] feelings. But that's the way it strikes me." Like Dempsey he feels guilty about his modest at-

tention and early saturation, but the fact that he is well informed
(he ranks fourth on information) and that Dempsey is not (he is
the poorest of the entire group) suggests that this feeling of a
saturation threshold is one with wholly subjective standards. One
makes one's own world of guilt for inattention in public affairs—
it is not a product of educational distinction.

The more DeAngelo talks, the more it seems that the cost of
democracy in the sense of conflicting and confusing advice is excessive. He concludes: "I can get pretty confused when you listen
to these political speeches. . . . Like I say, a guy gets out and
he sounds like he's the best there is. The next guy gets out and
makes a bum out of him. You don't know what to believe, really.
You know what I mean?" He manages fairly well—but chiefly
by restricting his interest to family, union, and sometimes a little
bit of Eastport. A constricted attention, anathema to civic reformers, tends to solve some of the bewildering problems for this man.

But while DeAngelo arrives at this confession circuitously,
Rapuano, the packinghouse clerk, hastens to tell me of his confusion and ignorance. Asked the same question as the others,
apparently the very word "confusion" is a signal to him. He says:
"Oh, certainly. Oh, of course. Sure. . . . Maybe they don't want
me to understand them—I don't know." So here, too, confusion
confounds the stimulus fatigue, and to this is added some sense
of humiliation that such confusion should persist.

In one sense these comments are most remarkable for what
they do not say. They are not anti-intellectual; they do not, except
for Rapuano's allusion, allege that their confusion has been arranged or that they are being deliberately misled. They do not
respond to their feelings of inadequacy—clearly enough stated by
Ferrera and Rapuano—by trying to show that the natural wisdom
of common men like themselves is a better guide to reality than
that of the "fancy," "theoretical," "overeducated" men who are
doing all this talking. McCarthy's war against Harvard had widespread backing in the circles I am dealing with, but it was, I think,
emotionally shallow, unsupported by attitudes such as might have
been forthcoming from these men who suffer from their confusion
more than do the others.

The major theme here is not ambivalence, but disorientation.
These men are not speaking of being torn between various attractive or hateful alternatives; they are speaking of uncertainty and
doubt. Partisanship might serve as a great clarifier, but these men

are not partisan. Firm and unambiguous group status would select for attention only the "right" messages, giving clear cues on what should be accepted and what should not. But these men, being Americans, are ambiguous about their social status, and what they have, often, suggests mutually incompatible solutions. They are alone, and they are "supposed" to be, in this matter. They are supposed to listen to all sides, to understand some of it, to decide on the merits; but they haven't the time to listen, they haven't the equipment and background to understand, they aren't guided by their experience to a decision.

Yet again, for an appraisal, we must put these four men, and the many others in America whom they represent, in context. Most men respond to conflict and confusion with greater tolerance, but even where they do not, one man's need for freedom in one area may support another man's in another area. The Lana Turner case, in which Lana's daughter stabbed her mother's lover, has a morbid fascination for Kuchinsky, and he seems to fear restrictions that would deprive him of such deliciously horrible items; Ruggiero likes the conflict and debate that come with an unregulated and open presentation of news—he likes to argue. Freedom of expression, at least as a principle, derives its support from such diverse and sometimes irrelevant motives as these, and each supports the other. Kuchinsky's love of prurient reading may protect Ruggiero's love of debate—and vice versa.

C
FREEDOM AND OBLIGATION

Recalling that these are the successful men of their occupational groups, the upper working class, the steady breadwinners who are admitted to a housing development, the family men whose families (except for Sullivan's) stay together—recalling this, look now at their work lives. Six of the men have two jobs. Woodside works as an auxiliary policeman when he is not on duty with the railroad; Ruggiero works in the post office when he is not serving as maintenance clerk for Eastern State University; Sokolsky is a janitor in one place and a factory hand in another; Mc-Namara works on the books of his old employer on Saturdays and Sundays—and so forth. The time available for civic affairs, adult education, speculative thinking, self-improvement, and community work is not great.

The others are not much better. This is a time of recession; Costa is very worried about the cutbacks in his plant; already he is drawing some unemployment relief. Three more on the seniority list and O'Hara goes out too; he is worried but has not told his wife. Sullivan works intermittently on cross-country hauls as a man on various relief shifts; his time is not his own, for if he misses the call to work he goes back down to the bottom of the list of men available for duty. Flynn, who has a supply service job, knows that within a short time he will be faced with the choice of moving to another town and commuting fifty miles a day, or finding another job—there is a reduction in force in his department. Thus the men who are "working" work under the threat of immediate and onerous penalties. They are not psychologically free—and certainly not carefree—to enjoy the opportunities for choice and the cultivation of the arts, of themselves, of the community.

Consider the family and home situations of these men. They live in a housing development where the apartments are neat, relatively modern, laid out with some green space around them— and small. Most of them are two-bedroom apartments; the living room is about 12 by 14; the bedrooms are smaller, and there is no dining room. The living room contains a sofa, an easy chair, other assorted furniture, and a television set. The entire family is in the living room, children on the floor, Father in the big chair, the grandparent, if there is one, off somewhere to the side, and Mother in and out of the kitchen—her domain. Under these circumstances, everything is shared, all news, problems, quarrels; privacy is minimal—yet consider how well off these families are when compared with, for example, immigrants existing in multi-family dwellings where "living quarters" were partitioned off by hanging blankets on ropes across the room. DeAngelo has six children, O'Hara has five, and McNamara has three. Even with one more bedroom, the density is high; the saturation of time and attention with family problems, domesticity, and bringing up the children is evident. One might well ask, What is the meaning of freedom under these circumstances?

As is well known, worries of any kind have a tendency to exhaust psychic energies and to preempt the mind; somatic worries are no different, and, to the extent that they are associated with pain, they may be worse, especially if their effects are crippling or, worst of all, endanger one's capacity to earn a living. In telling me about himself, his life and views, Costa told me a great deal that might be thought hurtful to the ego. But it was not until toward the fourth day that he mentioned—inadvertently and only in passing—some "trouble" he had. I let it go, but I noticed that as he went down the stairs he went very slowly, groping surreptitiously for support from the brick wall. On the fifth day I ask him about his health. He says: "Well, I had something when I was a little tyke that probably put my family in a hole for five years. It was the reason why I was never in the service—spinal meningitis. I have some aftereffects to this day." But he passes this off and goes on to childhood diseases. I ask him about the aftereffects. Nervously and deprecatingly, he says: "Well, I'm almost blind in the left eye, and my—[pause] well, let me see, how do I explain this? Well, my equilibrium is off balance." I ask him about how this affects his work. He says: "Well, you see, I can't get both sides to work the same way, so that if I try to lift something, it's hard for me to lift. I can't do any real manual labor. . . . I look big and strong, but I'm not. . . . I don't tell this to anybody who asks me, but it's hard for me to really do any manual labor." Costa, scared, telling me his biggest secret, gets by on the assembly line with this defect because he can work at a bench and because the heavy lifting is done by conveyors. But he must live in fear of the awkward moment when he may be asked to help with a load or to adjust something, and he will be revealed as a kind of "cripple" to the hard time-and-motion-study employer he now serves.

For Costa it is his eye and sense of balance; for Woodside it is a mysterious ailment that affects his stomach. When it strikes, he must be hospitalized. He thinks he has found the source in a pork allergy, but he isn't sure. In addition, one of his legs was crushed by a truck when he was an adolescent; and once, when I visited him some time later, he was laid up by a slipped disk. But that is only part of the story. "You see, my wife had a partial nervous breakdown, and my son was in the hospital—two years ago he was in the hospital fourteen times." He has asthma, but that was not the reason: "No, that was from different accidents. He was either breaking his collarbone or his arm, or putting a nail through his foot, or going through a plate-glass door. . . . Well, the doctor said that what sickness we've had, usually most people don't have for their lifetimes." Consequently, I am not really surprised when, asked about his major problems now, he says it isn't money: "It's my health. I'm sweating out what they call a four-year term. Once I get ten years on the department, then no matter what happens to me, my wife will get compensation. But if anything happens to me within the next four years, they can let me out and I won't get a dime."

Sokolsky has a lung infection; Dempsey has a "heart condition"; Rapuano and Johnson have ulcers; Kuchinsky's wife has claustrophobia and a fear of crowds that keeps her—and him—socially isolated. (As a roofer, Kuchinsky seeks to get advice from the doctors whose homes he works on.) The free mind—choosing a party to implement a philosophy, choosing a career that will give self-expression, choosing reading matter that will offer fulfillment, choosing friends and conversation congenial to the spirit—is confined within a framework of worry and occasional desperation. In this sense, one might say that the foundation of freedom is far less a matter of the laws than of the health of a people—and for Costa, Woodside, and the others, the First Amendment offers less freedom (that is, opens fewer options for choices important to them) than would a good public-health-insurance measure. And this is Eastport, not Karachi, Stanleyville, or Port-au-Prince.

The circumstances of their lives speak with a firm voice on this matter; their own discussion of freedom is more muted. Still, as they wrestled with the problem that bothered Rousseau, they turned, quite unlike Rousseau, to some of the aspects of their lives that we have limned briefly above. I remarked: "A famous man once said, 'Man is born free, and everywhere he is in chains.' Do you know what he meant by that?" Some of the men thought it meant a person had moved from a democracy to a dictatorship, or that a man had gone to jail, or that men were too heavily taxed. They are literal; the language of metaphor, while familiar, is less often used. But there were some who, responding to Rousseau's imagery, showed something of the quality of their lives.

DeAngelo, who says of freedom, "I don't have to worry too much about anything, you know?" turns to answer my question with a worried look: "Well, I don't know what you all mean by chains there. He's born free, sure . . . but he's tied down, you know; he's got a wife and family. He got to support them. His life isn't his own anymore. He can't do what he wants to do; you know what I mean?" For DeAngelo it is family responsibilities that impose chains on the free-born spirit of man. For Ferrera, though the family is less demanding, the routine of earning a living is more burdensome—but the idea is the same: "Well, he's shackled to the chains that bind him—in his everyday life—whether you exist in a democracy or otherwise. The end is inevitable—a constant struggle, a constant struggle for survivorship. And I can always picture survivalship with a kind of struggle and trying to get rid of the chains that bind you." And for Kuchinsky, as for many of the others, the chains are golden chains and the imprisonment is poverty. First he laughs uproariously at Rousseau's phrase, then says: "I'm right in the chain now, ha-ha-ha." I ask him in what way. "Money situations and work and stuff like that. . . . Well, it might mean that. I tell you, I think a lot of us are right in that chain business right now, [pause] held down. And nobody's got the key for that lock to unloosen it." Flynn agrees: "There's no question about it; we're all in some kind of bondage," and he finds many illustrations of the restraints, some of them personal inhibitions, that keep men from feeling, acting, and being free. Dempsey sees man "probably chained down to working all his life—struggling to get along." Some are cynical, some are resigned, some resentful—but many find relief in saying how unfree they feel, how securely the chains fasten them to their jobs and homes and responsibilities, and how very right Jean-Jacques Rousseau was.

One important implication of this reading of Rousseau for our times is that the men do not experience this seemingly wide range of choice as a burdensome thing because in most concrete instances the circumstances of their lives dictate what they must do. Speaking somewhat metaphorically: because they are Americans, and because they are not rich, they have already escaped from freedom into obligations almost beyond their capacities.

Democracy is an odd system. It requires that most men tolerate freedom and that some men hold it dear. Yet men are born unfree, infants with only such choices as their parents offer them, and with a world of choice foreclosed. Though as adults they are required to tolerate some degrees of equality, and are entreated to believe in the equality of man, they inevitably emerge from families in which, as children, they learn inequality long before they learn equality. Democracy asks men to support the rights of others to be heterodox, to say things that violate their moral and political codes, but they are brought up to believe in propriety and convention as a civilizing process. It is little wonder that democracy is a late product of history, and a painful achievement for some individuals.

Perhaps, on the other hand, we are not dealing with a late product of history but with a recurrent, ephemeral product, and perhaps, too, our democracy and our freedom are waning, or growing only to wither eventually. Our interview material speaks to the question of the cycle of democracy; our men, although they have a heavier burden of individual choice than the common man in other civilizations had to bear, are not ready to set their freedom aside. The undercurrent of malaise, of fatigue, of a longing to be free of conflict and choice is not the mainstream. They are still psychologically prepared to accept hard choices in such areas as licentious behavior and segregation with a sense of reality not greatly distorted by reference to their intrapsychic problems. But that is for the next chapter.

3

Freedom and the Control of Impulse

> The subjective function of character for the normal person is to lead him to act according to what is necessary for him from a practical standpoint and also to give him satisfaction from his activity psychologically.
> —ERICH FROMM, *Escape from Freedom,* p. 283

In what sense is the anxious man a free man? Is the compulsive personality capable of free choice? Christian Bay argues, along with some others, that there is no freedom for a man unless he has the psychological strength and health to respond to the real situations that confront him, fitting his means appropriately to his ends and choosing ends that are, in fact, broadly gratifying to him. In this sense, he says, "Freedom means a degree of harmony between basic motives and overt behavior." [1] Erich Fromm suggests a different but similar point when he says that positive freedom "is identical with the full realization of the individual's potentialities, together with his ability to live actively and spontaneously." [2] This implies, among other things, self-control. It was possible that among the Eastport men the self-control systems were

1. Christian Bay, *The Structure of Freedom* (Stanford, Calif.: Stanford University Press, 1958), p. 83.
2. Erich Fromm, *Escape from Freedom* (New York: Rinehart, 1941), p. 270.

not equal to their burdens and that consequently a special fear of freedom arose, a reaching out for the power of law and custom to help them with their problems of self-control.

In an effort to assess whether there was any such fear of freedom among the Eastport men, any more or less disguised belief that freedom was dangerous (in the special sense of leading to unrestrained, wild, or frightening behavior), I searched for subtle clues that the men, themselves unaware of these views, might offer. The evidence comes chiefly from the men's discussion of what would happen if we had more freedom, and how people behave when they "feel too free." By and large, what these men talked about in this context were the abuses of power by union leaders, politicians and, in one case, the FBI. If they turn to the personal behavior of the man in the street, they speak generally of his lack of control, or reflect some variation of Ruggiero's views: "I guess they get a little too cocky and, uh, take advantage. Then it starts to hurt, when you give 'em too much [freedom]." There is a strain of tolerance in their responses—except as they think of problems of Communism and subversion; two men who refer to the way in which Negroes might "get out of hand" with more freedom give it a social explanation—Negroes have been kept down so much in the South that they don't know how to use freedom when they come North. For twelve of the men there is very little to suggest a fear of freedom lurking behind the façade of conventional expression and approval of the official ideology.

There were only three men who referred to acts of violence in talking about the consequences of greater freedom or less restraint. Johnson, the enthusiastic, voluble electric-utility mechanic says, "I think there'd be a lot of—[pause] well, a lot of people—perhaps murders, stealing, and things like that—raping and all those things." Rapuano, the well-paid packinghouse checker, summarizes the freedoms we have, and wonders what people could possibly do with more: "I mean, if there's any more freedom to be had," he says, "what else could there be, except going around killing people? And I wouldn't call that freedom." He feels strongly about this, and goes on, "I mean, there isn't any more freedom that a person *could* have." And Sokolsky, a machine operator, and no master of his own temper, worries greatly about what others would do in the absence of legal restraints: "They would do anything they want— they would steal, they would kill, and nobody would stop them. . . . You have to have laws to keep the people in hand or else they're going to run away with themselves." Sokolsky is most explicit—the risk is that "people will run away with themselves" unless they are controlled by the strong hand of the law. All three mention killing, two mention stealing, and one mentions rape.

Our theory, familiar to psychoanalysis and common sense alike, is that men who have trouble controlling their own impulses will be likely to fear freedom in the personal sense. It is not that their impulses are necessarily stronger than those of others—that they are greater lovers or have strong perversions or are possessed by towering rages that frighten them; nor is it that they are weak men in the usual sense of being vacillating or suggestible or lacking in force and character. The concept is simply one of some area of life, or perhaps of more than one, where they have desires that they fear may break down their controls and get out of bounds. They are afraid of themselves, afraid that they will do something that they regard as "awful" but that, at least from the outside, may not necessarily seem awful at all, such as expressing anger.

We must do two things: we must account for the fact that most of the men face the possibility of greater freedom with equanimity; it does not alarm them, though they may not see where such freedom is needed. And we must account for the minority (Johnson, Rapuano, and Sokolsky) who fear the worst. If the theory is right, we should expect to see among those who fear freedom some evidence of a struggle with impulse and desires not apparent among those who do not. Certainly one place to look would be in the sex life of the individual, and another would be in the control of anger and its expression. The problems of controlling drinking, spending, and consumption in general represent a third area where, in our society, impulse and restraint offer a precarious balance. We shall look at that, too.

A

SEX: IMPULSE AND CONTROL

Men do not, even in the intimacy of the kind of quasi-clinical interview I conducted, say that they have barely repressed homosexual impulses, that they are worried about their virility, or that there are certain secret perversions they long for. But they will tell you, and did tell me, about their first sex experiences, their attitudes toward homosexuals, their feelings about teen-age delinquent girls, the importance of sex in marriage, and so forth. From such evidence, and much more, one can make inferences about the tension level of this area of personal life. Moreover, for eight of the men we have scores on a "sex-tension" test devised by Harold Lasswell and Arnold Rogow, which, although unstandardized and in its formative stage, gives information on some aspects of the problem.

It is so much harder to assess health, normality, functional behavior, than sickness, abnormality, dysfunctional behavior; yet the evidence of the modest level of sex tension among most of the men, I think, is there. It is apparent in the questions on homosexuality. So far as I could tell, there were no tightening of the throat, elaborate casualness, no great indignation, and little punitiveness. During the course of the biographies, at the time when they told me of their adolescence, there was only one who boggled at the unexpected question "How did you learn about sex?" and then, "Could you tell me something about your first sex experiences?" Sokolsky and Johnson did a little bragging—most emphasized how shy they had been. Those who had been in the service were invited to talk about their extracurricular life. Every veteran has heard it all before—the conquests and the failures. How important is sex in marriage? Again it was less what they said than the symptoms of worry such a question might bring forth.

The more objective evidence of the sex-tension scale can help only a little; it became available to me after half of the interviewing was done, and after I had interviewed Johnson and Rapuano. But it helps to portray the shared sexual ideology against which the special nature of the men who are afraid of freedom can be assessed. With little evidence of tension, these eight Eastport men tended to believe that "most people have some kind of sexual problem." With even greater unanimity, and no tension, there was agreement that "There is more sexual perversion than most people think." There was no tendency to think of sex as bestial, and a complete agreement that the human body is beautiful. In short, one might say that there was an acceptance of sex and the human body and even of some sex deviation without panic. On the other hand there was a moral concern with the problems of control: the movies and press were almost universally viewed as containing too much sex; the parental generation was thought to be more moral than the present one; almost everyone thought prostitution and homosexuality were wrong, even though no children were involved; and most thought people in public life should set better moral examples. So far, one might say the symptoms of an accepting attitude within a framework of morality and control as socially defined were reasonably healthy.

Some more difficult problems emerge in the evidence that seven of the eight thought that "most people are sexually inhibited," particularly if this is combined with the view of five of the eight that "most people today are promiscuous" (the terms were explained to most of the men). In the context of their life stories, these views suggested that they are saying "*I* am too inhibited" and "*They* are too promiscuous." Some of these promiscuous individuals, we see from other questions, are "young people" and "Negroes." And it is quite possible that some of the inhibition that these men have in mind is not their own but that of the other sex, since three of these men believe "most women are probably sexually cold." However this may be, the most common pattern is the belief that people are both promiscuous and inhibited and, by inference, that others are promiscuous and I am inhibited, or perhaps that I have impulses I inhibit, while others have impulses they don't inhibit. They are bad; I am good. They are lucky; I am deprived. If this is so, and if it is nevertheless true that most men tolerate the general idea of a relaxed and free society, we would say that it is because they do not feel anxious about their own control system, believing it to be, if anything, somewhat over-developed. At some level they may be more concerned about their own lack of spontaneity and capacity for expression than they are about their capacity to control their various sexual impulses.

This is what society has made of them. Their life situations are those of responsible men, managing their affairs for the benefit of their wives, their children, their neighbors, society—but perhaps not to their own inner satisfaction. Working and saving have given them a control system they do not need to worry about now—at least most of them don't. They are trapped in their social roles of husband and breadwinner—but, fortunately, they derive enough satisfaction so that they are not punitively envious of those they imagine still to be free—the young, the Negro, and perhaps the Bohemian, of which they may be only dimly aware.[8]

3. Of the three high scorers (out of eight tested) on the sex-tension scale, one of them, Ferrera, reveals almost no supporting evidence in the interview material that would justify a conclusion that in a broader context his life problems (which are substantial) stem primarily from sexual sources. Another, Sullivan, does indeed show other symptoms that suggest the validity of this high score, but there is much contrary evidence, too. Sokolsky is the third.

Sokolsky's interest in sex comes to our attention as he discusses his early dates. "I had plenty of them; that's the trouble. I had too, too gol-darned many. My older brother had very few." Then, as now, he was competing with a more favored (and more handsome) older brother. What did he do on these dates? "Just like any other boy, I tried to get what I could." He goes on to say that the main topic of conversation down at the shop is sex. "That's something I'd like to talk about. . . . What's going on today is rough." At this point in the interview, I usually ask about whether the respondent has met any homosexuals and what he thinks should be done with them. I try this here, but Sokolsky brushes it aside in favor of his solution to the sex problem: "The way I figure it, I think the government should do something about that—and have a place where a man could go to relieve himself. Like you have in different states; they have houses where a man can go and relieve himself. That's what they should have all over the country. . . . Like a man, say he's in the mood, goes, satisfies himself, and he's okay. That's why you have all these rapes and all that today." I suggest that the prostitute's life is a hard one, and Sokolsky answers, "You'd find a lot of them that would go for a job like that," but later he thinks most of the women he has known are somewhat cold sexually. He claims (contrary to fact) that Eastport has a large number of houses of prostitution, but says he has never been to one. "Since I'm married I haven't fooled around with any other woman. I don't feel I should take that chance, because you don't know if the woman is clean or not." The discussion continues, and it is getting late in the night, but Sokolsky is eager to talk about oversexed men and women and rape: "You read in the paper where this girl got raped here, this girl got raped there," and so on, with emotion, gestures, and an intensity of interest that carry him away from the world of home, factory, and his limping routine life as a janitor and factory hand. It is congruent with this interest to find Sokolsky, alone among these men, mentioning the problem of Negro rapists under a system of greater freedom.

Rapuano, the second of the three men afraid of more freedom, did not take the sex-tension test; the suggestion that he has such tension comes in another way. I became aware of some problem of this nature when I helped him on with his coat as we were leaving my office to drive back to his home. He snatched the coat from my hand, saying with great embarrassment that he couldn't stand to have people help him on with his coat. He recognized it as a problem, and thought that it might be something I could help him with. Later, reflecting on this incident, it appeared to me that it was the physical contact that disturbed him, although at the time I thought it might be something of the dependent role, or, as he perhaps interpreted it, the feminine role, of some-one being helped on with a coat. The incident was followed a few days later with Rapuano's account of "the way he learned about sex." He says first that it wasn't a problem for him. He used to sit around listening to others tell about their dates, but it "never made a deep impression" on him. Then "of course, as time went on, I became curious." Did you satisfy your curiosity? "Well, it took a long time. Actually, I was afraid—afraid of women, because I was always afraid that I may—well, maybe do something wrong that they didn't like, you know?"

On the same evening Rapuano told at some length about an episode during the war when by good fortune and planning he found himself in bed with a waitress in a strange city, and, as he says, "God damn, I couldn't do a thing with her." Instead of going back to his post in style on the scheduled train (a great treat in the service), Rapuano "took a troop train back, just to get away from those girls." Finally, Rapuano turned from his discussion of a woman candidate for mayor to the subject of "women cops." He said:

> I go across Main Street and I turn in, I think, on Maple Street, and there's one—one woman policeman there. My God she's pretty, and everything—she's got a pretty face, and geez—if there's anything that's not feminine, it's watching a woman doing this here—[motions traffic on with his hands] you know. I can't stand that. . . . That's something I can't stand. I think I'll take another route to work. . . . I could see a fat woman, maybe, in the middle of the street, doing that, but when you get a girl that's really pretty over there—it's really unfeminine like—my God.

It is clear enough that for Rapuano there is something about this fused boy-girl figure that is intolerable—the pretty girl in the masculine clothes sets off a nearly explosive charge of anxiety. Rapuano is a family man, a father, a virtuous citizen; but the symptoms of sexual tension upon occasion come bubbling to the surface.

Weighing the evidence, then, we find two men with problems of sexual expression and control. We said earlier that there were three men who seemed to have somewhat morbid fears of what "people who feel too free" might do: Sokolsky, Rapuano, and Johnson. Now it appears that two of these men are the same as those with problems of sexual expression and control: Rapuano and Sokolsky. The theory, then, has such confirmation as this evidence will bear. It is easier to spell out for Sokolsky: he talks about freedom and rape, freedom and sexual license in the same breath. When he worries about what people might do if they got too free, he worries about their sexual behavior. But the trail is not so clear with Rapuano—perhaps because his inclinations are more deeply repressed than whatever it is that is bothering Sokolsky. Moreover, they are more frightening to Rapuano; they threaten him with an unbearable sense of guilt, and hence take more subterranean routes in their expression and are reflected in more morbid consequences. If our guess about Rapuano is correct, and the theory valid, they may be seen to emerge in the fear of murder, perhaps his own. But, even if these interpretations are correct, this is only a beginning, for beliefs, like behavior, have many sources.

B
FREEDOM OF ANGER

As children we are told not to strike our brothers, or even to quarrel with them; in church we are told, "Love thy neighbor as thyself"; the law has penalties for violence against others; it even has provisions against the use of "fighting words." But the anger wells up within; the hostility will not down; the mind and will are often—very often—not master of our emotions. Hence we are engaged in a struggle for control, a struggle in which society sometimes takes a hand. It would be plausible if the men of Eastport were to be concerned about the relaxation of that controlling hand, lest their own control be insufficient.

Again we must report that for the most part this seems in truth not to be the usual case. Reporting on "the last time you got angry or lost your temper," they tell of events that do not bear the marks of rage or show the symptoms of a struggle for control, although they do worry over the incidents.

Eleven of these men, while not "sweet" and sometimes not gentle, are not bothered with problems of hostilities they cannot express easily and without much damage to others. If they get angry, they "blow," as they say, and let it go at that. Or, like

Dempsey, they live on a monotonous emotional plane; or, like Flynn and Ruggiero, they find successful sublimation in their work. Only two seemed angry with me in the interview sessions, Sullivan and the "overeducated" Farrel, and both for the same reason—they resented the subordinate status of the interviewee. Their "faith in people," their impression of a benign government, their level of tolerance, are not those of an alienated, frustrated, and angry group of men—but of a group who can live easily within their modest budget of anger.

That is the picture for most of the men—but there are four who present a somewhat different profile; Johnson is not among these, but Rapuano and Sokolsky are. Rapuano, as one might guess from his intense outbursts on doctors and Communists, has a certain volatility of emotion he first denies then recognizes: "Well, I get mad, sure. I wouldn't say easily. I get mad at—oh, yes, very often, sure." He describes an incident when he lost his temper because he didn't like the way one of the boys in the factory recently talked to him in front of his nephew. He reports it this way:

> So I told him, I says, "Look" I says, "You talk to me that way once more, and I'm going to hit you right in the stomach." I told him, you know. He's bigger than me, but he didn't say nothin'. He's one guy I wouldn't want to be friends with, see? . . . It wouldn't take me long to, you know, just belt him one.

But as for fights—and this man is forty-two—it has been a year and a half since he had one. He didn't like his helper, and when his helper protested the way he spoke to him and threatened to knock him down, Rapuano said to him:

> "Well, if you're going to knock me down, let's go outside and you knock me down," see? And we were outside and I hit him five times, and that was it, see? He doesn't come to me any more and tell me he's going to knock me down any more, see? And in fact he's doing better since I hit him. I think I ought to hit him more often. [pause] Oh, yes, I think I broke a rib on him and loosened a couple of teeth.

But along with the anger there is love, genuine love; speaking of his son, he says, "I'll grab ahold of him and kiss him and what not, and I'll tell him I love him and all that there." This is not a cold angry man; it is a warm, impulsive man, quick to anger. He fights with Communists on street corners; he had a habit of turning over ash cans in Jewish neighborhoods before he reformed (I find no traces of this kind of rabid anti-Semitism now); he fires off a post-card to Khrushchev to "shut your big fat mouth." His fear of freedom, as we have discussed it above, is fed by a secret fear of what an angry man might do without the restraints of government and society and convention and family to help him out.

Rapuano thinks people in general will go too far if they have greater freedom; but, as one might expect, in view of his record, he thinks one of the central dangers is the abuse of freedom by the Communists. This trenchant fear of Communism, unique among the men, has a special meaning to Rapuano that is only dimly revealed by the interview material. At the end of our many hours together, the last question asked and answered, I mentioned that his feeling about Communists was a little different from that of the others, and asked him why this might be. With a tremor in his voice, and breathing hard, he says: "I have a very, very strong feeling about Communism. I can't—I—to me, an American Communist is—it's—I can't explain it. It's just—there's not words to describe how I feel about that." He searches for words, and says: "I don't like to see people in chains. . . . I don't like to see people more or less slaves to other people. I don't like to see people told what to do." To the hard-working Rapuano, the personal meaning of slavery, of submission, of being dominated is suggested by the discussion of his sexual confusion. It is only a tentative inference, and the reader must decide what weight it will bear, but I think Rapuano's fear that the Communists will "enslave" him and "dominate" him has its source in a fear that his wish to be attacked or "dominated" or even "enslaved" by men will be acted out or discovered. Together, these two problem areas of sex and anger, with possibly a single source, have led Rapuano into a classic political pattern—that of the militant heresy hunter.

Like Rapuano, Sokolsky, too, is an angry man. Within the past year or so he threatened to punch his older brother if he got too "exclusive"; when his younger brother said something he didn't like to his mother, "I just turned around and, boom . . . I really hit, up and hit him, right across the face." In appraising his own character, he says: "Once in a while I get hotheaded. It takes me a long time to, but when I do—boom, I'll explode. [pause] I can't think of any other bad points about myself." Speaking of himself as a child, he says, "I wouldn't take any—small as I was—I wouldn't take any sass from anybody. Boom, I used to take off, and boom, that was it."

In his discussion of freedom, Sokolsky, more than any of the others, is concerned with legality, but it is a flexible legality. Often it seems as though he is saying that circumstances and desires must inevitably lead people to break the restrictions on their behavior that are provided by law and that human nature is uncontrollable. At other times he seems to panic at the thought of these uncontrollable desires and the fragility of the law. It will be recalled that in his discussion of sex and delinquency, Sokolsky advocated government-operated brothels as a useful solution in Eastport. But, on the other hand, he "strongly disagrees" in the sex-tension scale that "our laws regulating sexual behavior are far too strict." Speaking of law and restraint in general, he says, "The law's all right, as long as they just don't break them, [pause] which they are today," and he goes on to report that robbing and burglary are rampant in Eastport. He adopts a tolerant view toward this— it is because of the depression (early 1958) and men seeking food for their families. If you put them in jail, the city has to take care of the children—a poor solution. But the next minute he reports, as we have said earlier, that any relaxation of restrictions, any increase of freedom will mean that people will steal, kill, "and it would be an awful mess of a country." He bitterly opposes the treatment of the Negroes in the South, particularly in Little Rock. But in Eastport, if the laws were relaxed, he says, "I think they would really run wild." In this confusion, this struggle between conscience and desire, law and liberty, Sokolsky finds freedom a tenuous thing—desirable but infinitely dangerous. And so it is. But it is not so dangerous as Sokolsky thinks, because others—at least the others in Eastport that make up my little group—do not go "boom" so easily as Sokolsky.

C
THE IMPULSE TO CONSUME

In the discussion so far, turning the facets of emotional life to see how they might fit, as with a jigsaw puzzle, into the patterns of an ideology of freedom, we have found it not so difficult to find a "fit" for two of the three men who, it will be remembered, spoke of increments of freedom in terms of the release of the dark forces in mankind: murder, theft, rape. These two, Sokolsky and Rapuano, have problems of anger and problems of sexual tension. But there is a third member of this group, Johnson, who, like the others, saw men released from control as wild and rapacious; yet he has neither a terrible temper nor such marked problems of sexual adjustment. But, as we have noted, he is an emotional man, an impulsive man. Have we some tentative explanation that is a clue to this aspect of his ideology?

Johnson's problems center upon his inability to restrain his consumption impulses. At the most obvious point, these refer to oral intake. Although the problem is within his capacity to manage, Johnson has a drinking problem; he ranks second from the bottom in a rating scale on control of alcoholic indulgence. Of himself in youth he says, "I was always a big eater," and he worries today over his tendency to put on weight. For an active man he is somewhat heavy. His talk about good times is concerned, more than that of the others, with food and places to eat; and, in the telltale language of the body, his ulcer announces the unconscious tendency of the stomach to "nurse" on its own lining.

These matters speak of problems of oral indulgence, but as far as Johnson is concerned, the problem is focused upon money. Consider, with a little patience, three answers to completely different questions spaced at different times throughout the interviews. On the first occasion I ask Johnson if he has worries and, if so, what he worries about. He says: "Even though I'm happy-go-lucky most of the time, I do a lot of worrying. But most of my worries involve money. It seems as though they're practically all based on it." Since this answer is not so different from others, we might ignore it, but the theme comes up again in a unique way. Asked about the main lessons life has taught him, Johnson says:

> Well, we'll have to go to money again. My primary trouble in my life has been money—getting involved in things, you know? . . . And I know what the answer is, but I just can't seem to get there —not to move so fast to spend that money, gaining things that you don't actually need, which I have learned, and believe me, I have been doing, for some time. . . . Here, about two years ago, if I didn't like my car, boom, I'd go out and sign the papers to buy a car. Or I wanted a suit of clothes; I'd go down and get a suit of clothes. I have learned a lesson there.

He certainly is conscious of the problem; but though he was still substantially in debt, he was planning some rather elaborate vacations when I talked to him.

In our discussion of Utopia, I asked Johnson what he would not have to do in Utopia that he does in the everyday world we live in. He said: "I could look everybody in the face and say, 'I don't owe you a dime.' That would be one of my main things."

And in a minute or two he reflects back on this, and says, "Believe me, I'm a great dreamer, but this I know: if I could ever get out of debt, I would never be foolish again in those ways."

The problem, of course, extends in all directions. It makes him somewhat grasping. He has arranged some rather shady insurance deals with a local garage man so that he could collect for a dent in his bumper from a woman who grazed him slightly but who did not put the dent there. He does some repair work on the side, and if he thinks the householder does not know the price of materials, he overcharges. These are matters that bother him considerably; he is shamefaced about them. But the temptation to grasp so that he might consume was more than he could stand.

So also with his judgment of other men. In his view all men are grasping; all men, particularly politicians, are out to "make a buck" in any way they can. They are not malicious and they do no real harm; but that is the nature of man, as he sees man through the prism of his own character.

It is with evidence of this kind that I arrive at the conclusion that Johnson's fear of freedom is, like that of the others, based upon a problem of impulse control. He has only the most tenuous direction of these impulses; he is in a constant struggle with them, usually winning in the struggle, but by a slender margin. In such circumstances it is quite plausible to believe that he welcomes social controls and fears freedom. He welcomes them not only because he fears what he might do if they were less binding but also because he fears the penalties that he might incur *and that he would deserve* if he transgressed or overindulged. He mentions stealing, perhaps, because this is close to his own illicit desires, the grasping impulse he must struggle with. He mentions raping because it is close to his problem of seizing and enjoying what he wants—now, without thought. And he mentions murder, not because of his hostile impulses but because, one might say, he fears that this is the appropriate end of those who let themselves go, as he fears he might.

D

EGO STRENGTH, EMOTIONALITY, AND FREEDOM-TENSION

There is one thing in common among the men whose sex, anger, and consumption problems we have discussed—they are all emotional and impulsive men. It is important to make clear that emotional, expressive people are not the only ones who have trouble with control of their emotions; indeed, the very tightness of lip of the repressed, the coldness of the quietly cruel, the deliberation of speech of the man who fears to wound because he wants to kill—all show evidence of control problems that may be far worse and are infinitely more blameworthy than those we have dealt with above. Nor are these three men under discussion the only men who are expressive—Ruggiero is one of the most mobile and quickly expressive of men. These are, let it be said again, those with affective problems that seem troublesome to them and bear a discernible relation to their attitudes toward freedom and restraint.

At an early point in the analysis of these fifteen men, my research assistant, David Sears, and I attempted to make an informal assessment of the ego strength of the men. The criteria for this assessment are set forth in Appendix C; briefly, they deal with aspects of impulse control and capacity to deal effectively with certain environmental demands. We examined their capacity to control their tempers, to spend in moderation to meet their most pressing needs, to drink in moderation, to accept defeat, to plan for long-range goals, and to relate their aspiration levels to their probable achievement levels. We also weighed their control over moodiness and prolonged periods of depression.

Three of the five men with the least "internal" ego strength (contrasted with the strength to deal with external or environmental demands), as these factors measured it, were, from the weakest to the least weak: Sokolsky, Rapuano, and Johnson. These are the men we have been talking about. Thus there is a general theme, a latent structure, lying half hidden in the pattern made by each specific problem of impulse control—the general theme of ego strength. Elsewhere we have discussed the relationship of such strength to political participation; it seems to be a close one.[4] Now to this we must add that only the strong egos can support a free society, can bear the burden of choice, can accept the responsibility for internal control in the absence of social control.

Those who do not have this control in sufficient strength to enable them to enjoy freedom, or to contemplate its extension without extravagant concern, may not yet demand a closed society.

4. Robert E. Lane, *Political Life: Why People Get Involved in Politics* (New York: The Free Press of Glencoe, 1959), pp. 147–55.

After all, their ideology is multiply determined: Sokolsky's Jew-ishness will make him shy of many restrictionist movements; John-son and Rapuano dislike positions of subordination—they will not easily yield to anything that implies a personal domination. They are not searching for an escape from freedom; they are merely expressing their freedom-tension. At the same time, each desires and fears restraint. And if he should transgress, he desires to be assured forgiveness.

Fromm stresses the importance of Protestantism in individual-izing man's relation to the universe, creating the basis for a more general "individuation" of men, a quality he thinks characteristic of modern times.[5] The men who are struggling with this prob-lem "escape from freedom" in a specific way: they seek to integrate themselves in a "band of brothers," a solidary group that will re-lieve them of their burdens of individual responsibility and choice. What I am suggesting here is somewhat different; I suggest that the burden of freedom for modern (and ancient) man comes from relying on an inadequate system of personal controls. For him, therefore, the solution is the reinforcement of convention, the specification of behavioral codes, the demand for sanctions against licentious behavior, the encroachment of the criminal code upon the area of individual choice. This is another escape from free-dom, based upon another and different kind of personal need. One of the problems of political theory has been, of late, to ac-count for the nonauthoritarians who seem only tenuously sup-portive of a free society. Perhaps these three men, Rapuano, Sokol-sky, and Johnson, suggest a source for this frail support, a source in the problems of impulse control, an *impulsion syndrome*, which contributes something to this accounting system.

A contrast to the present situation is offered by the Puritan colonies on the American continent three hundred years ago. For them, too, there were control problems emerging from the trou-blesome impulses—as there always are for every society—but the means of handling the situation were different. We might say that they increased the problem for each individual by making the level of control required almost unendurable; but at the same time they helped him with his problem by giving him both a "Puritan conscience" with which to shackle his wayward impulses *and* a social control system that reinforced the conscience at every turn. Twentieth century America works in precisely the reverse

5. Fromm, *op. cit.*, pp. 40–102.

manner—the expression of sex impulses, including deviant ones, the expression of anger in children and adults, the indulgence of appetites of all kinds are regarded with tolerance. At the same time the society fails, as Riesman has pointed out, to create the conscience and the code to guide this new freedom; moreover, society does not easily reinforce this conscience and code with church, press, and school as was done in the Puritan days. Thus the vagueness of what is allowed and the inadequate control system contribute to the freedom-tension of modern society.

4

The Fear of Equality

Life depends, not upon birth and status, not upon breeding or beauty, but upon effort, effort that will be rewarded in riches, in material goods which are the sign that the effort was made, that one has in the language of childhood been "good."
—MARGARET MEAD, *And Keep Your Powder Dry*, p. 55

"Among the novel objects that attracted my attention during my stay in the United States," said Tocqueville in the opening lines of *Democracy in America*, "nothing struck me more forcibly than the general equality of condition among the people. I readily discovered the prodigious influence that this primary fact exercises on the whole course of society." [1] Some sixty years later, Bryce comments, "The United States are deemed all the world over to be preeminently the land of equality." [2] But what is it that impressed Tocqueville and "the world" as equal? Is it the equality of men at birth that Jefferson said was self-evident? Tocqueville had in mind something else, and so did Bryce. Tocqueville found their material equality "the fundamental

1. Alexis de Tocqueville, *Democracy in America*, Phillips Bradley, ed. (New York: Knopf, 1945), I, 3.
2. James Bryce, *The American Commonwealth* (New York: Macmillan, 1910), II, 810.

fact from which all others seem to be derived and the central
point at which all my observations constantly terminated." [3] But
some sixty-five years later, Bryce could not agree, for he found that
the growth of great fortunes had altered the scene since Tocqueville reported on it, and, moreover, "we may expect these inequalities of wealth to grow." [4] In a parallel way, Tocqueville found
that Americans were remarkably similar in education and intellectual ability,[5] while Bryce found that the proportion of those
with a superior education "rises faster than does the general
level of the multitude so that in this regard also it appears that
equality has diminished and will diminish further." [6] But in spite
of these differences, Bryce and Tocqueville agreed on one thing:
the social relations among Americans of all conditions of life had
an equalitarian style to them that distinguished Americans from
the citizens of other nations:

> The equality of estimation—the idea which men form of other
> men as compared with themselves [says Bryce], it is in this that the
> real sense of equality comes out. In America men hold others to
> be at bottom exactly the same as themselves . . . the admiration
> felt [for a great man] may be a reason for going to see him and
> longing to shake hands with him, a longing frequent in America.
> But it is not a reason for bowing down to him, or addressing him
> in deferential terms, or treating him as if he were porcelain and
> yourself only earthenware.[7]

This sense that we are all made of the same common clay, a
meaningful, if figurative, translation of the idea that we are all
born equal, is hard to capture in words, difficult to describe, de-
ceptive to native and foreign observers alike. For example, a contemporary of Bryce's, Hugo Münsterburg, tries his hand at it thus:

> The American labourer does not feel that his position is in-
> ferior; he knows that he has an equal opportunity with everybody
> else, and the idea of entire equality does not attract him, and
> would even deprive him of what he holds most valuable—namely,
> his self-initiative, which aims for the highest social reward as
> recognition of the highest individual achievement.[8]

3. Alexis de Tocqueville, *op. cit.*, I, 3.
4. James Bryce, *op. cit.*, II, 811.
5. Alexis de Tocqueville, *op. cit.*, I, 51.
6. James Bryce, *op. cit.*, II, 812.
7. *Ibid.*, p. 817.
8. Hugo Münsterburg, *The Americans* (New York: McClure, Phillips, 1904), p.
323.

The unrealism that shades this historic discussion of the American workingman with a persistently rosy hue affects Münsterburg's concept. Certainly the American laborer knows that he receives less income, less deference, less preferment in public places than the middle-class men. He knows that his position is inferior but he responds to this in a special way. He is not so blind as to think he has equal opportunity with everyone else; but he knows that he has more opportunity than he is using, more, perhaps, than he can use. He certainly does not seek "the highest social reward," but rather, only an increment of those rewards that come as a consequence of a little better job: an increment of income, status, and recognition. But in one sense, Münsterburg is right: "The idea of entire equality does not attract him." It is a matter worth exploring.

A

EQUALITARIANISM
AND WORKING-CLASS MOVEMENTS

The inequalitarian drift of income and education that Bryce thought he detected in the United States of his time seems to have been arrested. The richest 1 per cent of the people received between 12 and 13 per cent of the national income payments (before taxes) after the First World War; they received between 8 and 9 per cent after the Second World War.[9] The bite of the progressive income tax and inheritance tax, the provision of social security, unemployment insurance, and subsidized programs of public housing and public health have further reduced the disparities between the rich and the poor. Bryce refers to the "finished luxury of the villas" at Newport, but since then Newport has become only a shadow of its former self, as Cleveland Amory shows in *The Last Resorts*.[10] The equality of opportunity, the chance to rise in the world, is at least as great today as it was thirty years ago, and the probability of a decline in status is, in fact, less.[11] In some ways we have come back a little closer to the equalitarian-

9. United States Bureau of the Census, *Historical Statistics of the United States 1789–1945* (Washington, D.C.: U.S. Government Printing Office, 1949), p. 14; and supplement *Continuation to 1952* (1954), p. 1.
10. Cleveland Amory, *The Last Resorts* (New York: Harper, 1952).
11. See Natalie Rogoff, *Recent Trends in Occupational Mobility* (New York: The Free Press of Glencoe, 1953), pp. 61–63.

ism of Tocqueville's time. Where does the energy for this movement come from? Who is behind it?

Since 1848 it has been assumed that the drive for a more equalitarian society, its effective social force, would come from the stratum of society with the most to gain, the working classes. This was thought to be the revolutionary force in the world—the demand of workers for a classless society sparked by their hostility to the owning classes. It was to be the elite among the workers, not the *Lumpenproletariat,* not the "scum," who were to advance this movement. Just as "liberty" was the central slogan of the bourgeois revolution, so "equality" was the central concept in the working-class movement. Hence it was natural to assume that whatever gains have been made in equalizing the income and status of men in our society came about largely from working-class pressure.

But on closer investigation the demands for greater liberty or "freedom" prove to have been of an ambiguous nature. The middle classes sought freedom of speech and action in large part for the economic gains that this would give them, and moralized their action with the theology of freedom. But the freedom that they gained was frightening, for it deprived them of the solidary social relationships and the ideological certainty that often gave order and meaning to their lives. On occasion, then, they sought to "escape from freedom." [12] The older unfree order had a value the earlier social commentators did not appreciate.

There is a parallel here with the movement toward a more equalitarian society. The upper working class and the lower middle class support specific measures, embraced in the formula "welfare state," that have equalitarian consequences. But, so I shall argue, many members of the working classes do not want equality. They are afraid of it. In some ways they already seek to escape from it. Equality for the working classes, like freedom for the middle classes, is a worrisome, partially rejected, by-product of the demand for more specific measures. Inequality has values to them that have been overlooked. It is these attitudes on status and equality that I shall explore here.

12. Erich Fromm, *Escape from Freedom* (New York: Rinehart, 1941).

B

HOW TO ACCOUNT FOR ONE'S OWN STATUS?

Attitudes toward equality rest in the first instance upon one's attitude toward one's own status. Like a large number of social beliefs, attitudes toward equality take their direction from beliefs about the self, the status of the self, one's self-esteem or lack thereof. It is necessary, therefore, first to explore how people see themselves in American hierarchical society.

The American culture and the democratic dogma have given to the American public the notion that "all men are created equal." Even more insistently, the American culture tells its members: "achieve," "compete," "be better, smarter, quicker, richer than your fellow men"; in short, "be unequal." The men I interviewed had received these inequalitarian messages, some eagerly, some with foreboding. Having heard them, they must account for their status, higher than some, lower than others. They must ask themselves, for example, "Why didn't I rise out of the working class, or out of the 'housing-project class,' or out of the underpaid office-help class?" And, on the other hand, "Why am I better off than my parents or than the fellows down the road in the low-rental project or than the fellows on relief?" Men confronted with these questions adopt a variety of interesting answers.

Is It Up to Me?

The problem of accounting for status is personally important for these men only if they think that their decisions, effort, and energy make a difference in their position in life. Most of my subjects accepted the view that America opens up opportunity to all people, if not in equal proportions, then at least enough so that a person must assume responsibility for his own status. Thus O'Hara, a maintenance mechanic in a factory, in a typical response, comments that the rich man's son and the poor man's son "have equal opportunity to be President . . . if they've got the education and the know-how." But, he goes on to say, "Some of them have a little more help than others." This is the constant theme: "All men can better themselves"; the circumstances of American life do not imprison men in their class or station—if there is such a prison, the iron bars are within each man.

There were a few, of course, who stressed the differences of opportunity at birth, a mockery of the phrase "all men are created equal." Here, as only rarely in the interviews, a head of steam builds up that might feed radical social movements. But this is true for only a few of the sample. Three or four angry young or middle-aged men deny the Jeffersonian phrase. Rapuano, the packinghouse clerk, says:

> How could you say we were born equal when, for instance, when I was born, I was born in a family that were pretty poor. You get another baby born in a family that has millions.

And Kuchinsky, a roofer, says:

> Are we created equal? I don't believe we are, because everybody's got much more than another and it's not right, I think. Of course, ah, we have no choice. I mean we can't do nothing about it. So we're not as equal as the next party, that's for sure.

And Ferrera, a shoe salesman, says:

> All men created equal? Ah, very hypocritical, 'cause all men are not created equal—and—I don't know—you really pick some beauties don't you? . . . The birth of an individual in a [social] class sort of disputes this.

To these men, then, subordination and life position are attributable not so much to the efforts of the individual, something for which he must assume responsibility, as to the circumstances of birth, over which he has no control. Yet for each of those men the channels of advancement were seen as only partly blocked. Rapuano, for example, says elsewhere that income is generally proportionate to ability. Like the theme of "moral equality," the theme of differential life chances from birth is easily available. What is surprising is not that it is used at all, but rather that it is used so infrequently.

C
REDUCING THE IMPORTANCE OF THE STRUGGLE

When something is painful to examine, people look away, or, if they look at it, they see only the parts they want to see. They deny that it is an important something. So is it often with a person's class status when the reference is upward, when people must account, not for the strength of their position, but for its weakness. How do they do this? [13]

In the first place they may *insulate* themselves, limit their outlook and range of comparisons. Ferrera, who says, "It's pretty hard for me to think there is anyone in the upper class and I'm not in the upper class," slides into a prepared position of insulated defense:

> I think a lot of people place a lot of stress on the importance of social classes, [but] I feel that I have a job to do, I have my own little unit to take care of. If I can do it to the best ability that is instilled in me at birth or progress through the years, I feel that I rightly deserve the highest classification you can get. I don't particularly like the headings, "upper, middle, working, and lower."

It is a resentful narrowing of focus in this case: two years at an inferior college may have led to ambitions that life then failed to fulfill. Contrast this to Woodside, a railroad guard and auxiliary policeman with a Midwestern rural background, who accepts the "categories" of social class rather willingly. He says, after dealing with the moral and intangible aspects of equality, and after being asked, "Are there any people whom you regard as not being equal to you?"

> Well, that is a tough question. Well, in fairness, I'd say all people are equal to one another in his own category. When I say category, I mean you couldn't exactly expect a person that had very little knowledge to be, we'll say, should have a position where a person with a lot more education had it.

Equality must be treated within classes, not between them, to be meaningful—and in this way the problem of placing oneself becomes tolerable, or sometimes rather gratifying.

A second device for reducing the impact of class position is to *deny its importance*. This is not to deny the importance of

13. "The fierceness of the mobility race generates tensions too severe for some people to bear, and fear of failure in the race generates a sense of insecurity which is highly injurious. Denial of status deprives the individual of one of his deepest psychological needs. . . . It follows, then, that even where status has been publicly renounced, individuals continue to manifest, in a variety of ways, a deep psychological craving for the certitudes which it offers. The hazards and insecurities resulting from absence of status have sometimes caused an impulse, as Erich Fromm expresses it, to 'escape from freedom.' " David M. Potter, *People of Plenty: Economic Abundance and the American Character* (Chicago: University of Chicago Press, 1954), p. 106.

getting ahead, but to limit this to the problem of job classification or occupational choice—nothing so damaging to the self-esteem as an ordering of persons on a class scale. Rapuano, resisting the class concept, says:

> I don't think it [social class] is important. I mean, whenever I went and asked for a job, the boss never asked me what class I was in. They just wanted to know if I knew my business. Oh, yes, and I don't think in politics it makes any difference.

Others maintain that for other countries social class is important, but not for Americans. There are rich and poor, perhaps, but not status, class, or deference levels to be accounted for.

A third device for reducing the significance of the struggle for status and "success" is *resignation,* a reluctant acceptance of one's fate. When some men assume this posture of resignation one senses a pose; their secret hopes and ambitions will not down. For others it rings true. When Dempsey, a factory operative, speaks of his situation at the age of fifty-five, one believes him:

> It's hard, very hard. We seem to be struggling along now, as it is, right here, to try and get above our level, to get out of the rut, as you might say, that we're probably in right now. . . . [But] After you get to a certain age, there, you stop—and you say, "Well, I can't go any further." I think I've gotten to that point now.

But when Sokolsky reports that he is contented with his station in life, it does not seem authentic:

> Being in the average group [he wouldn't assign himself a class status] doesn't bother me. I know I make a living—as long as I make a living, and I'm happy and I have what I want—try to give my family what they want. It doesn't bother me—no. I'm satisfied.

But then he adds, "I hope to God my children will do better than their father did."

Contrast these views with those of Johnson, a mechanic who says: "I feel someday I'll be better off. I feel that way because I believe I have it within me to do it"; and with Flynn, a white-collar worker, who answers:

> No, I'm nowhere near satisfied. It seems to me every time I start to move up a little bit, all the levels move up one step ahead of me. I can't ever get out of this area. I have a certain desire and willingness to do something extra.

D

THE WORKING CLASS GETS ITS SHARE

When comparing their status with those lower on the scale, however each man may define it, it is easy to point with pride to achievement, material well-being, standing in the community. But satisfaction with one's self and one's friends depends on seeing some advantage in one's situation vis-à-vis those who live and work on a higher status level. At first this seems to be a difficult task, but in many simple ways it can be easily done. Our sample, for example, found ways of ascribing greater happiness, power, and even income to the working class than would be found in the upper class.

The equality of happiness is a fruitful vein. Lower income and status are more tolerable when one can believe that the rich are not receiving a happiness income commensurate with their money income. "Are the rich happier than people who are just average?" O'Hara does not think so:

I think lots of times they're never happy, because one thing is, the majority of them that are rich have got more worries. You see a lot more of them sick than you do, I think, the average. I think a lot of your mental strain is a lot greater in the higher class—in the rich class—than in the other.

And Johnson says:

Well, even though this rich man can go places and do things that others can't afford, there's only certain things in life that I think make people happy. For instance, having children, and having a place to live—no matter where it is, it's your home . . . the majority of these big men—I don't think they devote as much time and get a thrill out of the little things in life that the average guy gets, which I think is a lot of thrills.

Indeed, hardly a man thought the rich were happier. And yet, O'Hara says, on another occasion: "What is the most important thing that money can buy? Happiness, when you come down to it." Perhaps he means that money buys happiness for the average man but not for the rich. In this way he can cope with a mild envy by appropriating happiness for himself and "his kind."

Power, like happiness, is awarded to the working (or lower-middle) class. The sheer fact of numbers gives a sense of strength and importance. Costa, a factory operative, says, for example, "People like you [the interviewer] are the minority and people like me are the majority, so we get taken care of in the long run." Whether a person sees himself as middle class or working class, he is likely to believe that most people belong to his class. This being true, his class, people like him, become the most important force in electoral decisions. O'Hara puts it this way:

> The biggest part of the people in this country are working class. And I think they've got the most to do with—they've got a big part to do with running this country—because the lower class, a lot of them don't vote, when you come down to it, they don't have the education to vote, and your upper class isn't that much —isn't as great as the other, so really when you come down to it, it's your working class that's deciding one way or the other.

Not only do they "have a big part to do with running the country," they are crucial for the economy. This is not only as producers—indeed, no one mentioned the theme romantic writers on the laboring man and the immigrant have often employed— "they cleared the land and built the cities." Rather it is because of their power to shatter the economy and their power to survive in a depression that they are important. Kuchinsky explains this as follows:

> I think the lower class of people are the important people. I think so because of the business end of it. Without us, I don't think the businessman could survive. I mean if we don't work— of course, they have the money, but, ah, a lot of times during the crash, which was an awful thing, too, I think a lot of 'em lived so high that they couldn't stand it any more when they went broke, and they committed a lot of suicides there. But we were used to living that way, it didn't bother us.

Today, as perhaps never before, the working-class man can see his status loss, compared to white-collar workers, as a loss compensated by income advantages. Thus DeAngelo, a machine operator and shop steward, reports:

> You got people working in offices, they might consider themselves upper class, y'know, a little better than the workingman. But nine times out of ten the workingman is making more money than he is.

And in the same vein, Rapuano says:

> I certainly would hate like hell to be a white-collar worker in the middle class and making the money that the white-collar

worker does. I would rather be a worker in the lower class, and making their money, see?

Of course, this assignment of income advantages to the working class hinges upon a narrowing of the range of competition—but this is the range that makes a difference for these men.

E

MORAL EQUALITY

Another device for dealing with subordination in a society where invidious comparison with others is constantly invited represents, in effect, a borrowing from an older classical or religious tradition—an emphasis upon the intangible and immeasurable (and therefore comfortingly vague) spiritual and moral qualities. The only clearly adequate expression of this religious view was given by McNamara, a gentle and compassionate bookkeeper, who said: "All men are created equal? That's our belief as Catholics," implying some sort of religious equality, perhaps such an idea as is captured in the phrase "equality of the soul." Woodside, a Protestant railroad guard, takes, in a way, a secular eighteenth-century version of this view when he says that men are equal, "not financially, not in influence, but equal to one another as to being a person." Being a person, then, is enough to qualify for equal claims of some undefined kind.

But it seems probable that when men assert their own equality in this vague sense, typically phrased in something like O'Hara's terms: "I think I'm just as good as anybody else. I don't think there's any of them that I would say are better," something other than moral or spiritual equality is at issue. These moral qualities are what the educated commentator reads into the statement, but O'Hara means, if I may put words in his mouth: "Don't put on airs around me; I'm trying to preserve my self-respect in a world that challenges it; I therefore assert my equality with all. I won't be pushed around; I know my rights"; and, to the interviewer, "Just because you're a professor and I'm an oiler, it doesn't mean you can patronize me." And when Sokolsky, a machine operator and part-time janitor, says, in the interview: "The rich guy—because he's got money he's no better than I am. I mean, that's the way I feel," he is not talking about moral or spiritual qualities. He is saying, in effect, to his prosperous older brother and his snobbish wife, "Don't look down on me," and to the world at large, "I may be small, but I will protect my self-esteem." These men are posting notices similar to the motto on the early American colonies' flags, "Don't tread on me."

Speaking of moral virtues, we must observe how easy it would have been to take the view that the morality of the middle levels of society was superior because the rich received their wealth illegitimately. None of my clients did this. Nor did they stress the immoral lives of the wealthy classes, as did Merton's sample some sixteen years ago—a commentary, perhaps, upon changing attitudes toward the upper classes taking place over this period.[14] The psychic defenses against subordination available in stressing moral equality or superiority were used—but only rarely.

F
PEOPLE DESERVE THEIR STATUS

If one accepts the view that this is a land of opportunity in which merit will find a way, one is encouraged to accept the status differences of society. But it is more than logic that impels our men to accept these differences. There are satisfactions of identification with the going social order; it is easier to accept differences one calls "just" than those that appear "unjust"; there are the very substantial self-congratulatory satisfactions of comparison with those lower on the scale. Thus this theme of "just desserts" applies to one's own group, those higher, and those lower.

So Kuchinsky says: "If you're a professor, I think you're entitled to get what you deserve. I'm a roofer and I shouldn't be getting what you're getting." Furthermore, confidence in the general equity of the social order suggests that the rewards of one's own life are proportionate to ability, effort, and the wisdom of previous decisions. On ability, Costa, a machine operator, says:

> I believe anybody that has the potential to become a scientific man, or a professor, or a lawyer, or a doctor, should have the opportunity to pursue it, but there's a lot of us that are just made to run a machine in a factory. No matter what opportunities some of us might have had, we would never have reached the point where we could become people of that kind. I mean, everybody isn't Joe DiMaggio.

14. Robert K. Merton, *Mass Persuasion: The Social Psychology of a War Bond Drive* (New York: Harper, 1946).

And on the wisdom of earlier decisions, Johnson, the electric-utility mechanic, says:

> I don't consider myself the lower class. In between someplace. But I could have been a lot better off but through my own fool-ishness, I'm not. [Here he refers back to an earlier account of his life.] What causes poverty? Foolishness. When I came out of the service, my wife had saved a few dollars and I had a few bucks. I wanted to have a good time. I'm throwing money away like water. Believe me, had I used my head right, I could have had a house. I don't feel sorry for myself—what happened, happened, you know. Of course you pay for it.

But the most usual mistake or deficiency accounting for the rela-tively humble position is failure to continue one's education ow-ing to lack of family pressure ("They should have made me"), or youthful indiscretion, or the demands of the family for money, or the depression of the thirties.

The Upper Classes Deserve to Be Upper

Just as they regard their own status as deserved, so also do they regard the status of the more eminently successful as appro-priate to their talents. Rapuano, the packinghouse clerk, reports:

> Your income—if you're smart, and your ability calls for a cer-tain income, that's what you should earn. If your ability is so low, why, hell, then you should earn the low income. ["Do you think income is proportionate to ability now?"] I would say so. Yes.

But there is a suggestion in many of the interviews that even if the income is divorced from talent and effort, in some sense it is appropriate. Consider Sokolsky again, a machine operator and part-time janitor, discussing the tax situation:

> Personally, I think taxes are too hard. I mean a man makes, let's say $150,000. Well, my God, he has to give up half of that to the government—which I don't think is right. For instance if a man is fortunate enough to win the Irish Sweepstakes, he gets 150 —I think he has about $45,000 left. I don't think that's right.

Even if life is a lottery, the winner should keep his winnings. And DeAngelo, a machine operator, comes spontaneously to the same conclusion:

I think everybody needs a little [tax] relief. I mean, I know one thing, if I made a million dollars and the government took nine-tenths of it—boy, I'd cry the blues. I can't see that. If a man is smart enough to make that much, damn it, he's got a right to holler. I'm with the guy all the way.

Because he is "smart enough" to make the money, it is rightfully his. Surely, beyond the grave, there is a specter haunting Marx.

The concept of "education" is the key to much of the thinking on social class and personal status. In a sense, it is a "natural" because it fits so neatly into the American myth of opportunity and equality, and provides a rationale for success and failure that does minimum damage to the souls of those who did not go to college. Thus in justifying their own positions, sometimes with reference to the interview situation, my clients imply, "If I had gone to college (like you), I would be higher up in this world." Costa, a machine operator, speaks this theme:

Now, what would be the advantage of you going twenty years to school so you wind up making $10,000 a year and me going eight years to school, making $10,000? You would be teaching the young men of tomorrow, the leaders of tomorrow, and I would be running a machine. You would have a lot more responsibility to the country as a whole than I would have. Why shouldn't you be rewarded in proportion?

McNamara, a mild-mannered bookkeeper who went to night school to get his training in accounting and bookkeeping, emphasizes education in response to the question, "Do you think it's easy or hard to get from one class to another?"

Well, I think it's hard because . . . not because of the class itself, or what the influence they have on you, but you just seem to reach a certain point, and if you don't have it, you just don't —you don't make the grade. I've found that to be true. I always seem to be one step away from a good spot. And it's no one's fault —it's my fault. I just don't have the education—just don't—just don't have what it takes to take that step.

And Sokolsky, machine operator and part-time janitor, says, in his justification of income differences:

A man that gets out of eighth grade—I don't think he would have the ability to do the job as a man that got out of college.

But later, he says, of politicians and businessmen:

If a man with more education has been in politics, he should get the job, but if there's a man that, let's say, just got out of high school, and he's been around in politics all his life, I think he should have a chance too. It's how good he is. There's some big business people who just haven't got it. [But] there could be some men with a gift of gab—maybe just out of eighth grade—they could sell anything.

What is it about education that justifies differences in income? In the above interviews it is clear that education is thought to increase skills that should be suitably rewarded. Furthermore, it appears that the time necessary for educational preparation deserves some reward—a recurrent theme. With education goes responsibility—and responsibility should be rewarded. But there is also some suggestion in the interview material that the pain and hard (unpleasant) work associated with going to school deserves compensation. People who did not like school themselves may be paying homage to those who could stick it out. It is a question whether O'Hara, a maintenance mechanic, implies this when he says:

> I think a person that is educated deserves more than somebody that isn't. Somebody who really works for his money really deserves it more than somebody that's lazy and just wants to hang around.

In this and other ways, education serves as a peg on which to hang status; and, like "blood," whether a person got the education or not is not his "fault," or at least it is only the fault of an irresponsible youth, not a grown man.[15]

The Lower Classes Deserve No Better than They Get

By and large those in the lower orders are those who are paid daily (not weekly) or are on relief; they live in slums or in public housing projects (but not middle-income projects); they do not live respectable lives; they have only grammar-school education; they may have no regular jobs. Closer to home, those slightly lower in status are people like "the lady next door who has a little less than I have," the man who can't afford to take care of his kids properly in the project, people who spend their money on liquor, the person with less skill in the same line of work.

The rationale for their lower status turns chiefly on two things:

15. Contrast de Tocqueville: "I never met in America a citizen so poor as not to cast a glance of hope and envy on the enjoyments of the rich or whose imagination did not possess itself by anticipation of those good things that fate still obstinately withheld from him." *Democracy in America*, II, 129.

their lack of education, and therefore failure to know what they want or failure to understand lifesmanship, and their general indifference. It is particularly this "not caring" that seems so salient in the upper-working-class mind. This is consonant with the general view that success is a triumph of the will and a reflection of ability. Poverty is for lazy people, just as middle status is for struggling people. Thus, Ruggiero, a building maintenance man, accounts for poverty by saying, "There's laziness, you'll always have lazy people." DeAngelo, a factory operative, sees it this way:

> A guy gets married and, you know, he's not educated too well, he doesn't have a good job and he gets a large family and he's in bad shape, y'know what I mean. It's tough; he's got to live in a lousy rent—he can't afford anything better.

But DeAngelo takes away some of this sympathy the next moment when he goes on to say:

> But then you get a lot of people who don't want to work; you got welfare. People will go on living on that welfare—they're happier than hell. Why should they work if the city will support them?

In general, there is little sympathy given to those lower in the scale, little reference to the overpowering forces of circumstance, only rare mention of sickness, death of a breadwinner, senility, factories moving out of town, and so forth. The only major cause of poverty to which no moral blame attaches is depression or "unemployment"—but this is not considered a strikingly important cause in the minds of the Eastport men. They are Christian in the sense that they believe "The poor ye have with you always," but there is no trace of a belief that the poor are in any way "blessed."

G

WHAT IF THERE WERE GREATER EQUALITY OF OPPORTUNITY AND INCOME?

We have examined here the working- (and lower-middle-) class defenses of the present order. They are well organized and solidly built. By and large these people believe that the field is open and that merit will tell. They may then deprecate the importance of class, limit their perspectives, accept their situation reluctantly or with satisfaction. They may see the benefits of society flowing to their own class, however they define it. They tend to believe that each person's status is in some way deserved.

How would these lower-middle- and working-class men feel about a change in the social order such that they and their friends might suddenly be equal to others now higher or lower in the social order? Most of them wouldn't like it. They would fear and resent this kind of equality.

Abandonment of a Rationale

Changing ideas is a strain not to be lightly incurred, particularly when these ideas are intimately related to one's self-esteem. The less education one has, the harder it is to change such ideas. Painfully, these men have elaborated an explanation for their situation in life; it helps explain things to their wives, who take their status from them; it permits their growing children to account for relative social status in school; it offers to each man the satisfactions of social identity and a measure of social worth. Their rationales are endowed with moral qualities; the distribution of values in the society is seen as just and natural. While it gives satisfactions of an obvious kind to those who contemplate those beneath them, it also gives order and a kind of reassurance, oddly enough, to those who glance upward toward "society" or the "four hundred." This reassurance is not unlike the reassurance provided by the belief in a just God while injustices rain upon one's head. The feudal serf, the Polish peasant, the Mexican peon believed that theirs was a moral and a "natural order"—so also the American workingman.

The Problem of Social Adjustment

Equality would pose problems of social adjustments, of manners, of how to behave. Here is Sokolsky, short and heavy, uneducated, and nervous, with a more prosperous brother in the same town. "I'm not going to go over there," he says, "because every time I go there I feel uncomfortable." On the question of rising from one social class to another, his views reflect this personal situation:

> I think it's hard. Let's say—let's take me, for instance. Supposing I came into a lot of money, and I moved into a nice neighborhood—class—maybe I wouldn't know how to act then. I think

> it's very hard, because people know that you just—word gets
> around that you . . . never had it before you got it now. Well,
> maybe they wouldn't like you . . . maybe you don't know how
> to act.

The kind of equality with others that would mean a rapid rise
in his own status is a matter of concern, mixed, of course, with
pleasant anticipation at the thought of "telling off" his brother.

Consider the possibility of social equality, including genuine
fraternization, without economic equality. Sullivan, a truck driver,
deals with this in graphic terms:

> What is the basis of social class? Well, things that people
> have in common. . . . Money is one, for instance, like I wouldn't
> feel very comfortable going around with a millionaire, we'll say.
> . . . He could do a lot and say a lot—mention places he'd been
> and so on—I mean, I wouldn't be able to keep up with him . . .
> and he wouldn't have to watch his money, and I'd have to be
> pinching mine to see if I had enough for another beer or some-
> thing.

And, along the lines of Sokolsky's comments, Sullivan believes
that moving upward in the social scale is easier if one moves to
a new place where one has not been known in the old connection.
Flynn holds that having the right interests and conversational
topics for the new and higher social group will make it possible
—but otherwise it could be painful. Kuchinsky, the roofer, says:
"I suppose it would feel funny to get into a higher class, but I
don't believe I would change. I wouldn't just disregard my friends
if I came into any money." Clinging to old friends would give
some security in that dazzling new world.

DeAngelo, a factory operative, also considers the question of
whether the people of higher status will accept the *arriviste*, but
for himself, he dismisses it:

> I wouldn't worry much about whether they would accept or
> they wouldn't accept. I would move into another class. I mean—
> I mean—I don't worry much about that stuff. If people don't want ·
> to bother with me, I don't bother with them, that's all.

These fears, while plausible and all too human on the face of
it, emerged unexpectedly from the interview material designed to
capture ideas and emotions on other aspects of class status. They
highlight a resistance to equalitarian movements that might bring
the working class and this rejecting superior class—whether it is

imaginary or not—in close association. If these were revolutionaries, one might phrase their anxieties, "Will my victims accept
me?" But they are not revolutionaries.

These are problems of rising in status to meet the upper classes
face to face. But there is another risk in opening the gates so that
those of moderate circumstances can rise to higher status. Equality of opportunity, it appears, is inherently dangerous in this respect: there is the risk that friends, neighbors, or subordinates
will surpass one in status. O'Hara has this on his mind. Some of
the people who rise in status are nice, but:

> You get other ones, the minute they get a little, they get big-
> headed and they think they're better than the other ones—where
> they're still—to me they're worse than the middle class. I mean,
> they should get down, because they're just showing their illiteracy
> —that's all they're doing.

Sokolsky worries about this possibility too, having been exposed
to the slights of his brother's family. But the worry over being
passed by is not important, not salient. It is only rarely mentioned.

Deprivation of a Meritorious Elite

It is comforting to have the "natural leaders" of a society well
entrenched in their proper place. If there were equality there
would no longer be such an elite to supervise and take care of
people—especially "me." Thus Woodside, the railroad guard,
reports:

> I think anybody that has money—I think their interest is much
> wider than the regular workingman. . . . And therefore I think
> that the man with the money is a little bit more educated, for the
> simple reason he has the money, and he has a much wider view of
> life—because he's in the knowledge of it all the time.

Here and elsewhere in the interview, one senses that Woodside
is glad to have such educated, broad-gauged men in eminent positions. He certainly opposes the notion of equality of income.
Something similar creeps into Johnson's discussion of social classes.
He feels that the upper classes, who "seem to be very nice people,"
are "willing to lend a helping hand—to listen to you. I would
say they'd help you out more than the middle class [man] would
help you out even if he was in a position to help you out." Equal-

ity, then, would deprive society, and oneself, of a group of friendly, wise, and helpful people who occupy the social eminences.

The Loss of the Goals of Life

But most important of all, equality, at least equality of income, would deprive people of the goals of life. In this they are like the working class of Middletown: "Its drives are largely those of the business class: both are caught up in the tradition of a rising standard of living and lured by the enticements of salesmanship." [16] Every one of the fifteen clients with whom I spent my evenings for seven months believed that equality of income would deprive men of their incentive to work, achieve, and develop their skills. These answers ranged, in their sophistication and approach, across a broad field. The most highly educated man in the sample, Farrel, answers the question "How would you feel if everyone received the same income in our society?" by saying:

> I think it would be kind of silly. . . . Society, by using income as a reward technique, can often insure that the individuals will put forth their best efforts.

He does not believe, for himself, that status or income are central to motivation—but for others, they are. Woodside, whose main concern is not the vistas of wealth and opportunity of the American dream, but rather whether he can get a good pension if he should have to retire early, comes forward as follows:

> I'd say that [equal income]—that is something that's pretty— I think it would be a dull thing, because life would be accepted— or it would—rather we'd go stale. There would be no initiative to be a little different, or go ahead.

Like Woodside, Flynn, a white-collar worker, responds with a feeling of personal loss—the idea of such an equality of income would make him feel "very mad." Costa, whose ambitions in life are most modest, holds that equality of income "would eliminate the basic thing about the wonderful opportunity you have in this country." Then for a moment the notion of his income equaling that of the professional man passes pleasantly through his mind: "Don't misunderstand me—I like the idea"; then again, "I think it eliminates the main reason why people become engineers and professors and doctors."

16. Robert and Helen Lynd, *Middletown in Transition: A Study in Cultural Conflicts* (New York: Harcourt, Brace, 1937), p. 447.

Rapuano, whose worries have given him ulcers, projects himself into a situation where everyone receives the same income, in this case a high one:

> If everyone had the same income of a man that's earning $50,000 a year, and he went to, let's say ten years of college to do that, why, hell, I'd just as soon sit on my ass as go to college and wait till I could earn $50,000 a year, too. Of course, what the hell am I going to do to earn $50,000 a year—now that's another question.

But however the question is answered, he is clear that guaranteed equal incomes would encourage people to sit around on their anatomies and wait for their paychecks. But he would like to see some leveling, particularly if doctors, whom he hates, were to have their fees and incomes substantially reduced.

That These Sacrifices Shall Not Have Been in Vain

The men I talked to were not at the bottom of the scale; not at all. They were stable breadwinners, churchgoers, voters, family men. They achieved this position in life through hard work and sometimes bitter sacrifices. They are distinguished from the lower classes through their initiative, zeal, and responsibility, their willingness and ability to postpone pleasures or to forego them entirely. In their control of impulse and desire they have absorbed the Protestant ethic. At least six of them have two jobs and almost no leisure. In answering questions on "the last time you remember having a specially good time," some of them must go back ten to fifteen years. Nor are their good times remarkable for their spontaneous fun and enjoyment of life. Many of them do not like their jobs, but stick to them because of family responsibilities—and they do not know what else they would rather do. In short, they have sacrificed their hedonistic inclinations, given up good times, and expended their energy and resources in order to achieve and maintain their present tenuous hold on respectability and middle status.

Now, in such a situation to suggest that men be equalized and the lower orders raised and one's own hard-earned status given to them as a right and not a reward for effort seems to them desperately wrong. In the words of my research assistant, David Sears, "Suppose the Marshall Plan had provided a block and tackle to Sisyphus after all these years. How do you think he would have felt?" Sokolsky, Woodside, and Dempsey have rolled the stone to the top of the hill so long, they despise the suggestion that it might have been in vain. Or even worse, that their neighbors at the foot of the hill might have the use of a block and tackle.

The World Would Collapse

As a corollary to the view that life would lose its vigor and its savor with equality of income, there is the image of an equalitarian society as a world running down, a chaotic and disorganized place to live. The professions would be decimated: "People pursue the higher educational levels for a reason—there's a lot of rewards, either financial or social," says Costa. Sullivan says, "Why should people take the headaches of responsible jobs if the pay didn't meet the responsibilities?" For the general society, Flynn, a white-collar man, believes that "if there were no monetary incentive involved, I think there'd be a complete loss. It would stop all development—there's no doubt about it." McNamara, a bookkeeper, sees people then reduced to a dead level of worth: with equal income "the efforts would be equal and pretty soon we would be worth the same thing." In two contrasting views, both suggesting economic disorganization, Woodside believes, "I think you'd find too many men digging ditches, and no doctors," while Rapuano believes men would fail to dig ditches or sewers, "and where the hell would we be when we wanted to go to the toilet?"

Only a few took up the possible inference that this was an attractive but impractical ideal—and almost none followed up the suggestion that some equalization of income, if not complete equality, would be desirable. The fact of the matter is that these men, by and large, prefer an inequalitarian society, and even prefer a society graced by some men of great wealth. As they look out upon the social scene, they feel that an equalitarian society would present them with too many problems of moral adjustment, which they fear and dislike. But perhaps, most important, their life goals are structured around achievement and success in monetary terms. If these were taken away, life would be a desert. These men view the possibility of an equalitarian world as a paraphrased version of Swinburne's lines on Jesus Christ: "Thou hast conquered, O pale Equalitarian; the world has grown grey from Thy breath."

H
SOME THEORETICAL IMPLICATIONS

Like any findings on the nature of men's social attitudes and beliefs, even in such a culture-bound inquiry as this one, the new information implies certain theoretical propositions that may be incorporated into the main body of political theory. Let us consider seven such propositions growing more or less directly out of our findings on the fear of equality:

1. The greater the emphasis in a society upon the availability of "equal opportunity for all," the greater the need for members of that society to develop an acceptable rationalization for their own social status.

2. The greater the strain on a person's self-esteem implied by a relatively low status in an open society, the greater the necessity to explain this status as "natural" and "proper" in the social order. Lower-status people generally find it less punishing to think of themselves as correctly placed by a just society than to think of themselves as exploited or victimized by an unjust society.

3. The greater the emphasis in a society upon equality of opportunity, the greater the tendency for those of marginal status to denigrate those lower than themselves. This view seems to such people to have the factual or even moral justification that if the lower classes "cared" enough, they could be better off. It has a psychological "justification" in that it draws attention to one's own relatively better status and one's own relatively greater initiative and virtue.

4. People tend to care less about *equality* of opportunity than about the availabiilty of *some* opportunity. Men do not need the same life chances as everybody else; indeed, they usually care very little about that. They need only chances (preferably with unknown odds) for a slightly better life than they now have. Thus: Popular satisfaction with one's own status is related less to equality of opportunity than to the breadth of distribution of some opportunity for all, however unequal this distribution may be. A man who can improve his position one rung does not resent the man who starts on a different ladder halfway up.

These propositions are conservative in their implications. The psychological roots of this conservatism must be explored elsewhere, as must the many exceptions that may be observed when the fabric of a social order is so torn that the leaders, the rich and powerful, are seen as illegitimate—and hence "appropriately" interpreted as exploiters of the poor. I maintain, however, that these propositions hold generally for the American culture over most of its history—and also that the propositions hold for most of the world most of the time. This is so even though they fly in the face of much social theory—theory often generalized from more specialized studies of radicalism and revolution. Incidentally, one must observe that it is as important to explain why revolutions and radical social movements do *not* happen as it is to explain why they do.

The more I observed the psychological and physical drain placed upon my sample by the pressures to consume—and therefore to scratch in the corners of the economy for extra income—the more it appeared that competitive consumption was not a stimulus to class conflict, as might have been expected, but was a substitute for or a sublimation of it. Thus we would say:

5. The more emphasis a society places upon consumption—through advertising, development of new products, and easy installment buying—the more will social dissatisfaction be channeled into intraclass consumption rivalry instead of interclass resentment and conflict. The Great American Medicine Show creates consumer unrest, working wives, and dual job-holding, not antagonism toward the "owning classes." And, as a corollary of this view:

6. The more emphasis a society places upon consumption, the more will labor unions focus upon the "bread and butter" aspects of unionism, as contrasted to its ideological elements.

We come, finally, to a hypothesis that arises from this inquiry into the fear of equality but that goes much beyond the focus of the present study. I mention it here in a speculative frame of mind, undogmatically, and even regretfully:

7. The ideals of the French Revolution, liberty and equality, have been advanced because of the accidental correspondence between these ideals and needs of the bourgeoisie for freedom of ecomonic action and the demands of the working class, very simply, for "more." Ideas have an autonomy of their own, however, in the sense that once moralized they persist even if the social forces that brought them to the fore decline in strength. They become "myths"—but myths erode without support from some major social stratum. Neither the commercial classes nor the

working classes, the historical beneficiaries of these two moralized ideas (ideals or myths), has much affection for the ideals in their universal forms. On the other hand, the professional classes, particularly the lawyers, ministers, and teachers of a society, very often do have such an affection. It is they, in the democratic West, who serve as the "hard core" of democratic defenders, insofar as there is one. It is they, more frequently than others, who are supportive of the generalized application of the ideals of freedom and equality to all men. This is not virtue, but rather a different organization of interests and a different training. Whatever the reason, however, it is not to "The People," not to the business class, not to the working class, that we must look for the consistent and relatively unqualified defense of freedom and equality. The professional class, at least in the American culture, serves as the staunchest defender of democracy's two greatest ideals.

5

Some Sources of Support
for Democratic Methods

> For the vast majority of Americans the term "democracy" has no connotations beyond "political forms after the American fashion."
>
> —GEOFFREY GORER, *The American People*, p. 222

> It would be an exaggeration to suggest that the twentieth-century American was more democratic than his nineteenth-century forebears but accurate enough to say that his democracy, having been more effectively challenged, was more self-conscious and rationalized than at any time since Lincoln.
>
> —HENRY S. COMMAGER, *The American Mind*, p. 408

Some writers employ the term "democracy" in a broad social framework, including within it the relationship between social classes, among ethnic groups, and the general interpersonal relations of a community. In such usages, "equality" is the ingredient that gives the experience of democracy its savor, and "average" is the concept that gives it a certain odor.[1] Others focus more upon the governmental institutions of a polity, seeing in the arrangements for expressing the will of the people, the es-

1. See, for example, Robert and Helen Lynd's report on the advantages of being "average" in their *Middletown in Transition: A Study in Cultural Conflicts* (New York: Harcourt, Brace, 1937), p. 123.

sence of the idea. Under these circumstances the idea of majority rule is the essential ingredient. A third variety looks to the protection of the rights of the individual, his freedom of expression, and the surrounding freedoms of religon and press and assembly that protect him from trespass, generally from governmental trespass. For these, the idea of minority rights is usually considered to be the jewel for which the democratic setting is valuable.

A

THE IDEA OF DEMOCRACY IN EASTPORT

What the men of Eastport have in mind, as they focus in an associative and connotative fashion on the term "democracy," is nothing that is quite like any of these. It is, in fact, neither majority rule nor minority rights, but something of a hybrid—majority rights. This concept is a variation of the central theme that was most enthusiastically endorsed in the discussion of freedom: it is the right of the majority to do what is conventionally approved. The word "freedom" is most swiftly, and most usually, associated with the word "democracy"—like this: "The way I look at democracy, the biggest fact is freedom. . . . Everybody is able to voice their opinion, and as long as they're on the right track, be able to do what they—what is right." Woodside, who is speaking here, almost said "do what they *want*" but his conscience intervened. O'Hara, with none of Woodside's Midwestern conscientious inhibitions, says clearly that democracy is to "do pretty much what you want the way you want, without being forced by the government to do otherwise." But the freedoms he mentions are conventional ones, and he emphasizes the freedom "to get ahead" if you have enough "push." Democracy as a popular concept centers in the freedom of the nondeviant individual to do what the majority thinks right.

Inasmuch as the ideas of equality and of freedom are explored elsewhere, I shall turn to the Eastportian idea of political democracy or popular government, their ideas of the trustworthiness of the electorate, the circumstances when popular government might better be abandoned, the extent to which the rulers can share power with the ruled and get anything done. To bring the matter to a focus, I shall use a measure embracing five criteria for this purpose, a measure that we shall call the "democraticness scale":

1. Willingness or reluctance to deny the franchise to the "ignorant and careless"; degree of elitism or restrictiveness concerning political participation; trust or scorn for "the masses."

2. Patience or impatience with the delays and confusions of democratic processes; appreciation or lack thereof of the protections afforded to minorities involved in these delays; degree of understanding of the policy advantages in "letting everybody have his say."

3. Willingness or reluctance to give absolute authority to a single leader in times of threat; provision or lack of it for ultimate responsibility in Congress and reversion of power to elected officials; relative preference for speed, decisiveness, expedition in contrast to deliberation, consultation, and consensus.

4. Where democratic forms are followed, degree of emphasis (and often disguised approval) of underlying oligarchical methods; appreciation or depreciation of consultative methods; degree of skepticism of popular requests or arguments not backed by sanctions.

5. Belief that the future of democracy in the United States is reasonably secure, or belief that it is uncertain, with various named or nameless contingencies likely to destroy it; appreciation or depreciation of the stability of social institutions, permanence of popular democratic preferences; presence or absence of a "secret" desire to participate in a great personal and social purgative movement.

Judged by these measures, Eastport is a democratic city; these are democratic men. Their views on the quality of the electorate (the first criterion) are sometimes scornful, but except for three men who argued for some kind of screening process to eliminate "the ignorant and careless," they all agreed that everyone regardless of qualification should have the vote. Ruggiero, Eastern State's maintenance clerk, speaks for the others: of the vote by the "ignorant and careless" he says, "There's only one way for democracy . . . we have to trust 'em with it." Ruggiero's view of the nature of man is more like that of Rousseau—basically good, spoiled by the commercialism and selfishness of society.

In addition to their support for the free and open universal franchise, Eastport also accepts with equanimity the confusion and disorderly processes of democracy (with reservations on "bickering" in the Administration) in an age when democracy is challenged to be "efficient." Here again, Woodside is representative (with four exceptions) in his views. He is not the no-nonsense policeman with the impatient night stick. Speaking of democracy, he says: "Oh, definitely it does [create confusion], because everybody has a chance to voice, and the time it is all thrashed out and everything, definitely there is a lot of time wasted—but it's good. It's time not wasted because regardless of how small or how big you are, everybody's opinion is heard, and it's balanced out, and I think that is the most important thing, regardless of time."

Challenged on whether it would not be best, "if there were another war with a threat of atomic bombing of this country," to establish a temporary dictatorship in the hands of the President, most of the men shied away from the notion of even a temporary dictatorship, even in the hands of the President. Costa, an assembly-line operative, thinks his emergency powers and war powers are already strong enough, O'Hara, a maintenance mechanic and oiler, argues "your Congress—that's what you elected them for—they should be able to straighten him out when he's going the wrong way"; and Johnson, the electric-utility mechanic, who says he has often thought of that problem, says, "I don't think any one man should run the show . . . because maybe the wrong man is there—you never know . . . that's too big a decision for one man to make."

When they turn to examine the democracy of their own organizations, the Hilltop Council, the unions, the veterans' organizations—they have some critical things to say, but generally they find the procedures measure up to their somewhat vague ideas of what the democratic process should be. As we shall see in a minute, there is a world of experience of fumbling consensual procedures among these men; and they accept it.

Finally, as to the future of democracy: "Well, I think we'll probably go right along with democracy," says the bookkeeper, McNamara. "It's flexible enough to make the necessary changes in the so-called atomic era." Johnson, a mechanic, agrees, and, like Henry Steele Commager, he finds that democracy "has been tested in quite a few ways in the past years—for instance, this segregation problem." How much of this faith in democracy is based on a want of imagination, a belief that the future will be like the present, or on a simple traditionalism, is hard to say. Sullivan, a truck driver, says of democracy, "I imagine it will always be pretty much the same as now." Of poverty in this country, he says, "I imagine we'll probably always have it [pause] the same as we do now." Although it is certainly true that the twelve who believe in the future of democracy are more likely to be its supporters than the three who do not, yet we must not confuse this dilute traditionalism with a deep and searching confidence in the capacity of democracy to solve its problems or see in it more than a kind of conventional, if useful, support.

Taking into account these and other, perhaps adventitious reasons for the support of democracy and the belief in its future, it is nevertheless true that most, indeed almost all, of the men both understand the frailties of popular government and accept it, with their eyes open. They know that ignorant and careless men, by voting, are helping to direct their own destinies; they acknowledge and accept the confusions and delays of parliamentary procedure; they are concerned over the need for swift, centralized power in emergencies, but they would want such power protected from abuse; they are not cynical about the uses of democratic procedures in their own local organizations; they believe democracy has a future on this continent and perhaps more broadly around the world. They believe these things—why? Why do these Americans, representative of working-class Eastport, and of New Haven, Springfield, Baltimore, Akron, Flint, and a large portion of urban America, adopt the ideology of popular government so completely?

B

AMERICAN SUPPORT FOR DEMOCRATIC FORMS

There have been many explanations for the hold democratic forms have had on the American mind. At least ten come to mind:

1. The support for popular government is derived from an intellectual lineage tracing back to Montesquieu and Locke and, some would say, Harrington. The men of Eastport are the inheritors of these views, however diluted and "brutalized" the ideas may have become in their passage through time and social strata.

2. The American support of popular government is a product of the American frontier experience, where men learned equality and self-help, and the practices of mutual respect and assistance.

If the Turner thesis—that the main product of the frontier was democratic man—has been somewhat eroded of late, it still serves as a focus of attention.[2]

3. Potter has challenged and developed this view,[3] so that it is the abundance of the American economy that has sustained the support of democratic ways and popular government. Where there is abundance—and particularly where there is a growing abundance—it is easier for the privileged to yield and accommodate, for, in absolute terms, they give up nothing. Similarly, it is easier for the underprivileged to contain their political tempers because, after all, they are relatively well off and becoming better off all the time.

4. Germane to this view, but basically different in that it does not rely on growth, is the tracing of American support of popular government to the system of land distribution that prevailed from the earliest colonial (New England) times. The decision, whether forced or not, to permit men to become freeholders, each with his own plot of land, a decision carried out in the West by the Homestead Act and reinforced by irrigation and other policies today, might be said to have given an economic or property basis for an easy growth of popular government. At least Harrington and Jefferson considered a population so based to be a democratic requisite.

5. The geography of continents, not farms, has been said to have provided the continuity of history, the internal peace and security of a nation, the freedom from threat and invasion that permits and encourages the growth of popular government.[4]

6. It has been said that the religious practices of the early nation gave it the initial democratic bent and that these practices have nourished our popular institutions.

The Puritan church in particular and the Protestant churches in general have provided for self-government among the church members or at least among a selected group of elders.[5] Lindsay emphasizes this aspect of the support for representative govern-

2. Frederick Jackson Turner, *The Frontier in American History* (New York: Holt, 1920).

3. David M. Potter, *People of Plenty: Economic Abundance and the American Character* (Chicago: University of Chicago Press, 1954).

4. Daniel J. Boorstin, *The Genius of American Politics* (Chicago: University of Chicago Press, 1953), pp. 8–35.

5. See Curtis P. Nettels, *The Roots of American Civilization* (New York: Crofts, 1936), pp. 164–169.

ment in the history of English parliamentary government.[6] It is even more true in the American experience.

7. The relation between self-government in churches and in governments is easier to understand than the relation between what is called free private enterprise and popular government, although it is certainly the case that the men of Eastport are convinced of one aspect of this close relationship. (The one thing they are sure a democratic government should *not* do is to tell a man how to run his business.) Still, it has been argued rather cogently that the experiences men have in choosing among employers, in trying their hand at their own businesses, in assuming responsibility for their own economic destinies leads them to prefer or even insist upon a form of government that gives them some "say" in public affairs.

8. There have been arguments of another kind, ones that turned upon the original "national character" of the English stock. Their emphasis upon rationality (Hume, Locke, Bentham, Smith), their capacity to compromise, their pragmatic tempers, their close relationship to the world of things (that is, mechanical ability), and so forth, are said to have provided the basis for an industrious and stable government; and to have led them to prefer the incremental advantages of a government of compromise as contrasted to the more ephemeral advantages of a government of purer principles.

9. On the other hand, it has been argued that the refreshing admixture of immigrant idealism brought here by men fleeing from tyranny abroad has sustained the American experiment in popular government.

10. Finally, there are current theories of the nature of American child care and early socialization wherein the child is taught his own worth, responsible independence, and how to share in family government, which purport to show why Americans support popular government.[7]

6. A. D. Lindsay, *The Modern Democratic State* (London: Oxford University Press, 1943), pp. 117–121.

7. See, for example, Erik H. Erikson, *Childhood and Society* (New York: Norton, 1950).

C

EXPERIENCE WITH DEMOCRATIC FORMS
IN EASTPORT

> The way in which people behave is all of a piece. . . . It would be impossible suddenly to introduce "democracy," which is a word for a type of behavior and an attitude of mind which runs through our whole culture, through our selection of candidates for office, our behavior in street cars, our schools and our newspapers, into an undemocratic society—as it would suddenly to introduce feudalism into a modern American city.
> —MARGARET MEAD, *And Keep Your Powder Dry*, p. 20

One thing is clear: unless a traditional way of looking at things is regularly reinforced by the experience of living men, it will gradually be extinguished. Perhaps this will take generations or longer (Kardiner says that much in the Plainville personality is a dysfunctional residue of what was functional to medieval man); [8] perhaps it will take only a short time; but at the same time that tradition is absorbed, it is eroded, however slightly, and turned into something a little different. One must look, then, not only at what have been the historical forces shaping the American tradition of democracy that, as conventional, culture-bound men, Eastportians absorb, but also at the forces shaping the lives and outlook of these men in their own daily existences.

It is striking how few of the influences said to reinforce the democratic orientation of the American nation over the course of its history can be said to have a firsthand, immediate bearing on the lives of these men. They have not themselves read Locke, Montesquieu, Madison, Jefferson, or their own Constitution. As we shall see, the phrase "a government of laws and not of men" leaves them bewildered. They have not lived on a frontier, never, for the most part, in open country at all. They have not owned land, as a homesteader or as a householder; they are not, in this sense, given an independent economic basis for criticism of government or, more important, the corporation. Most of them have not experienced laissez faire as an entrepreneur experiences it, and those that have must report mixed satisfactions. Dempsey tried his hand at a restaurant addition to his house and lost his savings; Ferrera has been in several bankruptcies; Johnson seeks

---

8. Abram Kardiner and associates, *The Psychological Frontiers of Society* (New York: Columbia University Press, 1945), pp. 418–448.

to open up a gardening business on his own, but this is still largely
a fantasy in his mind; few of their parents were small businessmen
—but Ruggiero's father tried tailoring on an independent basis
and lost much of his money, and Ferrera's father had to close down
his barbershop because of illness. One or two, it is true, have
somewhere in their family backgrounds a successful small businessman: Johnson's aunt has a beauty parlor, Woodside's brother
has a radio repair shop, Rapuano's brother has a grocery store—
but this is hardly enough to provide these men with those economic experiences that are said to link laissez-faire economics to
democracy. They are all now employees, and their experiences
here do not help to contribute to a belief in self-government; they
apply at factory gates or in employment offices for positions where
they have only minimal "say" in what takes place. A union may
help, but only a few have been close enough to the processes of
union organization and collective bargaining to speak with clarity
and feeling about them. Yet for a few, like Sullivan, Costa, DeAngelo, and Woodside, there is something of value in this union
experience that deserves examination, and to which we shall
shortly return.

Most of these men are Roman Catholics; their churches do
not vest much control in lay boards, councilors, vestrymen. Holy
Name Societies seem to have elected officers, but they are rather
tightly controlled. The Catholic world is caught between the
hierarchical medieval vision and the new Western style of life.
They have not been protected from the influence of war by the
Atlantic ocean; born, for the most part, during or shortly after
the First World War, they have lived through the Second World
War and the Korean War, and many of them have been in the
Armed Forces at one time or another. Five of the men are of
Irish descent, six are of Italian descent, two are from Eastern European stock (a Polish Catholic and a Lithuanian Jew), one is half-
Scandinavian, and only one is Anglo-Saxon. Thus, at least two-
thirds of the men are from Eastern or Southern European gene
pools and cannot be said to share in whatever is thought to be
inheritable from that cherished Anglo-Saxon—and perhaps Scandinavian and perhaps Irish—temperament. If, on the other hand,
it is claimed that their parents came to America in search of freedom, and thus were self-selected for their faith in popular government, it must be said that the Italian-American parents, more
than the children, supported Mussolini, and according to some

(McNamara is one) the Irish parents were more prejudiced against other racial and ethnic groups than they themselves are.

Finally, turning to the question of early experience, we cannot find any evidence that these men were encouraged, as children, to believe that they were, so to speak, voting members of the family household or that they could control their group destinies by group action. The evidence here is obscure; perhaps many of them were encouraged in this way. We have found only four instances where the son's relations with their fathers were marked by cold or hostile feelings creating a serious and permanent damage.[9] But in general it is the middle class, and not the working class, that helps a child to internalize the values and capacities congruent with democratic systems.[10] Is it the schools, with their middle-class teachers and value system, both parochial and public, that induct these men into the uses of democracy? Their classrooms may not have had this spirit (although some always will); still, the student councils, the civics events clubs, even elections of team captains may convey a democratic message. Perhaps Ferrera first learned the ways (and pleasures) of democracy in his election to captaincy of the football team in Eastport High.

With a few exceptions, then, must it be said that the forces that shaped the democratic heritage of a nation are now so attenuated, or operate in so different a milieu, that they are no longer serving to reinforce, generation by generation, the democratic ideal among living men? For these men of Eastport, is it largely the absorption of a past not quite their own, and conformity to the present as they find it, that leads them to support the ideal of popular government? Not quite. Here, I think, one must distinguish two different kinds of experience. In one, a person may have a set of experiences in a society that, while not really relevant to the political order, nevertheless create for him a *general* sense of satisfaction that leads him to accept and endorse the political system of his society. This is a little like the "halo effect" in judging persons; if a teacher likes a child's manners, she will see him as brighter and handsomer than she otherwise would. Thus if a person likes the opportunities for education and self-advancement in a society, he may tend to like everything about that society. It is, too, a little like the process of stimulus general-

9. See below, Chapter 23.
10. See a summary and interpretation of this literature in my *Political Life: Why People Get Involved in Politics* (New York: The Free Press of Glencoe, 1959), pp. 227–228.

ization: if a person, say, responds favorably to a monetary reward, and this is reinforced, he may respond favorably to other rewards that can be seen as having monetary value. Partly it is that the causes of social phenomena are so obscure that any institutions that are associated in one's mind with a satisfactory situation may be thought to have some causal relationship to that situation. In any event, the satisfactions the men of Eastport receive from certain aspects of career and family life do seem, by some one or all of these processes, to generalize to the political and social order in which their careers come to fruition and their families have their existence.

Following this line of argument, perhaps the most important single factor in the Eastportian support of the general society of which popular government is a part is the economic and social position of these men relative to that of their fathers. They are all, with, I think, only two exceptions, markedly better off than their fathers. Each man has not only stepped into his father's shoes; he has ordered a larger size. But it is not only in this comparison that these men of Eastport fare well; they fare well economically with respect to their own expectations (except for the dream of a house of their own). It is true that they are in debt, that they were, at the time, seriously worried about unemployment and layoffs, that many had illnesses that caused them long, deep hours of anxiety, that they had postponed a number of gratifications to achieve their respectable status, and that now, in some ways, they had forgotten what it was like to "have a good time." But while all these things are true, the rewards in pride, in a sense of responsibilities met, in the companionship at the shop, and the supportive affection of wife and children, and in the small indulgences their budgets permitted, all kept them positively oriented toward the society of which their government is a part. In a rewarding life, however painful it may be at times, convention and the going order are anchored to bedrock.

But there is a second kind of experience, which is more specifically related to an enduring affection for the ways of democracy: it is experience in democratic procedures in small groups. Their church, it seems, leads them into this understanding only a little way; their schools a little way further. The voluntary groups that the men belong to, the labor unions, the veterans' organizations, the community councils and Parent-Teacher Organizations, catch the men at different ages. They mean different things and serve as vehicles for a variety of needs, but almost all of them have elected officers, parliamentary procedures, majority rule tempered by minority rights, and other aspects of what might be said to be popular government. People are often facetious about these aspects of their organizations; sometimes they are cynical. The men of Eastport were neither. Ruggiero, the university maintenance clerk, speaking of the Disabled American War Veterans, says, "I'd say yes [they are democratically run]; because they vote fairly, I mean you have your caucuses . . . you have a little more fight in it than you would in the, uh, religious organizations." DeAngelo, speaking of his union, says, "I think they're run democratically—don't force any issues on anybody. I mean, like the way we run it, if we have a meeting with the company and they were discussing work practices or something—anything that we agreed upon in there is not binding until we have a meeting with the body, and the body is the deciding factor." Sullivan, a truck driver, who has had his differences with the union, reviews the situation briefly: "I don't know so much about the [democratic] way the union is run. [pause] The national leaders—I guess they don't care what goes on as long as their money keeps coming in. They're not interested with the actual running of it . . . so I guess your local committees and your regional committees are— I think it's run pretty democratic." Sullivan is hard to please, outspoken, and bitter about some of his experiences—his endorsement is, therefore, a meaningful one. This is the most usual view, and it extends even to social clubs. It is so usual that the men sometimes wonder whether there is another way. Sokolsky, speaking of his Young Couples' Club, says, "We have elections once a year and the people we like we vote in. . . . What other way is there?"

At Hilltop there is a Community Council with responsibilities for representing the tenants before the management, for supervising recreational facilities, for taking up matters of general interest such as road repairs and dogs running loose. Some of the men go to these meetings and consider themselves members, while others do not. Sullivan has been on the council, Flynn has been an officer of the organization, and several of the men have supervised sports or have otherwise been associated with it. What do they learn? Sullivan says the Hilltop Council is democratically run. Flynn, a most respected person around Hilltop, says, "I happen to be in a position in the ones [organizations] that I do belong to, to see that they are democratically run. . . . Maybe some people in the same organizations might differ. I think an attempt is made to see that all viewpoints are expressed." Most agree with him; a few, as he says, are skeptical.

On balance, the Legion posts, the lodges and the unions, the PTA's and the community councils are schools for learning, in an enclosed space, what the wider democracy of the nation requires. Not least of all, they teach the imperfections, the hesitations, the halting progress of democracy, and so prepare their members for a more realistic and informed view. At least in part, popular government survives less because men are aware of its crowning virtues than because they are adequately prepared for its galling vices.

D

CHARACTEROLOGICAL REINFORCEMENT
FOR THE DEMOCRATIC FAITH

But the generalization of satisfaction and the reinforcements of experience are not enough to explain the adoption of democratic ideals by the men. People do not support conventional ideals, with the understanding conviction these men show, without a set of personal qualities congenial to those ideals.

Among these is, first, the assumption of responsibility for their own fates by the men of Eastport, for each believes himself to be the master of some portion of his environment as well as the captain of his soul. A combination of this individualism with the characterological ego-strength that undergirds it leads the men of Eastport to accept *self*-government as the appropriate form of government. If their own destinies are in their own hands—something they accept—they must be given some "say" in the nature of government.

We said that, in the second place, most of the Eastport men have sufficient tolerance of delay, confusion, and ambiguity to suffer along with a procrastinating, hesitating legislature.[11] Our evidence suggests that one's tolerance differs a good deal with the nature of the matter that is ambiguous and how much you care

11. On the concept of tolerance of ambiguity, see Else Frenkel-Brunswik, "A Study of Prejudice in Children," *Human Relations*, 1 (1949), pp. 295–306; and "Intolerance of Ambiguity, as an Emotional Personality Variable," *Journal of Personality*, 18 (1949), pp. 108–143.

about it. Although, most of the men (three-fifths) agreed that "bosses should say just what is to be done and exactly how to do it if they expect us to do a good job," they and others think that "people ought to pay more attention to new ideas even if they seem to go against the American way of life," and they are willing to believe that "some of our most deeply held beliefs will be successfully challenged by science someday."

In a more qualitative and impressionistic way, I have reviewed the discussion on political parties, the records of Roosevelt and Eisenhower, the merits of several religions, the treatment of the Little Rock situation, and the attitudes toward urban redevelopment in their home town. The discussion is remarkably balanced; partisanship is held to a low level—almost deprived of its cutting edge; heroes are found to be of human proportion—in short, the ambiguities of life and politics are not only tolerated, they are elaborated upon. These Americans of recent lineage but impeccable pedigree have a high tolerance for ambiguity, a strong preference for hearing more than one side of an issue, and a capacity for accepting delay and confusion in the process of getting what they want.

The support of popular government is realistic; whence this realism? One way to answer this is to say it comes from the application of an established pattern; it is part of a more general way of thinking. This, then, is a third source of democratic support. Of course there are, in Eastport, certain autistic and romantic ways of losing touch with reality, as we shall see when we review the cases of three undemocratic men, and there are milder cases that are not so incapacitating. Some relied upon projective and self-delusive thinking, such as the belief that nationality makes no difference in making friends—denied by the names of their closest friends—or the wish to know less about unpleasant matters —a kind of denial, as in Costa's anger when the Chamber of Commerce published figures on rising unemployment. There were mildly obsessive ideas, such as Johnson's constant reference to people in every situation as, in the first place, "out to make a buck," as though men had only one motive (along with his probably delusory notion that he might come into some money someday). But the remarkable thing is the sturdy sanity of the group. Those who had special hatreds (Rapuano of doctors and Communists, Kuchinsky of Jews) felt grieved and injured rather than persecuted; no one (except Kuchinsky's wife) so far as I could tell had the mild forms of paranoia that one sometimes finds in everyday life. There were few delusions of powerful friends whom a person could call on to solve his problems—if he but chose to do so. The endowment of words like "progress," "democracy," or "Communism" with magical powers with the expectation that by manipulating them one could change one's life position, or the state of the Union, was evident, but only the magic of "education" seemed seriously disruptive of realistic thinking. The autistic inability to "hear" or "understand" what I was saying was present—as the Kuchinsky example will show—but was minimal. I could (when necessary) almost always break into the stream of consciousness and direct its flow to areas of relevance to the topic in hand. In short, these men were "there," and positioned themselves in a real world, dealing with it realistically. This realism, then, permitted them to make a reasonably accurate appraisal of the nature, process, and value of popular government, an appraisal that need not be disappointed, yet avoided cynicism.

Fourth, if popular government is to decide the circumstances of one's life, then not only must the public have the qualities that fit them for their responsibilities; each person must also have faith that others, as well as himself, in fact do have these qualities. Morris Rosenberg, who invented the "faith in people" scale, found that one's disbelief in the helpfulness, trustworthiness, sympathy, and cooperativeness of other people was clearly related to a belief that political authorities (or any authorities) cared little what one wanted or needed to have done, and to a disbelief in the feasibility of democracy.[12] Almond has found that there are substantial differences among several national cultures; with Americans generally *high* in faith of this sort.[13] The small evidence available to me at the moment of writing suggests that such faith in people in the United States is not only high but also fairly constant over geographical and social class ranges. (I compute Rosenberg's mean score based on his sample of about 1,500 Cornell college students to be 3.73; the mean score of the fifteen Eastport men was 3.67.) Moreover, to the statement, "These days a person really doesn't know whom he can count on," eleven of the fifteen men disagreed. Three of the four who agreed with this misanthropic statement (which is, in fact, part of an "anomie scale") are the men to be

12. Morris Rosenberg, "Misanthropy and Political Ideology," *American Sociological Review*, 21 (1956), pp. 690–695.

13. Gabriel Almond and Sidney Verba, forthcoming study of socialization in five countries.

discussed in the next chapter, who qualify as least supportive of popular government. Thus, the premise seems sound that a confidence in one's fellow men must precede a support for democracy, and in Eastport, as in Plainville,[14] the induction of citizens into society has given them such a trust in the nature of man as to make the postulates of democracy plausible.

There are three men, and only three, who *strongly* disagree with the statement "Nowadays a person has to live pretty much for today and let tomorrow take care of itself." These three men are, again, the undemocrats. Is it, then, that a support for democracy presupposes some appreciation of "today," some sense that life is worth living *now;* that it is not continually a preparation for possible future contingencies? A fifth characterological support for democratic forms may be a capacity for present enjoyment. Such enjoyment, unclouded by the kind of phenomena represented in Kuchinsky's withdrawal, Rapuano's confusions, and Ferrera's moody tempers, may help a man to find congenial the democratic way of life, with its focus on the pursuit of happiness, not honor or glory. This is not hedonism, but rather finding a pivot for the balance of self-indulgence and self-sacrifice that gives a little to indulgence. And, it seems, behind this is the idea that each man is worthy of some modest consideration—even if it is only his own self-consideration.

14. See Abram Kardiner and associates, *The Psychological Frontiers of Society,* pp. 345–350.

6

The Undemocrats

In the years following World War II one would not have expected to find much overt support for Fascism in Eastport—even among Italian-Americans for whom it had been a kind of nationalism—and certainly little overt Communism. One would expect, and one would find, more authoritarianism, more latent support for a hierarchical, closed society, whatever the name of the political system it embraced. But this authoritarian style and ideology is not the same as the opposition to popular government that we have called "undemocraticness."

Kuchinsky, the autistic roofer; Ferrera, the athletic salesman; and Rapuano, the packinghouse clerk, are the ones who, as I sifted their statements and weighed the evidence, seemed to qualify as opponents of popular government by the five criteria outlined in the last chapter. These criteria were, the reader will recall: (1) a scorn for the mass electorate, (2) distaste for the confusion and delay of parliamentary procedures, (3) a preference for temporary dictatorship in time of threat, (4) unrelieved cynicism about the democratic procedures in the organizations they knew, and (5) doubt about the future of democracy. How do these men qualify as undemocrats? From what personal qualities does this view draw nourishment? How does society encourage their undemocratic outlook?

A

KUCHINSKY: THE INPUT-OUTPUT PROBLEM

Kuchinsky, whose general political-information score was poorer than that of two-thirds of the others, holds that the ignorant and the careless should not have an equal vote ("A fellow's gotta be in a sound mind; I mean, he's gotta know what he's doing."); on the workings of democracy he says congressmen are "the bosses" and that "they hold back a lot on us." In response to my question on "temporary dictatorship," he grasps at the word "temporary," and says, "I don't think we should elect a fellow that wanted to be a part-time President. I think we should really go into it deeper and elect somebody that would take over the job permanently." On the Hilltop Council, whose meetings he has never attended, he says: "No, *we* don't run it, that's for sure. . . . I think it's run by the higher people." He thinks we won't know about the future of democracy for a couple of years, by which time the then current recession should have been resolved. Here and elsewhere he seems to identify democracy with prosperity—and this is about the only concept the word "democracy" suggests to him. When he was first asked for its meaning, almost his sole response, repeated twice, was, "Geez, I can't think of it now."

Departing from the undemocraticness measure, we would find many other grounds for considering Kuchinsky's support of popular government tenuous, for example, his belief that Congress has been standing still since McCarthy died, and his support of Hitler (with the reservation that he "overran his shoes"). Certain of Kuchinsky's hatreds also help round out the picture. Although he is moderate in his views on Communism, and accepts his Negro neighbors without anxiety, he hates unions and Jews. He is thus selective in his ethnocentrism, and although he feels particularly strongly about the ways in which Jews "control" the economic life of Eastport, he ranks in the low third of the authoritarianism scale. He is not a classic "authoritarian"; but he is a frail support for a democratic polity. How then to account for Kuchinsky's undemocraticness?

Kuchinsky's home life was hard, but he did not fear his father and he had an indulgent and affectionate mother. In this his childhood experiences in the home of an immigrant foundry worker, while not democratic, were not psychologically damaging in any extreme sense. In school, on the other hand, he had great difficulty, and in explaining this he says: "I got hurt back years ago. . . . I mean, I fell off a roof, damaged the head, so that didn't help me much. But I don't consider myself a dumb person." (One wonders to what extent his self-image is composed of a picture of a boy with a "damaged head" who made good anyhow.) He left school after the eighth grade, getting working papers when he was fourteen or fifteen. Thus, much of the democratizing experience of school was never made available to him. He went right to work in the foundry, quit to work in an arms plant during the war, and learned to be a roofer immediately thereafter. By this time he was married and had a child, and gradually the withdrawal from group and social life that now characterizes his leisure time led him into his present somewhat isolated existence. In this kind of life, deprived of school and union, PTA, lodge, or even veterans' organization memberships, it is hard to see where he might have experienced much of the democratic way of doing things.

Kuchinsky is among the three with the least faith in people, a quality associated with belief in popular government. On the other hand, while he is not anomic and has no particular gift for weighing both sides of a question, he is not intolerant of ambiguity. It is the unreality of his thinking, his confusion, and his inability to deal with abstractions that seem to form one pediment to his undemocratic ideology. The other is a particular kind of weak ego. Here we turn to the reality problem, with a brief glance at some possible sources. In the first place this confusion is a product of his low level of education and intelligence, though he has a kind of practical intelligence that permits him to earn rather more than average. In the second place, he is at the margin of two very different cultures with conflicting values and even cognitive processes. Both parents are emigrants from rural Poland; his wife is Polish; and his father-in-law and mother-in-law (both Polish) live with him and his wife. Apparently they do not speak English—or at least not well—and have never been naturalized. His church is the one Polish Catholic church in town. His views on such matters as "freedom" and "democracy" and the American standard of living express how it must seem to people "on the other side"—a very live and salient reference group for him. In this Polish culture, then, he finds reinforced the superstitions, the fatalistic ways of thinking, the traditionalism, and the general world perspective that Thomas and Znaniecki have spread out in rich profusion in *The Polish Peasant*.[1] Against this he must balance the prevailing culture of his neighborhood, his work crew, his boss, the media—in short, the non-Polish milieu that abrades his Polishness at every stage. This problem of culture conflict is shared by some of the others—but his situation is far and away more full of conflict than that of the others. Confusion, eclecticism, and a sense of the unreality of things is not an unnatural product of this situation.

But in the third place, a special combination of exposure and insulation, of input without output, that lies at the source of the confusion, is the particular matter I wish to explore in Kuchinsky's life. Like a man with a thirst when the bars open up, Kuchinsky drinks in the media: "Nights I come home after work . . . when the news comes on the TV I like to sit there and listen to the news and see what's going on. I think it's very interesting and I think I'd be lost without it. If I don't hear it—I get up early in the morning, six o'clock—I turn that thing right on in the morning to get the news, y'know, to see what happened in the morning or what happened during the night. See what's going on—they made any progress in Washington, or stuff like that." He reads the news in the papers (but likes the headlines best) and can tell about some of the stories he has read: an accident of some kind overseas, a burglary in a neighboring town. Among the magazines he "read up a lot on New York *Confidential* magazine," and holds that the accounts must be true because "if it's not true they won't print it." There is a very considerable exposure to news, current events, gossip here. Like everyone else, he is selective about what he sees and what he retains. In a ranking where "one" is high and "fifteen" low, he ranks eleventh in his knowledge of government (civics), thirteenth in his knowledge of events ("what Congress is doing these days, and so on"), but seventh in his knowledge of political personages. Thus what he tends to select from the input is the gossip, the personalized and concrete and often somewhat scandalous revelations of political and other public figures.

Kuchinsky, as we have said before, is an isolated man. He alone

---

1. See William I. Thomas and Florian Znaniecki, *The Polish Peasant in Europe and America* (New York: Knopf, 1927), Vols. I and II.

belongs to *no* voluntary groups (except his church) and is kept from much informal social life by his wife's mental illness. He dreads factory work and has sought out the roofing job partly because it offers a humanly more manageable situation, a crew of men whom he works "with" and which, I judge, gives him the kind of social support he most needs. It is almost his only human contact outside his family. Although part of the time he is working in isolation, the times when he has opportunities to talk with the other men on the crew (and he gets along well with them) are devoted to discussion of "vacations and fishing and what I'd like to do if I had some money," but, as he says: "I don't personally care to discuss too much of politics. Y'know, I mean, while working or anything like that, I don't think it's the proper time and place for it. I mean it takes you away from what you're doing." Conscience alone does not enforce this: "When the boss is around you can't just stand around discussing politics. I don't think he'd go for that too much. Not unless it was on his part." [The boss is a Republican.] Moreover, since some of the men, too, are Republicans, and Kuchinsky is a lifelong Democrat, he feels challenged, although he won't admit it: "There's nobody gonna change my mind about nothing—like I say, if I feel I need a change I'll make the change myself, and there's nobody going to tell me." He says his wife's opinions are most important to him, but elsewhere he says: "She follows in my footsteps, more or less. I don't believe she'd change." She is even more isolated than he is, burdened as she is with fear of crowds and almost incapacitating paranoia. At one level, then, we must say that inexperience with ideas, abstractions, and the vicarious understanding of events that comes from "working through," in however blunt a fashion, accounts for his failure to absorb the prevailing democratic idea.

I am certain that Kuchinsky's obfuscation of politics and undemocraticness come from a more permanent and enduring mental set than is reflected here, but the point I am making—and it bears on a wider audience dealing more broadly with other matters—is that a heavy input of media-presented political material without adequate opportunity for discussion, verbal formulation, and translation into one's own terms, and rebuttal, may lead to the kind of disassociated thought that Kuchinsky so clearly illustrates. Figuratively one might say that the mind will sour an idea unless it is ventilated. And if the bacteria content is as great as in

Kuchinsky's intake (particularly *Confidential*), the rate of spoilage will be high.

It is not going too far afield to notice that Kuchinsky's situation is similar to the situation often reflected in a revolutionary and postrevolutionary era. With a high political input, accompanied, perhaps, with much undercover malicious gossip, the nation under a dictatorship provides little opportunity for vicarious and verbal testing of ideas. Discussion "down at the shop" is guarded and rarely useful for this purpose—catharsis, rather than reality-testing, is likely to be emphasized. There is no chance in such a situation, as there was little for Kuchinsky, to throw out an idea before a group of men who will bat it around, perhaps not for its own sake, but for the sake of solidarity, phatic communion, the sharpening of wits and claws. Thus there is no seasoned public in such a time and place—only a populace that has heard much and verbally tried out very little. Again, the input-output problem.

A second significant pediment to Kuchinsky's undemocraticness lies in his inability to deal "on equal terms," so to speak, with the outside world. He ranks third from the bottom in the variety of ego strength that deals, not with the control of impulses, but with the "mastery of the environment." He also ranks third from the bottom on a dominance scale. He is among the four lowest in his conception of the power of the citizen to change things principally by voting (citizen efficacy). At many junctures in the interviews he reveals himself to be a dependent person with strong nurturant needs, fearful of responsibility or leadership. Although he was very—and loosely—articulate with me, in a group of friends he says of himself, "I'm a good listener. . . . I like to listen and I like to see what the next guy has to say," and over and over again he describes himself as "easygoing" and "I don't argue at all with anybody." This distressingly weak grasp on the environment and search for those who have such a compensatingly firm hand comes out in many ways. Speaking of the wisdom of elected leaders, Kuchinsky says, "Eisenhower, he knows what the people need there and what we need here." Responding to a question on who runs the government, Kuchinsky says, "It's the boss. . . . There's an organization that runs it." It is a managed society that we live in, but the management knows what our needs are and, if it is possible—if it doesn't cost too much—they will serve the popular interests.

This is the very heart of the political outlook of the Polish peasant: the political order is part of the nature of things—supplication might help, but there is no question of sanctioned demands, of self-assertion, of popular determination. And, of course, the Italian peasant and the Irish peasant are but little different. What is striking, then, is the general way in which men of Eastport have cast off their peasant metaphysics and robed themselves in the pragmatics of an urban democracy. But Kuchinsky is different from the others. It is as though the stratum of human civilization in which we are mining suddenly produced a specimen from an earlier period—and the processes of acculturation were laid bare by this sudden contrast.

B

FERRERA: DISILLUSIONMENT AND FANTASY

Ferrera, a shoe salesman, weighs over two hundred pounds, stands six feet four in his stocking feet, and, dressed in his business suit with his hat pulled low over his eyes, might inspire a mild terror in the hearts of people he approached casually. It would be misplaced; he is usually a man of peace. He earns his place among these undemocrats on all five counts, but the most revealing insight into his social outlook comes when he deals with the future of democracy. It is worth pausing to examine:

> Well, I feel that we are a decadent race. I feel that [pause] within a hundred years we may see the demise of America—unless something is done about it. But I think we are on the way out. ["Decadent in what way?"] Well, it's too much corruption that's rampant from the—the—the highest categories of our races—top advisers all the way down. There's too much vice and corruption [pause] too much [pause] too much *rottenness*. I don't know what other words to say, but [pause] all down the line it's got to give way to [pause] history. I think it's history repeating itself unless something is done about it. Now what could be done I don't know. But I feel sincerely, I feel deeply that unless something is done, this country is headed right toward the dogs. ["If we're on our way out, do you see any other country rising to take the role of leadership?"] Yes, I see the Russians; they're definitely taking over the lead, the Russians, or the Chinese.

A few minutes later he adds an amazing addendum and qualification to this position; he says, "The only staying power I could think of would be the power of the churches." This "figures," so to speak, and I accept it as the view that the only way to save America from the Communist nations is through the church. But I am wrong; that is not what he meant. He explains: "If the church was given the freedom once again in Communist-inspired countries, I think this 'prophecy' [of American downfall, mentioned above], if I may call it that, would definitely be true." At one blow, he takes the curse off the foreign victors, sanctifying them, so to speak, and assures America's downfall. It is a neat device.

Why does he scorn popular government? Why is he so skeptical of the forms of democracy, and why does he foresee the demise of the American system in a hundred years? Some of the elements of his experience and personality that contribute to our understanding of Ferrera's politics have been discussed above, but there are three that deserve a further examination: (1) his romantic unrealism, (2) his narcissistic disappointment in himself, and (3) his belief in a philosophers' stone that will lead him to success. Because of the first of these, his lack of a close, sure touch with the world as it is, he has had more than a dozen jobs since the war, clung to a failing company when everyone else abandoned it as bankrupt, and spent almost a year unemployed as a consequence. In his discussion of freedom he longs for a retreat away from the world, the life of a recluse—and his images of freedom, government, Utopia, are curiously "poetic," with the symbolism of big white clouds occurring several times. In a general appraisal of himself, he says: "I don't reason properly—I'm not a very logical person. In arguments I find myself saying some ridiculous things—I think they're so farfetched. . . . I'll come out with a rebuttal that will leave the person aghast. They get amused by it— 'What the hell did you say that for?'—Of course, they don't say it. . . . That's the type of guy I am." Nor does he listen when other people talk. In short, in many ways the evidence cumulates that Ferrera cannot predict the way the world of people will behave.

Ferrera's lack of a realistic approach to the world around him is unlike Kuchinsky's—it is romantic rather than autistic—but it has some of the same results. He does not absorb the lessons of the democratic culture; his experiences offer lessons that are distorted in the translation; his fantasy (something Kuchinsky lacks) keeps him from meshing his means with his ends.

Turning to Ferrera's self-absorption, his disappointed scrutiny of a hero's remains, we find him saying mournfully, "Well, I became an introvert as a result of [pause] making the wrong decision as far as the college was concerned and brooding over the fact that I had—hadn't completed my education and not being drafted into the services and all that stuff. I guess that developed into some form of neurosis." He has, more than others, a set of adjectives that come easily to mind when he speaks of himself: "I'm a humble person," "I would say I was a friendly sort of a guy," "I am a very stubborn person—and very impulsive," and so forth. He is keenly aware of his moods and psychic states: speaking of his recent bankruptcy and joblessness, he says, "I was very much beside myself; I have never been affected as I have been for the past few months; I was very upset; I felt as though I were caught so that I could never be free." He reports his psychic struggles to overcome his introversion, to go out into the world more, to listen more attentively when others are speaking to him. Because of this absorption in himself, he is not open to experience.

He is, moreover, if I am permitted hyperbole, a disappointed narcissist. He remembers his youth as a golden age. He was the only three-sport captain in his high school; he was offered any number of athletic scholarships to various universities, and even "performed in Madison Square Garden." How could such stardom help but create a kind of narcissistic concern with self? And in the dim recesses of his youthful happy-go-lucky mind, he wondered how it would end. He says now, looking back on his youth: "I've been a fatalist. I never expected to pass my twenty-first birthday. I have a friend of mine who is a general foreman, and every time he sees me he says, 'It's good to see that you've passed your twenty-first birthday.' . . . It was just a childish feeling that I had; I couldn't envisage anything in the future. As a matter of fact, even now I can't." It is as though life stopped for him when he left college and cut off his athletic glory, the cheering crowds, the first choice of all, the constant attention, a cornucopia of narcissistic supplies. The disappointment in this love affair, then, comes from the sad recognition that the man of thirty-eight he now knows inhabiting this fine frame is, after all, only a modest shadow of that bright youth he once knew.

Introversion, concern for a conscious attention to one's own mood and motive and psychic situation, need not lead to undemocratic views; but narcissism is likely to, and disappointed narcissism is an even more potent predisposing agent. The person who is disappointed in himself, in his status in the eyes of the world, is also disappointed about the world that sees him this way. If others do not appreciate him as he would like to be appreciated, they must be something less than men; Ferrera thinks of them as sheep, and if they are sheep, they are unlikely to be able to run a community council democratically, or to be worthy receptacles for decentralized power. In short, disappointment with the way others see you leads easily to a disappointment with others in a more general sense—in their judgment, their skill, their intelligence, their very worth in the eyes of God.

The third lineament in this brief character sketch needed before we can grasp the origins and meaning to Ferrera of his undemocraticness is his idea that somehow, somewhere, there is a philosophers' stone, a fountain of youth, a secret key to unlock a door in the garden wall that will yield him the lost fame and fortune he still seeks. At some points it seems to take on the idea of predestination—as in his phrase "some seem to be chosen to perform extraordinary things, while others are just meant to be cast into oblivion." Elsewhere it seems more like the usual notion of "getting the breaks"—"That's been one of my pet peeves, fortune. It's always been my argument that a man is not really self-made." And then he goes on to explain the good fortune of a man who, sticking to his more or less routine job, rises with the rising fortune of his business. He contrasts this with his own experience: "I've had many opportunities to do things," he says ruefully, "but I've never taken advantage of them." And hence life has meant for him "the shattering of many beautiful dreams." He could not recover that lost paradise where the secret door opened at the touch of his athletic hand.

It now remains to put together this portrait: Ferrera, the undemocratic man. The key to it is self-disappointment: the world that once gave him hero's honors, failed, as he feared it might, to accord him a man's success. The lad whom he learned to think so highly of, and of whom he expected such great things, disappointed him; even his parents, who "expected big things of me, inasmuch as I had done such a wonderful job in high school," could not help but be disappointed. Thus it is that he has come to feel that the world, society, people have failed him. They promised him everything and gave him nothing. When he tried to recover his Midas touch, all turned to ashes. People, then, are not trustworthy; they do not care what happens to you; they will not help you out; there's no use planning for the future because the future died when he left the playing fields. And, since this is the case, by analogy and by preference, one might as well think of the United States democracy as a doomed affair, with its golden youth behind it. All this is made more plausible by the unreality of Ferrera's world, the curdled romanticism that still grasps at the promises of "confidence men," as he terms the people he has had to deal with.

C

RAPUANO: PSYCHIC HOMELESSNESS
AND THE UNDEMOCRATIC WAY OF LIFE

We have met Rapuano before, and we shall meet him again. He is mentioned as the man who lost his identity; he is an impulsive man whose fear of freedom was analyzed in Chapter 3; and he is, like Kuchinsky and Ferrera, a "cabalist" thinker (Chapter 7). He is also a true undemocrat. Of the electorate, he says: "Just because a man is—just because he's a human being, doesn't make him smart enough to vote. He's got to have intelligence." His feeling about the democratic process is that democracy "gets in its own way," what with the Fifth Amendment, the slowness of Congress, bureaucratic inefficiency, and so forth. His solution to this is to "streamline" the government—a marvelous popular term with its mechanical and engineering overtones. Because of this slowness—in which, unlike most of the others, he does not find positive advantages—he feels the President should have, if not a strict dictatorship, "some unlimited powers." He rehearses the time involved to get something done if the President does not have these powers: "a week to call Congress together, another week before they start talking about it [the important new matter] . . . two years before they pass it . . . another three years before they gave the money." The organizations he has belonged to differ: the unions are not run democratically because "they were telling us to vote for a certain candidate," but the Veterans of Foreign Wars, having failed to make this error, seem to get a clean bill of health. There is in general, however, a tendency for Rapuano to see secret forces behind the democratic façade. And as for the future of democracy, it seems that another depression like the one in the thirties would finish us off. "My God," he says in anguish, "if we ever had anything like that again, it ain't going to be hard to sway some people to run to Communism."

Rapuano is not a Fascist—he does not have the hero-worshiping and other symptoms that characterized Ferrera, nor the admiration for the Nazis Kuchinsky showed. He is not even an authoritarian—he is among the three lowest scorers on the authoritarianism scale. Is he ethnocentric? He says: "There's nothing wrong in being social, or going to a party where there may be a couple of Negroes in it, but I definitely wouldn't want to go to a party where there's a majority of Negroes. [pause] I mean, let's face it, I hate to see anybody, you know, being pushed around, and being in the minority, because I know damn well that if I was in the minority, I'd feel it, too." He returns to this theme of being the only white couple at a Negro social event, and then, referring to Negroes at white gatherings, says: "I wonder how they feel; whether they'd be uncomfortable. I suppose they'd be uncomfortable, just like we would." He was the only man who considered in a feeling way how it must be to be one of *them*. No, I do not believe he is ethnocentric, in the usual sense of the term.

Like Ferrera, Rapuano has had democratic experiences, has shared in power and watched the deliberative processes of democracy take place in small groups. He almost completed high school; school was no burden for him, as it was for Kuchinsky. Indeed, he says with a somewhat embarrassed pride, that he graduated from grammar school with honors. With his intelligence, his openness to experience, he learned from school something about the conventional American way of electing rulers and sharing in policy deliberation. He has been a member of a union; he is a member of the Veterans of Foreign Wars; he has participated in electoral canvassing in his neighborhood. It is not for lack of an opportunity to see and learn about democratic forms that he is an undemocrat.

Rapuano says he would like to go back to any part of his childhood, if he could; his problem was a cultural one, not a family one. Like Kuchinsky, he was caught in the cultural dilemma of the immigrant's son, confused by the conflicting demands and identifications, torn by the alternating prescriptions of home and school. But unlike Kuchinsky, Rapuano developed and preserved a large number of friends and identifications outside his closed cultural group. His was an outward-looking, not an inward-looking, orientation. Still, the cultural conflict left a set of scars, and must be regarded as the first of a set of circumstances that injured the democratic "nerve" in the growing youth.

His personal qualities provide some clues—and some puzzles. He is not a dependent personality like Kuchinsky, eager to have the world run by some stronger hand. He is only slightly below average in the dominance scores and somewhat above in the sense of political efficacy. But more convincing is the way in which he *selected* a career, rather than falling into an available vacancy, and the way he has built up his role in the packinghouse so that it now represents an important part of the operation. He can control the environment much more easily than he can control his impulse life. He has a curiously uneven tolerance of ambiguity: he examines both sides of a wide range of issues; he sees the gray and the shade, as well as the black and the white, in his reports on political leaders. Typical of this circumspect quality of thought are such comments as this on India: "It seems that they agree with the Russians more than they do with us, but then again if we did help them, maybe something would come of it. Maybe the people would realize that we're trying to help them." His intolerance comes out when the subject of domestic Communism, or of gangsters, comes up; he rails at the courts for protecting them. Calm and tolerant in repose, in anger, when certain targets are mentioned, he is extremely intolerant. The special sexual as well as social meanings of Communism to Rapuano that I have suggested could, if I am right, account for this specific intolerance—contributing a second specific reason for his undemocraticness.

He does not have difficulty in controlling moods of depression; he is not narcissistic, or introverted, as is Ferrera. But he has, as we have seen, powerful angry spells, and almost intolerable struggles controlling his anger. In examining the freedom-tension of some men, we have seen something of the etiology of this problem; suffice it to say that it is also at the base of this undemocraticness. Finding himself full of inacceptable impulses, he will expect others to be the same way. If they are the same way, they will not serve as a model electorate, or as reasonable legislators, and certainly the future of democracy cannot be assured. This is the third source, then, of Rapuano's failure of support for popular government.

The fourth source has to do with another feature we have explored before: Rapuano's loss of identity. In religion, national origin, political party, class status, and even sexual matters, Rapuano shows signs of ambivalent identification or loss of identity. I would argue that the most likely intellectual development for a man where nothing is anchored, nothing, including his concept of himself, is secure, is to put a high premium on stability, order, decisiveness, rationality. This is, I think, what has happened to Rapuano. Since confusion about himself, combined with ambivalence about political matters, and uncertainty about his occupational future are constantly framing questions in his own mind, and have made him chronically worried and badly ulcerous, he cannot bear more confusion and indecisiveness in his world— such confusion as may appear in legislative processes. Since he is often painfully aware of his own lack of knowledge relevant to a decision, he emphasizes the need for the electorate to be more knowledgeable and informed. Finding it difficult himself to decide on policy matters, he insists that the President have the powers for quick decision. He is not really pessimistic about the future; but, projecting onto other people his own indecision, he worries about what people will do when tempted. Marginal man, a man without psychic country, he becomes, understandably, an undemocrat.

D

THE SOCIAL PRODUCTION OF UNDEMOCRATS

Here are three men who, instead of supporting the democratic ethos of the American society, detract from its strength and character. They could be radical or conservative, in the usual sense; either is quite compatible with the criteria distinguishing undemocraticness. What has gone wrong here? What is there in the social order that has bred these social outlooks?

One thing that has gone wrong is that in each case there is a marked weakness in coping with the real world; the explanatory systems are distorted; the reality principle seems easily dislodged. In saying this, we are focusing on cognitive failures in contrast to the usual focus on affective and personality disorders. And in making this focus, we can turn to the daily experiences of these men to see what they teach them; not to the internalized experiences that produce personality changes.

For all three of the men the two worlds they have lived in—immigrant parental family, native American birth and rearing—have been disorienting; for two of them, Kuchinsky and Rapuano, the division has been traumatic. (These are two of the four men *both* of whose parents were immigrant.) This bilateral cosmos has often provided two versions of reality, two explanatory systems, two competing models. For the unusual person, such a marginal position may provide the opportunity for genuine free choice, genuine philosophic synthesis. For others, it undermines confidence in the self and imposes too heavy a burden on the cognitive mechanism. The effort to understand is overwhelmed; the selection of what is real and true becomes eclectic, "far out." There is considerable evidence that this is what has happened here.

Society provides for most men opportunities for "batting the breeze" with their fellow men; this is not merely useful in guiding men in the group culture of which they are a part; it is also a kind of vicarious trial and error of ideas, a testing of the "far out" interpretation. It is the isolated farmer, the uncommunicative peasant, who have the greatest difficulty in understanding the events over their narrow horizons, for they suffer from an inability to develop, through conversational testing, explanatory models that they can use elsewhere. As we saw, Kuchinsky cut himself off from this process and lived in a fantasy world, partly as a consequence of this. The urban industrial world is a better place for developing realistic thinking to sustain democratic forms, because in that setting there are so few who find it possible to cut themselves off from conversation the way Kuchinsky did.

Both Rapuano and Ferrera suffered from lack of perspective on themselves at crucial times; Ferrera could not adjust to a situation where the glory of his youthful athletic prowess would wane; Rapuano could never "find himself," discover a core of personal identity. To the extent that the culture encourages wishful thinking about assimilation, about the chances of "rising in the world," about the kind of lives people are likely to lead, it creates a dissonance between the individual as he knows himself and his life, and the self and life promised to him. The unfulfillable social promise that leads a person to be disappointed in himself distorts at the source the instrument he has for testing reality.

□ □ □ □ □ □ □ □ □ □ □ □ □ □ □

Power in Society and Government

7

Cabalism—
The Political System of Undemocrats

> In our time, the conspiracy theory of events has gained ground. Along with those suspicions, there is an accompanying decline of moral temper.
>
> —DANIEL BELL, *The End of Ideology*, p. 193

Few men, except as they are consumed by destructive impulses, can sustain a belief in anarchy. If they destroy in their imaginative interpretation of the world some one principle of social order, they will be forced to discover another, perhaps based upon a backstairs view of life that they do not admit into the parlor of their minds. The undemocrats discussed in the last chapter were skeptical of the claims put forward by a conventional democracy that power is or can be widely shared, that democratic forms are not really a sham engagement with an empty ritual. Therefore it comes as no surprise to find that an inquiry to discover whether or not Eastport entertains a conspiracy theory of social power points exactly to the three undemocrats (Kuchinsky, Ferrera, Rapuano) and one other (Sokolsky). Unable to tolerate the idea of *no* social control, too realistic to believe that society was in fact anarchic, moved by psychic needs and guided by projective interpretations that make one view more congenial than

113

others—these men adopt a view of social control that we have termed *cabalism,* based on the term "cabal," "a secret association of a few designing persons."

A

CABALISM AND SOCIAL CONTROL

The belief that there is a secret, inscrutable, generally self-seeking, often illegitimate group behind the scenes with control over the men who hold the titles of office has certainly been widespread. Sir Henry Maine argues against the very possibility of democracy because those with money will always buy the votes of those without—thus an economic elite will always govern.[1] Mosca and Pareto, among others, believe that democracy is a façade behind which the "plutocrats" really rule.[2] Throughout Europe, Michel's doctrine of an "iron law of oligarchy" has a wide currency, suggesting that wherever there are the appearances of democracy, there is in fact an undercover control by some special group of insiders.[3] C. Wright Mills has found a power elite, which, he says, "really" governs America.[4]

Indeed, the theme of secret conspiratorial power in government is endemic in America, and not always without substance. For the Greenbackers it was the banks, for the Grangers and Populists it was the railroads and the trusts; for the Lincoln Steffens municipal reformers it was usually the transit and utility interests who corrupted the democracy that tempted them. At the lower fringes of respectability, for the Know-Nothings it was the Catholics, and later, for the Coughlinites, it was the Jewish international bankers; for the McCarthyites (with slightly greater plausibility) it was the Communists.

The idea that there is some secular but distant and incomprehensible power in the world controlling the destinies of men has many versions. It is important to distinguish the cabalism that we are here discussing from the "establishmentarianism" of the British working class, the Marxist version of capitalist control of democracy, and the "usurpation complex" described by Adorno

1. Henry Sumner Maine, *Popular Government* (London: John Murray, 1885), pp. 29–31.
2. Gaetano Mosca, *The Ruling Class* (New York: McGraw-Hill, 1939); Vilfredo Pareto, *The Mind and Society* (New York: Harcourt, Brace, 1935).
3. Robert Michels, *Political Parties* (New York: The Free Press of Glencoe, 1949).
4. C. Wright Mills, *The Power Elite* (New York: Oxford University Press Galaxy, 1959).

and his associates. Hoggart describes the British working-class view of an elite powerful "they." " 'They' are 'the people at the top,' " he says, " 'the higher ups,' the people who give you your dole, call you up, tell you to go to war," and so on.[5] This usage is prevalent throughout Europe. Usually "they" means "the powers-that-be," says a recent *New York Times* account of political jokes in Europe. "They" are the Establishment. But "establishmentarianism," if we may use this term, lacks precisely what is most significant about the cabalist view: the discrepancy between legitimate overt forms and covert reality, the conspiratorial nature of power. Marxism itself is ambiguous on this score. On the one hand the rule of the bourgeoisie, the temporarily legitimate heirs to the feudal landlords, seems overt: "The executive of the modern state is but a committee for managing the common affairs of the whole bourgeoisie." [6] On the other hand this control is done in underhanded manner by bribery and deceit. In a sense, Marxism has it both ways—the Wall Streeters, robber barons, bourgeoisie have the waning legitimacy of a passing historical period, but because they are losing it—indeed, have lost it—they become conspiratorial by the elapse of time.

A third variety is suggested by Adorno in his discussion of the "Usurpation Complex" the heart of which is the belief that only the economically strong have the right to govern. In this view the democratic government that is not close to these interests lacks legitimacy because it seems to lack strength. "Their idea of the strong man, no matter in what glowing personalized terms it may be expressed, is colored by an image of real strength: the backing of the most powerful industrial groups." [7] Dissonance between economic and political strength for these men creates the same kind of uncomfortable feeling that dissonance between social status and political power creates for others. In these views the conspirators have come to power—and that is what is wrong.

It is easily possible to identify cabalism with paranoia: the idea of a secret and all-powerful group controlling one's own destinies along with the national destinies seems congruent at the very least with paranoid symptoms. But it is not an essential feature of the cabalist philosophy, for it is not at all necessary to think

5. Richard Hoggart, *The Uses of Literacy* (Boston: Beacon Press, 1961), p. 62.
6. Karl Marx and Friedrich Engels, *Manifesto of the Communist Party* (New York: International Publishers, 1932), p. 11.
7. T. W. Adorno, Else Frenkel-Brunswik, Daniel J. Levinson, R. Nevitt Sanford, *The Authoritarian Personality* (New York: Harper, 1950), pp. 685–686.

of the cabals as having a personal interest in oneself—indeed, none of our cabalist thinkers felt personally persecuted. It is more a principle of social control than a principle for accounting for one's own fate in the world. None of the men sought to explain their modest status by a conspiracy theory of events.

The characteristics of cabalist thought are quite other than these. The first premise is:

1. There is some unofficial quasi-conspiratorial group behind the scenes to manipulate and control public affairs.

In a sense this is merely an explicit formulation of the implication in the code of the undemocrat that democratic façades are shams; here it is revealed who it is that "really" runs things. Curiously, it is always a group, never a single man. Even if a specific name is mentioned, like Ford or Du Pont, it is the family, the "Fords" and the "Du Ponts," or, perhaps, "people like Ford and Du Pont." This permits the conspiratorial element to enter; it allows for a "plot."

2. Each cabal group is responsible to no one but itself; its power is checked, if at all, by only the most tenuous and ineffective forces.

The whole idea of *responsible* power is antithetical to the way of thinking of the cabalist; he is searching for an absolute power to relieve him of anxieties arising from having swept away the conventional idealized explanation. Of course, there is the possibility of "wheels within wheels," with some shadowy superpower at the center; but never is there the notion that power is responsible to the people on whom it is exercised. This reintroduces the sham that the cabalist thinker tries to smash; it suggests that most (to him) implausible notion of the control of the stronger by the weaker.

3. There are two kinds of cabals; on the one hand, there are the high status big-businessmen, international bankers (not Jewish in the Eastport version), "Fords and Du Ponts"; on the other hand there are the low-status racketeers, Jews, union-bosses, "immoral elements," Communists.

The true cabalist will work with both in devising his explanatory system, but he has very different attitudes toward the two. Toward the high-status cabal he is somewhat respectful and not quite certain about their "real" legitimacy. Here he shares in the "usurpation complex" mentioned by Adorno. In this part of the discussion there is a sense of the inevitable—it's got to be that way; this is in the nature of things, resignation, a more-in-sorrow-than-in-anger (or perhaps, for Ferrera and Rapuano, more-in-envy-than-in-anger) kind of feeling. But somehow the sorrow or even the envy is a denatured variety; since this corresponds to the natural order, there is almost relief that events are, after all, under control. And, as we have pointed out elsewhere, there is very little of the indignation against big business that characterized the period of antitrust legislation or the fight against monopolies and cartels. One senses here the feeling that this is a legitimate conspiracy, a traditional plot, a cabal of the authorized elite.

The other group, the low-status, indeed, negative-status, cabals (Jews, Communists, hoodlums, and "immoral elements") were conceived in a different image. They were not inevitably in charge of things—indeed, they could be controlled and even punished if people would only come to their senses. That they should be punished was clear enough—there was little resignation and no satisfaction in a state of affairs where they were "getting away" with their illicit management of events. The level and character of emotional commitment was likewise different—the problem of influence by the low-status cabal was upsetting; the question of control by the high-status cabal was not.

4. The cabalist argument is protean; for the same person it will focus now upon the international banker and now upon the Communist. No one cabal will do for all occasions.

Cabalist thinkers use *both* high-status and low-status cabals—and more than one of each status level. The man who saw international bankers making wars also saw "criminal and immoral elements" dominating California; the man who saw Communists running the Democratic party also saw a secret corrupt group running New York City. Moral problems are likely to be assigned to the low-status cabals; in the Eastport version there is little emphasis on corruption in high places. Economic problems are assigned to high-status cabals for they, after all, do not *subvert;* they *run* things—and in their own interests.

5. The affairs, meetings, and decisions of the group are secret and not understood by most people who take things at face value; therefore it is a special gift of insight that permits one to penetrate reality and see the outlines of what is happening.

The constant refrain in cabalist thinking is "things are not what they seem." Thus it has the special advantage in conversation of giving the cabalist thinker an apparent sophistication; he is the master inside-dopester, who really needs no dope at all, but assumes it. The authoritarian is eager to believe that there are great secret sexual "goings-on"; the cabalist is eager to believe there are conspiratorial "political goings-on."

These two points (4 and 5) taken together reveal cabalist thought as a kind of philosophical principle, a cosmogeny, or explanation of the beginning of things. Everything happens because some small, unseen, and unofficial group wanted it to happen that way. Returning to the question implied in some explanatory schemes (Chapter 20), Who willed it? the answers for the cabalists are different from the most usual answers in Eastport. For the cabalist thinker, every event is willed.

6. The method of the cabals—the way they create wars and depressions and revolutions—are obscure, but they involve extraordinary, almost supernatural powers.

The cabalistic thinker rarely spells out the channels of influence, or makes explicit the sources of cabalist power or the reason why those over whom they exercise their power do not play one cabal off against another. These accounts are more convincing, of course, shrouded in mystery. Indeed, mystery itself is most attractive to the mind of the cabalist thinker. The mystery, however, is more the mystery of religion than of magic,[8] but it is the religion of the netherworld, where there are, on the one hand, princes like Lucifer, and on the other, those like Lucifer's other self, the snake.

The application of this style of thought to the problems of the day is easy, too easy. But it is easy, too, to dismiss all imputations of "deals," of secret power, or discreet control. Somehow a balance must be achieved. How shall one appraise, then, the various cabalist-style arguments that give to the munitions makers a special determinative role in "causing" the First World War, how judge the influence of Communists in causing us to abandon Poland at the Yalta Conference, the influence of the "old China hands" in bringing Communism to power in China? The material is available, if anyone with such an intellectual bent cares to put such a cabalist construction upon it. It is only when he passes beyond reality limits and becomes suffused with projective and mystical thinking that he qualifies as a cabalistic thinker.

8. At least this is true if we use Malinowski's use of the word "magic," "a body of purely practical acts, performed as a means to an end." See Bronislaw Malinowski, *Magic, Science and Religion* (Garden City, N.Y.: Doubleday, 1954), p. 70.

B
FOUR MEN AND THEIR CABALS

Eleven of the Eastport men seemed free of cabalist thinking; they saw power as generally shared and limited, and they viewed legitimate power as superior to and containing, in the long run, the power of private groups. Four men exhibited in significant degree the symptoms of cabalist interpretations of social control. Let us examine their views and, briefly, recapitulate certain features of their lives. Three of them, Ferrera, Rapuano, and Kuchinsky, as we have said, are familiar as "undemocrats"; the fourth, like two of the others, is familiar as one of the men who was fearful about the excesses of a more free society. We shall start with him.

Sokolsky

A slight man in his late thirties of Russian-Jewish extraction—though not, as he says, "a very good Jew"—Sokolsky finds himself approaching middle age with a repetitive factory job he does not care for, living in a town he would leave without regrets, outclassed by his brothers and sisters, and, at the time of the interview, in debt because of the cutback in employment at his plant. His cabals emerge in several contexts. He finds that Presidents generally, and Eisenhower in particular, take orders from party bosses: "They're telling him how to run this country. . . . We [the fellows down at the shop] figured he's a general and he knows what to do—but he's taking orders like anybody else." He believes that the recession was brought on by a conspiracy of manufacturers who wished to punish labor and to show who was in charge. In mentioning the things he would not like to talk about with his friends, he lists "big-business control of government." The reason he wouldn't like to talk about it is that "they've got control of it now, so . . . I mean I don't see any sense in talking about it when there's nothing we can do about it." And elsewhere he says: "Big business is running this country today. There's nothing we can do about it, but they're running it." Jay College is keeping industry out of Eastport; the sons of the rich have complete sexual liberty and are getting away with it. In short, the rich and powerful have things all their own way.

Rapuano

Both Sokolsky and Rapuano are friendly men, have good relations with their shop associates (in spite of Rapuano's temper), and express themselves with a free flow of emotion in the interviews. They do not exhibit the typical stance of a paranoid; they are not looking over their shoulders for someone out to get them; they both rank high in the "faith in people" scale. Nevertheless, Rapuano is worried about cabalist groups operating behind the scenes to exercise their strong and usually evil power. Here, for example, is his view of Communists:

> I thought [Senator McCarthy] was a great man. I've thought that when they censured him in the Senate—I thought that was part of the scheme of the Communist conspiracy to do that, and they succeeded. Now there's a man that fought for—for this country. He fought for people like me, against Communists, and yet they tied his hands and censured him. I think that killed him more than anything else. I thought he was a great man. We should have more people like him.

The Communists ran from him like rats from a fumigator when he exposed the Democratic party. New York City, he believes, has been taken over by a group who "use it to their own advantage." As for Eisenhower, "There's somebody that put him there who's running the party. . . . It stands to reason that there would be."

Kuchinsky

The Polish-Catholic roofer whose wife suffers from claustrophobia and fear of crowds, Kuchinsky, sees a quite different set of cabalists at work. His cabalism took a classic form: the Jews run everything. They run the unions, business, and, of course, the banks. What is hard to remember in reading the following excerpt is that the spokesman is a decent man in his personal relations, solicitous of his mentally ill wife, kind to his children, with a controlled temper on his job:

> LANE: How about subversive elements in this country: Do you think there are many subversive elements in America?
> KUCHINSKY: [pause] Now, you'd have to explain that question to me a little more.
> LANE: Yes, say, Communists.
> KUCHINSKY: Well, ahem, yah. I, ah, I believe there is, but I don't think they're gonna amount to much here. Because, I'll tell you why. . . . It's not well organized here. You'll get it and

you'll have it. You'll never put it out of this country, that's for sure. But, ah, like I say, it'll never be too strong here, cause I think the people are a little too smart. I think it's one race that's in there. I won't mention the race. [Has mentioned it before.]

LANE: Well, we might as well mention it. You think it's the Jews?

KUCHINSKY: Yah, yah. But I believe that, ah, in the Jewish organizations, I believe there's an awful lot of Communists there. . . . We've been reading it right along. I mean it's been proved right along, and, ah, nine out of ten mostly Jews. . . . They've controlled the biggest part of this country. So I mean, that's the situation there. I don't think, ah, like I say, ah, if we watch 'em and keep our eyes open, I don't think they can overrun this country, that's for sure.

LANE: When you say *they* control the biggest part of this country, you mean the Jews do, not the Communists?

KUCHINSKY: Oh, yah. I'd say the Jews run this country, that's for sure . . . both labor and business—and money. Because any business you go to today or any stores you go to today, 95 per cent of 'em are Jewish. Every business downtown is practically Jewish.

LANE: How do you think they got that?

KUCHINSKY: Well, ah, like I say, I believe it's, ah, I believe it's a lot of nerve.

The style of thinking that calls such cabalists from the netherworld affects the view of other aspects of society. Across the seas "the Communists are boss in Germany and France . . . you have a gang . . . you have to overrun a gang." And in Washington the political bosses—"they're the fellows, they're the Government, they're the ones that are running the country." And nationally: "I think Du Pont and all of them people, I think they really control a lot of it. They're the big ones. They're the fellows that really run the country, too, with that money." This is not pluralism, but a tendency to see among a limited number of groups whatever group comes to attention as endowed with unlimited power. The word "really" does the trick: the Jews "really" run things; the party bosses are "really" in control; and the Du Ponts "really" run the country. It is a plea to look beyond appearances, a verbal wink, and, in this case, a peasant's sly nod to show that he knows what is going on beneath the cover of a moral façade.

Ferrera

A shoe salesman, Ferrera is a large, strong, dark man, impulsive (as we saw in Chapters 3 and 6), sensitive, moody, sometimes disoriented—with a strong capacity for friendship and an occasional show of violence. His cabalism is often suggested rather than overtly stated. There are wheels within wheels, it seems. Eisenhower takes his orders from Dewey, and "Mr. Dewey gets his orders from Wall Street. Mr. Dewey is Mr. Big, but there is somebody just a little bit bigger than him," someone shadowy and obscure. The unions "have a little more than a lot to do with" running the Democratic party, and the unions are "Communist-inspired." More than that, "their business agents are hoodlums." In some sense, Ferrera sees a conspiracy of immoral elements, criminals, and vicemongers. He can't understand the light sentences they draw when convicted; he believes, as reported above, "that we are a decadent race," and finds this decadence particularly strong in Hollywood; indeed, "I understand that the entire State of California is beginning to stink." But his most vivid picture of an all-powerful conspiratorial group arises in connection with the origins of war:

> I'm led to believe that the fate of the entire world is controlled by a group of men—six or seven, or possibly ten—whether they're still—whether they still have the control that was—a—well known in the First World War—I'm speaking of the House of Rothschild [and some other vaguely remembered banking house] . . . I believe that there are a few men who control the finances of the world and I believe that there are a few men that manipulate the strings—I don't know who they are, just a very passing acquaintance I have with that thing, not much is said about it, but I know there are men extremely influential—the one that I know offhand in prior times was William Randolph Hearst.

A little learning has exposed Ferrera to some earlier radical mythology, and he has seized it and made it his own.

C
THE PERSONAL SOURCES OF CABALIST THINKING

How to account for a conspiratorial picture of the world, even in these relatively mild and nonincapacitating forms? It is striking that the relationship between such fear of conspiracy and authoritarianism is almost zero; there is no evidence that these men, more than others, are anomic; we do not find evidence either of social anxiety or—and this is surprising—of neurotic anxiety. This last item is surprising because, as noted above, the cabalist symptoms show a prima facie closeness to the phobias that form the core of our neurotic anxiety tests. (On this test, Rapuano was high, Sokolsky was middle, and Ferrera and Kuchinsky were low.)

These men, then, are not neurotic in any usual sense; they do not share the symptoms of the paranoid—tightlipped, fearful, whispering that someone is after them. They are not schizoid, either, even in the way in which Adorno's "cranks" and lunatic-fringe character types exhibit schizoid tendencies in their socio-political fantasies, although they do have a more tenuous grasp on reality than do the others.[9] Nor, except for Ferrera, can one see in their interpretation of secret power abroad in the world, an easy rationalization for their own frustrations or failures. On the contrary, Kuchinsky shows every symptom of a man who feels that he has "arrived," speaking with scorn of those who have not been so fortunate and foresighted as he in learning a valuable and valued trade. Sokolsky, also frustrated, blames his situation on his position as second son who had to be sacrificed to the first, and his own lack of a business head. Rapuano, satisfied with his economic progress, does not see any relation between his occupational problems and the Communists—his war with the Communists is on the symbolic level. Even Ferrera tends to blame his parents, himself, and an unappreciative world, rather more than "they" for his failure. It would be difficult and tortuous to trace a line of thought that relates the "power of the cabals" to the occupational, familial, or status frustrations of these men. It is, of course, always possible that aggressive feelings following upon frustrating experiences may be displaced upon remote and apparently irrelevant objects —but there is no more reason to believe that this is the case here than in any other area of life.

I have said that one source of cabalism is to restore to society some agent of public order after a general cynicism has swept away the power and authority of democratic institutions (and of course it works the other way, as well; a conspiratorial theory of human society makes democratic institutions seem implausible from the beginning). But in our explanation of conspiratorial thinking there is one theme that seems to bear especial weight. It is the relation between personal control and ideas of social control.

We turn here as we did in the discussion of freedom, to the question of ego strength, and to avoid obscurity I shall repeat the definition given earlier. Ego strength, as the term is usually employed, implies (1) a capacity to master and order one's impulse

9. T. W. Adorno and associates, *op. cit.*, pp. 765–766.

life in the interest of long-run satisfactions, plus (2) a capacity to cope with the stimuli and demands of the environment as they affect a person's life. Although theoretically there is some reason to believe that these two kinds of "ego strength" are associated with each other, efforts to measure them have not always found the separate measures to have this correlation.[10] In what follows we have employed a combination of objective test scores and the independent estimates of two persons intimately familiar with the fifteen cases to rank the fifteen men in terms of (1) mastery of impulses, and (2) mastery of environment, and (3) a combined ego-strength measure.[11] The scoring procedure is given in greater detail in Appendix C. In general, the mastery of impulse life was focused on capacity to control anger, control over spending impulses, moderation in the use of alcohol, absence of moods of melancholia, capacity to accept temporary defeats of life aims, effective implementation of long-range goals, and a fitting of aspiration level to a realistic appraisal of expectations—a sense of the probable. The mastery of environment included a capacity to deal with authority without anxiety, an apparent sense of control over the impersonal forces of life, an objective score on questions taken from Gough's dominance scale, and an estimate of how a person handles his career problems.

So much for the concept, the measures, their interrelationship, and our small attempt to achieve an idea of interobserver reliability. What strikes our attention here is that in the final combined score of ego strength, the person judged to be most deficient in this quality was Sokolsky, the next most deficient was Ferrera, and the third was Rapuano. These are the three lowest scorers. Kuchinsky, our Semitophobe, ranked exactly in the middle (one judge said seventh, the other said eighth). However, if we turn to the measures of mastery over the environment, on the face of it, a dimension more closely related to conspiratorial thinking, we find that again the three lowest are included in our four cabalist thinkers but that Kuchinsky takes the place of Ferrera, who ranks ninth on this measure. Thus, on either the overall measure or on

10. Elizabeth Douvan and Alan M. Walker, "The Sense of Effectiveness in Public Affairs," Survey Research Center, University of Michigan, processed, about 1955.

11. The correspondence between the two rank lists was substantial—only five differed in the two measures by more than two rank scores (one through fifteen), and only two by more than three rank scores. On the two independent judgments of the overall quality of ego strength, only one judgment was as much as three rank scores off. The scoring, of course, was done in each case without knowledge of the other judge's score.

the mastery of environment measure, or on both, each of the four ranks among the three lowest in the rank order of the fifteen men.

TABLE I

Rank Order on Measures of Ego Strength and Mastery of Environment of Four Men with "Conspiratorial Thinking" Patterns (in a Group of Fifteen)

	Ego Strength	*Mastery of Environment*
Sokolsky	15	15
Rapuano	14	14
Ferrera	13	9
Kuchinsky	7	13

The most immediate, and perhaps the most important, bearing of ego strength, or its lack, on cabalist thinking is not psychodynamic, however, but cognitive—or rather, experiential. The core of the question of ego strength is control: control over impulse life, control over environmental demands. These four men do not know the meaning of control. Being unable to meet and control their private environments, they do not know in general how public events are controlled, ordered, or brought about. Their failure is one of understanding; they do not know the way individual long-range decisions are made, let alone social decisions. They have not experienced on the personal plane the control of a small environment. How could they then imagine how the larger environment is ordered? That which is known from experience represents a kind of knowledge that is integrated into an orientation toward the broad, unstructured social world.

There is a second sense in which personal experience colors an understanding of the world. If society is the man writ large, and if each individual understands mankind largely from his interpretation of himself, those low in ego strength will likely see society in the grip of irrepressible forces that are constantly challenging the rather ineffective regulators. We do not have to reach beyond the bounds of plausibility to conceive a person who experiences himself as barely able to contain the impulses that surge up within him finding the same situation in society. It would be only "natural." Thus Sokolsky, fascinated by sex and worried about his own sex impulses, makes of the issue a social problem. And Rapuano, worried about his identity and place in society, repressing with difficulty his sneaking doubts about his Americanism, finds the domestic Communist menace almost uncontrollable.

Thus both the personal experience, or lack of experience in managing affairs, and the personal problem of repressing the "irrepressible" lead men into thinking of the world as governed by absolute, powerful, unofficial forces.

But the cabals were of two kinds: the unofficial, conspiratorial but legitimate high-status (business) groups and the illegitimate low-status usurper (Communist, Jewish, gangster) groups. Each man employed both in his explanations of the social order, and, so we shall argue, each served a useful but quite distinct purpose in his interpretation of the world. The references to the absolute power of business ("They're running things; there's no doubt about it") has a genesis going back to the somewhat riotous emotional life of these men. Unable to sort out and maintain a steady set of preferences, subject to whim and impulse, the possibility of maintaining a firm grip on any situation is slender. Yet *events must not be allowed to get out of control.* Chaos within breeds a need for control without. Now, we are not talking about projection but, as it were, compensation; a tendency to balance external control against the lack of inner control. It would be easier, no doubt, to see the President or Congress as running things—but here, if our discussion is more than an analogy, the deficiencies in experiencing a regnant ego or self make this less plausible than some system of powerful but unofficial control. So big business is made to fill the breach, and can be given the kind of absolute power that is psychologically most needed but is clearly hard to find in Congress or the President. It serves, then, to still the demand for a guiding hand, a conscious intelligence, a dominant force in society. It is a counterweight to the chaotic forces of drift and change welling up in anarchic fashion within the individual.

That is one half of the picture; the other deals with the rejection of impulse life, the effort to stamp on it, and the tendency to think of it as disagreeable, vile, unacceptable, contaminated by its association with sexual appetite, anger, and greed. The thing to do with such impulses is to destroy them, drive them out. They sometimes do get out of control; they always threaten control, but they are not themselves to be considered as regnant. The Jews, Communists, and gangsters of social life are, in this sense, like sex and anger in personal life. Or, in reverse, sex and anger are the individual's Jews and Communists and gangsters. They need a scourge like McCarthy (whom Rapuano said "fought for people like me") or Hitler (whom Ferrera said helped solve Germany's problems of poverty by eliminating the congenitally weak and whom Kuchinsky said "overran his shoes"). Unless we are misled, then, there is a fundamental relationship between one's internal experience of fighting against barely contained and inadmissible impulses, and one's external perception and reconstruction of society as threatened by some inadmissible and barely contained social force.

D
THE SOCIAL ROOTS OF CABALIST THOUGHT

Ambiguity of Control

The social situation, the social order that serves as the "ground" on which Eastport stands, contributes to the support of cabalist thought. The very obscurity of the agencies of social and political control makes it easier—as well as more necessary—to invent a personal set of governing groups. The separation of powers, the checks and balances, the federal structure of government invites this kind of sociological imagination. The economy is no "better." Reliance upon an "unseen hand" in the market place is uncomprehensible to many, if not downright ghostly. The social order is unstable, constantly challenged by technology, mobility, fashion. The ambiguity of control in a market economy in a pluralistic society, then, encourages the cabalist thinker in his imaginative interpretations.

Manipulative Theme

He may be led down this path by the very agents of the free society, in particular the debunkers of radio and television and the advertising men. In the British working class, says Hoggart, "Outside the personal life they will believe almost nothing consciously; the springs of assent have nearly dried up. Or worse, they will believe in the reducing and destroying things but not in assertions of positive worth: if you assume that most things are a 'sell,' it is easy to accept every bad charge, hard to accede to a call for praise and admiration. Some of the more powerful influences in modern society are tending to produce a generation expert at destroying by explaining-away. . . ." [12] And so the demo-

12. Richard Hoggart, *op. cit.*, p. 230.

cratic façade may be "explained away," destroyed, and one learns
that the "hidden persuaders" are at work, the "big bosses, they're
the ones." The manipulative theme of modern society reinforces
the cabalist mind. And in America, the panic over "being taken
for a sucker," which Gorer finds to be characteristic, may make
some especially vulnerable to this effect.[13]

Image of a Feudal Order

Many in our group are a generation or two removed from men
reared in Old-World beliefs. To what extent are their views colored by their ethnicity, their national origins? Kuchinsky is, in
particular, a transplanted peasant, with a peasant's superstition.
The political order of Poland was seen as part of the natural or
divine order of things, where events are established beyond perad-
venture of control; indeed, the idea of controlling events is hardly
admitted to the peasant mind. There is a strong suggestion that
Kuchinsky's anti-Semitism is transplanted, and so, also, when he
says the Du Ponts really run things, he may have in mind the
feudal lord. Similarly, Rapuano and Ferrera, figuratively speaking, may have an "ancestral memory" of the little village just
outside Naples where their grandfathers lived, which colors their
image of how a social order is controlled. Or, even more trench-
antly, both of them may have some more current knowledge of
the Mafia, about whom Senators Kefauver and McClelland have
developed a national concern. Nor is it unlikely that Sokolsky's
membership in a minority religion with ancient claims against a
dominant ruling group, excluded from status if not from power,
colors his social outlook. Perhaps, in several senses, cabalism is
a heritage of an ancient historical order of things, the image of
a feudal order projected on the American panoramic screen.

Americanism Anxiety

This ethnicity takes its toll on rationality through a special
kind of anxiety. Mead, and especially Gorer, have pointed out that
in America, unlike other nations, nationality is achieved, not a
matter of course.[14] If one's national identity, then, is, so to speak,

13. Geoffrey Gorer, *The American People: A Study in National Character* (New
York: Norton, 1948), pp. 178–179.
14. *Ibid.*, p. 188; Margaret Mead, *And Keep Your Powder Dry: An Anthropologist
Looks at America* (New York: Morrow, 1942), pp. 70–79.

up to the individual, he may often sense some Americanism anxiety based on uncertainty whether or not he has it in the proper measure, or, even more important, whether everyone knows he has it in that measure. One can demonstrate this by attacking the enemies of 100 per cent Americanism, Communists and, for certain groups, Jews. This latter point raises the ironic spectacle of the transplanted Polish peasant clinging to his Polish-peasant anti-Semitism and finding it perversely reinforced by his mistaken concept of Americanism.

Religious Styles of Thought

This is a secular culture we are talking about, in spite of the widespread church membership and the religious trimmings given to the rituals of politics, education, and welfare activities. If it were religious, or if it retained in more generous proportions the elements of magical thinking that have now become attenuated, though not eradicated, in the long journey of what is called civilization—if it were more religious or more magical than it is, the problem of assigning effective causes to the events of the times would be simpler by far. For then it is only a matter of choosing the God, the Devil, the demon or saint who is responsible for an event. But while civilizations outgrow the magical elements of religion, individuals may not. And when religion does not provide them with ready and familiar and even easy answers to their crude questioning, their "why's," they will invent their own, or seize upon those that lie in the half-educated stratum of society. The failure of religion to give any ready answers to the reason why things happen the way they do, the demise of effective theology and doctrines of divine and infernal intervention, creates a vacuum into which some men, panicked by ambiguity, rush with their talk of the cabals of the time. Is cabalism a product, then, of unacknowledged religious styles of thought persisting in a secularized society?

E

INOCULANTS AGAINST CABALISM

While these are some of the circumstances contributing to the development of cabalist thought, the fact remains that almost three-quarters of the men we talked to remain relatively immune.

Why should this be? Among the variety of restraining forces is the emphasis upon pragmatism that keeps the location of a cause close to the supposed effect, and avoids an elaborate architecture of explanations. Like the British, Americans are a prosaic people. As noted above, the widespread participation in a range of community, civic, and political activities, however trivial, however distant from the crucial decisions, gives to these men some sense of the way things get done in the American society.[15]

The ideology of Eastport, the pattern of beliefs that we have been describing, is not congenial to the cabalist idea. For one thing, the idea that some illegitimate cabal has taken over is most sympathetic to a general notion that this is, in fact, not *my* society, not *my* world. But these men are not alienated; a generation away from being legal aliens, they have embraced the going order of things that has permitted them to exceed their fathers and fulfill their wives' and children's expectations. They are glad to be a part of it. Perhaps as a consequence, certainly as a concomitant, they believe that the government is genuinely concerned about their welfare; it is a benign and solicitous government. Therefore they do not *need* and will not wish to invent another illegal government to take its place. Things are too good as they are. And as another aspect of this general sense of the appropriateness of things, they have conceded to the distribution of goods and services a kind of legitimacy. The rewards of this world go according to the announced and accepted principles: hard work, ability, merit, plus the Great Excuser, education. Finally, their concept of the nature of power as something like money (a natural analogy in a commercial society), available to those who work hard for it and seek it, forecloses the idea of an exclusive monopoly of power. But cabalist thought vests in each cabal an absolute power to do what it wants.

The typical Eastportian still believes it is possible in a democracy, though not always probable, to have open covenants openly arrived at.

15. Of course, this is not a guarantee. Ferrera, who believes that wars are decided upon by the international bankers, has, it is true, been active in Republican party precinct work, but the experience did not teach him the adjustive, mutual, accommodational nature of political power. He believes, for example, that the story of politics is completely summarized in the statement that political subordinates "are all a bunch of puppets—they all do as the big bosses tell them to do."

8

Power in Society

The top of modern American society is increasingly unified, and often seems willfully co-ordinated: at the top there has emerged an elite of power. The middle levels are a drifting set of stalemated, balancing forces: the middle does not link the bottom with the top. The bottom of this society is politically fragmented, and even as a passive fact, increasingly powerless: at the bottom there is emerging a mass society.
—C. WRIGHT MILLS, *The Power Elite*, p. 324

As things are today . . . most observers seem unwilling to take a straight look at the amorphous distribution of power in America. Sophisticated social scientists pin their hopes or fears on this or that elite, echoing the bottom dogs who feel there is a boss somewhere. Yet people fail to see that, while it may take leadership to start things running, or to stop them, very little leadership is needed once things are under way. . . .
—DAVID RIESMAN, *The Lonely Crowd*, p. 252

It is an elusive thing, power: two men, like Mills and Riesman, can look at the same society and see it distributed very differently. Hunter sees it concentrated in Regional City in the managers of the great corporations; [1] in New Haven, Dahl finds

1. Floyd Hunter, *Community Power Structure: A Study of Decision Makers* (Chapel Hill, N.C.: University of North Carolina Press, 1953).

it dispersed—specific to issues.[2] Brady sees the power centers in the great trade associations and their federations, the *Spitzenverbände*, the peak associations like the National Association of Manufacturers.[3] Lerner suggests a dual power structure: "Actually," he says, "the corporations and trade unions represent two galactic systems of almost sovereign power." [4]

But, fortunately, our problem is not to locate the power centers of society, but rather to reconstruct how a group of workingmen see it. Lerner says: "The run-of-the-mill American has shown a healthy concern for all phases of power," admiring the rich, worrying about federal power, "suspicious of trade-union power and church power even more than of corporate power, and suspicious also of military power—at least until the period of the world wars and cold wars." [5] Except for his remarks on "federal power" he has drawn the image with a vague accuracy; he senses how it must lie in the popular mind. Asked who has too much power in America, Eastport common men see both of Lerner's galactic constellations, labor first and big business and certain wealthy families second. These are, in fact, the only important power groups mentioned. The discussion on these overpowered groups, however, must find its place in the context of a more general picture drawn in the discussion about those who have "too little power," those who "really" run the government, those who run the political parties, the images of how government functions. In this context, then, attending to patterns of ideas, rather than specific phrases, certain general notions of the nature and location of power emerge.

A

UNION POWER AND BOURGEOIS SELF-IMAGE

There were more union than nonunion men among those expressing some fear, some aversion, some sense of alarm over the growth of union power. More of the men mentioned unions as "too powerful" than mentioned big business (but a few mentioned Du Pont and Ford—bringing the business total equal to union

2. Robert A. Dahl, *Who Governs? Democracy and Power in an American City* (New Haven: Yale University Press, 1961).
3. Robert A. Brady, *Business as a System of Power* (New York: Columbia University Press, 1943).
4. Max Lerner, *America as a Civilization: Life and Thought in the United States Today* (New York: Simon and Schuster, 1957), p. 318.
5. *Ibid.*, p. 397.

references). Unions were more likely than corporations to be the first mentioned. The men say, "I think certain unions are getting a little too powerful"; "A lot of unions are getting a lot of power"; "Some labor groups, I would say, have too much." What lies behind this fear of union power?

The reasons that men give for their distrust of unions are not obscure. They speak a good deal of the corruption that had then been in the news following the McClellan investigations. Surprisingly, they focus also upon the danger that unions will be too successful: Woodside fears the bankruptcy of small concerns. DeAngelo, a union steward, argues that the management of his own plant has been so easy on the union, so compliant toward union demands, that they are being priced out of competition. Rapuano uses the inflation argument: "Unions have just as much effect on the economy as big business has. If the people are making too much money, why *of course* the big business has to increase their prices to pay these people." These views suggest a kind of wages-fund argument, an argument based upon the belief that there is just so much available for wages, and if the unions are too successful and overdraw this fund, their members will suffer. A variation of this view is that management, not nature, will make them suffer: Sokolsky believes management created a recession in 1957–1958 to punish labor for its excessive demands. Thus union power is misused to enrich union leaders; when "successful" it may hurt labor more than it helps, and it may lead to retribution from the superior power of management.

But as they speak thus, hesitantly, about unions and their powers, it is as though there were some hidden strands of thought checking them, holding them back. They see that unions bring to working people such as themselves higher wages and, especially, greater security. With a few exceptions, their own experiences with unions, while mixing irritations with benefits, do not seem to be the source of their concern about union power. What holds them back, too simply, is that there is no place for strong identification with unions in their ideology; there are too many friction points; there is too much dissonance. Some of these ideological friction points we have considered, and others will follow; briefly, they emerge from the pattern of discussion somewhat as follows:

One of the most frequent complaints about unions is that they advise their members how to vote. To some this seems "undemocratic"; for others it is merely irritating. But it is irritating not simply because it is an "outsider" telling them what to think; it is irritating because *any* formal advice on this matter from any source is resented. The application of the *fear of being influenced* explored below has its most telling illustration here. Political opinions, as we shall say, are considered to be parthenogenic.

In another way a related theme is quickly surfaced in the union discussion: the *fear of partisanship*, and its obverse, the search for independence. Where there is conflict, the culture seems to instruct these men, there is probably something to be said for both sides, and the proper course is to *search for middle ground*. When management and labor conflict, union power against business power, some compromise is indicated. Thus Sokolsky, who hates his job in a bicycle plant: "I think they [unions] are asking too much . . . and the owners are getting a little fed up."

Union power is a subject loaded with tension and ambivalence because it assigns influence to low-status leaders, violating the bourgeois principle of harmonic social control: *power and status should be congruent*. Many people, not merely authoritarians, are upset when low-status people seem to command higher-status people. It is disturbing because it upsets stereotyped comfortable response patterns.

Unions raise for each individual uncomfortable questions about his own *class identification*, questions the Eastport common man faces with the greatest reluctance.

In the same way, unions pose the issue of individual ascent up the economic ladder versus collective protection in an occupational level beyond which a person does not aspire. Too great an identification with the union seems to imply to these men an abandonment of their own mobility.

Beyond this, there are several who see the union as engaged in conflict with society, and particularly with government. Since, as we shall see, these men generally believe that the national government is operated in their interest and distributes rewards fairly, they do not easily become partisans of antigovernment forces. "The union is more or less bucking the government," says Woodside, "and I think when you start bucking the government you're not doing any good for the regular layman" (his term for common man).

It is in these several senses that the union power seems dissonant with a broad social ideology, a way of feeling and acting and looking at the social order. These are bourgeois chemicals in the soil that stunt the growth of union power even in an industrial, urban, working-class community.

B

ECONOMIC POWER: FROM WAGE TO PRICE

As the Eastport men look out upon the social world, and particularly upon its economic aspect, they perceive not only that labor and business are powerful but also that this power is exercised in a certain way with certain results. In general, they are less concerned about the exercise of economic power over wages and income than they are about its exercise over prices and expenditure. In talking about the power of big business, not once do they mention the older fears of "exploitation"; rather they say: "Well, the government shouldn't allow monopolies . . . price setting by big corporations," and "I've heard it said that certain industries control steel prices because they control the furnaces," and "These automobile manufacturers and all of them—they go up on the prices whenever they want to." Moreover, as we have seen, union power offers a similar threat." Ruggiero, a building custodian, says: "I think wages are out of hand. . . . Years ago we bought just as much with the little money we had. The prices offset the wages." Even with unions the emphasis is not upon forcing higher wages, but upon restraining forces that might raise prices—a curious un-Marxian state of affairs, to say the least.

Some of the reasons for this shift from wage to price are transparent. But perhaps there are other, subtler reasons. The change of focus from production to consumption, reflected in the popular biographies of the media [6] and in other cultural changes,[7] may, indeed, help to explain this drift from concern over wage exploitation to price exploitation. A rising standard of living by itself would not do it; there is no evidence that poorer people pay less attention to commodity prices and less to wage scales than do their more prosperous neighbors. Rather the explanation seems to lie in the social concomitants of this rising standard: the rise of

6. Leo Lowenthal, "Biographies in Popular Magazines," in Paul F. Lazarsfeld and Frank N. Stanton, eds., *Radio Research 1942–1943* (New York: Duell, Sloan and Pearce, 1944), pp. 507–548.

7. See David Riesman, Nathan Glazer, and Reuel Denny, *The Lonely Crowd: A Study of the Changing American Character* (New Haven: Yale University Press, 1950).

cities, the changing sex roles, the advent of mass advertising, the expansion of leisure, and the bourgeoisification of the working class.

The focus upon price, on bargain hunting, on comparative shopping, on haggling is, in some ways, an urban focus, one dependent upon an impersonal market. In peasant Europe or rural America, where the manager of the general store or its European equivalent was a family friend, these habits were unknown. Thus the focus upon price grows naturally with the rise of the city and the city market. Moreover, buying of the daily necessities has been regarded as women's work; the many jokes about men earning and women spending offer a humorless testimony to this usual division. It is a division, too, freighted with considerations of male status; his wages gave a rough assessment to his social rank. With the "emancipation" of women, the emergence of the household where both parents were breadwinners (or, as in Eastport, where the woman comes on the job market when her husband is on short time or laid off) and the general fusion of many hitherto distinct sex roles, this maleness of the wage nexus and femaleness of the price nexus began to disappear.

One of the unanticipated consequences of an affluent society is the advertising mania that has filled the air and the presses with encomiums of products and paeans to consumption. More space and time are devoted to buying than to any other aspect of living. Wants for new products are created daily. While this puts a strain on the breadwinner to earn more, the first and nearest question is "How much?"

A working day that starts at six in the morning and ends at six in the evening leaves little time for cultivation of the arts of consumption, even though price in a penny-pinching way is certainly critical to such a life. But take four hours off such a working schedule and you alter not only the proportions of time devoted to work but also the proportion of time that can be devoted to a consideration of how to live, how to spend money. Holidays and weekends point to another similar consideration: Browning's Pippa, in mid-nineteenth century, had only one day off a year. Thus the price of commodities, as contrasted to the wage of work, is given a new importance in a more leisurely scheme of things.

These culture changes, and more, go into the bourgeoisification of the working class. Their higher educational levels, their concern for "appearances" in their quasi-suburban settings, their domestication in the sense that "the boys" don't go out together or gather down at the saloon or go to the fights the way they used to, but rather stay at home with "the missus" and watch TV, their capacity to buy hard goods, particularly cars and appliances, which lend themselves to "administered prices" better than groceries and clothes, and, associated with this, their installment-purchase debts and high fixed expenses—all these factors tend to make the "new exploitation" a matter of price and not of wage. The point should not be overstressed—but the evidence is unambiguous—the working-class men of today are relatively less concerned about their wage rates than about their expenditures. In a sense this is Omar Khayyám in reverse: "I often wonder what the workers sell one half so precious as the stuff they buy."

C

RELIGIOUS TOLERANCE
AND THE POWERLESS CHURCH

In Latin America, it is sometimes said, politics is a game played with only three or four powerful pieces: the army, the landowners, perhaps the urban masses, perhaps foreign capital, and the church. The Roman Catholic Church is a political power; it is rich; it usually controls education; it is organized in the rural areas as well as in the urban areas; its policy and advice are moralized and backed by impressive sanctions; it has discipline; it has an outside base of wealth, international influence, trained personnel, and it has God. This is formidable. In the Netherlands political divisions follow, with relatively few exceptions, Catholic-Protestant population fault lines. The "clerical" issue now losing salience in France has been a central political division at least since the Revolution. With some exaggeration, even for ten years ago, Lubbell writes of the American Northeast, "There are Catholic Republicans, of course, as there are Yankee Democrats, but, in the main, the bedrock cleavage in the East remains a Catholic-Protestant one." [8] And it is of America that Paul Blanshard is writing when he wrestles with the problem of the relation of the Catholic Church to civil liberties.[9] Against such a

8. Samuel Lubbell, *The Future of American Politics* (New York: Harper, 1952), p. 41.
9. Paul Blanshard, *American Freedom and Catholic Power* (Boston: Beacon Press, 1949).

backdrop as this, one wonders how the workingmen of Eastport will see church power, the power of religious groups, the uses and abuses of power by clergymen of differing faiths.

The question "Do you think any group has too much power in America?" is sometimes thought to be an invitation to express some variety of ethno-religious prejudice, most usually anti-Semitism. As noted above, Kuchinsky, a Catholic-Polish roofer, so interpreted it: "I'd say the Jews run this country; that's for sure. . . . Any business you go into today, 95 per cent of 'em are Jewish," and so on. But others did not. Interethnic slurs in the Eastport melting pot are dangerous, and Jews as well as others are the beneficiaries. Of the four Protestants and Jews, not one mentioned the Catholic Church. There are eleven lifelong Catholics —none of them mentioned the Protestant churches, nor did any of them show much evidence of dissident Catholic anticlericalism. Yet they are intensely aware of religious differences; Lubbell is substantially right: political alliances follow religious membership. What has happened to the question of church power or the power of "the Catholics" or "the Jews" or, as the Protestants would be called, "the Yankees"? [10]

There are a theological answer, a social answer, a personal one, and a political one. Asked about the dogma of their church, the religious beliefs that separated it from others, these men fumbled and grew still. They did not know. Asked what their religion meant to them, they said, more often than not, "salvation," but they did not hold that other religions failed in this respect. Flynn, for example, was eager to deny that Father Feeney's position, asserting that only Catholics were saved, had any standing in the modern church. Almost none believed that it was necessary for a man to be a member of any particular religion to lead a moral life, although with one exception all believed that a man must believe in *some* God to be thoroughly honorable and trustworthy. One would not be far from the mark to think of Eastport as having one religion with a variety of patron deities, a Jewish one, a Protestant one, and a Catholic one; there is something reminiscent here of a pantheistic religion with tribal gods. Listen to Costa, a sensitive and articulate assembly-line factory worker,

10. I am least sure that I am receiving from the Catholics and the Jews here the same kinds of answers that they would give a coreligionist. I have tried to balance my interpretation against the responses given by an Eastport Jewish sample to' a Jewish graduate student, and the responses given to an Italian-American student by an Italian-American sample in Eastport and New York.

explain what his religion means to him: "I'm a Catholic because I was brought up a Catholic. [pause] There have been Catholics in my family for hundreds of years, and nobody's ever turned. I was taught to go to church, and not to eat meat on Fridays, and all this is teaching from my mother and father. And I'm just going along with the [pause] same program that they instituted with my own children. Now, someday somebody's going to rebel, and there are cases where some of them do rebel. I—there's one thing I don't understand about the Catholic religion—why priests aren't allowed to marry." About half of the men show this anesthetized religious nerve, this affectless state of categorized religious membership.

This totemic view of religion, where each tribe has its patron God and tribal ritual, but no tribe sees it especially appropriate to export its religion, leads to identification without dogma. Each of the men was asked which of the following groups he would be most likely to trust and which he would be a little likely to distrust: veterans, Protestant, farm, Negro, business, Jewish, college, union, and Catholic. The most trusted group is the veterans' group (because "it's got all the others in it," because "it helps more people," and so on), but then the choice begins to hurt. Rapuano, having picked the veterans first, says, "If we didn't have the veterans' group—perhaps I'd probably—let's say, I'll be truthful with you, I'd probably pick the Catholic group." O'Hara, too: "Well, I think the veterans' group . . . Now, as I say, your church groups—you've got Protestant, Catholic, and Jewish. . . . I think they're all in their own line. I think they've got a good point, each one's looking out for their own. I wouldn't say the Catholic is any better than the Jewish, or better than the Protestant. ["How about for you?"] Oh, I would say the veterans' organization and the Catholic groups, of course, because being a Catholic."

There is an ethnic and religious interpenetration in Eastport that holds in check the libelous tongue, fractures the walls that separate Protestant from Catholic, as well as the inter-nationality barriers. Six of the fifteen men are either the product of a marriage binding together Catholic and Protestant or are themselves married to a member of the "other" faith. If someone inadvertently made a slurring remark about the power of the Catholic Church to Woodside, with his unimpeachable rural Midwestern forebears, he would learn that Woodside's wife is an Italian Catholic and his son, whom he loves dearly, is therefore Catholic. If someone remarked to O'Hara that they had the Yankees on the run in Eastport, he would discover that O'Hara's affectionate mother is a Yankee, though ethnically he identifies with his father's Irish Catholicism. Sullivan, whose father went to a Jesuit seminary, is married to a former Lutheran. Dempsey, the leader of a small, nonsectarian Protestant church, had an Irish-Catholic father. Farrel's wife is a Protestant from Maine; Johnson, whose mother was a Yankee and whose father was Danish, has become a Catholic because his wife and sons are Catholics. No wonder he says, on behalf of many of the others, "You know, all religions boil down to the same thing anyway, the way I look at it."

Finally, there are political reasons why these men of Eastport do not concern themselves with church power. The extension of the principle of the disestablishment of religion to the principle of separation of church and state has partially removed many of the political issues that elsewhere divide people on religious grounds. This has facilitated the emergence of another influential political circumstance: the political interpenetration of religion. Both parties include Catholics and Protestants and Jews, and each advertises this with a "balanced ticket." This makes it psychologically easier for the New England Catholic to vote Republican, which indeed he had been doing increasingly until 1960. Finally, the underlying tribalism to which we referred has a nationality base more than a religious base, and intra-Catholic, inter-nationality conflicts tend to push and pull people in and out of local party groups under pressure of local demographic changes. Thus church power, religious power, does not become identified with the power of one political group, as a rule; it is fluid, flexible, and cuts across a variety of other status lines. And because of this, as well as the personal interpenetration mentioned above, it is damaging to personal relations to raise the issue of religion in politics, and the code, so often expressed, "Religion and politics don't mix" is widely reinforced.

Whether or not this code is an overlay on a latent desire to employ the power of the church for political purposes, reflecting a strategy rather than a conviction, is not clear. Four of the men, including two of the most religious, started to say, at one point, that the churches had too little power in American society, and in every case, within the same breath, took it back. DeAngelo, round-faced, the skilled machine operator, who, with Flynn, is the most religious member of the group, says: "Too little power? Well, I don't know. Nothing I could say. Some people maybe would say church groups, but I don't believe in forcing these on anybody." Ruggiero says in the course of a discussion where nothing about religion had been mentioned for some time: "No, I don't know of any groups that are too small [weak]. Because I mean, when you come into politics, uh, I try to keep religion out of it." In these and the other instances, the very association of religious groups with the idea of lack of power is suggestive. Among the Roman Catholic group there is, perhaps, an ambivalence about church power in politics. Attitudes are made to conform to the official American code of separation of church and state by social forces and interpersonal considerations, but these may be in opposition to latent ideas of converting *religious* organization into political power, just as nationality-group membership has been so converted for now these many years.

D

THE POLITY OF ABUNDANCE: POWER ENOUGH FOR ALL

> Since the beginning of the nation the whole American atmosphere has been saturated with power—technological, economic, political, religious, military, financial. . . . There has been enough diffusion to give the nation as a whole the chance to revel in the feeling of abundant power.
> —Max Lerner, *America as a Civilization*, p. 398

Eastport can divide America into the rich and the poor, those who have it and those who don't. But the workingmen of Eastport cannot divide the nation into the weak and the powerful, because they see no one as weak. There are, indeed, reasons for not thinking of oneself as lacking in power; but what of others? When I asked, "What groups in society might have too little power?" the results of this discussion and of the general extended interviews as they dealt with this subject were, in a sense, surprising.

Farrel, with a superior education, thought easily of the disfranchised groups in the South, unorganized labor, the poor and disheartened everywhere. Not so the others. Elsewhere we discuss the lack of sympathy among the upper working classes for the members of the lower classes, the people on relief, the widows whose breadwinners have died, the old without pensions, the broken, the alcoholic, the ones that opportunity has passed by. Nowhere are they mentioned in the discussion of those without power, without protectors adequate to their cause in a dynamic, if impatient, society. On the margin of relief, themselves, many of these men resented those who were drawing relief checks. Having fought off the temptations of alcohol, often temptations that had been too strong for their fathers, they had little sympathy for those who succumbed. Along with the doctrine that each man's status was his own responsibility, there could be no thought that the poor and broken had too little power—they did not deserve more power. Indeed, there was some feeling that they had too much already, what with their electoral equality and their command over relief funds and city services.

Thus it was that more than half of the men, when asked if anyone had too little power in America, thought for a moment and said, "No," they couldn't think of any. Some of them went on to mention some groups—often symbolized as "Mr. Average Citizen," but it was clear enough from the hesitation and the frowns and the dislocated sentences that there was no clear picture in their minds of a powerless group in America. Is it the abstraction, the unfamiliarity with the idea that prompts this unwonted hesitance? Or is it, perhaps, as some would say, that Americans fear power, desiring every group and every man but themselves to be less powerful? It is, I think, neither. The sense that none are too powerless, except an amorphous public or a symbolic common man, is based first upon the idea that anyone who wanted to, and had the skills, could be powerful; just as anyone who wanted to, and had the skills and got the breaks, could be rich. The men explain this in their own terms.

Woodside turns in his chair and opens his eyes wide in an expression of great earnestness. "I think anybody that wants power will get it," he says, "and will get recognized for his power providing he does it the right way. I don't think of anybody that hasn't got what power he wanted if he went at it the right way." Clearly this is not confusion over an abstract term. Elsewhere he says, "Everybody has a little bit of power over another person, one way or another, regardless of whatever he does." He goes on to explain that I, his interviewer, couldn't have the power of his police chief in police matters, and the police chief would not have the power in academic affairs that he imagined I had. Thus power is distributed and comes as a concomitant of occupational role, persistence, and "going about it the right way." Johnson, the electric-utility mechanic, is somewhat less optimistic, but basically agrees. The group without power, "it's the majority of the citizens, themselves. Perhaps they're in a position to have something to say, but they don't realize it. I mean they're certainly in a position if they get together, to see things are done." The sleeping giant, the man who doesn't know his own strength! Flynn, too, argues that "a man who belongs to no group—as an individual, he is powerless," but goes on to point out that whoever is organized and represented has power. And Dempsey, vaguely but hopefully, says, "If you go out and fight for something, you're bound to get it, one way or the other, if you keep fighting long enough, I mean."

Power is dependent on organization and effort; those whom the gods would make powerful they first must organize. But the decision is your own; you have the right to organize, protected by freedom of association. This view offers a political principle of some importance to these men: *Freedom of association provides in the political field the basis for a rationale of relative power positions, just as free enterprise provides this basis for relative wealth in the economic field.* If one has little power at any given time, it is his own fault for failing to organize his interests.

One implication, perhaps a condition, of the idea that power is commensurate to skill and effort is that no one has a monopoly of power. There simply is not, in the usual perception of things, the picture of a more or less closed "power elite" such as haunts the mind of C. Wright Mills; except for the cabalists there is no sense that Wall Street runs things, that just behind the stage an Establishment is pulling strings, or a conspiratorial group that has usurped the legitimate powers of government. The Marxian view that the working class can have only such power as it takes away from the owning classes is alien to the concept of Eastport. Whatever the game that we are playing may be in this earthly life, it is not a zero-sum game.

Popular sovereignty is taken seriously, not just in the sense of electoral mandates and symbolic acts. Legitimate power lodges in the people, in society; one need not ask permission to exercise influence; one is already licensed to petition, to assemble, to organize and demand, and the license bears the stamp, not of government but of nature. One is born licensed to do these things.

Men whose grandfathers lived in rural parishes where the *patrono,* the priest, the chief of police controlled these things, seem to have lost all traces of family memories of this state of affairs. The feudal image of the world mentioned earlier seems, in this conceptual area, to have faded away in Eastport.

E
THE CODE OF SOCIAL POWER

Implicit in much that is said about the nature and distribution of power in society is a code that assigns legitimacy to some power, benevolence to some, effectiveness to some. Never articulated in this way, the code must be extracted from what is said, as the assumptions and premises of the common man of Eastport. That it may include contradictions is not surprising; the premises of much of our thought, of the thinking of one mind, is contradictory; but very often what seems contradictory is not more so than the "contradiction" between gravity and the levitation of a balloon—opposing tendencies seeking a balance:

It is better for power and status to go together; there is something disturbing about low-status individuals and groups exercising power.

Distant power is more likely to be "good" than nearby power.

Religion should be socially powerful, but churches should not exercise political power.

When unions get too powerful, (*a*) they are easily corrupted, (*b*) they demand too much, (*c*) they make prices rise, and (*d*) they will be punished by business.

Business power is more dangerous for its control over prices than for its control over wages.

There is social and political power available for anyone who makes the effort to seize it; usually he does this by organizing.

Governments are instituted among men, deriving their just powers from the consent of the governed.

Government (in America) has, and should have, all the power it needs to do what it wants, because it usually wants to do what is best.

There is nobody so weak that he can't protect himself against the power of others if he wants to. (If he is in trouble, his alderman or his congressman will help him.)

Since the rich generally deserve to be rich, they generally deserve the power that goes with wealth.

Powerful people shouldn't throw their weight around.

The best way to use power is by persuasion; people shouldn't be forced to do things they don't want to do.

9

Innocence Regained:
The View of Government from Eastport

Society is produced by our wants, and government by our wicked-ness; the former promotes our happiness *positively* by uniting our affections, the latter *negatively* by restraining our vices. . . . The first is a patron, the last is a punisher. Society in every state is a blessing, but government, even in its best state, is but a necessary evil. . . . Government, like dress, is the badge of lost innocence.
— THOMAS PAINE, "Common Sense," in *The Political Works of Thomas Paine,* p. 7

The generation which was taught by Paine that that government is best which governs least has left a deep impact on the American spirit.
— HAROLD LASKI, *The American Democracy,* p. 43

A

"A BUNCH OF MEN MAKING LAWS"

When Thomas Paine thought of government, he thought of its punitive, regulatory, inhibiting features. When lower mid-dle Eastport thinks of government, it thinks of other things. More than Paine, Eastport thinks of a benign, helpful organization, one working *for* the people, not merely restraining them. Thus, when McNamara thinks of government, he thinks of "a pooling of our knowledge for the welfare of everyone"; Woodside thinks of it as something "to fulfill your needs and wants as to the way you want things"; Ruggiero says he thinks of something "to make sure the people are taken care of." This is very different from the thoughts of government Paine expressed. When Eastport people think of government they think of *national,* not local affairs. In this sense Eastport is cosmopolitan; its horizon has been stretched by the New Deal and wars. It thinks of legislative functions, not administrative or judicial. Thus it thinks of making policy, not enforcing it, of stating aims and goals, as well as codes of behavior. Thus Costa: "It suggests a group of people elected by the people to formulate laws, and to make decisions, affecting the majority of the people, or benefiting the majority of the people—whether they be Republican or Democratic is not important." Government is *plural;* in only one case did an Eastportian (Dempsey) think of a single "ruler," the others mentioning a group. It is *dynamic,* adaptive, trying to meet new situations. Thus Ruggiero: "They get together and, uh, make laws to fit in with the modern times. Of course, you figure our laws of years ago—most of 'em are outmoded today." Generally, it is a *concrete* image, although Flynn said he thought of "organization" and Johnson said he thought of "security" when he heard the word "government."

These are the main themes. How might it have been otherwise? Had this been a socially alienated group, others would have joined Rapuano when he said that all he could think of was politics. "There ain't anything that's unpolitical that's government," he says. Perhaps, in one sense, he is right—but he means something more sinister, for the word "politics" has an unpleasant meaning in his vocabulary.

Had this been a society divided by sharp cleavages, others would have joined Sokolsky, who says, "Most of all, who is going to run it—that's what I think of now." Not what it does or how it is run, but *who* operates it—with an implied notion of government in the interest of a special group. Sophisticated? Perhaps. But this is the sophistication of the "wise guy," not the "wise man."

Had this been a group of "tradition-directed," although not alienated, men, they might have answered with Dempsey: "Well, someone to rule over us, probably [pause] to guide the people in the right way." But these are only variations to be contrasted to the main themes mentioned above.

B

THE WARM, FRIENDLY CONGRESS
AND THE MARTYRED PRESIDENT

[There is] a kind of folklore of Congress which gives it deep roots in the public mind. The people think of it at once as supreme legislator and supreme watchdog. In his legislative role the Congressman dresses himself up as the lawgiver. . . . But he has also hewn out the image of himself as the eternally vigilant guardian of the people's interests as against the tyranny of the "Administration."

—MAX LERNER, *America as a Civilization*, p. 416

The Theater of Power in the Age of Eisenhower

The political theory of the common man and his image of government focus, naturally enough, upon Congress and the President. In these institutions are gathered together the legitimate reins of power. Who runs things in government? A few said "party leaders," "big shots," "party bosses"—but generally these leaders are thought to have their seat of power on Capitol Hill; the legislature is their theater of operations. Others were more explicit about it—the inner circle of congressmen," "the congressional leaders." Many who thought "the people" ran things saw this as done through Congress, the agent of the people. Whether it is "the bosses" or "the people" or "congressional leaders," Congress in the fifties is the center of government; it is the main location of power (though, as we shall see, not necessarily of interest). Here Max Lerner, along with others, is wrong. He says, "When the American thinks of government, he thinks first of the President as its symbol." [1] More than two-thirds of the men said that of the three institutions, Congress, the Supreme Court, and the Presidency, it is the Congress that is most important. DeAngelo puts it this way: "Well, they all got their importance. I guess Congress seems to be the important one; they pass all the legislation; they pass all the bills; and they seem to run everything. They have the power."

Making laws, it seems, is the most visible product of government. Asked, "When you think of government, what do you think about?" a common response places lawmaking at the center of

1. Max Lerner, *America as a Civilization: Life and Thought in the United States* (New York: Simon and Schuster, 1957), p. 377.

things: "Well, it suggests a group of people elected by the people to formulate laws"; "Well, I think of a bunch of men; they get together and, uh, uh, they governmentize our country, lead us, make laws"; "It's a way of taking care of ourselves by choosing leaders and laws." In the fifties, it was hard to locate and appraise the President's contribution, his influence, initiative, policy, responsibility; but the enactment of a law is definite, concrete, important. And the process of *making* one in Congress is public and dramatic, often with an uncertain outcome until the very end. "It's here in Congress that the ideas are brought and presented as bills," says Ferrera, "and it's here that they are discussed and either passed or voted down. . . . The President would be the least important." Thus, under Eisenhower, the President presides over government, but he has lost control. The congressional leaders, says DeAngelo, again, "they are running the country. The President is only a figurehead, y'know what I mean." But in the sixties, as in the thirties, this image surely is different.

In this view the Congress is more important than I expected it to be; the President is less important. The emphasis upon law, the deemphasis of leadership, are contrary to what is often said of the common man's personalized image of governmental institutions. The view needs modification. Speaking of the past, the men speak of Presidents, not Congresses. Speaking of the recession, they are hurt that Eisenhower has been so delinquent, rather than angry that Congress has been so slow to act. Speaking of elections, they speak of presidential elections, not congressional or senatorial elections. Speaking of their surprise and wounded feelings over the American failures in rocketry, they discuss the defective intelligence, foresight, and action of "the Administration," not the Congress. Perhaps one can reconcile their views of the current power of Congress with these other phases of their image of government in two ways. One is to allocate time periods differently: past time is for the Presidency; contemporary time is for Congress. Another is to separate responsibility for initiative and responsibility for decision: the President must initiate, the Congress must decide.

Congress, it appears, is an "oral" agency—the congressman's job is one of talking and listening, often quite informally. He is rarely pictured in debate on the floor of the Senate or the House; rather he is seen meeting the folks from back home streaming endlessly through his office; he is answering his mail, traveling to see his constituents. He seems to receive his information and advice in conversation directly from the common man, the people. Not so the President. He *studies* matters, something he can do alone. When he is with others, he *tells* them; he does not listen. Sokolsky says of the President, "Maybe he's at his desk three or four hours a day, and the rest [of the time] he's supposed to be—maybe in the White House there, in the living room, studying the different bills." The idea of presidential advisers is vaguely threatening, partly because it suggests "influence in high places" and partly because it hints at presidential uncertainty.

Congress is responsive; the President is more autonomous. This follows, in a way, from the idea that Congress has an ear cocked for the voice of the people, while the President listens to inner voices. It also follows from the idea that the President proposes, the Congress disposes. Thus DeAngelo thinks of the President as maneuvering from outside: "Most anything that has to be passed, he knows about it. He's informed of it. I suppose he's trying to push his own bills through, you know? I mean, he's got to think of *his* wants." But Congress is not passive—congressmen are positively enjoined to be active supervisors of the public wants. For O'Hara the good congressmen are "not just going along with the party . . . they're looking out for the welfare of all the people he's representing."

Congress looks inward toward the nation; the President looks outward to the world. Congressmen have special duties to their home districts; they are custodians of popular welfare. The President is the custodian of popular safety, national destiny, the conscience of the people. Congress expresses the impulsive immediate needs; the President has a longer view. Congress offers "secondary gain"; the President offers a chance to fulfill the life goals of the nation. Perhaps this is the reason that in normal times they write to their congressmen, if they write at all. In times of national emergency (major depression, conscription, humiliation, as in the missile lag) they write to the President.[2]

Congress is in no way frightening; it is comfortable. The Presidency is, if not frightening, a little awesome, calling, in the imagination, for more deference. Congressmen *have* to be nice to you; it is their job. Every agent of a powerful congressional public-relations team is devoted to presenting the image in each

2. See my *Political Life: Why People Get Involved in Politics* (New York: The Free Press of Glencoe, 1959), pp. 67–74.

case of a friendly, attentive man, interested in "you." The collective image reflects this. Congress, moreover, has no police arm: the congressman is not surrounded by policemen, secret-service men, military aides. He not only will not hurt you; he hasn't the punitive means of doing it (unless, of course, you happen to be "subversive"). But the President is the head of an executive branch with bite: FBI, armed services, secret services. He is surrounded by guards.

If the President is a conscientious, an autonomous, a nonpartisan figure, how shall he adjust to an office that is at the very focus of all the major national pressures? If others are not supposed to be privily influential to the Great Man, what shall we do with the politics that surround the office? The cabalist mind has an answer: "President Eisenhower is not a big wheel. Tom Dewey is the big boss" (Ferrera). "It really surprised us. We figured he's a general and he knows what to do. . . . But he's taking orders like anybody else" (Sokolsky). The noncabalist democrat rejects this idea: "I don't think Ike would let them tell him what to do. If he didn't think it was right, I don't think he'd let it be" (Johnson). But a congressman is *supposed* to listen to T. Dewey and J. Doe and R. Roe, although he too must pursue his own version of the public interest.

The loneliness of the President, as these men see him, contributes to a suffering image; not Zeus but Prometheus, not Jehovah but Christ. In a vivid conceit Ruggiero explains his picture of the President's job:

> It would be, uh, if you take a vise, only, instead of two parts, the vise would have maybe ten or fifteen parts to put around his head, and then every once in a while giving a squeeze on each one of 'em. That's exactly what I . . . that's how I feel as far as his Cabinet, see? He's got a problem with labor, this guy's squeezin'. This other fella's havin' trouble with the War Department, or something like that, he starts squeezin'.

And Rapuano says: "He's got to satisfy everybody, let's say in all parties, whether it's his own party or the opposition, he's got to satisfy them both. And that's a tough job to do." No one ever saw a congressman suffering in this way. Without being a comic figure, he lends himself to a lighter treatment. Senator Claghorn never appeared in the Eastport interviews, but the congressman's image on the public stage is to be contrasted to *Abe Lincoln in Illinois* or *Sunrise at Campobello*. The president is a tragic figure, at least in the fifties.[3] Not the dignity, not the eminence, not the prestige of the President's job—the crushing responsibility of it: that is what strikes these men. So badly do they want him to be responsible that they make him so—even if he is on the golf course. O'Hara, a maintenance mechanic and oiler, asked how he would describe the President's job, says: "It's too much mental strain where he's got so many people that figure he's leading them. . . . I guess a lot of them probably have a lot of trouble sleeping at night, just thinking and worrying . . . even now when you've got a lot of unemployment throughout the country, I imagine he thinks about it. I mean I think if I were, I would." The awful importance of these decisions is what strikes Woodside: "His actions would make a great deal [of difference?] in making our country a better country or a bad one by the way he handled himself in his decisions. . . . I don't think there's any goofing off on that job." Says Johnson, a mechanic, "I think it's always on his mind." Elsewhere these same men express disappointment in President Eisenhower's second-term performance; they fear that he is indifferent to their fate and, more generally, to the fate of the unemployed (this is the winter of 1957–1958), but they cannot easily accept this conclusion. The idea that *nobody* is in charge of things, the idea of leaving the economy to the "unseen hand" of the market and the polity to the play of forces around Congress, is not easy to accept. In their interpretation of government, then, these men vest the President with a responsible concern for their welfare and a capacity to decide big issues commensurate with his eminence.

Johnson says: "When I think of government, I think of [pause] security. It makes you feel secure when you get good government." This is true for all the men, though they do not say it so clearly, but the security may be of several kinds, and the psychic welfare, like its material counterpart, may be unevenly distributed. Shortly we shall examine the benignity of government, here something of the source of that general support is indicated. From the Congress, and more particularly from the idea of home-state con-

3. Max Lerner suggests some sources for President Eisenhower's heroic-homely appeal: his "father image was at once authoritative, kindly, and carefully kept above the party battle (although he was a shrewd politician) and he rounded out his image, as American fathers often do, by incurring a heart attack and having an intestinal operation" (*op. cit.,* p. 377). Incidentally, Eastport is almost unanimous in saying that Eisenhower is *not* a politician.

gressmen, these men derive a sense of protection, of a friend in power, of an accessible person who is not likely to be protected by a number of secretaries. The right of petition here is expressed in personal, human contact, not through paper forms and proper channels. Flynn once petitioned for a change in civil-service rules and, with others in the same position, sent a delegation to Washington. They got what they wanted. Ruggiero sees Morreli, Eastport's congressman, on the problems his friends in the post office want taken care of; he is warmly received. The congressman's self-interest is seen as closely congruent with the economic prosperity of his district; his interests correspond to the interests of men like these Eastport fifteen, and this is true regardless of party. It could happen only in a society where class and ethnic political divisions are seen as fluid, where every Democrat is seen by a Republican congressman as a potential convert, a person worth wooing.

The President gives another kind of security; at least he does in normal times. He is a strong arm against the outside world; he is a national protector, and has the stature to be one. He does not have this soft side, this slightly lovable venality—hence he reinforces the voice of the superego; he calls for a higher morality; he is a protector against our weaker natures—the side of our selves that might cut taxes when we should keep them high to pay for defense. He cares deeply about what happens to the nation and the people and the values for which this country stands. Part of what makes congressmen so appealing is that they are not so seriously committed in this way; they are more human. But what makes the President appealing is that he is not "all too human" like the rest of us; while not quite a hero, he is supportive of whatever small heroic qualities we have in us, at the very least, of our moral selves. Perhaps it will be misunderstood, but in a figurative sense Congress is the group-adjustment leader; the President is the task leader; Congress is the mother, the President the father.[4]

4. Geoffrey Gorer, who is often as exaggeratedly right and wrong as a caricature, reverses the family-state comparisons, but with the same effect: "To a certain extent the pattern of authority in the state is reproduced in the family: it is as if the father represented the executive, the mother the legislative, and the neighbors, headed by the schoolteacher, the judiciary authority. The child is in the position of the public, playing off one authority against another, invoking the system of checks and balances to maintain his independence" (*The American People* [New York: Norton, 1948], p. 44). The idea of "the public" (instead of, say, the NAM and the AMA) playing off Congress against the President is, to say the least, ridiculous.

C

THE BUREAUCRACY: NARCOSIS AND NIRVANA

The popular feeling about government bureaucrats combines mistrust, dislike, and contempt with a degree of fear. . . . Americans are suspicious of any kind of elite, and the bureaucrats come closer to looking and behaving like an elite than do the professional politicians in Congress or in other government posts.
—Max Lerner, *America as a Civilization,* p. 411.

No one in the Eastport group sees civil servants as having much power; certainly they do not see them as dangerous to our liberties. No one reveals a lurking sense that the bureaucrat can borrow the power of government to enhance his own failing strength in life—as Lasswell suggests may be the motives of some civil servants.[5] The bureaucrat is not dangerous, or powerful, or important. Nor is he generally embraced in the euphoric picture of a beneficent government. Almost half of the men referred at some point to the less ambitious, less hard-working qualities of men attracted to jobs that are generally seen as offering lower pay, slower advancement, and greater security. Thus Ruggerio, a bundle of nervous energy and drive with a second job in the post office, says of civil servants: "They are the persons that are afraid. . . . They're just hiding, that's all they are. Because they have no ambition." Like a *narcotic,* the civil service helps them to sleep through life.

Not everyone, of course, has the same jaundiced view of the administrative branch of government and its occupants. Costa, on the ragged edge of being laid off, says: "Maybe those people were a little smarter in picking a field where there's more security. I think that if I knew twenty years ago what I know today, I'd be working for the government." For him, employment by the government also has this "escape" motif, but it seems to be a kind of escape from the pain and troubles of this world—a happy serenity —*nirvana.*

Sorting out those who think the civil service (and often this means post office) is too confining for the ambitious, or gives security in lieu of income, or offers a haven for those who do not work so hard, we find about seven men whose own jobs are not

5. Harold Lasswell, *Psychopathology and Politics* (Chicago: University of Chicago Press, 1930).

much different from those of the other eight in the group. (These are not, for example, the white collar or the better paid—or the reverse of these.) They differ from the other eight, by and large, in their expressive, emotionally charged life styles. They include the angry men we have mentioned (Rapuano, Sullivan, Ferrera, Sokolsky); the impulsive, volatile men like Johnson and, again, Sokolsky; the quick, nervous, ambitious Ruggiero.

On the other side, those who view civil servants as in no way different from others and who treat the civil service with respect are, generally speaking, the more "responsible," the more sober, the more disciplined, and the more emotionally restricted group. Their life styles seem to involve a lower affectual tone—indeed, a certain monotony; their discussion is less colorful; the words they select are rarely extreme. This group, then, includes Farrel, whose voice is captured on the tape with no force or expression; Woodside, whose conscientious earnestness prevents him from emotional outbursts: Costa, who takes back such critical thoughts as escape into language; McNamara, with his friendly, gentle, but always low-keyed moderation in all things. It also includes Dempsey, whose lack of energy and owlish imperturability, combined with what must be a very modest I.Q., do not support many expressions or emotion.[6]

If it is true that the men who are emotionally more expressive, more extreme, more likely in discourse to produce an opinion than a statement of a factual nature are, for one reason or another, likely to look upon the civil service with distaste, one source of this widespread negative attitude toward bureaucracy is suggested. The civil service is associated in many minds, and in these men's minds to some degree, with regulations, red tape, restrictions. In the literature on bureaucracy, much is made of the depersonalizing effect of the stress on a standardized product, of its reliance on routine and convention to protect itself from variations due to the personal values, whims, and emotions of the individuals who occupy the offices. It is clear enough, on this reading of the situation,

6. The coincidence is not perfect; three men who seem to accept the civil service and civil servants as relatively able and ambitious men do not share this emotionally disciplined personal style. Two of them (Kuchinsky and DeAngelo) structure the problem differently: they see civil servants as men trying to get ahead politically. The other, O'Hara, an expressive and friendly man, accepts the civil service as an area of relatively good jobs with one kind of payment—continuity in service and security—instead of higher payment per week or year. But he does not feel that the distinction between those who accept one and not the other is an invidious one in any way.

that these expressive and less disciplined men would find such a situation a strain; the devaluation of emotional life must appear not only confining; it also suggests a kind of castration of an affective life that is an integral part of their life styles. Impatient men, they cannot easily yield to the demands of everything in triplicate and "by the numbers." Their alienation from the bureaucracy, therefore, suggests one of the sources of intemperate opinions about the welfare state, or bureaucracy, or big government on the part of the entrepreneurial class, or the self-made man. Ideology rests on temperament and its many vicarious lives. The imagination of the self now in one situation, now in another, as well as "interest" and logic, gives color and direction to a social and political point of view.

D
THE CRITIQUE OF GOVERNMENT

For Eastport, good government is not necessarily moral government. This is not what they look for. Nor is good government characterized by any particular structure; federalism, electoral-college reform, reorganization of the executive branch (with one exception), all these are matters of considerable indifference. The American Constitution, they believe, is the last word in governmental arrangements, and the matter is eternally settled. No, good government in Eastport is *responsive* government; better government is more responsive government.

Bickering

The greatest impediment to responsive government is bickering: "The government right now should cut down on all this bickering between the Armed Forces. There's no reason for a lot of it." "There's too many people telling everybody else what to do. There's too many chiefs and no Indians." "I think he's [Eisenhower's] got a lot of people bickering along with him." "People fighting with one another and not getting together."

No doubt part of the trouble lies in the checks and balances of American government that make the amount of "bickering" greater because there are many coordinate and independently powerful authorities who may and do express views that are neither those of the Opposition nor those of the Administration.

Yet there are reasons to think there is something special at work here. For one thing, as we have noted, Eastport is quite willing to believe that "democracy creates confusion and prevents important things from getting done," without being disturbed by this at all. There is almost no raillery at Congress (which is said to be the most important part of government) for its talkativeness. They do not at all accept Dempsey's view that the three branches of government "have to have someone over them to tell them whether they're stepping out of line or not . . . and [therefore] naturally the President should have more power than the other two."

The special intensity of feeling about bickering comes, I think, from its interpretation as "answering back" in a hierarchical setting where subordinates are usurping authority they should not have. Moreover, the difference between debating and bickering is that the one is sanctioned as part of expected political role performance, while the other is outside the expected role. The general feeling is that public differences outside the roles of campaign speaker and legislative debator become public quarreling, and hence unseemly, even disorderly. Finally, because they do not associate "issues" or "principles" with such reported "bickering," the men of Eastport fill in the gaps in their knowledge with an easy *ad hominem* argument—these are conflicts over power.

A Government of Words

Congressmen, as we have said, are associated with oral activity, bureaucrats with paper work. For all men, but particularly for working-class men, this wordiness has a vaguely threatening, somewhat distasteful quality. Sullivan, the truck driver, speaking of congressmen meeting their constituents, feels that in this flow of words "lots of times they've nothing to say"—a futile and embarrassing enterprise. Woodside, the railroad guard, says of the bureaucrat, "I imagine he would have the position of going through a tremendous amount of paper work." Johnson, a mechanic, and Rapuano, a clerk, distinguish between the civil servant who is out in the open doing something important and the man in the office who is shuffling papers around. Wordiness, whether spoken or written, produces among all people—but especially among working-class people—an ambivalence that, as we have seen, is likely to attach to government, particularly a democracy.

The theme is a latent one; its incidence diffused and voice muted, it is still strong enough for us to ask whence this verbo-phobic attitude toward government. Men who are too fluent are disliked because their pace may be too fast for the attention and grasp and emotional affectivity of their listeners, creating for these listeners a problem of timing and response. In some manner, perhaps this is also true of a government of "words"—and not of men. Probably, too, the verbosity of government is reminiscent of school, evoking first an association with painful memories for some, and for many of these men a sense of guilt that they did not go further. Folk wisdom suggests that people who "talk too much" are "trying to put something over on you," concealing ignorance, diverting attention from the crux of the matter—whatever it may be. Leaders are usually not those with greatest verbal productivity in a group. These Eastport men are men who, for the most part, work with their hands; they have—or may have—an instinct of workmanship along these lines; they may have a craftsman's pride in a job well done. They cannot easily generalize this set of values from the shops they know to a "talking shop." The verbosity of government is, like any high-level policy-making or sophisticated administration, concerned with more or less subtle distinctions. Listening in to snatches of this discussion, the working-class man with his very blunt and undifferentiated perspective on the problems under discussion may utterly fail to understand what it is all about. He will see hairsplitting where the informed may see differences with enormous consequences. Talk and discussion often, if not usually, delay action; it is of the essence in the American democracy, at least, that everyone have his "say" in the matter, and there will be a strong tendency to avoid action if a strong and articulate minority asserts itself. But "men of action," such as manual workers and hard-driving businessmen, each in his own way, are not well endowed with patience and do not bide their time gracefully. It is of such stuff as this that the verbophobic response to government is created. But it is also too useful a weapon for those who hate the government on other grounds for it to disappear with better education and understanding of the nature of government. It is entrenched as a rationalization wherever positive government has its enemies.

Defection

Nathan Leites argues that one of the main themes in French politics is the fear of abandonment, fear by the populace that the authorities will abandon them, fear by the deputies that their leaders will abandon them, fear by the prime minister that his cabinet will abandon him.[7] In Eastport the nagging concern (rather than "fear") lest its representatives lose sight of the people's best interests is present as an important theme, subordinated as it may be to the dominant note of trust. It has several components. In its simplest form it is a concern lest the representative place self before duty; there is contempt for "the guy who is just taking the job for whatever he can get out of it, the prestige there is in it." There is a concern about loss of contact: "Congressmen know less and less about the people they are supposed to represent." Some express a concern, too, about the man who must leave his home district and go to a metropolitan, gay, seductive city: "The most important thing is to remember the things that he took with him to Congress, the ideals he was going to follow and the wishes of his people." But, curiously enough, one concern was hardly mentioned that in another era would have been central: there is little thought that the congressman will be bought off by "the interests" (although he might be helped by them now and then).

But if these fears of defection lie latent in the political mind of the upper working class and the lower middle class, rising to the surface obliquely, without that taste of bitterness characteristic of the alienated classes of Europe, they seem to be more or less forgotten when the men describe what it is that congressmen in fact do with their working days. As noted above, they are seen as reading their mail, listening to others; they are seen as receptive to communication from their constituents. The nagging fear of defection stays unobtrusively in the background. Thus it makes sense for them to *disagree,* as all but one did, with the statement, "I don't think public officials care much what people like me think." The fact seems to be that the antigovernment, anti-Congress educational campaigns of the National Association of Man-

---

7. Nathan Leites, "Images of Power in French Politics" (1960), unpublished manuscript on themes in the French political culture.

ufacturers, the steel, oil, and utility interests, and the medical profession, have been employing the wrong theme. The men of Eastport may—and some do—think of congressmen as spendthrift, not too efficient, talkative, and sometimes obtuse—but they do not think of them as cold, unreceptive to communication, and indifferent to their fates. And these are what matter to them.

Abandonment and defection by responsible, loved, and nurturant figures was not, for the most part, a feature of the life pattern of these men. There are, of course, exceptions: DeAngelo's father did run off—but his mother assumed a protective responsibility for him; Woodside's father did not serve as an adequate provider for the family; McNamara's father died when he was very young, and he was brought up by his mother and stepfather; O'Hara's father died when he was eleven, but his mother brought him up and protected him. Flynn's father drank heavily at times, but he loved his son and the two were very close. Throughout the lives of these men there were occasions—perhaps for half of them —when the demise, unemployment, frailty, or drunkenness of the father created situations that cause men to be generally suspicious that responsible authorities leave their charges, and defect, or lose an interest in them, or embrace another loyalty. But these events were not interpreted as abandonment by most of the men on most of the occasions. We have said elsewhere that the relationship of father and son is a central pillar of the foundations of political belief [8]—and so it is. On the other hand, it is significant that all these men had their own natural mother's nurturant care for their entire infancy and youth. Perhaps the sense that responsible figures defect and abandon their followers does not grow where this is the case. If the central problem with the father emerges as authority-tension, the central problem of mother-son relations may emerge, politically speaking, as nurturance-tension. Of course, this is hopelessly schematized; both mother and father represent both authority and nurturance. But, whether it is the Old World mothering or the New World momism, these men seem to have experienced nurturant mother care sufficient to protect them against a distrust of government or a fear that their protectors in government will abandon them.[9]

8. See below, Chapter 17.
9. For a discussion of the relation between politics and separation anxiety, see Sebastian De Grazia, *The Political Community* (Chicago: University of Chicago Press, 1948).

E

GOOD AND BAD GOVERNMENT POWER

Because of the belief in a harmony of interests, Eastport believes that public officials serve themselves by discovering and serving the general welfare, the public interest. Because of their belief that public officials seek, somewhat imperfectly perhaps, to serve the American people, the people of Eastport, the people at Hilltop, "me," they feel that the people are sovereign, and "I" am important. It is not necessary to discover, then, how it is that the people run things—*they run things by having their welfare serve as the criterion of policy*. They do not need to manage government, if they trust it to be run along these lines.

The government has many agencies with which to serve their interests. Some are more powerful than others; some are "better" than others. A code of good and bad political power to go along with the code of social power in Chapter 8 would look something like this:

> Court power is good; it represents the conscience of the nation and, like a conscience, keeps people from doing what they want to do but shouldn't. The Court speaks for our better selves.
>
> Presidential power is good when it originates in the President; it is suspect when it originates with advisers. Advisers are likely to be self-seeking and manipulative. Strong Presidents, in some unexplained way, "make up their own minds."
>
> Presidential power is usually "better" than congressional power because it is less "partisan"; the President represents all the people, but congressmen represent special areas, interests, and groups. The President is "united"; Congress is divided, hence factional. But congressional power may be influenced specifically for "me."
>
> Popular power is ultimate, supreme, original; but the people are less trustworthy than Congress, and individually vote for foolish and irrelevant reasons.
>
> Party power is worse than any other kind because it is (*a*) partisan, and therefore divisive, and (*b*) selfish, that is, the party leaders are more "out for themselves" than are other leaders.

□ □ □ □ □ □ □ □ □ □ □ □ □ □ □ □

Man's Relationship to Government

10

The Alienated and the Allegiant

> We must never see THE GOVERNMENT as something other than our-
> selves, for then automatically we become children; and not real
> honest children, but adults dwarfed to childhood again in weak-
> ness and ineffectiveness.
> —MARGARET MEAD, *And Keep Your Powder Dry*, pp. 165–166

> With practically no exceptions, Americans regard their own gov-
> ernment as alien; they do not identify themselves with it, do not
> consider themselves involved in its actions, feel free to criticize
> and despise it. This is most clearly demonstrated when Americans
> discuss American policies or activities abroad; it is "they" who
> have made this policy, taken this move, written this note—never
> "we."
> —GEOFFREY GORER, *The American People*, p. 225

A

THE IDEA OF POLITICAL ALIENATION

Political alienation refers to a person's sense of estrangement from the politics and government of his society. It may be
taken to mean a feeling that these public matters are not "my
affairs," that the government is not "my government," that the
Constitution is not "my Constitution"—in this sense, a disidenti-

fication. It implies more than disinterest; it implies a rejection, as in the psychoanalytic meaning of the term "alienation," but not in the Marxian version. Franz Neumann employs the term in somewhat this sense. He says, "The conscious rejection of the whole political system which expresses itself as apathy because the individual sees no possibility of changing anything in the system through his efforts . . . forms the core of what I characterize as political alienation." [1] Modifying this idea, making it more crisp and usable, we shall term political alienation a syndrome of three attitudes which may be expressed as follows:

1. I am the object, not the subject of political life—I have no influence and do not participate. Politically, I speak in the passive voice.

2. The government is not run in my interest; they do not care about me; in this sense, it is not my government.

3. I do not approve the way decisions are made; the rules of the game are unfair, loaded, illegitimate; the Constitution is, in some sense, fraudulent.

The opposite of alienation? Like health, it has been relatively little explored. Is it "integration," a wholeness where alienation is fragmented? The dictionary says the antonym is "reconciled," "united," or "reunited." We use the term *allegiant* to imply a unity with the "central values," the political processes, the moral integrity of the political system, a loyalty to and support of the going order.

B

CITIZEN AND GOVERNMENT:
ACTIVE OR PASSIVE VOICE?

Governments are instituted among men, deriving their just powers from the consent of the governed. . . .
—The Declaration of Independence

Among people in these poorer classes the image of a ruling class is very strong. Like some of the very rich, they believe the political world is a manageable one—but not by them: the "insiders," the "sixty families," or just plain "they" are in easy control of events.
—DAVID RIESMAN, *The Lonely Crowd*, p. 259

1. Franz Neumann, *The Democratic and the Authoritarian State* (New York: The Free Press of Glencoe, 1957), p. 290.

How can people express "their" will if they do not have any will
or conviction of their own, if they are alienated automatons,
whose tastes, opinions and preferences are manipulated by the
big conditioning machines?
—ERICH FROMM, *The Sane Society*, p. 185

Expression in the passive voice has been said to be the political
style of the peasantry of the world, the medieval serf, the Asian
villager, the Mexican Indian. David Riesman has drawn attention
to the way in which this sense of self as object in a world governed
beyond my control is a feature of a tradition-directed outlook on
life, and Daniel Lerner has given this traditionalism vitality in the
cultural setting of the Middle East.[2] While endogenous to country
life, particularly where this is isolated, poor, and illiterate, the
view of government as a distant, incomprehensible, unresponsive
power has its urban setting, too. "The world of 'Them,' " says
Hoggart, speaking for the British working classes, "is the world
of the bosses," increasingly, public officials. "To the very poor,
especially, they compose a shadowy but numerous and powerful
group affecting their lives at almost every point: the world is divided between 'Them' and 'Us.' "[3] Once this view was prevalent
in the immigrant ghettos of the industrial states. Handlin says of
the European peasant: "In the business of ruling he did not act,
was only acted upon." Then he came to America, and here:

> What was government that any immigrant should acquire a more
> favorable impression of it in the course of his journey? Govern-
> ment was a succession of malevolent obstacles in the way of get-
> ting to America. . . . In its name men found themselves betagged
> with strange papers, herded about like cattle. Its visible symbol
> was the outstretched, uniformed palm. Such, on arrival, was the
> newcomers' conception of [political] power.[4]

More broadly, we may look at a stratum of society—urban or
rural, the underdog stratum. In her "Portrait of the Underdog"
Genevieve Knupfer reveals his isolation from the group life
around him, his lack of broad social experiences, and his limited
circle of movement, his narrow range of thought and imagination,

2. David Riesman, *The Lonely Crowd* (New Haven: Yale University Press, 1950);
Daniel Lerner, *The Passing of Traditional Society* (New York: The Free Press of
Glencoe, 1958).
3. Richard Hoggart, *The Uses of Literacy* (Boston: Beacon Press, 1961), p. 62.
4. Oscar Handlin, *The Uprooted: The Epic Story of the Great Migrations That
Made the American People* (New York: Grosset and Dunlap, 1951), pp. 202, 204.

his gullibility and his lack of knowledge.[5] This is an irritated, frustrated, politically passive person, a person who is the object of governmental relations, not an active participant.

Most observers of the American scene have not seen this passivity; they have tended to follow Tocqueville ("The citizen of the United States is taught from infancy to rely upon his own exertions in order to resist the evils . . . of life")[6] or Münsterburg (in the United States it is "the privilege of every man to feel responsible for his town, county, state, and country . . . and by his own free initiative to work to better them").[7] But Bryce saw it and commented at length on "this tendency to acquiescence and submission, this sense of the insignificance of individual effort, this belief that the affairs of men are swayed by large forces whose movement may be studied but cannot be turned."[8]

The Voice of the Common Man in Eastport

Eastport's multitude speaks as Bryce feared they might on specific matters of individual influence and control, yet their conclusions about the nature of popular government seem premised on the line of thought suggested by Tocqueville and Münsterburg. Only four had ever written a letter to their congressmen, though they thought Congress responsive to such mail. Few had ever attempted to organize or petition for some policy advantage, though, as we reported earlier, they thought people could get what they wanted this way. The fact is that these men were pretty discouraged by the idea of *doing* something about any big problems. Here is Costa, disturbed over the cutback in defense spending and the consequent unemployment in defense industries, such as the one he works in. He is now on short time and therefore on short rations. What can he do about this situation? "Well, I don't know whether we, as ordinary citizens could do anything about it. Our policy's dictated from Washington." Kuchinsky, the roofer, worries about the recession; it is bad for the roofing business. What can we do? "If you do speak up . . . there's nothing done about it—they just go ahead." The missile lag concerns Rapuano, a

5. Genevieve Knupfer, "Portrait of the Underdog," *Public Opinion Quarterly,* 11 (1947), pp. 101–114.

6. Alexis de Tocqueville, *Democracy in America,* Phillips Bradley, ed. (New York: Knopf, 1945), I, 191.

7. Hugo Münsterburg, *The Americans* (New York: McClure, Phillips, 1904), p. 9.

8. James Bryce, *The American Commonwealth* (New York: Macmillan, 1910), II, 352.

clerk, but "I don't see what you or I could do about it—except at the voting polls. In one way, there's one of the little man's frustrations." This is the pattern: individuals, as ordinary citizens, can do very little about specific issues. This is an appraisal of the disparity between overwhelming problems decided at a distance by authoritative persons and the time, energy, social leverage, and knowledge the individual can bring to bear to change the nature of things. Plus the fact that the individual has no confidence that he knows how they could be done better. It seems unrealistic to expect anything very different.[9]

Eastport's common men find themselves politically impotent on most important specific issues, do not petition or write letters with any frequency, are dubious of the wisdom of the electorate on these issues, see elections as only partially successful instruments for imparting instructions to candidates, find themselves often confused by the complexity of public affairs, and tend to think of the elected officials as better judges of policy than they themselves are. How, then, do they come to have this sense of political importance?

One reason is that many of them have political connections and for local matters they *have* influence, can get close to somebody who may pretend to more authority than he has but who conveys to his circle of acquaintances the sense that they are in communication with important people when they speak to him. So much we have seen.

Another reason is that when they vote they do not at all see the relation between the proportion of their own vote to the total vote and the electoral consequences—as Bryce feared. Not one, for example, suggested that his vote for President was in any way less weighty than his vote for alderman—yet the local vote is something like 32,500 times as influential as the presidential vote. So heavily is the electoral idea buttered with a moral and conventional spread that such a concept is totally obscured.

A third reason is that the electoral process tends inevitably to give the voter a sense of importance, a sense that he is influential. After all, he is told this by the candidates and he can see that, for each candidate, he has something to exchange that the candidate

9. "Between the act of voting and the most momentous high-level political decisions is a connection which is mysterious. One cannot say that there is none at all, nor can one say that the final decision is an outcome of the voter's will. This is exactly the situation of an alienated expression of the citizen's will." Erich Fromm, *The Sane Society* (New York: Rinehart, 1955), p. 191.

wants—his vote. This idea comes through in many comments; here is one by DeAngelo, a factory operative who never goes to political meetings, never canvasses, never gives money, rarely talks politics. But he does vote:

> To me, voting is the thing, the right to put in the guy you want— that's the big thing. I mean, I know that over there they don't have that and they have a lot of trouble. The kid that was born to Princess Elizabeth—he is going to be the king someday. That's all there is to it. Nobody else is gonna run it, know what I mean? . . . Here, there's always a contest against each other try- ing to serve the people the best way they could to stay in power. And that's a good thing.

In this way the election transmutes the subject (as DeAngelo sees it) into a citizen. It is a symbolic act of enormous importance in leading men to speak of their relationship to government in the active voice, however confusing it may be in detail, however difficult to specify the nature of the control it represents, however inflated the claims made in the name of popular government. After all, voting for and against officials is what you do to govern- ment in an exchange where it does much to you.

A fourth reason lies, I think, in an identification I had not expected, a reference group that has all but disappeared from sight in the sophisticated analysis of politics and government. One expects an identification with a nation; it is called patriotism, and much is made of it. Called nationalism, it seems somewhat more suspect but strong and viable and dangerous everywhere. In Ze- nith and Middletown some expect identification with a commu- nity; people who never thought they had such loyalty often dis- cover that they possess something like it when they are abroad and find someone from their home town. Ethnic loyalties, religious loyalties, racial loyalties are, in America, strong but publicly de- preciated. Class loyalties are faint here, stronger abroad, but usu- ally dissolved by war. All these are familiar, hence somehow dis- counted. What seems surprising in Eastport is the viability of *the people,* the great undifferentiated class of humanity that somehow comes under this rubric as it has since the beginning: In the Constitution, "We the people of the United States, in order to form a more perfect union. . . ." In the Federalist papers, "the people [joined] in thinking that the prosperity of America de- pended on its Union. To preserve and perpetuate it was the great object of the people in forming that convention [1789]." [10] And now, in many vague, and some specific, ways, the common men of Eastport see themselves as "the people," the new populists. Fresh from the assembly line, Costa shows us, on behalf of most of the men, how this is done:

> I belong to the group that might have too little power. But, I mean, we—as long as we exercise our political rights, our voting privileges, a group of little men becomes a big group. ["When you say you belong to a group that might have too little power, what group is that?"] Well, what I mean to say—the point that I'm trying to make is that, being just an ordinary man, I don't have any outstanding attributes, and myself alone might get pushed around. But when there's millions of people like me—and I know there are—we get taken care of, because of the fact that we're a majority.

Once this identification is made, and the individual wraps himself in the power of "the People," he can find a foundation for thinking of himself as, in fact, the ruler of the nation. Almost half of the Eastportians said, in one way or another, that the people ran the government "really" or "basically" or in some more profound sense than meets the eye. They said it this way:

> I would say the electorate runs the government [Farrel]; The people run the government through their elected representatives [Costa]; I would say Congress [runs the government], the people themselves—which is the people [Johnson]; Well, it's supposedly the people . . . in fact that may be true. I think probably basically it is the people [McNamara]; The Congress. ["Who runs the Congress?"] I think the people [Sokolsky].

No doubt there is much of the civics text here, a little of the old-fashioned Fourth of July oratory now falling into desuetude. But they do mean it, too. They believe that the people are not only the source of power—something that, if "folk" is substituted for "people," can be totalitarian in a nasty way—but that elections, opinions, "pressures," operate somehow to bend policy as "the people" want it to go.

Finally, there is another reason and meaning to this version of popular sovereignty. They believe that their welfare is the criterion for policy. But this hinges on a concept of allegiant citizenship that we shall shortly develop further. In the meantime let us consider one consequence of this persistent belief in the power of the people.

10. John Jay, *Federalist Paper* Number 2 in Modern Library Edition (New York: Random House, 1937), p. 12.

Self-Esteem, Group Therapy, and Public Civility

Popular sovereignty is the right to be periodically "consulted" or, if not that, appealed to; it is the right to a friend, or the image of a friend, in power—one's alderman or congressman; it is the claim to participation in the exercise of great power, however small the fraction claimed; it is the expectation of small items of behavior from politicians and police that suggest that one is important, somebody worth caring about. It is the right to a modest self-esteem. It is what is missing when the Italian farmer tells his interviewer: "I feel that I just don't count as a person. No one cares one way or the other what happens to me or to my family. . . . All the officials care about is what we can do for them and seeing that they get their taxes." [11]

It has been said many times that men develop their images of themselves, achieve an identity, through a reading of the opinions of others, the cues given to them by institutional arrangements, their standing in court. There were four of the men in this sample who could not, by virtue of the nature of their work as machine tenders, find many "narcissistic supplies" in their routine occupation. There were about five whose wives worked; they could not find in their situation the small masculine pride that comes from being the sole source of the family income, the one on whom all must depend, the breadwinner. About three of the Italian-Americans felt that it was a slight disadvantage in Eastport to be an Italian-American. These were, be it remembered, the successful men of the neighborhood with much to give them a sense of importance and achievement—but, still, with much to make them doubt themselves and many little leaden weights to depress their sense of status and importance. In this context, popular sovereignty, interpreted as the sense, first, that the government *cares* about you, molds its policy to fit your needs when these are made clear, and, second, offers status and deference individually and collectively, is a source of public therapy and private morale. Popular sovereignty, if believed, gives back to the common man a little of the self-esteem that industrial and ethnically heterogenous society steals from him in other ways.

This restorative act has effects in many ways. Men who feel deprived of power and status may express their grievance in withdrawal and apathy—a common response. Or they may help them-

11. Hadley Cantril, *The Politics of Despair* (New York: Basic Books, 1958), p. 74.

selves to the trappings of power and status, becoming hollow men, pretentious, defensive. They may assert themselves with a willfully heavy hand on the levels of domestic power in their families, or become petty gauleiters in the office, or bullies in their lodges, neighborhoods, unions. Modest behavior is the product of self-esteem, not self-doubt. I am saying that the belief in popular sovereignty reinforces a view that "people like me" are important, powerful, esteemed by others, and so helps Eastport to walk with modesty.

C

GOVERNMENT FOR THE PEOPLE

Consider the implications of these statements:

The workers trust neither the government nor their employer. They have no confidence in them. Both are bitter enemies.
—French worker, quoted in Hadley Cantril,
The Politics of Despair, pp. 71–72.

They [the authorities] . . . "get yer in the end," "aren't really to be trusted," "talk posh," "are all twisters really," "never tell yer owt" [that is, about a relative in hospital], "clap yer in clink," "will do y' down if they can," "summons yer," "are all in a click [clique] together," "treat y' like muck."
—Working-class phrases in Richard Hoggart,
The Uses of Literacy, p. 62

When I vote, I listen to this fellow and I listen to that fellow and read this and read that. . . . I say to myself, both these guys are out someplace to make a buck—there again, you come to corruption. That's the way I figure it, you know? But who's going to help me most? But [pause] even though those fellows make a dollar, the way I look at it, I don't believe that they're going to do anything to hurt this country—any of them, because no one man could do this thing. It has to be done with a group of men, and these men are not going to allow it.
—Johnson, a mechanic in Eastport, U.S.A.

These quotations warn us that it is time now, once for all, to put the political "alienation" of the American common man into some kind of perspective. At the beginning of the chapter, Gorer is quoted as saying, "Americans regard their own government as alien." Laski, speaking of the "Spirit of America," says, "It is, indeed, suspicious of government, partly because it has a profound regard for freedom. . . ." [12] Max Lerner speaks of "American skepticism of all political power." [13] On the other hand, it is also agreed by these gentlemen that Americans believe, in the Lynds' phrase, "No people anywhere are better governed than are Americans." [14] It is a puzzle that our friend Johnson, the mechanic from Eastport, helps to untangle.

The French worker quoted above is *bitter,* desperate, truly feeling left out, in a word, alienated. The British workers seem best described in other terms; they are *mistrustful,* as Hoggart says; they are getting a "little of their own back"; they are grumbling, somewhat disaffected, even hostile—but there is a sense of community and communion along with the suspicion. Are they alienated? If so, it is in a different sense; they are separated from the authorities by a barrier partially of their own creation, and many who speak this way vote Conservative. Johnson, on the other hand, is certainly not a bitter man, nor does he seem so mistrustful as his British counterparts. He fills tape after tape with jocular comment about himself, his work, his early life, his boys, his vacation trips, how he sees the problems of society. He has exaggerated plans for the future. Yet, as we see, he is skeptical of the motives of politicians—more so than most—skeptical of his friends, not above engaging in a shady deal or two—but regretful afterward. Athletic, but a little chubby, hard-working and ambitious, a good union member, he embraces the society that gives him scope for his energy and permits him to dream of better times. He combines both the extreme suspicion of corruption and self-interest in the group—and the extreme identification of the going order. Thus he shows how foreign commentators—and some of our own—can be misled by the idea that statements about "corrupt politicians" imply a belief that these politicians are not, at the same time, working hard for the public welfare, for "the people," for the Eastport men themselves.

The Nature of Allegiance

Government for the people—in what sense? In the first place, when they think of the congressman or the mayor or the President

12. Harold Laski, *The American Democracy* (New York: Viking, 1948), p. 43.

13. Max Lerner, *America as a Civilization: Life and Thought in the United States Today* (New York: Simon and Schuster, 1957), p. 377.

14. Robert S. and Helen M. Lynd, *Middletown in Transition: A Study in Cultural Conflicts* (New York: Harcourt, Brace, 1937), p. 321.

doing his daily job, they think he has in mind the welfare of the nation or of his particular constituency—and this is true of even the more cynical men. When they think of "government," they think of a positive, supportive, nurturant organization. Asked how government affects their lives—surely a question tapping the funds of irritation, frustration, and resentment that should accrue over taxes, regulations, conscription, failures to solve traffic problems, and the like—the men offer "thin" but constructive, positive answers. Ruggiero, an Eastern State University clerk, a little more articulate than the others, says: "They change your life, like this redevelopment here in Eastport. . . . They're the ones that made the minimum wage . . . define working conditions and things like that." Ruggiero is able to criticize the government; he is thought to be a little dangerous in the post office where he works because he says Russia is not all bad, but, fresh from his custodial job in an office building, looking up from his height of about five foot five, he stands foursquare behind an allegiant view of government. So also Flynn, a railroad supply clerk: How does government affect his life? "My son can gain assistance from the government for his education which he probably wouldn't otherwise get . . . housing programs, that so many people have been able to own their own homes." Government, then, is not only for the people; it is also for *me*.

The alienated man not only believes that government is failing to serve his interests; he believes that it is also serving some other set of interests, either those of a rival class or of "the vested interests" or of some hostile, disliked, rejected group. Just as the cabalist thinks some such group has seized power, so the political alienate believes that such a group is receiving the rewards to be given by a biased government. And of course, the two go together. Only four men were cabalists, and even they do not stress the "alienation" of governmental rewards; they do not themselves feel personally aggrieved.

But in this generally euphoric picture of the nature of government, there are some discordant answers. As reported elsewhere, Rapuano thinks only of politics when he thinks of government; he sees congressmen as having rackets and going on junkets; his first impression of government's effect on his life is conscription. Ferrera, asked if he thinks government is doing the right things, says he can't think what they are doing, but "I don't think they are the right things." His view of the civil service is expressed rather poetically, "full of sound and fury . . . performing some menial task," and his first idea of how government affects his life is "by reason of its tax program," while locally, "poor planning and financing has caused tremendous hardship." Here, then, are two men who qualify as politically alienated in a way that the other cabalists (Sokolsky and Kuchinsky) do not.

The politically alienated man longs to be embraced, nurtured, included, but he seems not to be drawn to the welfare states that promise him, in a dilute but useful way, just these qualities. The fact is that he does not see the welfare state. After Rapuano has said that government affects his life through conscription and then mentions taxes in a rather casual and nonindignant way, he goes on to say: "Otherwise, they've never bothered with me, and I never bothered with them. . . . I have nothing to do with the government; no, I've never had anything at all to do with them." And Ferrera stumbles into his alienated position as follows: "Well, it most affects me, I guess on its—I don't know—most affects my life, by reason of its, ah, tax program, ah, ah, oh. It endeavors to do something about the cost of living. [pause] This is a field I do very little thinking of." Living in a publicly supported housing development, some of their children going to public schools, having drawn unemployment insurance checks, worried about the Russians, and particularly about the "missile gap," why should these men not even see the welfare state around them?

These are men, be it recalled, who have problems containing their anger and who may need to reinstate a jungle world where anger is legitimate, functional, necessary. Such angers are out of place in a more orderly society and a more humane world. Within the breasts of Rapuano and Ferrera there is a tug of war: each needs a humane world to embrace him and relieve his poignant sense of homelessness. But each needs the jungle world to assure him that his anger is appropriate in the nature of things.

Alienation versus Divorcement

While two men, Rapuano and Ferrar, cannot see the welfare state that envelops them, and, instead, feel only the pinch of taxes and the pain of things gone wrong, there were others who were quite oblivious of all government, apparently aware neither of its benefits nor of its burdens. Three men (Dempsey, Kuchinsky, DeAngelo) believed that the government was run *for* them but failed completely to see how government affected their lives. A strong allegiant, Dempsey, says, "I couldn't say that they affect me in any way that I could see. [pause] They don't hold me down. If I don't want to go ahead, why that's really up to me; they might even try to help me." Kuchinsky can't think of any way the government affects his life: "I think we've got what we want. Of course, we'd like to have more, but, ah, it's a tough thing. I mean, we've been treated pretty good by the government in this country." And DeAngelo comments, "It hasn't much effect on my life, you know. It could affect my life, I suppose, if they passed labor laws that could hurt me." A few minutes later he discusses the way government helps Eastport. Clearly not alienated, the distance here between individual and government is still substantial. They are *politically divorced*.

The explanation here is simple. These men are among those with the fewest social group memberships; they are those for whom the shop and the home are totally preoccupying; they are eleventh, thirteenth, and fifteenth on the political-information scale. Two of them, Dempsey and Kuchinsky, would not stir out of their houses to be interviewed. Dempsey apparently was "left back" in school; Kuchinsky did poorly in school and is still worried about a fall he had on his head when he was a child; DeAngelo's father abandoned him when he was an infant, and he and his mother lived on relief funds for many years. With these capacities, experiences, and skills, one expects and finds a very limited social horizon. Government is over that horizon for these men.

D
THE RULES OF THE GAME

> Beneath the alternating exasperation and apathy of the voters . . .
> are the convictions that no people anywhere are better governed
> than are Americans, that such weaknesses as appear are not due
> so much to the institutions as to the inevitable failings of well-
> meaning but "poor, weak human nature," and that in govern-
> ment, as in the rest of the culture, progress is inevitable.
> —ROBERT and HELEN LYND, *Middletown in Transition*, p. 321.

The Lynds are right; one cannot easily find in Middletown, Eastport, or America a man who is "against" the Constitution. Symptoms of this facet of alienation, signs of a disaffection for the rules of the game as played on the fields of American politics, if present at all, will be more subtle. Perhaps one might identify them by asking what one would like "to see different in this country." Is there anywhere in a discussion of such dissatisfactions, some suggestion of a change of regime, a fundamental change in what may be thought to be "democratic hypocrisy"? Not at all; those who were most critical of the electorate, skeptical of the democratic procedures in their own organizations, most ready to believe that democracy had a shaky future, that is, the *undemocrats,* say: "I think I'm pretty well satisfied" (Ferrera); "I'm happy the way I am" (Rapuano—but he says this after a rather moving plea for greater economic security). The cabalists believe that illegitimate groups have usurped control; there is implied here some sense that the rules of the game are inadequate to protect legitimate interests and that there is a discrepancy between the formal rules and the actual rules. But there is no whisper of a suggestion of constitutional reforms or any change of regime.

The alienated citizen might easily seek a resolution of his problems through some charismatic leader who, with magical powers, rises above the Constitution. Like Louis XIV and Mayor Hague of Jersey City, the leader then *becomes* the regime. Eastport had a kind of nostalgic wish for another Roosevelt during the "Eisenhower recession" of 1957–1958, but Roosevelt himself is appraised in a balanced human way. He is a political leader, not a magician. The two most withdrawn men, Dempsey and Kuchinsky, show symptoms of looking for solutions in "another fighter" to get things moving again. But that is all—a rather faint trace, visible, a little disturbing, but in perspective, not a search for a great man to replace a worn-out constitution.

We look further afield in the fantasy world of ideal types. In the discussion of government in an ideal society, in Utopia, something interesting happens. For the most part, as the men describe the government of Utopia, it takes on a familiar shape. O'Hara, like the others, is no chiliastic thinker, but he can imagine a utopian government. "I mean where it's a democracy, where you can do what you want to do, with law and that—just like more or less what we've got here." Sokolsky says, "I think we would have the same kind of government, because [pause] I can't think of any other government that could beat this kind." A few, like Costa and Woodside, fear that perfection means uniformity, and reject the idea. A few others, like McNamara and Ruggiero, feel that perfection means that government would be unnecessary in a society where everyone is perfect. (For them, indeed, government is the badge of our lost innocence.)

But two other men set up as an ideal a form of government where there are powerful authorities who are checked, if at all, only by the most tenuous popular control. We have met them before, among the cabalists, among the undemocrats, among those suffering from the confusions of freedom: Rapuano and Ferrera. Their testimony is of interest. What kind of government would there be in a perfect society?

> RAPUANO: [pause] Well, there certainly would be a simple government. . . . There wouldn't be too many people making the laws or governing the people, for one thing. It probably would be more or less like a council. And there wouldn't be any voting every year or so—that would be out. If a man dies, then we'll vote for somebody else—you know, put in a new man at the head of the council, for one thing.
>
> LANE: It would be a lifetime membership on the council?
>
> RAPUANO: I would say so, yes. [pause] Of course, if he happens to be, let's say, well, let's call him a radical, the first thing to do is you just grab him bodily and just eliminate him. But it's pretty hard to do something like that . . . where there's an enormous population. I mean, those things are all right on an island where there's maybe three or four hundred people. . . . But, I wouldn't mind living on an island, believe me. Oh, gee, I sure would.

It is all there: the dislike for elections, the desire for simplicity and peace as contrasted to the confusion and conflict of a democratic society, the "bodily elimination" of dissidents, the radically different rules of the game. Looking only at this facet of the syndrome, we have found in the fantasy material one of the symptoms of political and social alienation.

Both Ferrara and Rapuano are big men, but Ferrera is more athletic, tougher, yet also more introverted. Both are given to mood swings, both susceptible to fits of anger. Ferrera is more "moral"; he has just been speaking of "brotherly love" in Utopia. Here are his views on a utopian government:

> FERRERA: Well, in the accepted sense, yes, there would be [government]. There would be something similar to what we have today, with definite leaders, subleaders, all the way down the line.
>
> LANE: Who would the leaders be? Who would run things?

FERRERA: I can't picture anyone but the elders—
LANE: Elected, or—
FERRERA: Yes, elected. No, no, possibly another way of qualifying
to be a leader. I think that Utopia probably wouldn't have
elections; possibly would have qualifications—and—something similar to that, and if you lived to be eighty years old,
you would probably qualify for leadership or some part of
leadership.[15]

Again the rejection of elections, the deemphasis on popular control, the hierarchical simplicity, the venerable and venerated
authorities, all amplify Ferrera's latent political alienation; he
would like another set of rules, another kind of regime.

There are two—but only two—who speak in this vein. Here
again we find, overwhelmingly, an allegiant society, allegiant
even in fantasy life.

Glancing backward now, we find that the overwhelming majority of the common men of Eastport (seen through our sample)
are politically allegiant—not alienated from government or society. Although it is true that they sometimes speak in the passive
voice about their role in government, and cannot see how they
can change the course of events in any important way, they nevertheless conclude that in the long run in their role as "the people"
they do in fact run things. Eastport believes that government in
America is operated in its behalf; it believes that the rules of the
game are fair, effective, indeed, "given" in the nature of things.

But there are two men, Rapuano and Ferrera, who qualify on
two of the three criteria, as political alienates: they do not find
government operated for them; they harbor a secret and basic
dissatisfaction with the rules of the game. The roots of these feelings do, of course, draw nourishment from other areas we have
examined—the cabalism, the undemocraticness, the fear of freedom—but they have another source, homelessness. It is worth
exploring.

15. The next exchange is amusing and reveals the independence and the jocular
hostility of Ferrera. I ask him, "What kinds of things that you do now would you
not have to do in Utopia?" Ferrera: "One thing, I wouldn't be doing this." Lane: "I
might." Ferrera: "Ah, we would assume that in Utopia you understood all these
problems."

11

Homelessness:
The Roots of Political Alienation

Political alienation, we have said, is the tendency to think of the government and politics of the nation as run *by* others *for* others according to an unfair set of rules. It is more than a *traditionalist's* sense that these things are part of the natural order over which he has no control, for the traditionalist has no belief that it could or should be otherwise. He does not feel alienated from his government because he never felt allegiant or integrated or in some way a part of it, and he never imagined that that was a possible state of affairs. Similarly, many of the men who say the government has no effect on their lives, the men who are *divorced* from government, are unaware, withdrawn, have a limited threshold—but they do not wish it otherwise and do not hold in their minds the possibility of an alternate arrangement. The politically alienated man is aware of the alternatives and grieves over his losses.

Personal Alienation

The most reasonable inference is that political alienation is but a symptom of a more general personal alienation, a concept to which many have contributed. For Schiller and Hegel, it implied a divorce between the self as subject and the self as object. For Feuerbach it implied the giving away of some part of the self, the sensibility, to the sphere of religion.[1] For Marx it referred to the giving away of men's creativity and work satisfaction in exploitative industrial situations. But it is in Fromm's discussion of "Man in Capitalistic Society" that the broad contours of personal alienation become clear.[2] He says:

> By alienation is meant a mode of experience in which the person experiences himself as an alien. He has become, one might say, estranged for himself. He does not experience himself as the center of the world, as the creator of his own acts—but his acts and their consequences have become his masters, whom he obeys, or whom he may even worship. The alienated person is out of touch with himself as he is out of touch with any other person. He, like the others, is experienced as things are experienced. . . .[3]

He becomes an object of his own manipulation; he seeks to sell himself, to use his personality as an instrument; he develops, in one of Fromm's phrases, the "marketing personality." This syndrome is a complex one; it includes four major elements: (1) objectification and abstraction of the person from his environment, (2) manipulation of himself and others for certain extrinsic ends, (3) nonintegrated personality functioning (a split libido), and (4) rejection of some parts of the self—as when a person changes his name, his accent, his personal background to repackage himself into a more marketable item. (Notice it is rejection of the self, not of society, that is implied here.)

Is Frommian personal alienation, defined in this way, the source of political alienation? In the Eastport milieu, it is not. As one examines the evidence in the work life and friendship patterns of these men, it becomes increasingly doubtful that the aspects of personal alienation described by Fromm have a close relationship to the political alienation suggested by Franz Neumann, and more broadly developed above.

Homelessness

It is the idea of homelessness that seems to have the most direct bearing on the political alienation of Eastport, an idea

1. For some comments on this history of the idea of alienation, see Daniel Bell, *The End of Ideology: On the Exhaustion of Political Ideas in the Fifties* (New York: The Free Press of Glencoe, 1960), pp. 337–342, 393.

2. Erich Fromm, *The Sane Society* (New York: Rinehart, 1955), pp. 78–208.

3. *Ibid.*, p. 120.

expressed by A. E. Housman in lines that, because they have a resonance with the malaise of our time, have become familiar to many:

> And how am I to face the odds
> Of man's bedevilment and God's?
> I, a stranger and afraid
> In a world I never made.

The idea that this is not *my* world, nor made for me, has a special meaning of its own, with certain basic themes. It includes (1) the feeling that human companionship is too shallow and transient or, figuratively, the search for the human relations of the hearthside, (2) the lack of a sense that there is a certain place where I belong (and where others will recognize that I belong), (3) the feeling that there is no special and defined job there waiting for me to do it, and hence the fear of loss of usefulness and function in society, (4) the sense of doubt about how to play the roles that as father, husband, worker, citizen, an adult must assume in society. It is a commonplace to observe that the changes that have transformed society from a basis in status to a basis in contract, from *Gemeinschaft* to *Gesellschaft,* from rural folk community to urban complex have imposed on each person the need to make his own friends, create his own place in society, find his own occupation and define his own roles. This has been called individualism; here we deal with the psychic burden of individuation, the sense of homelessness that occasionally stirs in all of us but that in some becomes a prime mover of emotion. That is the case with Rapuano and Ferrera.

These two men, cabalists, undemocrats, political alienates, are not depersonalized, do not treat their friends or themselves as objects, enjoy warm, active, friendly relations with others. In analyzing the relationships established with me during the course of the interviews, I came to believe that four men were engaged in some (relatively minor) pretenses, efforts to create an impression that was somehow false to their primary natures and feelings. Neither Ferrera nor Rapuano was among this group. By this criterion they were "sincere," and apparently were not rejecting some aspect of themselves they wanted to hide. They did not try to manipulate me or "sell themselves" to me. Nor did it seem that they were merely using their work life to advance careers; they were totally involved in their work problems. In these aspects of their personalities these were not Frommian alienates.

COMPANIONSHIP   But, in the sense described, they are home-less, although their homelessness revealed itself in different ways. Both are concerned about depth of personal relations, the problem of intimacy. Ferrera seems unable to get enough of it; he finds in-adequate the friendship style of Eastport and particularly the way his life has been lived there. He has many friends; he reaches out toward people, includes them in his masculine, athletic orbit. He says, "I feel that in the city of Eastport I have about—-literally thousands of friends, people I can stop and chat with . . . but as for close friends, I'd say that I have about six or seven intimate friends, possibly ten or twelve all told close friends." But in an-other moment, he says (and only he says this), "I'll tell you frankly, I don't really have one very close friend, and, ah, I think I am a little sorry that I don't." While Ferrera doesn't find this intimacy, this complete repose and sense of deep mutuality, Rapuano, who is looking for the same thing, does find it. What does he like about a friend? "I like them because, I mean, when I'm with them, I can be at ease, and talk to them as I want to. I don't have to put on any airs, or try to fake, you know, my tone of voice, or speech, or something like that. [pause] In other words, I like to, I like to be down to earth, I mean, act myself, and with the friends I have, I could do that." This problem of peeling off layers of pseudoself is reflective of the issue that confronts Rapuano at every turn—the problem of identity. In friendship, real friendship, he can re-solve this. The point is that both men are looking for the same thing—something quite different from the "common interests," mutual favors, "fun," or even "protection of privacy" motifs in the other discussion.

PLACE   In like manner, both men feel they do not have the kind of roots in the community that they need; they do not have such a sense of belonging that if they left Eastport there would be something missing in their lives. This is, it is true, not so surpris-ing for Rapuano, who is one of three men not born and bred in the Eastport area—but neither is Woodside, and he has a sense of belonging to the people of the area. Rapuano asked how he would feel if he had to leave Eastport, answers: "It's just a place where I'm making a living, I guess. . . . There isn't anything I'd miss about Eastport, really." Ferrera is a little more reluctant: "Well, I'm sure I would miss my parents; my relatives, and, ah, my dear friends—but I wouldn't hesitate to do it [move]. I don't know,

I've been saying it right along. Many a time I wanted to pack up and leave, but she [his wife] wouldn't move. Oh, this goes back—I wanted to take off a long time ago. Just go. I'm that type of person." In a later section we discuss the failure of localism; for these men the failure is more complete; it is the total failure of community to provide an emotion of warmth and a sense of rightful place; in short, the sentiment with which a good fiction writer can endow the phrase "my home town."

FUNCTION   Men normally find their sense of usefulness and purpose fulfilled in their work experiences. Their work gives them, or can give them, a private sense of accomplishment, creativity, and even mission, as well as the public rewards of status and income. As noted above, both Marx and Fromm felt that the work situation of the workingman in industrial society led to an impoverished sense of fulfillment and creativity. We return to this later, but here it should be said that in the Eastport group only five men disliked their current work situation, two basically because they were machine operators with dull repetitive jobs, and one because of the cutthroat atmosphere engendered by the company's efficiency-conscious management. Two men disliked their jobs not so much because of the nature of the work that they did as because they longed to be small businessmen, proprietors—and, especially, their own bosses. Rapuano was the fifth. He must keep track of packinghouse supplies, endlessly worrying about innumerable items and paper forms. One might say of him that his malaise is exactly the reverse of that of the alienated man; he cares too much, he is too involved. First he turns to the extrinsic rewards of work—status and prestige—and then gets to the problem that gnaws at his vitals. Of the future of his job, he says:

> There isn't any future in that job. I mean as far as I'm concerned, this is about as high as I could go. . . . ["Are you cut out for this type of work?"] Well, not the way I feel, I'm not, no. In the condition that my health is in today, I'm not cut out for it, believe me. If I was feeling well and didn't have this ulcer, I'd probably like the job, see. Those things [worries about supplies and the boss's failure to help him] wouldn't bother me so much, see? I mean those things are—why, they just become enormous problems, you know what I mean?

This man is not distant from his work; he is overwhelmed by it.

But Ferrera is a puzzle. Since he left "college" where he spent two years on an athletic fellowship, he has been a gas-meter reader, started a paint shop, went back to teachers' college in physical education, got a job selling beer, drove a truck, purchased a small store at the same time he was working for a large selling concern, gave up the selling job, sold out the store, started up a vending-machine business with some others, gradually saw this go bankrupt, was then unemployed for a year, and, just at the time of the interview, had embarked upon a salesman's job for a wholesale shoe agency, with another "big money-making idea" on the side. Each position at the time seemed promising, with great potentialities; the present selling job has the same quality—perhaps with greater probability of success. Of his present job, he says: "I like it. I like to work because I like people—that's why I stayed in sales so long, because I just enjoy people a great deal and people seem to take to me—so it should not be too difficult [to make a success of it]. And I like the subject matter, because I know I'll be doing good." But asked what he is cut out for, he says, thinking of his past, "I don't know what I'm cut out for; I really don't," and in the beginning of his work history he says: "I can never find myself. . . . I can never straighten myself out . . . it took me a very long time (he is now 38) to finally find my way clear . . . so I floated around." Like Rapuano, he is overinvolved in his work; and also like Rapuano, a few months previous to the interviews (when I first called him) he was depressed about his work situation. He was unemployed and demoralized. It is fair, I think, to classify this complex set of attitudes as a search for purpose, function, usefulness, a search for something the American society does not easily provide, but which one finds ready made in a familial, homely community. In his work life, Ferrera, like Rapuano, is homeless.

ROLE   One reason it is so hard for foreign observers to understand America is that the roles that men play are even less well defined here than abroad; they are more often subject to change (what was correct for Mother this year may be incorrect next year), more often learned on the spot by people not to that particular manner born, prescribed by cues so subtle that they are easily missed. A German philosopher once said to a friend of mine that compared to the "flinty" opposition of his compatriots, American opposition was "cottony.") An examination of Eastport's interpretation of the "good citizen" role reveals almost no focal point: it includes most of the qualities of the good man, the good provider and father, the attentive follower of news, the active leader, the moral example and, of course, the conscientious voter. But we already know that Ferrera and Rapuano, who are un-democrats and cabalists, are skeptical of the utility of voting and uncertain about the degree to which they can control events or be heard by men with power. Their role as husband and provider is a matter of concern—at least for Ferrera, who upbraids himself for having failed to provide a steady income for his wife and family.

As fathers these men are generally successful: they are loving, if impulsive and moody; they are solicitous; they strain to be of help to their children. But they show two patterns of uncertainty that are not present in the discussions of the other men. The patterns come to light as the men discuss the question "Do you think there is any special way of bringing up children in a democracy where there is as much freedom as we have here?" All the men except Rapuano mention, along with other things, some need for control, for discipline, for moral standards. To sample these comments, we find O'Hara, a mechanic and oiler, a partisan of a free society and privacy for children, saying: "Too many people figure their children can't do wrong. I mean, you can't do that either. You always—you should always figure when you were a kid, you did wrong, and I means yours can do the same thing." McNamara, a bookkeeper, a strong political liberal, says: "I think control is important to children—up to a certain age. And they seem to have lost that control in the school. In an effort to do good, they perhaps have done a little harm." Woodside, a railroad guard, is more moral; he says in his earnest manner, "If the child has a good basic foundation, and he's believed in certain things like going to church, being a good citizen, taught right from wrong, I say you've got a good citizen." Compare these views—and the others are all similar in some part—with Rapuano's views:

> No, no—I wouldn't say there's any special way of bringing them up. . . . Bringing them up—just bring them up. I mean, if you have any special way, I think you'd spoil the kid. [Let him] run around the way he wants to run around. Of course, there are limits to what he could do. [But] if you tried to, let's say, put a fence around the kid, he's going to probably turn bad. Let him be free—let him do what he wants to.

Progressive? Liberal? Premissive? It embodies something of these. But recall that Rapuano is the man who believes that if people have more freedom they would be "going around killing people," who says of Communists, "I don't think the Constitution was to protect people like that," and who picks fights with "agitators" on the streets. This is not the expression of a philosophy of freedom; it is an expression of a man who, in his paternal role, lacks the confidence for guidance, is uncertain of his own standards, and so fails to provide moral standards for his children (although he is a moral man), and who, although he may not abdicate his paternal role, leaves it vague, unstructured, incomplete—and all in the name of freedom.

Ferrera's is a different problem—he represents almost the classic middle-class dilemma posed by the conflict between the older, moralized parental pattern and the "newfangled" advice of the experts. Is there a special way of bringing up children? Ferrera is caught, apparently, not only in the crossfire of the "experts" but in some conflict with his wife as well. He is so insistent (speaks of himself as having a stubborn trait) that one suspects a host of doubts kept in their places by only the strongest show of will. He says:

> Well, I don't know if you can call it a special way, but if you bring up the children to do what you think is right, and, ah, teach them to be God-fearing, and—I think if you do not listen to all that tripe—or read all that tripe that people are writing . . . [He trails off.] It's my opinion that these so-called experts of child psychology are just writing—oh, I'm talking about magazine articles, and of course there's lots of very funny people in the child-psychology world—some who deserve a great deal of credit; but educators—I'm thinking too of educators—but there are an awfully lot of people who . . . don't know the dardnest thing about bringing up children. . . . *I insist that what I think is right is right, whether the child agrees with me or whether my wife agrees with me or not*—I feel that in the eyes of God I am doing the right thing.

True confidence does not need to insist, under cover of God's authority, in this fashion. True confidence, too, could read, digest, and use advice. He says that he is "severe in certain aspects of childhood," and since his wife tells him he has a terrible temper, in an angry and frustrated mood he may well insist on doing what he thinks is "the right thing in the eyes of God" just to reassure himself about his mastery of the parental role (child psychologists notwithstanding). This is sporadic; other people are, as he says, drawn to him—no doubt his children are, too. But of all the men, only Ferrera mentioned conflicting advice on the parental role. Both men, I think, are more in doubt, more conflicted, engaged in a more worrisome search for the right parental role than is true of the other men in Eastport.

Strangers upon this earth, "homeless" in their hometown, Ferrera and Rapuano, although more active politically than others, do not feel that they are part of a meaningful democratic process, and are skeptical of the worth of elections. Indeed, frustrated as they are in their search for purpose, intimacy, certainty, they could hardly be expected to embrace a governmental and political system that failed them in these crucial respects.

Men who are in some measure alienated from the democratic style of government and who support McCarthy and who exhibit symptoms of social aggression are thought to be authoritarians with high "F-scale" scores.[4] As it turns out, Ferrera ranks 2.5 on authoritarianism among the fifteen men, and Rapuano, with much less education, ranks 13.5, that is, in the most equalitarian fifth. These men differ greatly on the treatment to be accorded sex criminals, the worth of the artist and the professional man compared to the businessman, the need for discipline among young people, and the exactness with which bosses should tell their men what to do. This highlights the fact that the homeless man is theoretically very different from the authoritarian. Where the authoritarian bases his human relations on calculations of strength, and seeks subordination to the strong and domination over the weak, the homeless man seeks a penetrating intimacy in human relations, which he may not be able to find. Whereas the authoritarian conceives of his own group as the center of things, and others as "strangers" and outsiders, the homeless man constantly finds himself as the outsider, the stranger trying to enter or find a "we-group" to join. The authoritarian seeks the extrinsic status and income rewards of work life, while the homeless man seeks satisfactions on the job, finds challenges in the problems, looks for companionship where he works. Though both the authoritarian and the homeless man dislike the ambiguity of ill-defined role structures, their styles of resolutions may be different, for the homeless man essentially is looking for fulfillment of his need to be useful, to find a congenial purpose in each role;

4. See T. W. Adorno, Else Frenkel-Brunswik, Daniel J. Levinson, R. Nevitt Sanford, *The Authoritarian Personality* (New York: Harper, 1950), especially Chapter VII.

he looks for meaning, while the authoritarian looks for simplification, definition, authority, order.

Yet both are led to view the democratic order with skepticism.

Allegiance and Homelessness

What of the others, men like Costa, a factory operative, who feels his life has been something of a failure; or Dempsey, a drill-press operator, too old to change his job but eager for respite from industrial life; or Flynn, faced with the need to move to another location because there is a "reduction in force" in his branch of the railroad supply business? Indeed, what of the now formidable literature on the human casualties of urbanization, industrialization, atomization of society? In one guise or another, as anomie, alienation, anxiety, depersonalization, and now homelessness, the symptoms of the human costs of modern civilization are coming to light. It is all there in Eastport, too: the tragedies and sufferings, the disappointment and regret. There are five men who would leave the community with little regret, three men who hate their jobs, two workingmen who yearn to be small proprietors, many wrestling with their ethnic identities—their Jewishness, their Italianness, their Polishness—many men seeking "the American way" in a vain effort to find the indistinct blaze marks on the mythical, changing golden path.

But the conditions of life that produce these casualties also offer many rewards, for while some men hate their work, most find it interesting, challenging, often exciting. While some men would not mind leaving friends and familiar places, most would mind, and do have a sense of place and home. While all men struggle with various role interpretations, most have a sense that they know what is expected of them, and can do it. And while the intimacy Rapuano and Ferrera want is not easy to find, some do not want it, and most find great satisfaction in their shopmates, their bowling friends, their wife's friends' husbands, even their neighbors. In this balance of anomic and nonanomic, alienated and nonalienated, homeless and nonhomeless feelings, the positive rewards of living have, in fact, reinforced a political style that is, for most, democratic, nonconspiratorial, allegiant.

12

The Mind of the New Collectivism

Let a people believe in government-omnipotence, and they will be pretty certain to get up revolutions to achieve impossibilities. Between their exorbitant ideas of what the state ought to do for them on the one side and its miserable performances on the other, there will surely be generated feelings extremely inimical to social order. . . .

—HERBERT SPENCER, *Social Statics,* p. 319

No people ever had less reason to fear the arbitrary abuse of governmental power, yet Americans have been traditionally reluctant to yield power, and they still tend to deflate it.

—MAX LERNER, *America as a Civilization,* p. 355

[The] constant tendency [of Americanism] is to shrink, whether internally or externally, from collective action on the ground that because collective action must involve coercion, it destroys that power of self-regeneration in man without which no reform is ever fully achieved.

—HAROLD LASKI, *The American Democracy,* p. 738

A

FROM INDIVIDUALISM TO COLLECTIVISM:
THE ROAD TO EASTPORT IN THE FIFTIES

Writing to his friend Elbridge Gerry in 1799, Thomas Jefferson said, "I am for a government rigorously frugal and simple, applying all possible savings of the public revenue to the discharge of the national debt." [1] Some sixty years later, John Stuart Mill stated the principle of minimum government in its classic form: "The sole end for which mankind are warranted, individually or collectively, in interfering with the liberty of action of any of their number, is self-protection. . . . The only purpose for which power can be rightfully exercised over any member of a civilized community, against his will, is to prevent harm to others. His own good, either physical or moral, is not a sufficient warranty." [2] But in Eastport, in 1958, Kuchinsky, a roofer, says of the government: "I don't believe there's too much of anything that they could stay out of. I think they're in most everything today." We are in his kitchen; I ask him if he thinks that's right. He looks thoughtfully at the stove, and nods his head firmly: "Yah, I think so. I think it's a good thing. Even that segregation business, I think the government should have something to say about it." The idea of minimal government, lingering in many American opinions, has almost vanished from the political mind of the common man in Eastport. What has happened?

Reviewing a similar change of attitude in England over the nineteenth century and the first decade of the twentieth century, Dicey notes the changing duties of government encroaching bit by bit on Mill's principle and the earlier Benthamite philosophy of government. [3] He observes the growth of poor laws, of health and unemployment insurance, of the protection of unions and other groups from judicial action, the increasing regulatory and equalizing functions of taxes, and many similar matters. In each case he attempts to show how these violate the principles of minimal government and maximal individual choice, and he seeks to explain these legislative changes by accounting for certain elements in the public opinion of the British people during this period. In an introduction to a second edition, published in 1914, he searches for the causes of the most recent changes. First, he says, is the realistic perception of the "patent facts which impress upon ordinary Englishmen the interdependence of private and public interests." These are witnessed in the impact of a strike

1. Frederick C. Prescott, *Alexander Hamilton and Thomas Jefferson* (New York: American Book Company, 1934), p. 327.

2. John Stuart Mill, "Essay on Liberty," in *Utilitarianism, Liberty, and Representative Government* (London: Dent, 1910; Everyman ed.), pp. 72–73.

3. A. V. Dicey, *Lectures on the Relation between Law and Public Opinion in England* . . . (London: Macmillan, 1914).

on the general welfare, the influence of communicable diseases, and other, now long-familiar citations of this nature. A second recent cause, says Dicey, is "the declining influence of other movements" that once held such promise of widespread benefits as to form panaceas in the public mind. Here he contemplates nationalism and the unification of Italy and Germany abroad, and the evangelical and moral reform movements at home. As they achieved some of their immediate objectives and failed to achieve others, it appeared that they would not solve all the ills of the world, after all, and so men turned toward Socialism or collectivism. Third, Dicey suggests that the "intellectual weakness" combined with "moral virtue" of the prosperous classes in England led them to accept what he regarded as specious arguments for collectivism because of their moral appeals. Fourth, the advent of parliamentary democracy gave to the special interests, including the working classes, a leverage in government that they exercised in their own behalf. Fifth, he says that England was somewhat influenced by the rise of Socialist doctrine and practice abroad, while, sixth, the combination of real suffering and class conflict, together with a better perspective on the possibilities of change due to a wider distribution of education, led men to seek specific relief for poverty and working-class disaffection.[4]

American legislative experience has paralleled the British in the drift toward the kind of thing Dicey calls "collectivism." The various state regulations of grain elevators, slaughterhouses, child labor, hours and working conditions of women; the passage of the Interstate Commerce Act of 1886, the Pure Food and Drug Act of 1906, the Federal Trade Commission and Clayton Acts of 1914 being only some of the major landmarks in the period Dicey was writing about. The most important legislation came later, however, during the two world wars—the New Deal and the Fair Deal—and embraced not only regulatory measures such as those mentioned but, more important for our purposes, as we shall see, a series of welfare measures with a dramatic change in the public mind. The road we have been traveling has been called "The Road to Serfdom," and it has been defended as leading to freedom under planning, increased democracy, an extension of the liberal spirit.[5] In various guises, the governmental arrangements

4. *Ibid.*, pp. liii–lxxxvii.
5. Friedrich A. Hayek, *The Road to Serfdom* (Chicago: University of Chicago Press, 1944): Barbara Wootton, *Freedom under Planning* (Chapel Hill, N.C.: University of North Carolina Press, 1945); Herman Finer, *Road to Reaction* (Boston: Little, Brown, 1945).

required to administer this new "collectivism" have (after Belloc
had appropriated the name the "Servile State") been termed the
"Administrative State," the "Welfare State," and, in a military
version, the "Garrison State." The needs of wartime allocation of
resources, the gradually more and more visible requirements of
central intelligence and guidance in a modern economy, and the
humane desire to protect men against the hazards of modern industrial—and agricultural—life, conspire to increase the role of
government year by year. This has an obvious economic foundation; it is moved by a political organization of interests and a governmental machinery to enact and administer the changes. It is
also grounded in a set of attitudes and beliefs about the relationship of man to his government. Let us explore these.

B

PRINCIPLES OF COLLECTIVIST THOUGHT

*The main focus of attention is on use of government to solve
social problems, not the use of social instruments to solve government problems.* Eastport believes that the major problems of
our time are defense, unemployment and depression, redevelopment and housing, educational deficiencies, juvenile delinquency
and moral slackness, traffic, the high cost of living and inflation,
desegregation and race relations. Eastport does not think that
corruption in government, governmental interference with people's private lives, governmental reform of any kind, taxes or the
public debt are major problems. The focus of their attention is
what can be done to improve society, not what can be done to
improve government.

Broadly speaking, the means adopted to relieve social ills can
be individualistic, as with Bentham and James Mill, or collective.
If individual, they may turn on ways of improving moral character, relying on church and family. Or, focusing on skills, example, training, the approach may emphasize education, public
or private, early or adolescent. A few men, Ferrera, DeAngelo,
and sometimes Flynn, stressed moral or religious reform as a solution to the problem of delinquency, disorder, race prejudice, but
rarely poverty and war. Almost everyone laid great store in improved education, but this was supplemental to the main theme.
By all odds the most important instrument for reform was government. The question Eastport posed then was always, What

can *government* do to help solve the major problems facing America today?

The government is charged with unlimited responsibility for the general welfare. It probably has always been true that the electorate blamed the government for depression; at least the tendency for the electorate to vote against the "ins" in periods of depression suggests this. But this may have been a kind of "anomic activity," like smashing machines or barn burning at a time when the government's responsibility for prosperity was not a part of the American creed. Today it is embodied in law (the Full Employment Act of 1946), and Eastport, in a rather vague, backdoor fashion, accepts this as approved doctrine. This is part of a more general belief that the government is responsible for discovering and seeking solutions for *all social ills*. This is the drift of answers to the questions on "What kinds of things do you think the government should do?" Thus Johnson says, "They should do everything they can to see that the people have what they need, like giving them an opportunity to work." McNamara says, "I suppose government should provide for social welfare, defense, and anything that has to do with life and liberty for the people that are being governed." The scope is totally inclusive; the responsibility is perfectly clear.

The problems will yield to appropriate governmental action. Not long ago many people would have agreed that "any attempt to fix by law the rate of wages was antiquated folly." [6] Fromm, referring to the official capitalist doctrine regarding economic laws, says, "*We* are the producers of our economic and social arrangements, and at the same time we decline responsibility, intentionally and enthusiastically, and await hopefully or anxiously—as the case may be—what the 'future' will bring. . . . These [natural economic] laws are above us, and we are their slaves." [7] There is a trace of this in Eastport; more people believed that there will always be poverty than did not, but they were melioristic if not optimistic on this score—a great deal could be done about it. The same might be said of the threat of war. Speaking of the Russians, DeAngelo says, "I don't think we'll be able to do anything with 'em"; and there is a strong tendency to believe that there will always be wars. Yet these men are not fearful of atomic bombing,

6. A. V. Dicey, *op. cit.*, p. xlix.

7. Erich Fromm, *The Sane Society* (New York: Rinehart, 1955), p. 138, his emphasis.

and they generally support the United Nations; they have not at all retired into "Fortress America." The sad, familiar vein of thought represented by Sullivan's comments on corruption, "There is nothing the government can do about people lining their pockets; that's all in nature, I mean, it's human nature," is thin and worn, and not worth mining. It is a fair judgment that Eastport believes that man, through government, can improve his lot in almost any direction; he can change economic laws, and need not be a slave to any circumstances.

These general "collectivist" tendencies are, however, modified by another principle, *the doctrine of limited noninterference.* Certain practices and certain institutions are sometimes said to be best left alone. Among these, private business has a claim to "privacy" from the government. Thus Costa, a machine tender: "The government shouldn't step into private industry and try to tell them how to run their business," and Sullivan, a truck driver, "The government should not try to run individual businesses." But this common man's version of Chamber of Commerce doctrine, individualistic in the abstract, suffers great erosion when individual issues emerge. For example, Costa believes the Wagner Act was "the best thing that ever happened to the working man," and he argues for stronger policing of pricing practices of big business. Sullivan believes that if the government handled the economy properly, "the recession never never would have happened"—it is government's responsibility, not the individual's —or "nature's"—"I don't think there's anything *an individual* can do about it." Still, there is a hesitance, a restraint, here that is the heritage of economic individualism in the Spencerian manner.

If Spencer has left his mark, so has Calhoun. Ruggiero says of the national government: "Well, they shouldn't get into, uh, anything on the local level, or on the state level. I think they oughta leave some of the state things alone." Federalism, as well as states' rights doctrine, has some support—but again it is violated in detail, even by Ruggiero, who when he thinks of "government" thinks almost exclusively of national government. Few people care much about the trespass of national government upon state and local government—the national government is certainly not an "outsider" as opposed to "their own" local government; the national government is equally their own, and richer and more honest.

The third area of government restraint bounds the question of race relations. Flynn speaks most explicitly for this view, but others imply it or suggest that the government moves too rapidly in the South. Asked if there is something the government should do about the segregation problem, Flynn says, "Oh, I think a better question than that would be, 'Is there anything the government shouldn't do about it?' " and then he goes on to elaborate his philosophy of laissez faire in race relations, based on the view that drawing attention to the problem only makes it worse.

Noninterference in these matters has roughly the same standing that isolationism has in foreign affairs; it is purely a matter of expediency and choice. By interfering, the government "only makes matters worse," gets involved in situations that are too complex and tricky to be handled from Washington, produces side effects that were unintended and unfortunate. How different this is from the natural-rights claims to the sanctity of the person and his property, which is nature "mixed with" his labor; "it hath by this labour something annexed to it that excludes the common right of other men." [8] And how far from Spencerian admonition against "a man who, in the presence of all the wonders that encompass him, dares to announce that he and certain of his colleagues have laid their heads together and found out a way to improve upon the Divine arrangements. . . . Irresistible evidence is at length establishing a belief in the law of supply and demand, as some thousands of years ago it established a belief in the law of gravitation . . . our wisest plan is to let things take their own course." [9] And how far from the philosophy of a recent President, "We cannot extend the mastery of government over the daily life of a people without somewhere making it master of people's souls and thoughts. That is going on today. It is part of all regimentation." [10] But in Eastport in the fifties, the common man was much more worried about governmental inaction than about governmental trespass.

The government is rarely seen as interfering with one's own personal liberty. Only Rapuano's reference to conscription, some few desultory references to taxes, and two comments about highly

8. John Locke, *Two Treatises on Civil Government* (London: George Routledge, 1884), p. 204.

9. Herbert Spencer, *Social Statics; or The Conditions essential to Human Happiness specified, and the First of them Developed* (New York: Appleton, 1878), pp. 323, 333, 334.

10. Herbert Hoover, *The Challenge to Liberty* (New York: Scribner's, 1934), p. 203.

contingent regulatory legislation implied that government was regarded as a personally restrictive agency. It may blunder, it may not be honest, but it is not restrictive. In part, this is because, as we noted above, the real restrictions, the difficult disciplines, are industrial and economic, not governmental. Perhaps for the common man it has been this way for a long time. In 1940 the *Fortune* Poll asked the question, "Do you feel that the federal government is now interfering too much with your individual freedom?" About half of the "prosperous" said "yes" while only 17 per cent of the "poor" said "yes." [11]

Due process and the protection of the courts is primarily for people accused of crimes against property; not for those accused of violence, sexual crimes, or disloyalty. Some 120 years ago, Tocqueville said, "The rights of private persons among democratic nations are commonly of small importance, of recent growth, and extremely precarious; the consequence is that they are often sacrificed without regret and almost always violated without remorse." [12] Certainly this is a risk. But there is a difference in the nature of the regard for the "rights of private persons": crimes against property and conflicts between the state and the individual over property matters are given a preferred status and, in the minds of the Eastportian, given the full protection of "due process of law." It is those without the bounds of certain kinds of conventional morality that are so easily sacrificed. Thus those accused of stealing money from the government, the "corrupt," are treated tolerantly, but those accused of stealing "secrets" are met with high indignation. The person who refuses to sell his property to the local government, tying up the redevelopment program in legal action, is thought worthy of full protection; the person who refuses his loyalty to the Constitution and the flag is thought unworthy of such protection. People who worry about the behavior of the Negroes who come to Eastport from the South worry about violence and sexual morality, not stealing cars, robbery, or burglary. Yet within this context, the onus falls much more heavily on disloyalty than on sexual immorality. All but two or three men seemed unsympathetic to the men whose reputations were injured in McCarthy's search for subversives; yet all but one

11. Hadley Cantril and Mildred Strunk, *Public Opinion 1935–1946* (Princeton, N.J.: Princeton University Press, 1951), p. 107.

12. Alexis de Tocqueville, *Democracy in America,* Phillips Bradley, ed. (New York: Knopf, 1945), Vol. II, p. 326.

were sympathetic with the problem of the homosexual, suggesting care and treatment rather than punishment.

The central idea of government is service, not power. In a famous definition of government, Max Weber says "a political association . . . will be called a 'state' if and in so far as its administrative staff successfully upholds a claim to the *monopoly* of the *legitimate* use of physical force in the enforcement of its order." [13] Marx would turn this around; the state is a monopoly of illegitimate power because "political power, properly so called, is merely the organized power of one class for oppressing another." [14] Eastport thinks of government in terms primarily of making laws, a manifestation of power. But they are laws designed to serve the people, not to regulate the evildoers. They reflect much more accurately another view, the Greek view, that the state exists to make life good. [15]

Not the regulation of abuse, but the expenditure of money is the key to governmental remedial action. There are two competing themes in American economic reform movements: one dealing with currency and credit, the other dealing with the policing of economic behavior. The one, from the time when the Constitution was made to say "No state shall . . . coin Money; emit Bills of Credit; make any Thing but gold and silver Coin a Tender in Payment of Debts," through the great controversy over the Bank in Jackson's time, through the greenback movements, and through movement for a free coinage of silver, has sought to relieve the debtor class and, later, to stimulate employment. The other, represented by the regulatory legislation mentioned earlier, has sought to prevent the abuse of private economic power. The regulatory approach has nominated wrongdoers, named enemies of the people: the Granger movement pointed to the railroads and the elevator owners as the abusive "interests"; the Progressive movement leveled its artillery at "malefactors of great wealth"; and the New Deal pretended to shoot down "economic royalists" and did manage to hit the holding-company operators, reform the securities exchanges, and control some labor-baiting activities.

13. Max Weber, *The Theory of Social and Economic Organization*, Talcott Parsons, ed. (New York: Oxford University Press, 1947), p. 154, his emphasis.

14. Karl Marx and Friedrich Engels, *Manifesto of the Communist Party* (New York: International Publishers, 1932), p. 31.

15. See Charles H. McIlwain, *The Growth of Political Thought in the West* (New York: Macmillan, 1932), p. 10.

A change has occurred in the nature of economic demands that will influence the struggle for governmental assistance in many important ways. The advocate of "collectivism," the citizen demanding that government do something about the ills that trouble him, no longer needs a villain and/or need search for a target. He asks, in the case of a recession, for more government contracts in his area; in the case of squalor and slums, for more government housing; in the case of penury and misery in old age, for more government medical assistance to the senior citizens. It isn't necessary that he find someone who has misbehaved; all that is required is that the government provide the beneficial healing flow of funds to wash away his grievances. Ruggiero, a state University maintenance clerk, is most brief: "Well, I think with this recession it's—I think, uh, the government ought to spend more money." Johnson, a mechanic in a relatively secure job, faces the problem of the government and the recession: "The only thing I can see is that the government is going to have to release—I won't say unnecessary work—but new roads and some sort of building for projects, or something. They'll have to do it, between the state- and the government-sponsored money." Rapuano, a clerk, turns to a local problem, housing. He says: "They're spending a lot of money there, and I don't know where they're going to get the money from. [He mentions a big figure.] Where could they get that much money in a city of this size? But however they do it, it's a good thing. I don't mind paying for it"—the last, no doubt, a touch of bravado. Foreign policy is a real problem for O'Hara, a mechanic and oiler; he is quite critical. What should we do about it? "Well, I tell you one thing. . . . I think they should spend a lot more money on it." A few worry about the taxes—but very few. Almost none believe a balanced budget is important ("It's impossible"—Sokolsky). Costa and one other worry about relying on defense spending in an economy that, he says, "is supposed to be self-supporting," but his solution for the recession is more government contracts. A great green river flows from Washington, and it is no wonder that these men find that with a little irrigation from this stream the solutions to their problems would thrive like the green bay tree.[16]

16. Compare: "As the great majority of those who create the laws have no taxable property, all the money that is spent for the community appears to be spent to their advantage, at no cost of their own; and those who have some little property readily find means of so regulating the taxes that they weigh upon the wealthy and profit the poor, although the rich cannot take the same advantage

C

BELIEF IN GOVERNMENTAL POWER
AS A SUBSTITUTE FOR RELIGIOUS FAITH

> By the side of every religion is to be found a political opinion, which is connected with it by affinity. If the human mind be left to follow its own bent, it will regulate the temporal and spiritual institutions of society in a uniform manner, and man will endeavor, if I may so speak, to *harmonize* earth with heaven.
> —Alexis de Tocqueville, *Democracy in America,* I, p. 300,
> his emphasis

> Our culture is perhaps the first completely secularized culture in human history. . . . God has been transformed into a remote General Director of Universe, Inc.; you know that He is there, He runs the show (although it probably would run without Him, too), you never see Him, but you acknowledge His leadership while you are "doing your part."
> —Erich Fromm, *The Sane Society,* p. 176

As Dicey pointed out in his day, and as many have argued since, the new collectivism draws nourishment from technological innovation, urban living, both the exigencies of war and a new humanity among men, and the exhaustion of man's patience and belief in supernatural remedies. This last feature emerges from the biographical material of the men of Eastport. In many ways, belief in a powerful state is a psychological substitute for belief in a powerful God. It emerges most clearly when we look out from the windows of their lives upon the social scene. As industrial and clerical workers, they are faced with the uncertainties of tenuous jobs, mortgage and installment-purchase debts, irritation over parking and traffic problems in town, worries about inflation, uneasiness about the relations between Negro and white, and in other ways liminally or subliminally they are conscious of a social world that they have not the power to control. You may tell them that God is supervising these matters and that the means for change is prayer. The Eastport men say they believe in prayer— but they do not count on it. Now, if you tell such men that the government has not the power, the authority, or even the right

---

when they are in possession of the government. . . . In other words, the government of the democracy is the only one under which the power that votes the taxes escapes the payment of them." Alexis de Tocqueville, *Democracy in America,* I, 214.

to bring order in this common household, you have severed them
from all hope for a solution. The common man never did take
kindly to the social Darwinist idea that government was impotent
to improve his lot; it always seemed to him like the academic
hocus pocus that it was. Faith in an unseen hand is like faith in
a godless religion; it is only for the most sophisticated minds.

The equivalence of religious and governmental faith is apparent in several other spheres. A faith in a supernaturally inspired arrangement satisfies the need for a belief in order in
human affairs, a sense that however misguided and whimsical it
may be, there is a guiding hand. It is true that in Eastport a fear
of disorder and anarchy is stronger than a fear of tyranny at this
time. If you erode a man's faith in an active Superintendent in
the Heavens, you cannot at the same time destroy the faith in a
superintending presence here below.

More than that, the belief that there is a tenant at the seat of
power who generally agrees with one's own outlook promises
justice as well as order. It is easy for a man to show that God has
the same moral standards that he himself possesses and that God
is lenient when necessary and strict when advisable. Unless the
priests say otherwise, this view of things will prevail. But as God's
justice becomes less important, a just government becomes more
important—it becomes necessary to believe in a benign, solicitous,
and just governmental order.

A religion gives priorities to certain objects of attention, structuring goals, fantasies, offering solutions to the ever-present problem of sin and error, in short, providing men with agendas for
their waking hours. In a secular society of the American variety,
government has no such powers, but it is true that the leaders of
a competent and potent government may help to suggest a focus
for discontent, interpret the social world of nations and men, and
order and schedule efforts at solutions. They organize the competition against foreign powers, draw attention to the problems
of inadequate education, arouse concern for safety on the highways, inflation, segregation. How frustrating it would be to be
told from the beginning that government can only talk about
these things, never do anything effective about them!

A positive faith in one's political system, like a positive faith
in religion, reassures a person that he is properly connected to
the powers that be; he is not alienated, an outcast, a target for
punishment. He has been "good," and, like a good child, deserves

well of the authorities. One finds this view marked in the comments Costa, an assembly-line worker, makes on "the most important lessons life has taught" him. He says:

> Well, there are several. It is [pause] a wonderful thing to believe, no matter what you believe—religion or politics or whatever it is. It's a wonderful thing to have a real belief in something. . . . I'm not religious, but I like to feel I have certain beliefs about the Catholic religion that are good for me. I believe in the political system of the United States. I think it's good for me. It's good for anybody to believe that we have the right kind of system.

And the reverse of this state of faith and grace, the misery of the man without the law, is suggested when he says, "I think a person who does [thinks?] something against the law, or against his fellow man, doesn't feel happy about getting up in the morning, as I do, because there's nothing on my conscience."

There are close analogies in the ways in which individuals may proceed to effect changes in the established order. One aspect of this lies in the switch from prayer to petition, from John Calvin or Pope John to John Locke. These are, in many ways, equivalents, because they are more effective as expressive gestures than as instrumental means to create changes in the nature of things. Both are likely to be uttered in private, or perhaps in group meetings; neither is certain of delivery to the intended destination. Both depend upon faith in the sympathetic nature of the supposed auditor. Petition is, in the sense intended here, an expression of opinion, a request that the authorities do *something* about a situation, relieve a grievance, and above all care about the welfare of the petitioner. The force of Christianity comes from Christ's reputation for caring about the humble. Democracy feeds upon the same substance. If one creates a god to do these things for you, one must believe that he *can* do them—if he wants to. So also with government; one must believe that government can, "if it wants to," solve one's problems.

The secularism of these predominantly Catholic men of Eastport is clear enough. It is true that when they were asked "Why are we here upon this earth?" many responded in terms of fulfilling God's plan. The meaning of religion for many was personal salvation in the strictest Christian sense. Yet divine intervention was rarely mentioned; the importance of dogma was profoundly minimized so that a position of religious tolerance could be easily and consistently maintained; and there was hardly a man who saw anything special about the way a member of his religion might look at political phenomena. Being a good Catholic or a good Protestant or a good Jew in the civic world meant simply being a good man, nothing else.

There is a historian's perspective to the view that belief in effective government is a working substitute for a belief in a personal and directive church or God. Certainly the antagonism between divinity worship and state worship, as in the Nazi regime and the current Soviet ideology, is supportive of this position. Indeed, a long and quarrelsome history of dispute between church and state, from Amenhotep to the Emperor Julian, from the Holy Roman Emperor Henry IV to the English Henry VIII, from Roger Williams to the Jehovah's Witness cases, suggests how each considers the other a rival not only for temporal power but also for controlling the agenda of life. If one gives up belief in divine rule, he must accept the belief in human rule; and if legitimacy is not conferred by God, it must be found in an only slightly less mystical belief in the sovereignty of the people.

13

The Shores of Utopia

The sources of utopian political thinking may be hidden and constantly changing, constantly disguising themselves. While political curiosity and interest have been largely driven out of the accepted sphere of the political in recent years by the "crisis" mood of the press and of the more responsible sectors of public life, people may, in what is left of their private lives, be nurturing newly critical and creative standards.
—DAVID RIESMAN, *The Lonely Crowd*, p. 372

The utopianism of America seemed far more realistic than that of Europe, since the material basis upon which it could be built was not exhausted until about a century after the foundation of the republic.
—HAROLD LASKI, *The American Democracy*, p. 730

A

A FALSE DREAM OF UTOPIA

It is a far cry from the plain row houses and communistic property arrangements of Sir Thomas More's *Utopia*, to the bourgeois heaven of the Eastport working class. It is like the distance between New Harmony and Levittown. In lower middle Eastport today, what is a perfect society, an ideal society, a modern Utopia?

How would it be different from what we have now? What would people do for a living? Who would run things? How would people behave? Are we getting closer to it as the years go by?

As they struggled with these matters, Eastportians showed not only what features of social perfection were important to them but also what features were not so important and what features of society were regarded as too sacred to dream about. "Well," says DeAngelo, a skilled machine operator, "a perfect world is where everybody believes in God." This reminds us of what others did not say. The idea of divine intervention on earth, of a New Jerusalem, is as distant from the thoughts of these men as any world view could possibly be. No more is there reference in any view of a "workers' commonwealth," and certainly not of the dictatorship of the proletariat; indeed, the dictatorship of the bourgeoisie is more nearly what is envisaged. And, too, except for one vision of an island paradise, none of these modern Utopias are sensuous. Quite the opposite. What has happened to the "fun morality" that Martha Wolfenstein says has taken over among children and film stars?[1] What of the allegedly licentious impulses of a postwar generation? There is almost nothing here to tell us how people would "enjoy themselves" in Utopia, nothing on their "good times." And, indeed, when one considers the nature and the poverty and infrequency of the "good times" these men remember in their own lives, one sees that it is not in their experience to imagine a Utopia of fun and good times. That is not the way they view the world.

Nor is Utopia an escape from work. Flynn, in his worldly-wise manner, sees an abundance of goods for everyone, but "at the same time they have enough activity—whether this be in the form of work or hobby or what it happens to be—something that falls within their own interests to keep from going stale." "You still have to work," says DeAngelo. And Ferrera, a salesman, tempted, but remaining on the Puritan axis: "Where there is labor involved, how can it be Utopia?" ["Do you think in Utopia that people wouldn't work?"] "It would be hard to say that they worked, as we understand work." ["Do you think people would be happier if they didn't work?"] "No, I can't imagine people not working." But there is a minority whose Utopia is, as one said, "semiloafing."

1. Martha Wolfenstein, "Fun Morality: An Analysis of Recent American Child-Training Literature," *Journal of Social Issues*, 7, No. 4 (1951), pp. 15–25.

How is one to interpret the fact that men do not think of family life, marriage, or sexual relations when they speculate about the perfect society. No doubt the present arrangements seem founded in immutable laws of nature and morality; quite literally change is unthinkable here. Yet other Utopians find these topics absorbing. Even St. Thomas More suggests that young men and women be introduced to each other naked before they are betrothed—so that they may not be deceived about what they are contracting for. It is probably not only conventionality, however, that prevents Eastport from thinking about these matters. The fear of licentious thoughts draws a silken curtain about this topic for most men, though of course not for all.

Of all the social institutions in whose toils these men are enmeshed, the industrial work life, the class system, the family and the church, private property itself, only the government seems widely amenable to change, so little rooted in the inevitable and natural scheme of things. They are taught this way. Where in grammar school and high school (or, most places, in college) is the family system portrayed as one of several models of procreation and economic sustenance for the young? Where, too, is the church with its religion portrayed as one of a number of solutions men have devised for their reassurance and comfort? Can one imagine a thorough-going exploration of the advantages and disadvantages of title vested in private persons, cooperatives, corporations, communities, governmental authorities, or international agencies? These men are horrified at the notion of equality of income, but they will entertain the idea of nonelected governments; they reject it, but it is not an unthinkable idea. The fact is that certain things, like private property, supernatural worship, and a given code of sexual morality, are sacred; governmental arrangements are secular.

The class relations in Utopia are very like those in Eastport, except that there are no very rich and no very poor. O'Hara, a mechanic and oiler in a large factory, is quite happy with his status as an honest workingman; he says: "The biggest part of them [in Utopia]—you're not really going to get all of them—are middle class. I think you're going to have high, and you're going to have low." DeAngelo, a machine operator, stresses the fact that you're going to have low: "I don't say that in the perfect world everybody has got to have the same amount of money. . . .

I mean, if everybody was equal and had an equal amount of money and didn't have to work, you wouldn't have nuthin', you know what I mean?" Utopia is not an escape from class differences, but a regularization of interclass relations, a sweetening of them, such as is implied in Sullivan's hope for "a more perfect labor-management set-up," and, more clearly, in Johnson's flattening out of the bottom scale: in Utopia everyone "has a position— not just working."

Utopia, in the Space Age, is primitive; it is a glance backward to the peace, the quiet, the simplicity of an earlier time. Instead of a Brave New World, this is a return to the days of the ancients. Sullivan, the truck driver, shelters his Utopia in an Ancient Greek marketplace; Ruggiero returns to a bartering system; Woodside is reminded of "the good old days"; Rapuano says it's "like they live in the South Pacific . . . they swim and fish, and they sing and they dance, and they eat, and that's what they live for." But no one said it was where you push a button and your car is clean, you push another button and, presto, you are in Los Angeles. There is an excitement that goes with technical progress; but somehow the idea of a perfect society seems to ground itself in older virtues, older ways of doing things, paradise lost.

Above all, Utopia is a place of conventional morality and good human relations. "I mean with everybody getting along, without so much robbery and violence of different sorts. . . . I think it would be a wonderful society." "Well, first, there'd be no crimes. . . . I think they would be very nice, because they wouldn't want for anything." It is conventional in its appearance, too. Like Levittown, or any middle-class development, it has single-family houses, curving drives, picture windows, and standardized variation among the houses. Indeed, the first impression is that Utopia is only the upwardly mobile dream in universal form.

But as we penetrate the heart of the dream, it becomes clear that what these men seek would not be found in the homes of the bourgeoisie today, for they ask for something the bourgeoisie does not have. They seek less for material comfort than for relief from worry; they seek success, but they seek equally for relief from the pressure to be more successful; they want a world of congenial human relations where they are accepted for what they are, not for what they would like to be or feel they ought to be. They do not know it but they are dreaming a false dream. Levittown is not Utopia.

B
UTOPIA IS NOT ENOUGH

Perfection and Monotony

The builders of Utopias are, in a way, trapped in a design for uniformity by the logic of their calling. Each of the great utopian architects, Plato, Campanella, More, Fourier, Owen, and even Butler and Bellamy (leaving aside such satirists as Swift, Huxley, and Orwell), wrote as though there were only a single solution, or at least a single best solution, to the social problems of his time. Not only that, but within each utopian society there is a terrible tendency toward uniformity and a deadly lack of chance variation, whim, and eccentricity. Plato stipulates the circumstances of eating, the details of education, the commonalty of wives and children, and one receives an overwhelming impression of conformity and monotony—reinforced by the exclusion of such poets as may criticize the gods and heroes or teach violence. Campanella likewise provides for a monotonous communism of family life; More has every house so exactly identical that when people move into each other's homes, as they are required to do every ten years, they will not be inconvenienced. Huxley provides an island apart for those who think for themselves—that is, the deviants. It is only in the light of these observations that what at first appears as a curious illogicality and mental aberration among the men of Eastport makes a kind of sense.

Woodside, for all his police work, worries about the very idea of Utopia in these terms: "Well, in order to have a perfect society, anyways the way I would look at it, the people would have to think and act alike, and in order to think and act alike it would be that everybody would have to be doing pretty near the same thing . . . but with the way things are now, people are thinking different and doing different things. It would have to be a dictatorship. You'd actually be told what you could do and couldn't do, where it would be to the extent that you'd fear doing otherwise. . . . A few would actually put the hammers, so to speak, right over your head, and if you did otherwise, you'd be demolished or smashed. You would be erased out before you could do otherwise. I mean, I wouldn't want society that way—far be it." Although, of course, the logic is shaky—perfection is not perfect—the penetrating insight into the political framework for an imposed Utopia is almost brilliant.

Costa, an assembly-line worker, has the same reaction, although Costa's fulsome praise for the "American way" suggests one source of his distrust of reform. He says: "I don't know whether there ever could be a perfect society without everybody thinking alike and doing alike, and in a free society I don't think that could ever happen, because once that happens, it wouldn't be a free society any more. Somebody from a position of power is telling you what to say and what to think." Costa would not even discuss it; perfection, as he saw it, was incompatible with his values. Sullivan, the truck driver, who has just said Utopia would involve a uniform morality, freedom from illness, and a "perfect labor-management setup," pauses, and says, "Well, to make it a little more brief, I'd say the place where everybody thought pretty much the same."

In these and similar views there is the notion that the world would go stale and flat if all disagreement were eliminated. This is, it may be noted, the same fear that illuminated the fear of equality we mentioned earlier. The power to enforce such sameness frightens people—they fear the implied dictatorship. Thus the fear lest they lose their freedom goes hand in hand with the fear that they might be, in the end, not only equal but identical. But there is another argument for something less than perfection. Ruggiero, a university maintenance clerk, speculates that people would know when they had reached their peak of achievement or earning capacity in a perfect world, and this would take away one's ambition and the very salt of life. Moreover, foreknowledge of one's life span is destructive of morality. "Knowing when you're going to die—some people would really raise hell. They'd believe [in God] in their last month, or something like that, when they'd been pretty bad. . . . But not knowing is the best part. You just have to be good all the time, because you don't know when it's gonna be."

What all these have in common is the fear of anonymity, the loss of identity that a perfect society envisioned in these terms would impose. Who am I, indeed, if I am like everyone else? The little qualities of character, the small graces, the talents and skills learned so laboriously—to lose all these things is to lose oneself and, in a sweep of fate, to lose the "earnings" of a lifetime of effort. Of course it is too much. The effort of some to stem the course of Communism in America is, in many latent ways, reinforced by this hardy, if confused, sense that what one has made of oneself is in jeopardy.

Why should one-third of these men believe that the perfect society would involve an identical sameness of belief? (They might have argued, as some did, that there would at least be economic and moral differences, or as did Voltaire's opponents, that the best of all possible worlds must contain conflict and sin lest men fail to appreciate the good things they have.) Is it that school teaches a single "school solution"—namely, the one the teacher prefers? Does the Roman Catholic Church give these men the view that, as there is only one true religion, so there is only one true "solution" to each of life's problems? Is it a remote product of Aristotelian logic underlying many of the thought processes of our culture? We are said to be a conformist and other-directed society where differences of taste and dress, as well as belief, are discouraged. We have seen some evidence to support this view. Are these men here responding to this conformism? Would a "perfect picture" be symmetrical and repetitive? Would a "perfect garden" be in the eighteenth century Italian style, formal and clipped? All these men at one time or another have worked in factories; do they conceive of perfection in factory terms—perfectly turned-out replicas of the original model?

On the other hand, it is equally important that, unlike most of the famous authors of utopian schemes, these men reacted strongly against the idea of sameness and conformity. What this group of men is saying, after all, is, "If perfection is uniform, we do not want it."

Utopia and Progress

Among the many clichés about the American character, none is so well established as the American belief in Progress. The heart of the matter is that "things are getting better all the time"; that is, *things* are progressing. Technology is improving; we can do more with less effort; per capita income is increasing—the lot in life of the average man is improving. This is the American idea of Progress.

But there remains another question. Are *people* getting better? Some Utopians, Robert Owen in particular, founded his entire proposal on the proposition that human nature was what the environment made it, and hence was almost indefinitely perfectible. The Platonic view was of a different persuasion—people inherit their characters and, depending on the material, have a much more limited capability for change. Our Utopians, not so optimistic as Owen nor so pessimistic as Plato, tend to see men as limited in their capacity for improvement, being dragged and pushed into their better selves by technological progress—and by education. The skepticism is seen most obviously in those who do not think we are moving toward a better scheme of things: Sokolsky finds men too greedy; Sullivan says "you can't change human nature"; DeAngelo feels that people are too impious and are not trying to improve the social order, and hence life is deteriorating. But the human drag on a progressive movement is apparent in the views of the others, too. O'Hara thinks we are moving toward a perfect society ("We've got a pretty good chance"), but: "It will never be perfect, I mean you'll always have—human nature—there's always somebody will fight with somebody. I mean somebody's always ready because that's human nature." McNamara, holding that "we're getting closer" to Utopia, also feels that "it's quite impossible" for people not to be jealous of other's success. Ruggiero holds that we have things "much better than our fathers had it," but worries whether or not an increase in population means an improved average, for "you'll always find some bad eggs in it," and "it's gonna be harder." Things are moving ahead, but people are lagging; science advances, but morality stays still; we know more—and this inches us along the road of Progress, but our wayward character drags our heels in the dust.

C
WHAT MAKES UTOPIA GOOD?

The End of Anxiety

Everyone (but Costa) dreamed a little dream of some more perfect society, some society that came closer to the heart's desire. Few desire great wealth; almost all desire good jobs with something left over for such modest luxuries as car trips and perhaps even a small outboard motorboat. But the focus is not on material possessions; Utopia in this materialist society is quite otherwise. Good health, for one thing, is more important. But beyond all doubt the most important benefit Utopia might bring is relief from worry, surcease from anxiety, a lifting of the burden of doubt about the future that weighs heavily upon them.

Sullivan, the youngest of the group, a hard, compact muscular man, thinks for a moment of what he would not have to do in Utopia that he does now: "Well, I wouldn't have to worry about the doctor, and . . . well, I probably wouldn't have to worry about my job, or if it's going to be there, or if the business is going to fold up, or anything." Flynn, a railroad supply clerk, has other worries: "Well, I wouldn't have to be too concerned about how I was going to get the family educated—because all this would be provided for in this Utopia." Kuchinsky's problems are shared by many others; he says, to start with: "Well, I don't think we'd have to worry about the money situation. That's for one thing." This is echoed by Johnson, "I could look everybody in the face and say 'I don't owe you a dime.' " DeAngelo has a family of five boys and a girl; the oldest is thirteen. In Utopia, he says: "I wouldn't have to be workin' nights—my mind would be more at ease. I wouldn't have to worry about, you know, something happening at the house —y'know, somebody breaking in, or stuff like that." Ruggiero, the smallest but the richest man in the group, with a nervous energy that led him at one time to supervise three machines where others had been content with one, thinks that in Utopia "I'd be relaxed more. Maybe I'd have more children . . . if we could do a thing like that. In this kind of a world you could have as many as you want. We wouldn't have to—I wouldn't be worrying as much as I do today on different things."

The Age of Anxiety—in an affluent society—has found its spokesmen in these Eastport men. And these are the men with the more secure jobs, the more stable families, the superior personal organization and character! They are not asking for much— they never do; they do not want to be cocoons in a cradle-to-grave web of security (at least they do not ask for it). They want relief from worries about what would happen if they got sick. How will we see our children through their education? Will my job be there tomorrow? Is my family protected when I'm away? Could we afford to have another child? This is the burden they want Utopia to free its people of. For an affluent society, it seems like a small thing.

The People Are Nice in Utopia

America is the land, so it is said, of superficial human relation-ships;[2] it is where "human engineering and the science of social relations flourish; it is where psychoanalytical theory is translated into a science of interpersonal relations.[3] And all this, perhaps, is at the cost of deep, permanent, visceral friendships that have noth-ing to do with good "human relations." No doubt this is a prod-uct, in part of social mobility and a transient way of life—as well as of other things, but it may contribute to the American version of a more general Western industrial malaise. Individualism, what might be called "emotional autarchy," and loss of identity through loss of community and group anchorage are the burdens; the benefits have been less explored. In every society, of course, the conduct of human relations is a crucial matter for convention and regulation. How, then, out of the American milieu, out of the bourgeois Hilltop development on the outskirts of Eastport, do these men imagine that men behave toward one another in Utopia?

They stress "harmony," but not depth or warmth; the lack of disagreement, but not real mutual understanding; the avoidance of injustice, wrongs, hatreds, but not the closeness of companion-ship, not the solidarity of mutual trust, not the positive sense of love. This is the good human relations that they already taste, the one necessary, often, in a melting pot where language, culture, and age-old ethnic loyalties form rifts beneath a surface where it is dangerous to tread. Thus Woodside momentarily imagines a situation where "everything is going on fairly smooth for every-body," but he doubts whether this is possible in view of human differences; O'Hara says, in the fuller explanation, "I mean a place where people can get along with one another and not have much trouble." This, he says, would be facilitated if people were spread out more—"I wouldn't want to see it too crowded." John-son, a friendly man, goes somewhat further; he wants "friendly neighbors, close neighbors and friendly—with land between the homes, you know?" And how would these landed neighbors be-have? "Well, in my mind, they'd all behave nice." But, like Wood-

2. See Kurt Lewin, *Resolving Social Conflicts* (New York: Harper, 1948), pp. 1–31.
3. See Harry Stack Sullivan, *The Interpersonal Theory of Psychiatry* (New York: Norton, 1953).

side, at this point he gets cold feet: "I imagine," he says, "that's a thing that would never be." Sokolsky, too, explains the behavior of the Utopians with the same word "nice": "I think they would be very nice." McNamara explains a little more, "Of course, Utopia would be where everyone would get along fine, and no one would be jealous of anyone else's success or health or wealth or whatever they have." And just at this point, like Johnson and Sokolsky, McNamara withdraws. "But, of course, it's quite impossible," he adds, as though he were caught in some guilty act.

There is a tension in this discussion between, on the one hand, the concept of harmony, consensus, and order as somehow closer to "perfection" and, on the other hand, the support of a variety of opinions, choice, and pluralism with their implied conflict and disorder. As we have seen, Woodside rejects the perfect society because of its enforced consensus, but he also argues that "differences would lead you into either being angry or hateful to one another, and that usually leads to trouble." Others, too, show this confusion. Part of the problem is a confusion among concepts: a confounding of consensus with homogeneity, good human relations with conformity, niceness with sameness. The ideas of conflict within a framework of agreement, of loyal opposition, and of differences that enrich but do not enrage, somehow have not been brought to the level of conscious thought in this stratum of Eastport. In a way, they live the idea, but they would live it better if they saw the possibilities more clearly.

Some Utopias are restricted to a chosen people; they proceed on the assumption that if one could only cast out the devils in society the remainder would dwell in peace and harmony. Rapuano, as we noted above, says that his paradise island would be like that, for if he finds that a member of the Council there "happens to be . . . a radical, the first thing you do is to just grab him bodily and just eliminate him." Others, however, see Utopia as having "a bad apple" here and there, but they do not propose to eliminate them—rather they tolerate them, find a place for them. And tolerance, of this quality, it may be observed, is easier where personal relations are friendly but independent. Men who are treated only at arms' length can tolerate one another's defects more easily than they can in a more intimate relation.

Some useful functions of utopian thinking in an open society are to clarify goals for the society, to present a contrast between what is and what might be, to set standards for behavior and thought that are always just a little out of reach. Utopian thinking fails when it degenerates into moral homilies out of Sunday school, pictures of life drawn from ladies' magazines, or when it merely writes into a proposed social order a few of the highly personal desires an individual has sheltered in his own bosom. It fails of these functions when the Utopia is a vague prayer for relief, or a cloudy image of nice people in nice homes doing nice things. How could such a loosely drawn sketch provide the contrast between the present and a possible future necessary for guidance? On these grounds it must be said that the utopian thinking of the common man in Eastport does not serve society as it should. But then, he has no purposes developed and exchanged with others, no common goals whose pleasures are increased by being shared; he has no sense of a future beyond his own generation.

But there is another side, too; for the utopianism of Proudhon and the anarchists, of Robert Owen's community movement, of the Brook Farm experiments, of Upton Sinclair's End Poverty in California efforts have, more than once, distracted reform from the mainstream, sacrificed real gain now for illusory promises of greater gain tomorrow, and generally frustrated men of equal vision but greater practicality. It was Marx's and Lenin's rejection of utopian socialism that made their movement so strong, even in the early days.

So society loses the virtues of a clearer argument over goals, a clearer picture of present practice contrasted to other possibilities. But it gains stability.

PART TWO

o o o o o o o o o o o o o o o

The Sources of an Ideology

How shall we account for ideological stability and change? In the last chapter of this Part (Chapter 25), I suggest a modest paradigm to assist in accounting for ideological change:

> For any society: an *existential base* creating certain *common experiences* interpreted through certain *cultural premises* by men with certain *personal qualities* in the light of certain *social conflicts* produces certain *political ideologies.*

The data available through extended interviews illuminates some elements of this scheme only imperfectly. They tell us more of what the men see and experience than of what the community in which they live is really like; the operation of political, economic, educational, and religious institutions takes place largely out of their field of vision. Thus the existential base is slighted.

Something more is done with the experiences these men have. Here we report on their work experiences, their financial experiences, a few of their early family experiences, and try to show how these contribute to the shaping of the political mind of Eastport. Earlier, in the discussion of the sources of support for democracy, we examined some of the experiences these men have had with voluntary organizations; this has a bearing on the discussion in Section IV.

The most extensive treatment deals with the cultural premises of a political ideology, for the interview material is rich in this area. With some latitude I have used the terms "metaphysics," "ethics," and "epistemology" to classify this discussion, but there is another area, which I regret I did not explore: values.

The paradigm speaks of "personal qualities," for which one might substitute some more familiar phrase, such as Fromm's "social character" or Kardiner's "basic personality" or the common "national character." I wanted to avoid the controversies surrounding these terms—they are not central to my purpose. The discussion dealing with this subject (Section VI) is very brief, partly because I was somewhat dissatisfied with the inferences I might make, partly because I chose to develop the personality themes in connection with specific ideological topics. Certainly the discussion in Chapter 3 on ego strength and the discussion in Chapter 5 on "Characterological Reinforcement of the Democratic Faith," and the discussion in Chapter 11 on "a sense of homelessness" should be read into this analysis of personal qualities bearing on ideological change.

The treatment of the "social conflicts" in Eastport has no special chapter. The common men of Eastport disguise and repress and atomize their perceptions of conflict in society. With the aid of a community study, these conflicts might have been outlined; but it is significant that the mind of the common man reflects so little of this aspect of social life.

The accounting of ideological stability and change in Eastport is a partial account; it illuminates what is in the minds of the Eastport common man, leaving the real world somewhat in shadow.

□ □ □ □ □ □ □ □ □ □ □ □ □ □ □

Society and Experience

14

Eastport Social Patterns:
Opportunity and Community

> An individual in a given position of life who occupies himself
> with the concrete individual problems that he faces and then
> suddenly awakens to discover the fundamental conditions which
> determine his social and intellectual existence . . . is inevitably
> driven beyond the narrow horizon of his own town and learns to
> understand himself as part of a national, and later of a world,
> situation.
>
> —KARL MANNHEIM, *Ideology and Utopia,* p. 95

From the many social patterns of Eastport (the religious
pattern, the educational pattern, the pattern of politics, the industrial and commercial pattern), I have chosen two elements that
seem to me especially important in shaping the experiences of the
Eastport common man and therefore important in forming his
ideologies. These elements have to do with (*A*) the nature of
economic opportunity and (*B*) the nature of community life.

A
OPPORTUNITY

A man's economic life modifies his ideology, and of the ingredients of that life the opportunity to earn what he considers to
be a decent living is probably the most important. Beyond that,
the opportunity to increase his earnings (and status) from time to

time counts substantially in framing a social outlook. Using opportunity in these two senses, abundance and improvement, we ask how does economic opportunity in Eastport affect the experiences and the social outlook of the common man?

Abundance

The median income in 1949 and again in 1960 was slightly lower in Eastport than in comparable cities outside the South. The rate of unemployment hovered just under 6 per cent through most of this period, rising during the 1957–1958 recession to over 9 per cent. (A doubling of the Negro population in Eastport during this period probably meant that the incidence of unemploymen did not hit the white common man so hard, accounting for the fact that only two or three of our sample said they had been unemployed since the war.) But in spite of the slightly lower than (national) average wage rates and the low chronic, if selective, unemployment, Eastport was regarded by most Eastportians as having good times during this period. No major industries left town or closed down; rather, new government contracts caused an expansion of several of the larger employers. Memories of the thirties formed a contrasting background against which the almost full employment of the fifties seemed more than satisfactory. Both objectively and subjectively, the Eastport men shared in the national prosperity, the national abundance.

Escalation

Like the rest of America, Eastport is "leveling up"; the men of Eastport are on an escalator. Consider the comparisons in Table II between the situation at the beginning of the last decade and at its end.

TABLE II

	1949 or 1950	1960
Median income (constant dollars)	$2,714.0*	$4,281
Per cent of families under	($2,000) 36.2*	($3,000) 16.6
Per cent of families over	($7,000) 6.4*	($10,000) 15.4
Per cent unemployed	5.8	5.6
Median school year of adult population	9.1	10.1
Per cent foreign-born	15.8	13.2
Per cent nonwhite	6.0	14.9

* 1949 figures.

The income figures here, which take account of the roughly 27 per cent rise in the consumers' price index between 1949 and 1960, present a graphic picture of this escalation. In deflated dollars, the median income of Eastport increased 58 per cent in these eleven years, which is considerable even considering that 1949 was not a good year and 1960 was. Moreover, in more or less constant dollar terms (actually there is an overcorrection), there are about half as many families at the very bottom (under $2,000 in 1949, under $3,000 in 1960) and in the upper brackets over ($7,000 in 1949, over $10,000 in 1960). From this evidence it seems probable not only that the whole curve has shifted upward but also that the shape has also somewhat changed its character. However that may be, it is clear that Eastport's common men were sharing an *increasing* abundance in the fifties.

Advancement

A person may improve his standard of living by participating in a general economic growth (escalation) or by individual advancement through promotion or finding a better job. There is a mixed feeling about the opportunities for individual advancement among the Eastport men. Some, like DeAngelo, feel that they might be made foremen someday, or, like Ferrera, feel that in a new job they will earn more money. But relatively few believe they will make a major advance, say, from working class to middle class, and many believe that they will advance chiefly through "business picking up" or an increase in wage rates for the same kind of work they do now. What are the objective community conditions providing a realistic basis for the expectations of these men and others like them?

In the absence of detailed information on the patterns of economic opportunity in Eastport, I have constructed a rough index of the possibilities for advancement from each $1,000-income bracket to the next. It is somewhat arbitrary in three respects: it uses $1,000-income brackets (where, if we had the information, some relative scale would be better); it is based on the assumption that the total distribution of income does not change patterns during the period in question (whereas we suspect that it has become more equalitarian, as noted above); and it ignores dual job holding. Nevertheless it gives us a clue to the objective conditions for advancement facing these men. The central idea is that, if we regard reported incomes as attaching not to individuals but rather to roles or jobs or positions in the income structure, we shall then have a kind of "table of organization" for positions in that society. Taking this point of view, however rough it may be, we may estimate for each income level the number of total "jobs" on the income level just above them. The ratio between the number of "jobs" on level *A* and men on level *B* forms an *opportunity ratio:* if there are half as many "jobs" in the $2,000–$2,999 bracket as there are in the $1,000–$1,999 bracket, the opportunity ratio for the $1,000–$1,999 level is .50. These data are presented in Table III, and are shown graphically in Figure 1:

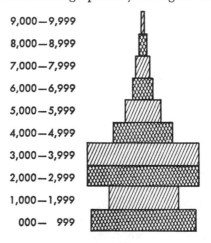

TABLE III

NUMBER OF FAMILIES IN EACH $1,000 BRACKET, EASTPORT, 1949

Income Bracket	Number of Families	Opportunity Ratio
Less than $1,000	9,470	0.66 *
$1,000–$1,999	6,275	1.60
$2,000–$2,999	10,245	1.00
$3,000–$3,999	10,295	0.53
$4,000–$4,999	5,470	0.61
$5,000–$5,999	3,340	0.53
$6,000–$6,999	1,775	0.57 †
$7,000–$7,999	1,035 †	0.57 †
$8,000–$8,999	605 †	0.5 7†
$9,000–$9,999	355 †	

NOTE: These figures represent estimates based on a 20 per cent sample of each census tract in 1949. We have adjusted the figures by eliminating the seventeenth census tract, which contained chiefly Jay College and its student body. Thus these are not exactly the figures reported in the *1950 Population Census Report.*

* This figure is distorted by the fact that a high proportion of 6,900 persons sixty-five years of age and over are included in the "less than $1,000" bracket. Since these persons are unlikely to be in the labor market, the opportunity ratio is much higher than this.

† These figures are based on an attempt to fit a constant rate of change over three brackets reported as a lump sum $7,000–$9,999. The number of men (jobs) allocated in this way is 1,995.

A glance at this figure and these data show us that the opportunity ratios in two of the lowest brackets are relatively large (for example, 1.00 or more). This would almost certainly be true of those in the under-$1,000 bracket, in spite of the lower opportunity ratio, because this bracket includes a large number of the 6,900 people who are sixty-five years of age or older, and some students as well. Thus those seeking advancement in this bracket might find the actual opportunities facing them very favorable. From that point on, the opportunity ratios decrease somewhat, although they remain fairly constant near the one-half ratio for the remainder of the series. (The last three are similar to one another because of the extrapolation procedure used.)

Within the sight line of these men, within the range of incomes people they know might earn, or, for some, within the range of their own maximum expectation, there is, at each $1,000-income bracket, a better than half "chance" that there would be an opening developing somewhere in the next higher $1,000 income bracket, as men in the higher bracket died or moved away or were themselves promoted. This permits a realistic expectation of incremental mobility; it permits men to look forward to advancement as they grow older. About eight of the men, by and large the younger ones, have this expectation.

Opportunity and Ideology

Almost all observers of the American scene have remarked on the American assumption that there will always be "enough." Some have said it accounts for the American's generous disposition of money, once he has earned it. Others have noted how this has freed him to experiment with his life, try something new, pull up stakes, leaving in each case some little area of security for an unknown venture.[1] David Potter, most notably, has explored the ways in which this assurance of a little more than enough has shaped American character and values.[2] This, he says, is the real significance of Turner's frontier—the feeling that there was more "out there." America is a land of plenty where one need not fight with neighbors for a limited supply. Moreover, the provision of abundance has made it possible for democracy to make good on

1. See, for example, Harold J. Laski, *The American Democracy* (New York: Viking, 1948), p. 35; James Bryce, *The American Commonwealth* (New York: Macmillan, 1910), II, 814.
2. David Potter, *People of Plenty: Economic Abundance and the American Character* (Chicago: University of Chicago Press, 1954).

its claims to provide opportunity. At the base of Almond's findings that Americans are more likely than the English or the Germans or the Italians or the Mexicans to say that "people can be trusted" may rest on economic abundance.[3] The idea that there is enough work to go around helps to explain why the Anglo-American production teams found that American crews worked at a brisker pace, erecting almost twice as much steel in a day as their British "competitors." The British never wanted to see a job finished because they feared there would not be another one.[4]

The social outlook of Eastport is saturated with the influence of the opportunity (abundance, escalation, advancement) that characterizes life in that city. It makes it possible and desirable to focus upon the near future when anticipations will be realized; these men do not need to live in the present, as the underprivileged of the London slums are said to do, or in an afterlife, or in a millennial world future. They can afford to be tolerant of economic and political opponents because they are not threatened with extinction; they are confident of provender and shelter no matter what happens. The risks of politics, like its stakes, are diminished; politics becomes less important. James Harrington argued that private landed property was essential for freedom—otherwise no one would criticize the Crown. In the assurance of a source of income, of work, there is something of the same foundation for free talk, free criticism, free grumbling. But the very fact that there is this foundation keeps the grumbling from curdling and embittering and alienating.

Opportunity helps men to achieve independence; it loosens social bonds; it *contributes to social-identity diffusion*. The poor, of course, know that they are poor and know that they belong to the working class. They are not involved in that struggle we see among about half of the men as to whether or not they are working class or middle class. But more than that, the poor are poorly educated because in their homes children are needed for their economic assistance. This means that, if they are the children of immigrants they remain "ethnicized," for education is the great assimilator. Reinforcement of the ethnic ties solidifies bonds that give a man a strong reference group, a strong social identity. Poverty makes for interdependence within a family; cousins, brothers-

3. A forthcoming study of socialization in five countries.
4. Anglo-American Council on Productivity, *Building* (New York and London, 1950).

in-law, uncles are required to help each other for mutual survival. This makes family a source of identification. Among the younger men in Eastport, this family identification is weaker than among the older men. In these many ways opportunity diffuses the social identities of men. This is the price of bourgeoisification.

Within this framework of opportunity, escalation has a special influence. Both Scheler and Mannheim believe that "rising" classes are prospective in their thinking; [5] it should be true, and it is true, in the limited sense we have suggested, that Eastport does look forward to better times in the future. But, since there is no evidence that the rich have less of a future than have the poor (indeed, more men are in those brackets that might be called "rich" than ever before), it comes not as a "counterconcept," not contrasted to retrospective golden-age thinking, but as a communitywide shared vision of mutual gain and even mutual assistance. As such, this concept of a "rising community" in which all may participate is totally different from the rising class, seen in the "seesaw" model of status that the Marxian mind produces, where if one side goes up the other goes down.

There is another point to be made on this escalation effect. It was the case, as observed elsewhere, that the Eastport men tended to confuse, or at least not to distinguish between, a rising standard of living based upon promotion and the rising standard of living based upon the escalation effect. This means, quite simply, that they tend to assume that their escalation is a product of something creditable to themselves, just as the unemployed man in a depression thinks he is to blame and eventually believes himself to be a rather worthless article. Owing to this confusion, itself a part of the firmly founded belief that a man is responsible for whatever happens to himself, the escalation of his standard of living seems to enhance his self-esteem.

The expectation of rising to foreman, increasing the civil service rating a notch, becoming a "setup man" rather than an operative, is reasonably plausible in Eastport, given the opportunity ratios in the income brackets we are dealing with. In general this scope for incremental mobility tends to discourage elitist thinking or snobbishness. The higher the opportunity ratios, from

5. Karl Mannheim, *Ideology and Utopia* (New York: Harcourt, Brace, 1949), p. 212; Max Scheler, *Die Wissenformen und die Gesellschaft*, p. 201, quoted in Werner Stark, *The Sociology of Knowledge* (New York, The Free Press of Glencoe, 1958), p. 77.

level to level, the lower will be the incentive to think of oneself as belonging to a class of people who are somehow "special." Under these circumstances, too, one is more likely to know others who are mobile in either direction, men whose fathers were day laborers and men who fathers were barbers, and some whose fathers were small businessmen. The middle stratum will have a perspective on life enlarged by the variety of this passing parade. If passage is relatively easy (an opportunity ratio of, say, more than 0.33), the sense of desperation over "falling" in income or status is minimized. The panic over losing a position may be somewhat less. By lowering the frustration rate, a structure of this kind lowers the need for projective aggressive behavior. Under these circumstances they need not blame; they can afford to believe that people can be trusted; freedom is less dangerous, equality less urgent, democracy more plausible.

B

COMMUNITY OR DEMOCRACY?

The loss of a sense of community in American cities, and therefore in the places where most Americans live, has been widely mourned as destructive of personality and social health.[6] I have spoken of this earlier, in the discussion on homelessness, and will again in the analysis of localism in Eastport, but here I wish to search the Eastport setting more insistently for the elements that make a genuine community in this present meaning of the term. Its meaning is similar to Tönnies' *Gemeinschaft;* it includes six elements.[7] First, in a "community" of this kind human relationships are intimate, enduring, based on a clear understanding of where each of the persons stands in the society. Second, a man's "worth" is estimated according to *who* he is, not *what* he has done—at least in the general estimate these two ingredients are emphasized this way. In this sense, status is ascriptive, not achieved. Third, roles are specific and consonant one with another. A man does not find his duties in one role conflicting with

6. This is one of the themes of a very rich literature on the effects of the city on the individuals who live in it. Among others, the following authors' works illuminate the problem: E. W. Burgess, Lewis Mumford, R. E. Park, S. A. Queen, Louis Wirth, and H. W. Zorbaugh. Indeed, while the sociology of knowledge has drawn attention to the class basis of social perspectives, these authors have done even more to show the urban ecological basis of a social outlook.

7. Compare Talcott Parsons, *The Social System* (New York: The Free Press of Glencoe, 1951), pp. 48–67.

the duties that devolve upon him from another role. Fourth, the members of a community are relatively immobile; neither in their physical nor in their social movements do they go far from their origins. Fifth, the culture of the community is relatively homogeneous; it must be so if roles are not to conflict or human relations to lose their intimacy. Sixth, the moral custodians of a community, family and church, are strong, their code is clear, their injunctions well internalized. This is a picture of James Whitcomb Riley's Hoosier village, of Thornton Wilder's *Our Town*, and of Eastport a hundred years ago.

Community in Eastport

Of the human relations of a metropolis, Louis Wirth says that they are limited to "externals," a fact that permits people of very different beliefs and customs to have social commerce.[8] Robert Park speaks of the "social distance" between individuals in urban areas.[9] No doubt metropolitanism does this to people, but American cities may be worse than others, for it is common for the European visitor, no stranger to cities himself, to mourn over the lack of intimate, enduring, social ties he knew on the Continent. On several occasions I have observed the "individualism" of the Eastport men, their use of "I" instead of "we," their fear of being too closely identified with any particular social group, their assumption of responsibility for their own lives and families, but not for those of others. Their life patterns daily reinforce these themes by fractioning their social life: their family life and work life are separated; they do not live in the neighborhood in which they grew up, and thus there is some spatial distance between them and childhood friends; they do not share their parents' friends; the men they meet at church (and a number say they make friends at church), are not the ones they go bowling with. In short, in Eastport, as in American cities everywhere, men have partial, external, and somewhat distant human relations with one another.

This is sometimes acknowledged and even approved by the residents of this noncommunity. Two men who were the pillars of liberal democracy had this to say: "A friend," said Flynn, the

---

8. Louis Wirth, *The Ghetto* (Chicago: University of Chicago Press, 1929), pp. 283–284.
9. Robert Park, "The Concept of Social Distance," *Sociology and Social Research,* 8 (1924), pp. 339–344.

president of the Hilltop Council, would be "a person who may be interested in the same subject and think pretty much along the same lines. . . . [But] I don't like friendships which bring people too closely together too frequently." And McNamara, a book-keeper, a "liberal," and a friendly man, says, "I don't believe in becoming too entangled in other people's affairs." (How different these were from the two politically alienated men who were searching for a kind of intimacy and support they could not easily find!)

Eastport life produces a situation where a man must handle several social roles that are not harmonized by a common culture, but may be in conflict with one another. Partly this is the problem of the division of labor; partly it is the problem of living a family life divorced from a work life. The strain imposed on the Eastport men by their need to "earn more" and at the same time to take a hand in the rearing of children was seen in their occasional feelings that they were not particularly good at either.

Eastport life is mobile; it requires of each man an adjustment to changing physical and social environments. One out of ten of all Eastport residents changed living quarters between 1949 and 1950. Four years after the interviews took place, eight of the fifteen men had moved. Attachment to place, to people, to rituals of living must be flexible, loose.

Eastport is heterodox. Within "the ghetto" or in "Little Italy," or in the heart of the Negro ward, there may be some homo-geneity, some reinforcement of a common core of values and cultural viewpoints. But Eastport, like many American cities is de-segregating. The Italian community, once concentrated in a few wards across the tracks, although still strong in these areas, is now much more widely dispersed. In the two census tracts with the highest median income, about 10 per cent of the population is foreign-born; in the two poorest (non-Negro) wards, where one would expect a much higher percentage, only about 18 and about 12 per cent of the population are foreign-born. In 1960, 15 per cent of Eastport was Negro, about double the proportion of 1950. (Roughly 30 per cent of the Hilltop population is Negro.)

For income as well as for ethnic distribution, there is both segregation and desegregation. A graphic frequency distribution of median income by census tracts shows most of the tracts, where most of the people live, stretched in a broad plain across the middle of the figure. Four-ninths of the tracts, inhabited by about two-thirds of the population, lie within a $500 range of the city median. Yet within each tract there are some wealthy as well as poor men; in the two poorest (non-Negro) tracts between 1 and 3 per cent of the families were (1949) living on $10,000 or more. (In the two richest tracts 20 and 14 per cent were in this bracket.) Like the foreign-born and the Negroes, the rich and the poor are both concentrated and dispersed. Hilltop shares a supermarket where the people of Stern Terrace, the poor man's public housing development, shop. It is located in the same parish, that is, church and parochial-school district, in which the prosperous inhabitants of the highest-income tracts live. In the course of a day Hilltoppers meet both rich and poor. It is true that the relations of these men to their poorer and richer neighbors are merely external and marked by social distance; nevertheless, they get a glimpse of another way of life that sometimes contrasts in important ways (as they see it) to their own. The reassurance of a "given" way of living is eroded by such contacts in such a milieu.

Eastport life tends to weaken the social institutions that provide the rules for moral behavior. This is particularly true of the family, whose functions have been taken over in part by school, guidance counselor, camp, youth organization, and so forth. It is also true at the adult level where the "established opinion" of a traditional community once served as a guide for moral judgment. Under these circumstances boys and men hear about many conflicting ways of evaluating things; their ears and eyes are tuned and focused to alternative ways of doing things, alternative codes and mores. The requirement of tolerance silences the church on many matters; its own diverse and heterogeneous membership makes bold pronouncements risky.

But one feature of the community structure that has a special bearing on Hilltop must be mentioned. There is a vast literature on the ecology of cities, locating the areas of homeless men, suicides, prostitution, mental breakdown, and so forth. By and large, the pathologies of personal and social disorganization occur in a patterned way, toward the center of the city, just off the downtown business district. Although modified by redevelopment, this was still substantially true of Eastport at the time of the interviews; but Hilltop, where these men lived, was on the fringes of the city, separated by empty space and a small wood from slum areas, red-light districts, flophouses, run-down tenements, and so forth. It encapsulated the bourgeois in these men and protected it from the bruising experiences of contact with disorganized areas of life.

Community and Ideology

There are those like Erich Fromm, William Kornhauser, and Sebastian De Grazia who argue that the loss of community, the *Gemeinschaft* society, and an integrated and coherent belief system have created malaise, anomie, and alienation.[10] Our findings and theory, on the other hand, suggest that it is the very absence of community that makes democracy possible. It is the failure to see the difference between a city state and a nation state that has given plausibility to this argument for community. Briefly, and for the sake of emphasis, we shall state the Eastport case one-sidedly and bluntly.

Community sentiments involve close and enduring loyalties of place and people; but politics based on friends and neighbors and loyalties to local parties make national, rational, and flexible politics more difficult.

Community encourages immobility; it makes it hard for men to achieve status and wealth on the basis of their merits, and this, in turn, undercuts much of the philosophy of a democratic system.

Community makes for traditionalistic ways, for at the very core of the community idea is the sentimental attachment to the conventions and mores of a beloved place; but democracy is based upon the widespread distribution of questioning and criticism. Without this criticism it moves too slowly to meet and deal with problems as they arise.

Community reinforces and encapsulates a moral code; it raises moral tension; it makes heterodoxy a more serious crime; but democracy, as we shall see, thrives on low moral tension where the question of blame is subordinated to understanding.

Community personalizes issues and events and explanations because familiar names and characters inevitably become associated with everything that happens. The ties to the people involved, who are known not merely as "flat" actors on a stage but in their more rounded wholeness, make the impersonal explanations necessary to democratic usages more difficult.

10. See Erich Fromm, *The Sane Society* (New York: Rinehart, 1955); William Kornhauser, *The Politics of Mass Society* (New York: The Free Press of Glencoe, 1959); Sebastian De Grazia, *The Political Community: A Study of Anomie* (Chicago: University of Chicago Press, 1948).

Community generates myth, lore, heroes, sagas, epics; these become embedded in the belief system and value system; men then employ them in their thinking, interpret current events in the light of these analogies. But modern democracy is more efficient in meeting the demands made upon it when events are interpreted by the common man, as well as by the elite, in the cold light of a rational model, where cause-and-effect chains are seen, so far as possible, with reduced sentiment and poetry. At least it meets some of the demands better in this style.

Community makes for solidary relationships among men. That is its great virtue. But democracy works best where men are relatively more free to combine and recombine in a flexible fashion and where, as in Eastport, each is a free-standing unit. Those seeking "intimacy" seek totalitarianism; nor is this a chance relationship.

In a village setting, a city-state, it is possible to combine these qualities of community with a kind of democracy, the town-meeting kind, or its extended versions. Where more than one of these communities must work together, not as a federation but as a part of a sovereign national unit, the possibility disappears, for in this larger, impersonal unit a whole new order of requirements suddenly emerges. Then, politics assumes many of the characteristics of the marketplace; men are divorced from their leaders, exposed to conflicting views, burdened with responsibilities for decisions with remote consequences, uncertain of their reference groups, mobile, and therefore often transient. The men who work the system must shed the qualities of the community man and assume the lonely role of the independent, isolated individual. In the nation-state some identity diffusion and a touch of anomie is necessary for democracy to survive.

15

Work Life in Metropolis:
The Reshaping of Democratic Man

The most important effect of the frontier has been in the promotion of democracy here and in Europe. . . . The frontier is productive of individualism . . . [and] frontier individualism has from the beginning promoted democracy.
> —FREDERICK JACKSON TURNER, "The Significance of the Frontier in American History," in *The Frontier in American History,* p. 30

Among contemporary men will there come to prevail, or even to flourish, what may be called The Cheerful Robot? . . . The society in which this man, this cheerful robot, flourishes is the antithesis of the free society—or in the literal and plain meaning of the word, of a democratic society.
> —C. WRIGHT MILLS, "On Reason and Freedom," in Maurice Stein and others, eds., *Identity and Anxiety,* pp. 115, 116

A
WORK LIFE AND IDEOLOGY

What men learn as they work for a living reaches far beyond their occupational interests; they learn a style of life, a manner of dealing with others, a habit of subordination or assertion. Jefferson's preference for a polity based on agriculture stemmed from his belief that the way of life of the small farmer promoted the stability of mind and the independent outlook that Jefferson thought were necessary to sustain democratic institutions. Speaking of the general way of life on the frontier, Frederick Jackson Turner says:

> The tendency is anti-social. It produces antipathy to control, and particularly to any direct control . . . the democracy born of free land [is] strong in selfishness and individualism, intolerant of administrative experience and education, and pressing individual liberty beyond its proper bounds. . . . That coarseness and strength combined with acuteness and inquisitiveness; that practical, inventive turn of mind, quick to find expedients; that masterful grasp of material things, lacking in the artistic but powerful to effect great ends; that restless, nervous energy; that dominant individualism, working for good and evil, and withal that buoyancy and exuberance which comes with freedom—these are the traits of the frontier, or traits called out elsewhere because of the existence of the frontier.[1]

It is with a sinking heart that one contrasts to this happy view the picture that has been graphically drawn of the man on the job today. Max Lerner says of the industrial workman,

> Life on "the job" tends to be a joyless life, squeezed dry of any zest in work. On most jobs the frame of the day is set by the time clock. On the assembly line especially, as in the auto factory, time is the master. . . . The tensions on his [the worker's] nervous system are great, but while he must concentrate on his work he does not become absorbed with it, since neither his creative faculties nor his imagination are caught.[2]

J. J. Gillespie says of the industrial worker.

> Work is becoming more repetitive and thoughtless as the planners, the micromotionists, and the scientific managers further strip the worker of his right to think and move freely. Life is being denied; need to control, creativeness, curiosity, and independent thought are being baulked, and the result, the inevitable result, is flight or fight on the part of the worker, apathy or destructiveness, psychic regression.[3]

1. Frederick Jackson Turner, "The Significance of the Frontier in American History"; the original 1893 paper reprinted in Turner's *The Frontier in American History* (New York: Holt, 1920), pp. 30, 32, 37.
2. Max Lerner, *America as a Civilization: Life and Thought in the United States Today* (New York: Simon and Schuster, 1957), p. 241.
3. J. J. Gillespie, *Free Expression in Industry*, quoted in Erich Fromm, *The Sane Society* (New York: Rinehart, 1955), p. 125.

And to an elaboration of this view, Erich Fromm comments, "Just as work has become alienated, the expression of the will of the voter in modern democracy is an alienated expression." [4] There is a substantial chorus of voices speaking these sad thoughts.[5] What are the terms of this indictment?

Industrialization and Democratic Skills and Values

It takes men with certain qualities to make democratic institutions function effectively. These institutions must be operated by men who can share power, not subordinating themselves uncritically nor rebelling against the authority of others, not seeking exclusive power for themselves. But, it is said, the discipline of modern industry does not teach workmen to share power; rather they learn, as Gillespie says, subordination in minute detail; they learn to accept goals set for them by others, goals they have no hand in framing; they learn that management is power and that management is not responsible to the constituency of men who work for it.

Democracy, in a unique way, requires the ordinary man to develop skills of judgment and criticism of leaders. These must be responsible, moderate, sensible; that is, they must fall within the bounds of a commonly accepted framework of values. Such skills in judgment and criticism, like other skills, come only with practice and experience. But modern industrial life, it is said, does not provide opportunities for such criticism; it is hierarchical in its command, like an army; decisions are often made "in the front office" or in a headquarters city completely out of reach of the men affected; except on trivial matters their views are not solicited. They are not learning democratic skills on the job.

There are many tasks in a democracy that are left to private initiative; indeed, democracy can function properly only if men organize to petition for the redress of grievances, and, failing redress, organize to defeat the men who failed them. But, it is said, work life in industry discourages initiative, stamps out the very

4. Erich Fromm, *op. cit.,* p. 184.

5. See, for example, Georges Friedmann, *Industrial Society* (New York: The Free Press of Glencoe, 1955); James C. Worthy, "Organizational Structure and Employee Morale," *American Sociological Review,* 15 (1950), p. 175. But the more serious industrial sociologists are skeptical. See the excellent summary of recent research by Robert Blauner, "Work Satisfaction and Industrial Trends in Modern Society," in Walter Galenson and S. M. Lipset, eds., *Labor and Trade Unionism* (New York: Wiley, 1960), pp. 339–360.

impulse to change, and produces in its place, as Mills says, "cheerful robots."

Democracy implies a capacity for group effort where coordination and cohesion come from forces within a group, not from the power or authority of the leader. In the ward committee, the housing development council, the union membership committee, and so forth, the tasks of democracy are done only when mutually harmonious, cohesive, and task-oriented personal relations are established. But, it is said, modern industrial life atomizes work life; individuals who work in factories do not work cooperatively but rather in isolation of others, or, perhaps, even in competitive antagonism toward others.

Underlying some of these qualities of initiative, judgment, capacity to share power, effective and harmonious relations with others, making them psychologically possible, is the more fundamental quality of self-respect, self-esteem. Men who think themselves worthy of attention will petition for change, while others will not—perhaps raging privately instead. Men with self-respect can engage in harmonious and *reciprocal* relations with others, while those who do not respect themselves must subordinate themselves with occasional outbursts of protest. Men must respect their own judgment before they exercise initiative or agree to share power. But, it is said, in several ways modern industrial life denigrates the worker so that he cannot respect himself. For one thing, as Marx claimed, he loses the opportunities for respect that come with the creation of a finished product, for his contribution is likely to be only a small, segmented part of a finished product. The satisfactions of good workmanship and creativity are constricted by the narrow discretion and skill afforded in some industrial work. The loss of control over his own movements, the management of his work life by others, the treatment of him as a machine or a soulless unit is said to dehumanize the man and to reduce his own sense of individuality and worth.

The indictment has a plausibility to it that is disconcerting; it must be evaluated in detail. But the indictment rests primarily upon evidence from the work life of the machine tender in a factory, and more especially, the mechanically paced assembly-line worker.[6] It would be appropriate to the case to separate such posi-

6. See Ely Chinoy, *Automobile Workers and the American Dream* (Garden City, N.Y.: Random House, 1955); Charles R. Walker and Robert H. Guest, *Man on the Assembly Line* (Cambridge: Harvard University Press, 1952).

tions from others in appraising the likely effect of work life upon democratic attitudes. There are four men in the Eastport group who tend stationary machines all day, one of them on an assembly-line basis. A national sample of a comparable urban income group would not show a higher proportion of machine tenders or of assembly-line workers. Only 9.6 per cent of the total work force are manufacturing "operatives and kindred workers," and of this a much smaller group work on assembly lines.[7] Even in the highly mechanized automobile industry (including all those involved in the manufacture, sales, repair, and servicing of automobiles), where assembly lines have reached their greatest use, "assembly line workers make up less than 5 per cent of all workers in this complex."[8] But, of course, if roughly representative, our sample is small; still, looking separately at this group of four Eastport machine tenders and the other ten (we omit the overeducated Farrel), we may fairly appraise the work experiences they have affecting three kinds of social attitudes: (1) their attitudes toward authority, (2) their attitudes and working relationships with their shop colleagues, and their sense of mutuality and engagement with others more generally, and (3) their attitudes toward themselves, their self-image and self-esteem as these are fashioned by the work situation.

B
EXPERIENCE WITH AUTHORITY

The four men who tended machines (Costa, DeAngelo, Dempsey, Sokolsky) had diverse relationships with their immediate superiors, their bosses and shop managers; it is not easy to characterize even these four men, let alone the ten others we shall contrast with them. It is certainly a fact that Dempsey's relations with management are remote, emotionally thin, passive. Asked how he gets along with his boss he says: "Well, half and half. Sometimes I disagree with him and other times I might agree with him. But I will never argue with him, because I figure if he thinks it should be that way, well, then, that's it. Then, if he wants to let it run that way, it's all right with me." There is no initiative; there may be counterassertion—but no rebellion;

7. U.S. Bureau of the Census, *United States Census of Population: 1950, U.S. Summary* (Washington, D.C., 1953), Table 124.
8. Robert Blauner, "Work Satisfaction . . . ," in *op. cit.,* p. 354.

Dempsey says his boss "knows his business . . . he never gets sarcastic." Costa, the assembly-line worker, hates the company for its time-and-motion studies and "cutthroat" atmosphere. Management is impersonal, cold, ruthless, efficient. There is no union or shop committee. He is under constant pressure and has minimum freedom; he would like to leave. What he is learning about authority relations is that all the power is on one side, that all the sanctions are in the hands of the leaders, and that influence is out of reach.

But now contrast these two situations with those of Sokolsky and DeAngelo, who also tend machines. Sokolsky makes parts for bicycle pedals; he has been doing it for fourteen years, and he hates his job. But his brother-in-law is the supervisor of his section, and this provides him with a little leverage, a little protection. When his bad leg is "acting up" he can stay home for a day and nothing happens to him. He admires his brother-in-law: "He's a man that can handle men. He could talk to a man and make him feel good." So he doesn't leave and he doesn't even accept a better job that might change this relationship. DeAngelo is on the margin of this machine-tending group; his machine is a complicated one and his position as a skilled operator gives him a little better pay than the others. His relations with his supervisors are relaxed: "It's an easy place to work in, y'know what I mean? The people who run it, they're easygoing. We don't have any special time to smoke or have coffee—we do that any time we want; we go down to the locker room. Of course, on my job I'm responsible for it, so, y'know, I have to be a little more on the ball than the other guys." But even more important is the fact that DeAngelo is shop steward; he bargains with the company and feels that the company has been more than fair. He must take up grievances the men bring to him, and sometimes in protecting a fellow worker he is forced secretly to agree that the man is a laggard employee and should be penalized. His relationship involves mutuality and discretion, bargaining with power at his back.

Now consider the situation of the others, also workers in an industrial civilization, also sometimes removed from the final product of their work, also subject to precise hours and rigid discipline. It will be recalled that there are two maintenance men in this group; working in factories, they are closer to the machine tenders and may be expected to have the relations with their su-

periors most similar to those pictured in the indictment. O'Hara
is one. How does he get along with his boss? "I have arguments
with him. I get along all right. I kid with him, and I think I can—
I can say more to him than a lot of them up there, because he
knows I kid a lot, and he'll give it to me. He's given me a kick
in the rear and more than once—just kidding, like, and I never
got mad about it where somebody else would. I remember one
time we were up there and . . . [he got his finger hit by a ham-
mer] and I laughed at him. I suppose he got hot. But I don't think
he's the right man for the boss. . . . The shift foreman [some-
one else] is fair. He wouldn't go up and tell you, 'Well, you've
got to do this and you've got to do that.' He'd say 'Will you go
over and do this?' and you didn't mind doing it for him." O'Hara
has discretion in some things; he does a little electrical work even
though he isn't supposed to; he advises on the condition of the
cranes and takes responsibility for their state of repair. Even
though the foreman with whom he kids is "not the right man for
the boss" and is, in fact, the son of one of the executives, O'Hara
moves in synchronized harmony with a management whose interests he has adopted and who recognize in him a man of discretion
as well as a man of humor and spirit.

Johnson's experience is a little different; as a mechanic in the
electric generating plant in a firm where his father worked, he is
known by management as almost a member of the family—they
speak of him as a "chip off the old block." He finds it possible to
use discretion in his work, to make suggestions to management.
And yet, the truth is that he dislikes the subordinate position, the
idea of young college men being brought in over him, and particularly the sense that he has a rival who might be promoted
ahead of him. Authority, he finds, is not impersonal nor arbitrary,
or deaf to advice. He has been closely associated with the union
leaders in the plant; he does not need them for grievance procedure but he knows they are there. Still, he would like not to
be under any authority; he would rather "be doing something
on my own."

The others present a variety of pictures. Of the clerical workers, McNamara works under a treasurer and an assistant treasurer
in one office; he says: "They're both very easy to work for—very
easy. And they get along with each other well. It's about the best
job I ever had." Flynn works for a railroad supply house; he hates

the paper work and the routine, but has autonomy and is allowed discretion on the job. When Ruggiero was doing office work he kept demanding more and more work from his superiors, and was given more and more discretion.

Several men work out on jobs where there is some discretion and where their relations with their bosses are manifest in review procedures and periodic checkups. Three of these are Woodside, the railroad guard and auxiliary policeman; Kuchinsky, the roofer; and Sullivan, the truck driver. Woodside must decide what to do when he finds a drunken driver—contrary to regulations, he sometimes drives him home so he won't lose his license. He must decide whether to jail a drunken husband beating his wife—he often persuades the man's wife to drop the charges and let the husband go to the YMCA to sleep it off. He occasionally must defend these policies when they come to light, and he finds the sergeant or lieutenant at the desk reasonable, if there is no public disgrace. Kuchinsky has some differences with his boss. "I mean, we disagree on a lot of things; I mean a lot of things that I think are right and should be corrected. I mean, I brought it up more than once, but, ah, you know how people are; they just don't like to give in." Yet on the whole "I feel this fella's been doin' all right by me . . . this fella's got no pressure on top. I mean he leaves me alone. He'll set me on a job, and that's it." Sullivan had the experience of being unfairly accused of responsibility in an accident, and was suspended for a week. He went to the union, and demanded that they help him or else he would hire a lawyer; he went upstairs to management and presented his case, and won. Authority yielded to him.

What these illustrations reveal about the authority relationships of men's work life in an industrial community is its variety. But they reveal more. They reveal, first, that even in the monotonous machine-tending jobs there are avenues for special pleading, levers for exercising a little power: the brother-in-law a notch up the hierarchy, the union steward. In the second place, they suggest the new element in authority relations where the job involves some discretion, for here the advice of the man on the line is indispensable. He is not only an object to be ordered; he is also a person to be consulted. Although from the outside it appears that there is little discretion for workmen in industrial society, the closer one gets to it, the more important the decisions seem. And, in the third place, these glimpses into work life show the possibility of a humanized relationship between boss and man, which has several beneficial effects, as we shall see later.

But the authority relationships must also be seen in another light. They are role relationships limited to the work situation; they do not move over into the private areas of a man's life. None of their superiors know much about the home lives of the men (except for Johnson and, perhaps, McNamara). What goes on at the shop and what goes on at home are two different things. Metropolis affords the shelter of anonymity—a boon as well as a human cost. It would be a rare thing for one of these men to do as the salariat do, bring the boss home for dinner. They do not consider, as Babbitt considered, whether the bosses would like their homes, their wives, their ways of life. The workingman has a kind of privacy from authority that, if he becomes upwardly mobile, he will soon lose.

And, similarly, the bosses do not become models for the envy and imitation of the men; at least, if they do it is only in very muted ways. More than among the junior executives, work authority is divorced from fashion authority, diet authority, opinion authority. Here is a little autonomy in a world where it seems to be a shrinking quality.

To a surprising extent, these men have incorporated management goals in their own work goals. O'Hara is hurt by wasteful practices in his large manufacturing concern. DeAngelo argues that management has been too easy in its negotiation with his own union. Rapuano builds a supply empire with a lucrative outside business, but he must do this on his own time, and with no special income in it for him. There are the frictions, of course; Kuchinsky will not supervise other men unless he is paid as a supervisor; on his outside job Sokolsky gets careless in cleaning office buildings because he does not like the foreman. But there is a kind of identity with the firm that makes authority only partially an external force compelling men to serve ends they do not accept as their own. Industrial authority, in part—and I shall not stretch this too far—is incorporated within the men, and speaks to them of a common purpose.

The relationship of employer to employee has always been thought to center on the conflict over the division of the proceeds of business. But the relationship also includes the fact of payment of employees by employers. Looking at this part of the relationship, the *fact of payment*, and not the fact that something is with-held as profits, the men of Eastport do not see the industrial au-thority as their enemy (although the industrial restrictions are seen as the main hindrance to their freedom).

Not forgetting the bitterness of a Costa, the passiveness and affectless dependency of a Dempsey, the reaction to fears of favo-ritism of a Johnson, we must in all candor say that the authority relations marking the work life of these Eastport men teach them something of worth for a practicing democracy.

C
WORKING WITH OTHERS

Frederick Jackson Turner believed that the frontier's most important contribution to democratic life was the manner in which it taught a variety of individualism. By this he seems to have meant a kind of self-reliance and opposition to governmental controls of any kind. Living and working alone with his family, the frontiersman learned how to get along by himself. This doc-trine went into the thinking of a generation of scholars, becoming a part of the arsenal of Sumner, Burgess, and other latter-day con-servatives.[9] Of the historians, the Beards say, "Turner's theory of individualism and civilization either possessed a greater survival power or American historians were less alert than economists." [10] We have reversed the Turner argument, saying, in effect, that democracy works best where men have learned by intense life experiences to work cooperatively together, sharing power, able to keep personal frictions and competitive maneuvering within a framework bounded by group purpose. This is hardly new; in this area Tocqueville understood what Turner forgot.[11]

What do the men of Eastport learn about the modes of com-mon work? The four machine tenders learn something different from the others. Dempsey works on drill presses; he stands at the machine more or less in isolation; if anything goes wrong he calls in the adjuster: "We don't have time to visit, you might say.

9. See, for example, Sumner's essays on liberty in *Essays of William Graham Sumner*, edited by A. G. Keller and M. R. Davie (New Haven: Yale University Press, 1934), pp. 285–357; John W. Burgess, *The Reconciliation of Government and Liberty* (New York: Scribner's, 1915).

10. Charles A. and Mary R. Beard, *The American Spirit: A Study of the Idea of Civilization in the United States* (New York: Macmillan, 1942), p. 364.

11. Alexis de Tocqueville, *Democracy in America*, Phillips Bradley, ed. (New York: Knopf, 1945), pp. 288–330.

You can't leave your machine. That is, you could, to take care of yourself, but other than that, to go around visiting—no—they wouldn't allow that. You couldn't really blame them. It's steady and it keeps me occupied." What about lunchtime or any other free time, coming and going? "Well, the few I mingle with, I get along all right with. I don't—as I say, I'm by myself, mostly." The picture of isolation, partly because of personal constitution, partly because of the circumstances of the job, is a clear one.

But it is to Costa, the assembly-line worker at the Standard Manufacturing Company, to whom we must go to learn the most vivid lesson of the hardships of social relations in the modern factory. He says:

> You see, we work on an incentive system, and it's a case of cooperative effort, but it's not cooperative reward. There's people in particular jobs that earn their own incentive, but it's from these people that I get work that makes me earn my incentive. So when I see people take shortcuts and make it more difficult for me in order to make it easier for them, it's very antagonizing. It's one of the most cuthroat places I ever worked in. I mean there's no sense of cooperation whatsoever. Everybody's looking out for Number One, and it's hard for me to work under these conditions. That's one of the reasons that I hate Standard Manufacturing as much as I do. But it's the system they have there that makes people think this way. . . . I mean there has always been a little give in all the other places I have worked. Standard will spend $20 with a time-study engineer on your back to save two cents. Well, it's that kind of place. So, when you work in that kind of place, you see, everybody has the same idea—get as much as he can, and the hell with the other guy. With me it's different and that's why it has been a physical strain on me, and a mental strain to work under these conditions. I'd like to get out of there, but I hate to go someplace else and start all over again, which is what it entails for a fellow like me. I have to go and start at the bottom, and I just can't afford it. So I stay put. Of course, my wife has no knowledge of these things; it's bad enough that *I* have to think about it.

Costa learns in daily bitter lessons that it is a jungle world where cooperation is discouraged, where men have no share in a common life, where they are set to working at cross-purposes, where initiative is squeezed out of life.

Sokolsky seems to have a freer situation at the shop; he moves around a bit more, mentions the way the fellows there talk sex and politics and what he has to say in these discussions. He has neither the competitive disregard of other men's rights nor the isolation of Dempsey to contend with; he learns something about joint contributions to a common end, but his contribution is limited to what he can do at his machine, a router. DeAngelo's situation is most relaxed; as he says, with some exaggeration, he could go to the locker room for coffee "every fifteen minutes" if he wanted to. The picture is one of each associating with like-minded man, for him, those who don't drink and who like to talk about sports: "most of the time we hang around, mostly it's in the shop; uh, [pause] we live in all different parts of the city, y'know, and guys don't hang around or work around the clock." But there has been an active bowling competition. The shop is a social place for DeAngelo; the work is cooperative, but, of course, planned from above. DeAngelo, elected shop steward, works well with others and learns the arts of grass-roots leadership.

What of the others? There is strong evidence that the two maintenance men, O'Hara and Johnson, have worked out successful social relations with their associates, relations that facilitate the industrial work to be done. Johnson, for one thing, has been offered the position of union shop steward, but declined it; O'Hara offers extra assistance to both management and men in the maintenance of their machines; he is on their accident committee representing the men; he works at the canteen and meets others in a social setting; he is, so to speak, a "figure" on the company grounds. Both of these men learn on the job to combine work with social intercourse, duty and "kidding" in a way the informal machinery of democracy can use.

It is not much different with the office workers: the railroad supply man, the bookkeeper, the part-time post-office workers, the supply clerk, the salesman, all talk about their work life as a social experience in which each has duties intertwined with the duties of others; the mistakes or irresponsibility of one become the headaches of another; and so each adjusts his moves to make the other's work something less of a burden. In this stratum there is a little more initiative: the credit union, the bowling team, the appeal to congressmen of postal clerks, the joint activities voluntarily and cooperatively undertaken teach a new level of interpersonal social responsibility.

Reviewing these and other cases, one can only conclude that

the anonymity of metropolis, instead of arising from the fragmented and desiccated work life created by modern industrial
and commercial society, rather finds its antidote in the social life
of the office and the shop. This is, of course, not community in
the folk sense, or the *Gemeinschaft* sense; it is limited to certain
phases of life, limited to certain areas and times, not enduring
like the intergenerational linkages of the village, not intense as
those relationships are. There is, it is true, something anemic
about these relationships as close friendships, yet they are usually
the most satisfying the men have outside their families. But in
the more specific terms assigned to this discussion, the social relationships necessary to sustain a democracy, the picture is not so
dark as has been painted.

Specifically, I think, there are four lessons taught in these daily
experiences, lessons notably absent in the situation Costa and
Dempsey describe. First is the plain necessity to mask, if not to
unlearn, eccentric and irritating and selfish qualities. Kidding, so
useful to establishing a friendly rapport, can easily unsheath a
sharper edge and wound a man who offends group mores. Second,
they are learning something about the articulation of work—not
the common planning or the initiation of work projects, but the
way in which the work of one man fits into the task of another.
This is most vividly clear in the negative case where men do not
take pains to make their product meet the next person's needs.
This is the lesson of the industrial discipline: punctuality, attention to detail, avoidance of waste, responsible work even without
supervision. The mañana persuasion is too hurtful to the group;
it atrophies under this pressure. As a consequence the social articulation of a voluntaristic democratic society is improved; party,
electoral, and governmental machinery work better for this
reason.

Bringing men together in places of work provides the social
basis for common organization and action, as Marx said it would.
And, as Marx prophesied, some of this organization and action is
designed to force concessions from employers, to deliver the combined strength of the work force in bargaining with the management. But, as it turns out, this is only one, and sometimes not the
most important, of the organizational offshoots of the collective
work life men share together. For, as a third lesson in social relations learned by the men of Eastport in their work situations,

they learn to organize team sports, to organize and support credit unions, to form committees to supervise their canteens or coffee-shops; there are committees to make presentations upon retire-ment or to raise money for a shower; they serve on management committees to reduce accidents, allocate parking space, and so forth. And, more politically, those who work for the government organize committees of protest on postal work conditions, reduc-tions in force, removal of facilities to another area, and many other matters. Their work life may not teach them this directly, but by bringing them together and providing them with common interests it facilities it.

We have argued that Kuchinsky suffered a kind of curdling of the political mind because of his high political intake and low opportunity for discussion, low conversational rehearsal of views, and low ventilation of opinion. The socialized work situation provides such opportunities in different degree for different kinds of jobs. Certainly Costa and Dempsey have less opportunity than others, but both DeAngelo and Sokolsky report in detail the political conversations at the shop. In the police locker room Woodside could talk about the local politics that affect his posi-tion; Sullivan, while waiting for his name to appear on the call-board, can find companions to talk politics with; Flynn's car pool includes some politically interested individuals. The reports of political talk at the shop do not suggest that it is central, in most cases; men deprecate the level of information of their shopmates, but, in the interstices of their accounts, it seems that political opinions are aired and weighed. O'Hara says of his friends, "I don't think I talk too much politics with them," but later he says, weighing the various influences upon his opinions, "In political matters, I think that the arguments we get in the shop have more to do with what you decide than anything. . . . I mean, in the shop you read something in the paper and right away you start hollering about something. I think you have more or less to go along with the way things go up there that could change your view one way or another, than any place." The hollering, the bantering, the kidding that Republicans take from Democrats and vice versa—these experiences bring the "way out" opinion nearer to the group norms, but while they homogenize opinions, they may also, in the American work culture, civilize them, too. At least this is what seems to be missing in Kuchinsky's work life.

D

DISPARAGEMENT AND ENCOURAGEMENT
OF SELF-ESTEEM

The argument here, as we have said, is that the democratic machinery can be operated only by men who estimate their own worth, as well as the worth of others, as significantly high. Yet much that is currently written on the effects of industrial life on mankind suggests a conspiracy of events to denigrate men.[12] Here it is hard to dissociate work life from the more general features of life in Eastport. In this more general sense we must say again that the combination of assimilation and mobility that these men show in contrast to their fathers (their superior incomes, occupations, ways of life) give them a substantial increment of those narcissistic supplies that sustain a tender self-esteem. It is also true that in their comparisons with contemporary others, the vicinity of Stern Terrace, with its low-income population, gives them a visible sense of achievement. But the more specific conditions of their work life, their life on the job, is another matter. Would it be that these men feel that they are expressing some individual talent, something each can do a little better than others, on the job? Do they feel that they are appreciated by management and associates, that what they have to offer is something people know about and need? Are they treated with respect as human beings, men with souls and a valuable emotional life, as individuals and not machines?

On the matter of fulfillment and self-expression, there is a set of useful clues in the discussion of the job satisfactions. Among the machine tenders, Dempsey says that what he "likes" about his job is "that it keeps me occupied and gives me a halfway decent living. When I get out of the shop I want to forget it." Costa, as we have said, hates his job and has almost no opportunity for self-expression there. Once he had a dream of being a sports writer on a newspaper; now, on the assembly line, he says: "I'm not particularly proud of my station in life and I don't blame anybody for that except myself. I think it's an awful thing when a fellow gets in his forties and the future is so uncertain. It wasn't the lack

12. In addition to the items in Footnote 5 above, and the more general discussion in Erich Fromm, *op. cit.,* see Peter Drucker, *Concept of the Corporation* (New York: John Day, 1946); Daniel Bell, *The End of Ideology* (New York: The Free Press of Glencoe, 1960), pp. 337–346.

of opportunity that made it this way. It was lack of initiative at the right time. . . . I don't blame anybody except my own lack of ambition. I should be able to do more, but I can't. I have my limits." Sokolsky says he can run any kind of machine, and today, "I run about twelve or fourteen different machines." I tell him he must be expert by now, and then suddenly the façade falls away: "Oh, but I'm sick of it. I don't know why I never looked for another job. I don't know why. Well, maybe because I was scared to take the chance. That's it—see, the trouble with me is I have no push. If somebody pushes me, I'm all right; but otherwise I just stay still." Later we come back to his job making bicycle parts, and I ask him if he thinks he is cut out for this kind of work. He says, briefly, ruefully: "To be honest with you, yes. I don't know anything else." How different is the tone and substance of DeAngelo's feeling about his work:

> I feel lucky. I've found something that I'm suited for, y'know what I mean? Like the first box shop I ever went to, well, I learned how to run the machines in no time at all. I mean, I had no difficulty in setting 'em up or putting jobs on 'em, y'know; and y'gotta know a little bit about 'em, y'know. Seems like I've been where I am now maybe ten years. I know quite a bit about the job; I know quite a bit about the machinery. Seems like I picked a lot of knowledge up more—a lot more—than a lotta fellows been working there a lot longer than I have. Maybe it's because I take an interest in it, y'know? I mean a lotta fellows, their machine breaks down and y'know, you call a mechanic over—the union says certain things a mechanic's gotta fix. So a lotta guys will just take off and when it's fixed they'll come back. But I was never like that, y'know. I stick around and find out what's gotta be fixed, y'know? That's why I learned quite a bit more about a machine than a lotta fellows have.

It is three to one among the machine tenders—three who hate their jobs, feel unfulfilled, feel that they have failed, acknowledge their lack of ambition, believe very little in themselves. And DeAngelo, who likes his work and thinks if he stays there he will be foreman, something he thinks he could do and do well.

Of the other men, only a few do not like their jobs. O'Hara, a maintenance mechanic temporarily reduced to being an oiler, says: "Last year they were setting up a new job, and I think I took the job home with me too much. I'd sit and think, and I wasn't paying attention to what was going on other times—at home even. . . . I think that I have a tendency lots of time to talk shop more out of the shop than a lot of them. But, of course, it's something I enjoy doing, so of course if you enjoy doing something, you'll talk about it more. With some of them it's just a job. With me it's a way of living." And Sullivan, the truck driver, says: "To me, it's interesting. I could never explain it to you; it's something you have to see for yourself. It's just that there's so much of it . . . and there's not the least monotony to it." Kuchinsky, the roofer, feels he has special skills for his line of work; Woodside feels completely fulfilled in being now, after years of planning, an auxiliary policeman as well as a railroad guard; Flynn finds the challenge of his supply job exciting; McNamara says that closing out the books every month offers him opportunity for creative solutions to problems. Only Rapuano, the supply clerk, and Johnson, the maintenance mechanic, long to be doing something else. Perhaps it is not high enough, but ten of the men, one machine tender and nine of the others, two-thirds of the group, find satisfactions in their work life that make them feel good about themselves, feel that their skills are challenged, and they meet the challenge with something better than competence. They feel that they have a function in society and do it well, that is, a little better than the other fellow could.

But if it were the case that their contacts with management were such as to undercut this modest sense of fulfillment, if they were treated as things, if their jobs tended to dehumanize them, they might find this self-respect crumbling away. We have seen some evidence on this in the analysis of men's sharing of authority and power, but there are other glimpses into this range of feeling sheltered by manly bluster and hardy defenses. Among the machine tenders, enough has been said to show that Dempsey and Costa feel that they are allowed almost no discretion, are extensions of the machines they work upon, are hardly trusted to decide anything for themselves. Sokolsky feels a little different; his brother-in-law superior, one step removed, "very seldom comes around, because he knows the work is coming through good." He feels trusted, if not fulfilled. And the importance of this feeling is brightly illuminated by the contrast with his situation on his other job, where he cleans off the desks and vacuums the rugs and sweeps out offices. There he doesn't like his superior: "I'm the kind of a guy, I like to kid around. He's the kind of a man you can't kid around with. That's why I'm very unhappy with the job. I'd like to have a job where I could work in harmony. You go in there and you don't have good feelings. You always have a kind of nervous stomach." Sokolsky's face is mobile, as he says this; the lines down the cheeks deepen, and the corners of the mouth move rapidly in a nervous gesture. One sees the cost to him of an impersonal, cold, dehumanized relation to the superior world of bosses and management; and through him one sees a truly formidable mass of men suffering from the coldness and the deflation when management's representatives do not "like to kid," or cannot "speak to a man and make him feel good."

DeAngelo is the fourth machine tender, and we already know he feels trusted by management, responsible for expensive material given to him for processing, responsive to the straw-boss authority he enjoys. He feels appreciated as a man and a worker.

Of the others, one catches glimpses of a dehumanized supervision. Some of the postal workers resent the fact that they are constantly under surveillance from windows above them; Flynn finds the bureaucratic forms and rules and property control an unhuman tangle of controls. But it is more usual for them to indicate, obliquely, how they are trusted, given a little discretion, left on their own a little more than most. The problem of getting along with management is less often how to adjust to an impersonal superior than the much older problem of adjusting to the moods and tempers and favoritism of their immediate superiors. Kuchinsky has quarrels with his boss, and says: "Sometimes it might be a bad morning for him, or something like that, but then later on he'll come back and agree with you, and he'll tell you, 'Well, I think you were right, there, so go ahead with it.' And I mean, I think it's something that might have upset him; maybe, uh, somebody is, like, behind on work. I think it takes a lot out of him." Sullivan's bosses are the traffic managers; he says: "Some of them are pretty old guys you can't please—kind of crabby. I've told a lot of them where to get off and I've always gotten away with it." Johnson, who has worked in a large utility for many years, says of his relations with his boss: "I don't feel as though he questions my ability in my work, or if I'm doing my work. How the hell would you explain the thing? It isn't jealousy in any way. . . . There's a very good friend of mine—we work together. Well, the boss really goes for this other guy, see? . . . He leans to this man an awful lot and . . . when he's not around, he leans toward me. . . . They're holding back a job down at the plant right now that may mean $20 a week to both of us—a raise.

They are undecided who to give this job to—him or me. . . . If they gave it to him, I would be hurt." There is nothing here of efficiency ratings, months on the job, days absent; rather it is an intensely human situation where, Johnson feels, in the end, they will give something to each because they didn't want to hurt either one.

At least in these two respects, sense of fulfillment and feeling that management recognizes the worker as a person and treats him with some trust and respect, work life in Eastport offers support rather than destruction, help for the never-ending struggle to achieve a sense of personal worth. This is the general impression; but it is both true and distressing that in these respects as in others, the machine tenders suffer the hardest blows. Moreover, as a glimpse into the social scale below these upper-working- and lower-middle-class men, we observe that in the most menial of the positions reported upon—the office-cleaning job Sokolsky maintains on the side—the boss-worker relationship is most hurtful. With a lower stratum of workers, a lower quality of boss may emerge, and the humanity of work thereby may suffer a doubly corrosive influence. But among the group we are observing, the work situations offer men ground on which to stand and declare to themselves and to the world, "I am a useful and a respected person."

E
WORK LIFE AND SHARED PURPOSE

If it were the case—as we now know it is not—that modern industrial work life creates a variety of man inimical to the democratic process and unable to work the machinery upon which it depends, we would be faced with a dilemma. The least part of this dilemma would be to explain how it is that democracy has developed in precisely those periods and places where industrialization has grown. Surely the rate of extension of the franchise is a close correlate of the rate of increased mechanization. Most recently Daniel Lerner has cogently argued that in the Middle East and elsewhere, the long slow process of political modernization takes off from the growth of cities—implying the industrial and commercial base of democracy rather than the rural base.[13] And

13. Daniel Lerner, *The Passing of Traditional Society* (New York: The Free Press of Glencoe, 1958).

Lipset has shown with brilliant force the high positive association between stability of democratic regimes in Europe and the British Commonwealth (and of certain democratic tendencies in Latin America) on the one hand, and such indices of industrialization as the percentage of males in agriculture and the per capita energy consumed on the other.[14] Everything points to the same conclusion: industrialization, increased wealth, increased urbanization, increased education, increased communication—all seem to make democratic machinery more effective, more loyally supported, more stable.

Rather than attempting to explain the apparent paradox posed by these data and the Fromm, Mills, Max Lerner, Marx alienation school, our task is now to show relation between these macrodata and our own microdata. It is a good fit. What we have found is that, with the exception of some of the machine tenders, and particularly of the one assembly-line worker, the workman in Eastport's industrial society has developed relationships directly with his boss and indirectly with management that permit him some autonomy and allow him to develop a sense of influence and a willingness to criticize authority moderately and effectively. This is done through the interstices of the large plant offered by the relative, special friend and, particularly, the union. Where he has discretion over some aspect of his work, he finds himself consulted as well as told. Where the situation is favorable, a kidding relationship between boss and worker gives a little (and often uncertain) scope for a nonhierarchical human relationship. The limiting of the boss's authority to a particular role relationship and to the on-the-job precinct, unlike feudal or village authority, makes room for the autonomy of workers and gives them scope and opportunity for criticism of management—a fact that helps to account for the modest and job-related aspects of this criticism. Moreover, the incorporation of the ends of management into the agenda of the workers themselves makes it possible to internalize some of the authority and to see the work process as a cooperative effort among men working toward the same goals. We shall return to this.

We find, like so many others,[15] that work life in an industrial society permits and even encourages social relations of a reciprocal

14. Seymour M. Lipset, *Political Man: The Social Bases of Politics in the Modern World* (Garden City, N.Y.: Doubleday, 1960), p. 52.
15. For example, see Blauner, "Work Satisfaction . . . ," in *op. cit.*, pp. 349–352.

team-oriented kind, although this is least noticeable among the machine tenders. The work situation socializes, homogenizes, and civilizes men—all three, incompatible as they may seem. It offers men the ground for joint extracurricular action, such as the organization of bowling teams and credit unions. It brings men together to talk; and they often talk about the events in the news, thereby rehearsing attitudes and exposing them to comment, including them in the process whereby men merge their experiences and bring them to bear on distant, complex, and unfamiliar situations.

We find, too, that in the shop and on the job the possibilities for expression and a sense of fulfillment are present, again with the exception of certain machine tenders. Most men talk about their work with genuine interest; a sympathetic and attentive listener is all they need. Moreover, the relations with their immediate superiors are, contrary to some impressions, not limited to the cold calculus of rating sheets, quotas, and incentive payments. They involve areas of trust, responses to mood and anger and, occasionally, praise; the kidding situation with its many psychic functions, seeking and receiving approval; they are treated not only as workers but also as human beings. This sense of function fulfilled and of a recognized humanity, we have said, contributes to men's self-esteem with all that goes with it.

The macrodata show us the fact of association between industrialization and democracy; these findings show us—in part—how the relationship is brought about. Of course, there is much more to it than this; the story unfolds more significantly in terms of education and wealth; but industrial work life, with its ancillary occupations, instead of offering hazards for the democratic spirit offers contributing factors of great importance.

Yet there is something lacking here that men in a democratic society need but do not have, and do not have an opportunity to learn in the fragmented work life of industrial society. They do not have a sense of common purpose. They join with others to perform tasks that often enthrall them, but each is a limited task, done within a limited role, for ends that are, in any major view of life, very narrowly conceived, indeed. It is not enough that they do incorporate some of the management's goals among their own. It is a common conception, and one that I share, that in order to experience a deeper and more satisfying sense of fulfillment it is necessary to see oneself as working toward a moral goal that embraces and benefits many other men and, preferably, deprives none. The work life of an earlier society, tribal, village, perhaps even feudal, may at times have offered such a broad justification of work, may, indeed, have given what is sometimes called "meaning" to otherwise trivial tasks. Perhaps this is not necessary to democracy; the democratic machinery works well enough in a plural, fragmented, open-ended and multiple-meaning society. But it is a question, at least, whether men live their lives well enough in these limiting circumstances.

16

Money and the Conservative View of Life

Americans talk far more about money than Europeans and generally value it far less. Incomes and prices are of great social importance for rating people and goods in relation to one another; until you know the income bracket of a stranger, and he knows yours, your mutual relationship is unsatisfactory and incomplete.
—GEOFFREY GORER, *The American People*, p. 175

The vast array of available commodities has become an American way of living, but it does not follow that Americans are more likely than others to confuse living standards with life values, or mistake good things for the good life.
—MAX LERNER, *America as a Civilization*, pp. 251–252

If the Eastport common man is a conservative, it is in a special sense. He is not opposed to change, does not take a dim view of human nature (for the most part), has no love of tradition and, although not equalitarian, does not stand for a social hierarchy, either; these are not the ingredients of his conservatism. But he is conservative in the sense that he has no program for structural changes in society, is markedly loyal to the prevailing system of government, believes in private property and capitalism, holds that he is living in a moral order where people get pretty much the rewards and punishments that they merit, and assumes a general responsibility for his own fate. We are arguing here that this range of beliefs finds sustenance in and is modified by the experience men have had with poverty and wealth, income and debt—in short, with money. Here, in many half-conscious experiences, lies the source of a commitment to the going order and a desire to make it work; here, rather more than in an elaborated understanding of or belief in capitalism, free private enterprise, an open society, or even democracy. In their first study of Middletown, the Lynds say that "as the study progressed it became more and more apparent that the money medium of exchange and the cluster of activities associated with its acquisition drastically condition the other activities of the people." [1] The getting and spending of money also drastically conditions people's social outlook.

Poverty in Childhood

Plato, Freud, and the Jesuits agree that whatever is learned early has a special importance to the adult; it is more likely to endure; it is more likely to be central to his philosophy. In their childhood, the men of Eastport learned about the importance of money, or the lack of it. Asked what they worried about as children, they report this aspect of their lives in different ways. To Rapuano the most vivid memory of childhood was his mother, *his mom,* hiding from the bill collectors. Woodside remembers wishing he were someone else in school because others had regular meals whereas he was never certain that there would be food on the table at home. Johnson's story is less dramatic—he needed money for less crucial things. Asked about his major problems as a child, he says:

> Well, of course, there's the question of money. I realized in high school that I'd have to—if I wanted to have any social life at all—I'd have to get a job early. I did. I used to work evenings and make a few dollars, enough to, oh, get some clothes for dates. That seemed to be the problem all the way through. It just happened to be the era we went through, I suppose.

Costa comes from an urban family; his father, the head of a household of eight, worked in a foundry and in good times made $30 a week or, if full employment lasted a year, $1,560 annually.

1. Robert S. and Helen M. Lynd, *Middletown in Transition: A Study in Cultural Conflicts* (New York: Harcourt, Brace, 1937), p. 21.

In the depression, of course, it was another story—or rather a variation on the same story, poverty. He says,

> We never had economic security or even reasonable security. It was strictly a day-to-day deal. . . . We went through a terrific depression. But I think the main thing I remember—both my mother and father had a very happy outlook on life, in spite of all the adversity and sickness. My mother was sick a lot. She spent a lot of time in hospitals. My mother died at the age of forty-eight.

DeAngelo, whose father was a "bum" and whose stepfather was left to his own devices after a few unsatisfactory years of married life, lived partially on relief. He says of money:

> [When] I was a teen-ager the problem for me was money. You know, lots of fellows hanging around—they had fathers working and, you know, very big jobs, you know. They went places I couldn't go, you know. It was possible that my mother would allow a little money to give me, you know. Of course, the kids didn't go too many places then, outside of the show. They always had money to buy candy or soda. I never had any, you know.

Some, like O'Hara and Ferrera, claim they had no worries as children and would like to live their lives over again in just the same way. Still, for a large number, more than half, the sense of grinding poverty, or perhaps merely relative deprivation, was a crucial and searing experience.

Did such experiences of poverty affect the social outlook of the adult who won through to an established middle position? And if so, would one expect the poverty to have made a man radical, or the relative success in later life to have made a man conservative?

One important effect of this experience with poverty as a child, this recollection that the most important problem in childhood was money, has been to increase the salience of money through the adult years. This is not money as a counter to buy pleasure—the Eastport common man is not a pleasure-seeking man—but rather to buy security. What is the most important thing money can buy? "Peace of mind" (Sullivan); "I guess that would be a feeling of security" (Flynn); "Well, it'll give 'em security?" (Kuchinsky). Woodside's childhood was the one most marked by poverty; today his salary is one of the lowest in the group, but unlike the others he has been able to save a little bit. Here is how he describes himself:

I'm always figuring ahead, looking ahead. To me security for my family is my main objective. If I should die tomorrow, I want to be sure my family is taken care of. If I got five dollars, I want to make sure I've got something to eat throughout the week. It's due to not having it back along—that I want to make sure that I've got a little security.

A second effect, a conservative one, too, is the effect earlier poverty may have on a man's attitudes toward modern youth, apparently so affluent, free, and (therefore?) wild. DeAngelo, who lived much of his early life on relief, and was on the margins of delinquency at times, speaks of contemporary juvenile delinquency in this way:

Oh, I know what's the matter—I know what it is. It's just money. People today—the mother and father's workin'. They don't give a damn; they give the kids spending money. What's he worried about playing for? He's happy hanging around the corner. He's got a buck in his pocket to spend—get into trouble. They got cars. You see more cars around these high schools now, for crying out loud, than you see in the shop, for crying out loud. They all got cars.

There are others who blame delinquency upon too much money. Some remembered incidents of childhood, some sense of the inappropriateness of early indulgence, some feeling that having unearned money is evil seems mixed here with a more mature belief that one grows into a wise use of money more slowly than many parents realize.

The third effect, and the most important one from our point of view, is the financial conservatism that is instilled by penury in childhood. Consider, in this connection, Woodside's reaction to the problem of a balanced budget. Woodside, it will be recalled, was uncertain as a child from day to day where the next meal was coming from—or whether it was:

Any country that spends more than they have are definitely in trouble. I think you've got to watch that line as to how much you can spend and how much you can't spend. I think it comes right back to—you spend what you have and try to think of other ways of raising more. The last depression I was only a child, but I think that had a great deal to do as to why the depression was on— because it was so much in debt—the country itself.

Woodside is only moderately conservative, but he knows the value of money; he fears largesse, splurging, uncontrolled expenditures. He understands one thing well—scarcity.

Costa, when I talked to him, was partially unemployed; his firm had cut back production and was working only a few days a week. He had applied for unemployment compensation. Now, and as a child, money was a scarce, frighteningly scarce, item. And so, when he is asked about problems confronting his state, he starts off this way:

> Taxes are too high. They're spending too much money. This relocation of Route A and this new highway. It's a great thing, but the city—the state have got themselves in such a financial mess over it . . . I think it's going to hurt the economy of the state for a long, long time. I think it will be a long time before the state ever gets that money back. I think that [pause] whoever authorized it was overlyambitious . . . so that's going to mean another deficit.

These are three men closest to the edge of starvation and constant penury in childhood: Costa, Woodside, and DeAngelo. Costa ranks among the two most politically conservative in the entire Eastport group, while Woodside and DeAngelo rank in the middle. DeAngelo is a Republican, and Woodside and Costa are independents; all three voted for Eisenhower in 1952 and 1956; none believes the working people should have more power; all respect the business elite in Eastport and nationally; all three worry about high taxes and the unbalanced budget. In all these respects they are slightly or substantially more conservative than others. We have argued elsewhere that businessmen who translate their own experiences into public policy draw upon their own morbid fear of debt when they regard the public treasury in a state of unbalance.[2] In the same way some working-class men, also drawing on their own experience, become fearful of "lavish" expenditures, debt, and governmental generosity. And, by and large, these men are more likely to be found among those who have now achieved some small security but who once lived in a state of want. Among reasonably secure adults, poverty and penury in youth do not make for radicals; they make for security-conscious, financially conservative, thrifty supporters of the going order. Such men are more frightened than angry.

Money Worries: Saving and Spending

We live in an affluent society; these men are "people of plenty." What should they worry about, then, in their daily lives? They

2. See Robert E. Lane, *The Regulation of Businessmen* (New Haven: Yale University Press, 1954), pp. 80–81.

are quite clear about this: "Oh, finances, mainly, my wife's health . . . everything else that I worry about, in one way or another comes back to money" (Sullivan); "I worry about the bills, I guess, and when I'm going to pay them off. That's the important thing" (Sokolsky): "Even though I'm happy-go-lucky most of the time, I do a lot of worrying. But the most of my worries involve money" (Johnson); "What worries me is the economic situation. I mean, I'm always afraid that things might go back to the way it was back in 1932" (Rapuano); "I don't worry a great deal, no. But I have times when I concern myself—back to economics, that's all. Especially in this day and age when things aren't going too well" (Costa). This is not like the poverty of their childhood; it is living at the margin of an uncertain income; it comes from high fixed expenses, a little debt, and a cyclical economy that periodically threatens disaster. Worried, anxious men are cautious men. And cautious men are conservative.

In these circumstances, of course, the logical thing to do is to reduce one's annual expenditures and save for the threatening contingencies of sickness, unemployment, the breakdown of equipment. Eastport knows this, but the fact of the matter is that except for a very few (Woodside, McNamara, Flynn) these men cannot save, and they suffer severe pangs of guilt on this account. Costa heaps ashes on his head:

> I go back to the bank to cash my check and I see people putting one dollar into the bank. I admire those kind of people, and I don't know why I can't be like them, but it's always been either big or nothing with me. That's one of the reasons I don't have a dime. [pause] You might think somebody with sense enough to know that would do something about it, but I don't seem to be able to buckle down.

Johnson, an impulsive man with an absorbing interest in money, speaks of the causes of poverty in personal terms, and then goes on to show how he indoctrinates his boys:

> I'm very strict with my children when it comes to a dollar. I tell them how to use a dollar, which I used to just throw away, and occasionally I still do. But I tell them in such a way—I tell them—I use myself as an example.

And Sullivan, quarreling with his wife over their accounts, says ruefully, "Well, I can say firsthand 'a penny saved is a penny earned,' because I wish I did."

It could hardly be otherwise. Under the pressure of clever advertising, which is always partially subliminal in its manipulation of unknown motives, invited to go into debt at every turn, living in a housing development where each inevitably compares his possessions with others, these Eastport men spend to the limit of their income, or beyond that limit. Most of the men are moderately in debt. Johnson is paying off his folly and has about $800 still to go. DeAngelo is paying off accumulated doctors' bills, and so is Woodside; Kuchinsky has fairly heavy installments due every month on his car. Thus, they are not only worried, they are, in their own eyes, guilty as well.

Yet once this has been said, the implications of this guilt must be sharply limited, for on the whole the working out of the guilt in other areas of life, or even in thinking about money, does not impose a heavy burden or involve much projective or unrealistic thought. These limits are illustrated in the way these men think children should learn about money. In their own childhood, they did not receive regular allowances; money came to them in three ways: a generous uncle or aunt gave them money upon the occasion of some visit; their parents gave them money for some specific purpose such as going to a movie or buying candy; they earned money by doing specific chores (O'Hara worked for a grocery, Costa sold papers, Ruggiero cleaned his uncle's backyard). But for the most part it was the lack, not the spending, of money that was the significant feature of their fiscal lives. In view of the poverty of their own childhoods, most of them growing into fiscal consciousness in the thirties, one might have expected a central emphasis upon children's saving. There is some suggestion of this, too, particularly among those who have endured the most poverty as a child. Woodside mentions how important it is to "show him [his son] how hard money is to come by and how important it is to *have* money." DeAngelo says, "I don't have much to give 'em and to teach 'em. . . . Well, I don't know, I guess you could teach him when he's young to save money, y'know." Johnson says: "The best way, I think, which I'm practicing, is to try and to tell him, 'If you can, save a few dollars. No matter how much it is, save it.' " Here is the canny peasant, the thrifty bourgeois.

But the main emphasis is upon *spending wisely*, maximizing long-range pleasures rather than maximizing thrift. This is even true of those who first mentioned saving, for DeAngelo proceeds, in the very next breath, to take back what he had just said: "Not to save it, y'know, but if he's got a couple of dollars, and he wants to spend a dollar or so, all right, spend it, but y'know, hold back a little of it." And Johnson says: "If he needs it for something important, then go to it. Then he'll have it, because that's why he saved it. . . . Not to buy foolish things." It is, indeed, this latter theme that is one of the two main ideas about money in Eastport: it is not saving for its own sake, for saving has no special virtue; rather it is spending wisely, planning, budgeting, maximizing the gratification of expenditures. As Gorer says of the American culture, by itself "saving . . . is not laudable." [3]

"When they say 'balance the budget,' " muses Flynn, "I guess what they mean . . . is to spend no more than your income. . . . Now, this is pretty hard for the individual, who has only relatively small responsibilities. How can you do it on the national level with accumulated responsibilities?" Like many others, Flynn sees the problems of the budgets and debts as they are illuminated by his personal experience. Since he and the others are great worriers about money and are in debt and have trouble saving, they might be expected to moralize the government's excess of expenditure over income and to take an indignant stand on this. Or, on the other hand, since in their dealings with their children they stress wise expenditure rather than saving, and since in their own lives they have a "worried confidence" that somehow the income will keep coming in and somehow the debts will be paid off and somehow things will be better, perhaps their loose (but worried) attitude toward money will control their attitude toward government debts and budgets. As it turns out, the latter is the case. Even Flynn, perhaps the most cautious man in the group, goes on to say about the balancing of the budget: "I think, for myself, it would appear that this is not the most important thing. . . . There are too many other influences, like a world situation, or defense, or the current economic situation." Dempsey says he thinks balancing the budget is important, "but it doesn't seem as if they're going to do it. . . . You're in the red, but it doesn't stop anything. . . . I wouldn't worry too much about it—I'm too old for that." Sokolsky says: "I don't think it matters, personally. I mean, something always comes up." McNamara, a bookkeeper and a careful man, says, "I don't think it's too important a policy, because after all, the government is just the people, and the funds you use are the people's money." Rapuano says balancing the budget is "immaterial" in the face of the threat from Russia.

3. Geoffrey Gorer, *The American People: A Study in National Character* (New York: Norton, 1948), p. 176.

The fact is that the exaggerated worries of the three men discussed above (Costa, Woodside, and DeAngelo) are exceptional. The budget and the national debt have not the symbolic value in lower middle Eastport that one might have expected and that one would certainly find in business circles. Nor should we, really, have expected it, for money thrift and saving, while a source of worry, do not have a moralized, Calvinist meaning in their personal lives. Here, then, is the gate in the conservatism of the lower middle masses through which is driven the golden chariot of the welfare state.

Rewards Are Earned

If one theme in training children on the use of money is "spend wisely," the other is *money must be earned*. Those with large families and more limited resources are inclined not to give allowances to their children, but the others do, and the condition is that they earn them. Costa says:

> Well, in our house we have a system. Our children have an allowance each week, but they have to earn it. And if they don't earn it, they don't get it. They have specific duties they have to perform during the week in order for—which I get paid on Friday, I give them each a dollar a week. . . . But the main point I'm trying to make is we like to have them feel that if they have something, they have to work for it.

Dempsey, as always, is more laconic: "Let them go out and earn some and they find out the value of a dollar very fast. I've seen it happen right here [a reference to his stepdaughter, with whom he has had friction]." Sokolsky, who stresses saving more than most, also emphasizes earning. Speaking of his older daughter, with whom he is currently having trouble, he says:

> She used to have an allowance, but I cut it out because for that she used to clean up her room—you know, straighten her room out and put her clothes away. But now she's getting, well, she just comes in and throws the things on the chair and doesn't make her bed.

Such a program requires coordinated oversight. Ruggiero's children are probably learning that there are quicker ways to get money than to earn it:

> Well, the best way is actually let 'em earn it. We tried to use that system in the house, but, as I say, my wife is, uh, a little too easy.

I'm not home enough to show a little more discipline with the kids. Not that they're bad or anything, but, uh, it's easy come, easy go with them, too.

And he harks back to his own yard-cleaning errand-running childhood when money was harder to come by and its value learned through work.

These sentiments are expressed with feeling; they are universally shared; the principle that there is very little gain without effort is endorsed as both true and moral. Surely, then, looking out upon an economy where some men seem to have acquired great wealth without commensurate effort would encourage a dissatisfaction with the going order; might, indeed, plant the seeds of a new urban Populism. It is not so, because the phrase "wealth must be earned" is given both meanings: only through earning can one acquire wealth, and whoever has wealth could only have acquired it by earning it. Not discontent, but justification for the going order emerges from this interpretation. Johnson expresses it clearly. Speaking of "the rich man," he says:

> I believe the man is smart enough to make money, he should have something to say. I'm not jealous of anybody that's got a million dollars. He's much smarter than I am—more intelligent. He knew the way to get it.

We take Johnson here because he is a test case; he is more cynical about human nature than most. It is, then, really true that these Eastport men hold that a rough justice is done in the rewards and punishments of life. And among the many experiences with money they may have, their experience as paymasters in their own homes reinforces their belief that merit is rewarded and that there is a kind of distributive justice in the world, rather than capriousness, favoritism, nepotism, and the like.

The Money Worries of the Rich

"The American talks about money," says Santayana, "because that is the symbol and measure he has at hand for success, intelligence, and power; but as to money itself, he makes, loses, spends, and gives it away with a light heart." [4] Max Lerner remarks about the American attitude toward money. "It does not become an end in itself except for the impoverished of spirit, who are to be found

4. George Santayana, *Character and Opinion in the United States* (Garden City, N.Y.: Doubleday, 1956), p. 115.

in any civilization." [5] Perhaps the lightness of heart has gone since Santayana's time, but it certainly is a fact that money is a counter in life's game (which is, however, not a game of pleasure). It is not "an end in itself," in Eastport. Indeed, it may be true that the Eastportians are happiest when they are *not* thinking about money, or even the things that money can buy. Except for the three men who hate their work as machine tenders (Costa, Dempsey, Sokolsky), the men are probably happiest when they are on the job and things are going well, or when they are relaxing at home with their families around them and the television grinding out some simple comedy, or when they are playing or supervising local sporting events. They are least happy when they start thinking about money; they think about money only to worry about it.

From this it might follow that the Eastport common man would envy the rich, for only the rich would be able to think about money without worrying, or, perhaps, not even think about it at all and just enjoy it. Since money is the main source of worry that the Eastport men think consciously about, to be relieved of this worry would indeed seem to promise them rather carefree lives. Yet it does not work that way. So firm is the connection between money and worry that even the idea of abundant money does not dissolve that tie. On the contrary, it is so fixed a constellation of ideas that the tendency is quite the other way— the more money a person has, the more he will worry about money.

Are the rich happier than the average man? Rapuano says: "Their problems are probably bigger and even more heavy than ours. . . . They're mostly worried about losing their money, and it's harder for a person who has money to lose it than it is for a guy that's never had it." McNamara agrees: "I don't think they're happier. They probably worry a lot about money, so their worries are tremendous." Sullivan suggests that health is more important than money, and adds: "A lot of money brings worries, too, different times. I think maybe the average man might be happier." Dempsey's views are like Rapuano's: "I think a rich person is worrying more about his money—whether he's going to hold it or whether he's going to lose it. The average person hasn't got enough to worry about." Some mention the simple joys of life, family and friends, as equally available to all, and more meaning-

5. Max Lerner, *America as a Civilization: Life and Thought in the United States Today* (New York: Simon and Schuster, 1957), p. 252.

ful to the average person, who, they believe, has a greater capacity for enjoyment. O'Hara believes the rich have more mental breakdowns; Sokolsky says they are arguing all the time; Sullivan cites John D. Rockefeller's restricted diet. Much of this is rationalization, and some of it is sour grapes. But there is no doubt that experience with money worries imposes a framework on the picture of the rich that distorts it in a certain way, gives it more somber colors, conceals the glitter, makes it less attractive. And viewing the life of the rich this way has a conservative effect on the social outlook of these plain workingmen of Eastport.

Expectations

"The ordinary American has come to assume that somehow the 'goods' will be there for the economy as a whole." [6] In saying this, Max Lerner overlooks the anxieties of the business cycle, but in general it is true; the fear that society will be poor, that the nation will suffer scarcity is minimal. No doubt this colors a man's belief about his own situation as well. About half of the men are now earning substantially more than they were five years ago; they have experienced the rising standard of living that puts the bloom on the American dream. It has come about in several ways. For Flynn it has been due to advancement in the large firm for which he works; for Kuchinsky it has been increase in the hourly rates of pay for roofers; for McNamara it has been partly due to promotions and better jobs as bookkeeper, and partly due to extra work in the evenings and on Sundays. Currently he works seven days a week. For Ruggiero, the most successful of all, it is due partly to a willingness to go back from office work to a more "menial" but better paid position, and a longer stint on his second post-office job. Progress comes in many ways to those who seek it— and to those who, like Kuchinsky or Dempsey, just go about their business and participate in the gains negotiated by others.

For those on this escalator, whether or not they choose to climb while they ride, there is reason enough to hold euphoric views of the American society and the ways and privileges of the rich. After all, Émile Coué had his greatest success in America where his doctrine seemed like a statement of the laws of nature: "Every day and in every way I'm getting better and better." With his expectations fulfilled in this way, why should a man resent

6. *Ibid.*, p. 347.

the rich, or feel alienated from society? It is the conservatism of the others that poses a problem, those who are *not* doing better now than they did some five years ago, and yet who share the American tolerance of the rich, and do not show their own frustration.

But those who are now no better off than they were five years ago expect to prosper in the next five years. Sokolsky, fourteen years on a job he dislikes, does not think that he will have a better job but that, instead, "I think business will get better." DeAngelo, too, believes that better times will make for steadier employment and more overtime in five years. Others expect to have changed their personal positions and in this way increase their incomes: but even these are counting as much on the expanding economy as they are on their own upward mobility. *All* of the men either had substantially increased their income over the previous five years or anticipated increased income in the five years to follow, or both.

Most of the mythology of mobility—it's source in rugged individualism and its product in working-class economic conservatism—is grounded in the idea of personal advancement through effort and merit. It originated in the nineteenth century; its American hero is Horatio Alger. There are a few such men among Eastport's common man (Ruggiero, Flynn, McNamara, Ferrera). But the main source of Eastport's economic optimism, and the main reason for these men's economic welfare (compared to the previous generation), is the progress made in the economy that we have seen in Chapter 14, the general movement from manual to clerical, from industrial to service occupations. Rising wages, increased productivity, shorter hours—hence overtime and the "leisure" to take on a second job—these are the main elements in their economic progress, *not* promotion from millhand to foreman, from apprentice to master craftsman, from clerk to accountant. In general the men know this: DeAngelo thinks in five years he will be better off because "right now there's no Saturday work, and that's what knocks me out." Johnson, with his ulcers, says, "As long as this stomach doesn't bother me seriously, I think it's going to be better." O'Hara says, "I hope the Democrats get back in and I think it's going to better."

Our discussion so far has, like the income tax, involved a five-year carry-back and five-year carry-forward perspective. But the ideologies of conservatism and liberalism, Algerism and Micawberism ("something will turn up"), are nourished by roots that penetrate earlier generations. There is little doubt that Freud was correct in the basic origin of the competitive spirit: we are all in competition with our fathers. In this competition the men of Eastport are winners (to the extent that men can ever be winners in a competition where Father already has won the prize). They are winners because there is hardly one of them who does not see himself as a step ahead of his "old man" and in this sense fulfilling the promise of the American scheme of things. Perhaps they did not need the economic victory; most of the Italians have at least one immigrant parent; the Irish are more likely to have an immigrant grandparent; only one of the men is of what is ambiguously called native stock. They are victors merely by their superior Americanism. But whether they needed it or not, they earn more money than their parents; they provide for their children with greater largesse; they are, by their own accounts, more sober, steadier citizens. And although swept along by an expanding economy, they feel that they have done this on their own. Costa says, speaking of his childhood:

> In those days, depending on the parents' station in life, they just liked for you to follow their footsteps, and I can remember my mother telling me when I was twelve or thirteen years old, that if I got a job in a factory like my father worked at, and stayed with them, and, you know, gave them a day's work, that I could build myself a nice life, working on a machine. Now I don't believe that today, and I would never teach my children that.

In a very limited sense, but an important one, one might say that in stepping into Father's shoes these men found them too small. The psychic satisfactions in this drama of the generations cannot be overestimated. When the deep personal satisfactions that such a discovery as this may bring to a man in adult life are linked to his social outlook, the world as it stands, the *status quo,* has gained a friend.

Budgeting and Planning

In Chapter 12, on "The Mind of the New Collectivism," there emerged a picture of men willing to give to government whatever powers it needed to deal with whatever troubles came to bedevil society. It sounded like the foundation for a planned society, if not actual Socialism. But because these men draw their ideas from their personal lives and not from the coherent theories presented in books, this inference is unwarranted. While the controversies have raged in the university presses over the feasibility of economic planning, whether or not it is possible to have "freedom under planning," and whether a planned economy is Socialistic and a "road to serfdom," the common man has had his own experiences with economic planning and his own debates. Like the larger controversy, his debate takes the form: Is it possible to plan ahead or are matters so unpredictable, so subject to uncontrollable variation, that it is wiser simply to take things as they come? Here we may refresh our memories of how the men think about planning their own lives. Some men are reasonably sanguine. O'Hara says: "Well, I would say to a certain extent you can make long-range plans. To a certain extent . . . but I wouldn't plan ahead and figure that it's really going to happen." McNamara thinks it's possible for some people: "If you're ambitious I think you can plan, and set a goal." But as for himself: "I'm not much for goal-setting. I don't know why—probably just inability to be aggressive has something to do with it." But most men are rather more skeptical than that. Sokolsky says: "You never plan ahead because it never works out. . . . Like we figured we were going to put so much money away for this, and we would have money for that, and boom, all of a sudden something comes up . . . boom it falls through." And Dempsey, whose own plans for a little restaurant in his home did fall through, says: "I don't think anyone can plan for the future, I mean for a length of time—you should never read a continuous story, because you never know whether you're going to finish it or not." Or Kuchinsky: "I don't believe they can predict from day to day. . . . Today you're here and tomorrow you don't know what's going to happen." As the men report their attitudes, even after due allowance is made for certain useful rationalization of their own lives, a clear sense of the unpredictability of society, of the economy, and of their own futures emerges. Not that their lives have been this full of change and crisis—but the uncertainties associated with threats of layoff, threats of illness, and threatened movements of firms, or strikes, harrow the nerves almost as much as the changes that do take place.

It will be within this framework that men must appraise the possibility as well as the desirability of governmental planning, of long-term policies, of urban plans looking toward a future across the generations, as was the case, say, when to build a cathedral took a hundred years. The paradox is clear: The more the uncertainty of their own lives makes government planning seem desirable, the more the experiences they have endured make successful planning against unknown contingencies seem improbable.

What's Good for Business Is Good for the Workingman

The experience of the workingman in American society leads him to believe that, generally speaking, business is the source of legitimate earned money and that government is the source of relief, welfare, charity. The processes by which business earns its money are familiar and, however dubious they may seem to those who dislike the commercial spirit or who follow the aesthetic leads of Ruskin and Carlyle, in lower middle Eastport they seem sound and fair. They are fair because they represent an exchange of one thing for another; they are sound because businesses, like people, and like children on allowances, must have *earned* their money in order to have it. It is for these reasons, among others, that the men of Eastport look to government to help business, and look to business to help them.

The most obvious and almost universal expression of this point of view comes in the many assertions that in this period of recession the government should expand its purchases from business, extend its contracts to businesses that are laying off men. Thus Rapuano, discussing the problems of his state, says: "If the government would stop taking contracts away from these defense programs, once they give them, I think we'd be better off. . . . Let the people work and earn some money." O'Hara agrees with this diagnosis, "If they start building up defense and they start putting out contracts, and there's more work, which there's going to be— people who are working on your missiles are going to start buying stuff," and everyone benefits. Even if the government has to contract for "obsolete material," such contracts should not be stopped. Sullivan says, "A lot of things that the government's making in factories as soon as they come out, they're surplus— which of course is good, too, because it keeps people working." This is a different story, a different orientation to government, from the story and the situation in the thirties when government aid was direct to the worker in the form of public works. Of course, there are still those who favor roads and schools. Sokolsky says: "They say they're going to—the missile program will put a lot of men back to work, but you come right down to it, how many factories are equipped to make missiles? . . . That's not going to put very many people to work, I don't think. I mean let them build roads. They're going to build more projects, schools, like that. That's good." But Kuchinsky scoffs: "Five or ten billion dollars on road construction. I mean, who's going to work on them, you or I? Everybody in this country can't work on road construction, that's for sure." And Kuchinsky, in this argument, seems to carry the day.

The argument for government aid to business has other aspects. If you give the money to business in the form of contracts, the government will get it back in the form of tax receipts. Flynn, who often deals with the government as a liaison man, puts it most lucidly:

> The greater production he [the businessman] has, the higher, no doubt, his profits will be, and if his profits increase . . . the increase to the government itself should increase. With this increased income maybe they can help to foster additional privately endowed programs.

Flynn, having created this enchanting spiral, turns and smiles: "This is a fantasy, most likely," he says. But the workingman knows without benefit of fantasy that as industry prospers, he prospers; when profits are high, his wages are good, and that only then is Saturday work, at time-and-a-half, a regular part of his income.

Not only should government support industry through contracts and orders, it should also ease the tax burden on business wherever possible. This is particularly true of state taxes, for the idea that industry is mobile and locates where taxes are lowest has a strong hold upon these men. Dempsey, an older man with no union in his plant and no seniority provisions to protect him against being laid off, looks to industry as the loyal tenant looks to the landlord. He believes that the state should "lower the taxes on industry so that they can come in here—different industries can come in here to operate on a substantial income for themselves, so that they would be able to pay halfway decent wages to the workingman." Ferrera believes high state taxes in his state have encouraged industry to go South. And O'Hara, no friend of the employer, says: "I'll tell you one thing, I think taxes are too high for some of these"—he pauses, takes a breath, and goes on—"all right, with these businesses, because they're knocking an awful lot of them out of the state. I mean, they're going down South where they don't pay their taxes."

Since the days of the Progressives, and certainly since the Populists, the attitudes toward government and business have weathered and changed. Today a new mental hospital, a new highway program makes men less happy than a new aircraft plant in the state—jobs are better and wages are higher in private industry. The government is not seen as the ally of the workingman against business abuse or exploitation, or as the ally of the small businessman against monopoly or rate fixing (except for some complaint over high prices). The accent falls on another business-government relationship. The government is a great nurse that helps ailing businesses to prosper. And it is business's nurse first, and only then nurse to the workingman.

These are but a few ways in which the feel and smell of money in his own hands, the experience with debt and saving, tell the workingman how the government should manage its fiscal affairs. If he were poor in childhood—and all these men were more or less poor—he understands scarcity and fears largesse. The poorer he was, the more likely he is to be frightened of debt. But as the experience of an uncertain but broadly plentiful economy and growing standard of living reassure him, he ceases to be so money-nervous, so tense about expenditures—his own and the government's. He worries, but he focuses on wise expenditure and not on saving or thrift for his children and his public officials. Although he holds that money must be earned, he interprets this to mean that whoever has money must have earned it, and so the great inequalities are justified. His own monetary expectations for himself have been generally fulfilled and, best of all, he has gone well beyond his father in his wealth as well as in his Americanism. This gives an added savor to a *status quo* that has its share of bitterness. Yet in spite of this rise in his life, he feels he cannot plan ahead, and, believing this, he is skeptical that the government can plan ahead either. It is not the planning aspect of the welfare state that attracts him. And, finally, he knows that good money, earned money and pay come from business, while less satisfactory money, relief money, comes from the government. Thus he looks to the government to keep business prosperous so that he can get the good earned pay; he does not look to government for a direct payment, if he can help it and if government can only make "times good again."

17

Fathers and Sons: Family Experience
and the Development of Ideology

> In America the family, in the Roman and aristocratic sense of the word, does not exist. All that remains of it are a few vestiges in the first years of childhood.
> —ALEXIS DE TOCQUEVILLE, *Democracy in America,* II, 192

> Where in Europe . . . adolescence would lead to a conflict with the father, and the necessity of either rebelling or submitting (. . . [in] Germany, first rebelling and then submitting), there is, on the whole, no necessity for such exertion in the American family. The adolescent swings of the American youth do not overtly concern the father, nor the matter of authority, but focus rather on his peers.
> —ERIK ERIKSON, *Childhood and Society,* p. 277

Loosely speaking, there are three ways in which a father lays the foundations for his son's political beliefs. He may do this, first, through indoctrination, both overt and covert as a model for imitation, so that the son picks up the loyalties, beliefs, and values of the old man. Second, he places the child in a social context, giving him an ethnicity, class position, and community or regional environment. He also helps to shape political beliefs by his personal relations with his son and by the way he molds the personality that must sustain and develop a social orientation. The combination of these three processes produces the "Mendelian law" of politics: the inheritance of political loyalties and beliefs. But while imitation and common social stakes tend to enforce this law, the socialization process may work to repeal it. It is the socialization process, the way in which fathers and sons get along with each other, that we examine in this chapter.

Some perspective is gained by noting a number of possible models of the way fathers through their rearing practices may affect their sons' social outlook. The German model of the stern father who emphasizes masculine "hardness" and "fitness" in the son, and who monopolizes the opportunity for conversation at the dinner table, is one that has been explored at length.[1] The Japanese father, partially deified like his ancestors, strictly attentive to protocol and detail in the home, is another.[2] The Russian father-image—the gruff, indulgent, somewhat undisciplined but spontaneous and warm individual—is a third.[3] And the American father is said to be more of a brother than a father, joined with his son under the same female yoke, uninspired but certainly not frightening.[4] Here is an image to compare with others and, as with the other models, its caricaturistic exaggeration nevertheless represents an identifiable likeness.

In our Eastport discussions we were dealing with a moderately "normal" group. We are not involved with the extremes of personality damage or the bottom rung of the social ladder or a highly socially alienated group. Unlike the studies of American Communists[5] or of nativist agitators,[6] this discussion is concerned with middle and normal America, with more or less adjusted people. This is an important point because our findings differ in certain respects from those of other studies, but they do not necessarily conflict with them.

1. See Bertram H. Shaffner, *Fatherland: A Study of Authoritarianism in the German Family* (New York: Columbia University Press, 1948); David M. Levy, "Anti-Nazis: Criteria of Differentiation," in Alfred H. Stanton and Stewart E. Perry, eds., *Personality and Political Crisis* (New York: The Free Press of Glencoe, 1951).

2. See Ruth Benedict, *The Chrysanthemum and the Sword* (Boston: Houghton Mifflin, 1946).

3. See Henry V. Dicks, "Observations on Contemporary Russian Behavior," *Human Relations*, 5 (1952), pp. 111–176.

4. See Erik Erikson, *Childhood and Society* (New York: Norton, 1950).

5. Gabriel Almond, *The Appeals of Communism* (Princeton, N.J.: Princeton University Press, 1954); Morris L. Ernst and David Loth, *Report on the American Communist* (New York: Holt, 1952).

6. Leo Lowenthal and N. Guterman, *Prophets of Deceit* (New York: Harper, 1949). For an interesting case analysis of father-son relationsships and virulent fascism, see Robert Lindner, "Destiny's Tot," in his *The Fifty-Minute Hour* (New York: Rinehart, 1955).

A

THE UNFOUGHT WAR OF INDEPENDENCE

The influence of the son's rebellious attitudes toward his father has often been said to be important in explaining radical movements, particularly "youth movements." The son's basic position is one of growing from complete dependence to independence. During the later stages of this growth he and his father must each make a rather drastic adjustment to the changing relationship called forth by the son's maturation. Under certain circumstances the son may rebel against the family and particularly against the father. Is this the typical American pattern—as Erikson denies? Unlike German youth, he argues, American youngsters do not rebel, although willing and able to do so, because the paternal discipline is not something to rebel against.[7]

We explored the question of rebellion, particularly in its political aspects, with our fifteen men and found that there was indeed very little evidence of the kind of relationship that Erikson describes in the German situation. Apparently, only rarely did a family-shattering clash of wills occur when the son thought himself old enough to behave as a man. The father-son opposition took relatively minor forms: the question of what hour to come in at night, the use of the family car, the son's conduct in school. Concerning the political expression of such rebellious feelings, there were strong indications that this subject remained on the periphery of the men's world of experience.

Although the major evidence comes from the biographical material, answers to a question on youthful rebellion or radicalism are revealing. Rapuano, a packinghouse supply clerk with a rather undisciplined tendency to vent his aggression on social targets (Communists and doctors), responds in bewilderment and finally denies any such tendency. O'Hara, a maintenance mechanic in a large factory and one of the more class-conscious men, is confused, and takes the question to mean rebellion against his brothers and sisters. Woodside, a railroad guard who rejected his father with venom, responds to an inquiry about his own youthful rebellion or radicalism:

I do remember through the depression that my folks mentioned that it seems as though more could have been done—that the

7. Erik Erikson, *op. cit.,* pp. 280–283.

parties should have made more means of work so that the poverty wouldn't be existing so much around you—and, not only around you—but with you yourself.

He turns the question of his own rebellion and radicalism into a family matter: the family was more or less disgruntled. Only one man, better educated than others, speaks of his own moderate radicalism in a way that could be interpreted as a search for independence from or opposition to his parents.

There are several reasons why political expression of youthful defiance failed to come off. One is the low salience of politics for the parents. Few of the men could remember many political discussions in the home, and some were uncertain whether their parents were Democrats or Republicans. If the old man cared so little about politics, there was little reason to challenge him in this area. Another reason is that when there is a need to assert independence there are ways of doing it that come closer to the paternal (and generally American) value scheme. One of these is to quit school. Four or five men sought independence and the economic foundations for a life no longer dependent on paternal pleasure by leaving school shortly before they were ready to graduate—thus striking directly at the interests of parents determined to see their children "get ahead in the world." Of course, this act had compensations for parents in need of money, but there seems to have been more of a genuine conflict of wills in this area than in any other. Quitting school, in some ways, is the American youth's equivalent of his European opposite of conservative parentage joining a Socialist or Fascist party.

Two reasons, then, for the apolitical quality of youthful revolt are the low salience of politics in the American home and the opportunity for rebellion in other ways. A third reason may be—to use a hyperbole—the relatively low salience of the father in the American scheme. We asked our men, "Who made the important decisions in your parents' household?" One replied that they were jointly made, two that their fathers made the important decisions, and twelve testified that mother was boss. The statement of Ruggiero, a university supply man from a remarkably happy home, typifies the most frequent point of view. Which parent was boss in his family?

I'd say my mother. My father was easygoing in the house. . . . We found that Mother ran the house exactly the way she wanted to. She took care of the money, too. Paid all the bills. She still does.

Now it may be that from a child's perspective that Mother is usually boss. But the near unanimity on this point is convincing, all the more so because the accompanying comments generally show no overlord in the background. Even in this immigrant and second-generation population Mom had taken over.[8] Why, then, rebel against Father?

There is a fourth reason for the generally low rate of political rebellion. In the American home a child is given considerable latitude. "Permissiveness" is the term used currently to express this idea, and although the term and idea are in bad odor among some critics, it is clear that the prevailing standards of child care even twenty years ago allowed a degree of freedom in school, neighborhood, and home not generally prevalent in Europe or Asia.[9] To a large extent, the boy is on his own. This is Erikson's point, but we can illustrate it in detail. Thus Farrel, a man from a working-class background whose schooling included graduate study, reports on his tendency to political radicalism in his youth: "I think there must also be the adolescent-revolt aspect, which was never acute with me. . . . There was, as far as I was concerned, no necessity for it to be acute; I didn't feel hemmed in by my parents." Rapuano talks of his "reckless" youth in which he ran free with other boys, and some of the men speak of their parents' preoccupations that gave them opportunity to live a "free life." Many of the boys had earned money for their own as well as their families' use by selling papers, working in grocery stores, or cleaning up the school. Nor was this freedom attributable to parental indifference. When Rapuano was struck by a schoolteacher, his mother (*not* his father) visited the school to beat the teacher with a stick. A free child assured of supportive parental assistance when in need does not need to rebel.

A minority of four or five of these children, however, had suffered under controls that seem strict by most American standards.

B

FOUR MEN WHOSE FATHERS FAILED THEM

Although it is true that the symptoms of *rebellion* are rather slight and that its political expression is miniscule, it does not

8. Cf. Margaret Mead, *And Keep Your Powder Dry* (New York: Morrow, 1942).

9. On this point, see Robert R. Sears, Eleanor E. Maccoby, and Harry Levin, *Patterns of Child Rearing* (Evanston, Ill.: Row, Peterson, 1957); and Robert J. Havighurst and Allison Davis, "A Comparison of the Chicago and Harvard Studies of Social Class Differences in Child Rearing," *American Sociological Review*, 20 (1955), pp. 438–442.

follow that the American son, particularly the son of immigrants, identifies with his father—introjects the paternal ideal, as the psychoanalysts might say—and accepts the male role as it has been played on the home stage. At least four of our fifteen men probably had experienced seriously damaged relations with their fathers, and even in the roseate glow of remembered childhood do not like the old man. Interpretation of this situation must be circumspect, since people are supposed to love their parents and are even commanded to honor them. During the interviews, however, interstitial comments, reportorial selection of incidents, and graphic silences, as well as the explicit expressions of like and dislike, present a clear picture of father-son relations.

There are, of course, many varieties of both bad and good father-son relations. In these four cases of damaged relations we note two patterns. One is *identification without affection*, represented by only one case. The other, the *rejection pattern*, is illustrated by three cases. This section briefly pictures the father-son relationships of these four men. In the following sections their political expression is explored.

Identification without Affection

The American youth, as we have noted, typically does not invest much emotional energy in a father rebellion on the European scale. But of course the latter does occur. And sometimes the process resembles the German pattern where the youth identifies with his father, struggles for his approval, gradually asserts himself against him as though assaulting a fortress, departs, and returns to be like him—another paternal fortress against his own son.

Sullivan, a truck driver and a former semiprofessional boxer, follows this tradition. Now, at the age of twenty-five, he stresses his respect for his father, but his report shows little affection. Of discipline he says:

> He was pretty strict—very strict. He'd been brought up strict, and in an old Irish family there, and of course, all the way through school it was very strict [the father went to a Catholic seminary]. So he was pretty strict with me, more so than with the two girls.

When asked about his father's good points he responds in the same terms, as though everything else were blotted out: "Well . . . [long pause] his good points were that he knew when to be

strict and when to be lenient." Except on the question of sports
(where the father gave instruction, but nothing is said of a good
time), there is little joy in this relationship.

Yet there is identification. The son has adopted his father's
strict manner. Sullivan had left his family because his wife would
not follow his orders about the management of the home; he
now sees that the children should, properly, give instant obedi-
ence. His rebellion—and he did rebel—is over:

> Oh, I knew everything when I was nineteen. Nobody could tell
> me nothing. Boy, oh, boy, I found out, though. That's one thing
> my father would always try and . . . teach me things, and offer
> advice and so on. But no, I wouldn't listen. He told me especially
> about discipline and orders and so on. I never used to like to take
> orders. I don't think I was in the service a month when I wrote
> and told him, "Boy, you were right. You said some day I'm going
> to say that—and boy, you are." The service was a good thing for
> me.

Sullivan is a "hard" man to deal with, not mean, but there is a
steely quality about him that reflects his experience in and
exaltation of the Army, as well as his father's values.

Rejection of the Father

Unlike Sullivan, three others, Woodside, Dempsey, and De-
Angelo, reject their fathers outright. There is no effort to cover
over their feelings, to take back the criticism, undo the damage,
unsay the words. Something within them is quite clear and solid
on this matter and they are not shaken by fear or guilt at the
thought of such rejection.

DeAngelo is a factory machine operative, whose father and
mother separated when he was an infant; he subsequently acquired a stepfather. Of his father, who lives in the same town,
laconically he says: "I don't bother with him." Of his stepfather:

> He was a good guy when he was sober, but he was bad when he was
> drunk. I never had too much respect for him. . . . When he was
> drunk he wanted to argue, you know. But my mother was bigger
> than him—didn't have too much trouble taking care of him. After
> a while my mother left him, you know, and we were on our own.

DeAngelo narrowly missed reform school when in high school—
from which the principal ordered him to leave, possibly through
a misunderstanding. But some maternally inspired internal gyro-
scope kept him on an even keel through a series of such adver-

sities. Today he is the father of six boys, a steady breadwinner, and union shop steward in the plant.

Woodside, a railroad guard with a conscience, remembers his childhood with horror because of the irresponsible, drunken behavior of his father and particularly his father's "outside interests" —women. He says, quite simply: "At one time I felt I'd hate my father—that if anything ever happened to him it would be a wonderful thing." But today he plays checkers with the pathetic old man and helps him when he's in trouble. He hated his father in the past for the beatings he gave his mother, the humiliation he brought on the household, and the physical suffering to the children: "It's a pretty gruesome thing to tell anybody that a father could neglect his kids so much. Believe me, a good many days I've seen where I had just water, and I was lucky to have water—for a meal for the whole day."

Dempsey is an older man who married a widow when he himself was forty, having previously lived with his mother and, until they were married, with his brothers. In comparison with DeAngelo and Woodside, his reactions to his father are more veiled and he identifies somewhat more with him. He thinks of him as "a hard-working man, the same as I am now, and couldn't get much further than I probably will . . . although my hopes are probably a little bit higher." But through the veil we see more granite than flesh and blood. Did his father have a sense of humor?

> Well, that I couldn't say. As I say, we were never too chummy with him. He never was a fellow to be chummy with us children. . . . He was one of them guys—it had to be it, or there was no way out of it.

There apparently were few family outings, little fun, and strict curfews. What things did Dempsey admire about his father? "Only that he was a hard worker, and gave us a chance to do— to choose what we wanted to—at the time [reference to choice of religion in which they chose the mother's religion]. Outside of that he was a very hard man." And a few minutes later he repeats, "He was a hard—a very hard and stern man."

C

THE POLITICS OF FILIAL ALIENATION

Having examined a modal American pattern of father-son relationships and isolated four deviant cases, we turn to an inquiry into the politics of these last four men.

Low Information and Social Interest

The question of political information is considered first, partly because it indicates the degree of interest in the social world outside oneself. Our measure of political information is made up of questions on local, national, and international institutions and events. The local events, in particular, are not usually learned in school, since they include such items as "Who is the local boss of Eastport?" and "How would you go about getting a traffic light put on your corner?" It is therefore especially significant that these four men, concerning political information, rank as the four lowest of the fifteen cases.

There are several reasons for this. The loss or lack of a secure parental model encouraged each of these four to frame his own life style and to engage in the lifelong business of self-discovery. Each man is his own Pygmalion. More importantly, the development of a personal sense of security, of being a loved and wanted and respected person, which is a bulwark against psychic conflict, is lacking. This lack seems to be borne out by the evidence of severe anxiety in all four cases. Dempsey and DeAngelo rank among the four highest scorers on the "neurotic anxiety" scale. Sullivan ranks third on a social-anxiety scale and shows evidence of severe sex tension as indicated by his top score in this area (and his marriage is breaking up). DeAngelo ranks fourth on this sex-tension scale. Woodside, while less troubled by sexual problems and not "neurotically" anxious, ties for first place on the scale of social anxiety; he is, by his own account and other evidence, a worrier, a searcher for all-around "security" and has somatic difficulties.

Anxiety can lead into politics as well as away from politics. People can defend themselves against anxiety by knowing more than others—or people may succomb to the demands of anxiety by knowing less. Generally in the American apolitical culture the anxious man does not employ politics as a defense against his conflicts. One of the little-appreciated benefits of such a culture is the low premium on politics for the anxious and neurotic.

Authoritarianism

Three of the four men score strongly on authoritarianism: DeAngelo has the highest score in the group, and Sullivan and

Woodside tie for fourth; only Dempsey's ranking is moderate. The genesis of authoritarianism and its close connection with father-son relations are well known. Here it is sufficient to note that in order to believe that people can live and work as cooperative equals or at least as trusting partners, a person must have experienced such a relationship. In their relations with their fathers, these men had no such experience.

Speak No Evil of the Political Leader

There is a third area of political outlook that seems to be shared by these four men with damaged father relations, a quality that in some measure sets them apart from the others. Although political lore would have it otherwise, people generally prefer to speak well of political leaders than to speak ill of them.[10] But the average citizen can criticize such leaders, designate those he dislikes, and weigh the good and bad points of each on occasion. Our four deviant cases found such criticism or even objectivity more difficult than the others.

Sullivan admires Monroe, Lincoln, Truman, and Eisenhower. He defends Truman against those who believe that his attack on the music critic was out of order. He defends Ike for the vacations he takes. When asked about political leaders he dislikes: "Well, from what I learned in history, Grant seemed to be pretty use-useless. . . . [pause] He didn't seem to do too much [mentions that he was a drunkard]. And [pause] I mean I don't dislike him, either, but—I don't dislike any of them." Question: "How about living leaders, or recent leaders, which of these would you say you had the least respect for?" Answer, after a pause: "Well, [long pause] none that I could think of."

Dempsey likes Washington and Lincoln, and, when probed, Wilson and Truman, for whom he voted. Asked about "any particular feelings about Dewey," he says, "No, I wouldn't say that." Roosevelt was "a very good man." Eisenhower is also a "very good man, doing everything he possibly can." He can think of no mistakes he has made.

10. In 1948 between a quarter and a third of a national sample could find nothing unfavorable to say about Truman or Dewey, but almost everyone could mention something favorable about both candidates. See Angus Campbell and Robert Kahn, *The People Elect a President* (Ann Arbor, Mich.: Survey Research Center, 1952), and Angus Campbell, Gerald Gurin, and Warren E. Miller, *The Voter Decides* (Evanston, Ill.: Row, Peterson, 1954).

DeAngelo says he doesn't particularly admire any political leaders. But: "I like them. I mean, I didn't think anything bad about them, y'know." Questioned about an earlier reference to Robert Taft, he replies:

> Well, I mean, I thought for being President, I thought he'd be a little better in know-how and savvy than Eisenhower, y'know. I ain't got nothing against Eisenhower—he's good, he seems to be honest enough, but I don't . . . I don't . . . I don't think he should have run again because I think his health is—his health was good enough.

DeAngelo has trouble expressing his reservations about Eisenhower even on the question of health. When asked specifically about people he dislikes, distrusts, or thinks to be weak or wrong for the job: "Well, I don't know, not offhand."

Woodside's views are a little different. He likes Eisenhower but is more willing to discuss his weaknesses (particularly his signing of an order to execute a deserter). He likes MacArthur as a "big man" and mentions Lincoln favorably. Asked about his dislikes and those he thinks did a poor job, he mentions others' criticisms of Roosevelt but then rushes to his defense, except to say that he thinks Eisenhower is "a little bit more mannish" than Roosevelt. The only political leader he mentions unfavorably is Adlai Stevenson, who strikes him as a man who could say "yes" when he means "no."

With the possible exception of this last comment, these remarks convey three themes:

1. Conventional leaders like Washington, Lincoln, and Monroe are admired.

2. The independent leader who doesn't let outsiders tell him what to do is admired—Truman would stand for no nonsense (Sullivan); Stevenson is too much influenced by his advisers (Woodside).

3. Authority figures are not to be criticized—an especially important point.

These four men are not notably deficient in their general ability to criticize or to express hostility. Why, then, do these four, whose relations with their fathers are strained, find it so hard to criticize political leaders in a wholehearted way?

In answering this question, Sullivan's case should be distinguished from the others. Sullivan feels guilty about his negative feelings toward the original political authority in the family. He cannot bring himself to express his hostility without quickly withdrawing his remarks and saying something of a positive nature. The expression of hostility to authority figures is painful, and Sullivan simply avoids this pain.

The other three men express outright hostility toward or unrelieved criticism of their fathers. Why not also of political authority? In the first place, there is a carryover of fear from the childhood situation that has not been obliterated by the adult emancipation. Men do not easily forget those childhood moments of terror when the old man comes home drunk, abuses the mother, or gets out the strap to deal with the child in anger unalloyed with love. Secondly, a combined worship and envy of strength exists, which father-hatred fosters in a child, for it is the father's strength in the family that penetrates the childish consciousness. Finally, there is the persistent belief in the futility and danger of countering and rebelling against authority. Although DeAngelo was a rebel in high school and was expelled, and Woodside stood up to his father, threatening him with a log behind the woodshed, both are successful now partly because they have curtailed these antiauthority impulses that threatened to bring disaster once before. Their consciences are composed of antirebellion controls; this is why, in part, they can be good citizens.[11]

Utopia and Conservatism

The basis for a hopeful view of the world lies in the self; the world is ambiguous on this point. In the self, the notion that we can move toward a more perfect society is supported by the belief that people are kindly by nature and considerate of one another. Moreover, when the idea of a better social order is developed even a little, the mind quickly turns to the nature of authority

11. The view that men with damaged father-son relationships do not like to criticize authority figures may seem to fly in the face of a popular interpretation of radicalism. This contradiction is more apparent than real. The effect of failure of socialization on normal populations is more likely to be apathy than radicalism. (See, e.g., P. H. Mussen and A. B. Wyszinski, "Personality and Political Participation," *Human Relations*, 5 [1952], pp. 65–82.) There are exceptions, of course, since relationships are always expressed as probabilities. In radical groups, moreover, the tendency to criticize authority figures is focused on those who are seen as illegitimate, usurpers, or leaders who are considered to be weak. This was Woodside's approach to Stevenson, and it was precisely the latter's "weakness," his lack of decisiveness, that Woodside criticized. Our findings are complementary, not contradictory, to other, similar studies in these respects.

in such a society. Is there a kind of authority that is strong and directive, yet at the same time solicitous and supportive of the weak in their infirmities—in short, paternal?

At the end of the discussion on Utopia, reported above, we inquired whether or not there is evidence that we are moving closer to such a society. Although the men were not asked if the world was possibly moving in the opposite direction, some volunteered this answer. Our fifteen men answered the questions on an ideal society as shown in Table IV:

TABLE IV

	Damaged Father-Son Relations	Others
We are moving closer to ideal society	0	8
We are not moving closer to ideal society	3	2
(volunteered) We are moving away from ideal society	1	1

The pattern is clear. Woodside first touches on the drift from a peacetime to a wartime society. Then, speaking of only the peacetime society: "Like we're in peace now, the society is about the same as it has been back along. . . . I would say that throughout history it has been about the same." Asked if people are happier now than they were a hundred years ago, he is reminded ironically of the phrase, "There's nothing like the good old days," and he digresses to say that people adjust so quickly to mechanical progress that their degree of satisfaction and dissatisfaction remains about constant.

Dempsey, as always, is more laconic. Asked the same question about possible progress toward a better society, he says: "No. I don't think so. I think we're going to stay on the same lines we are on right now."

And Sullivan: "Never. We'll never get any place close to it, I think." He first modifies his answer by noting that "prejudice" may decline, but is skeptical because "you can't change human nature."

DeAngelo takes the dimmest view of all: "I don't think we'll ever get any closer [to a more perfect society]. We're getting farther and farther away from it, I guess. All indications are we're moving away from it. There's not enough people trying to make the world perfect." Asked why we are retrogressing, he cites what he regards as the drift away from religion and the rise of Communism. These are perhaps the two most convenient pegs today on which to hang a deeply rooted pessimism regarding the social order.

Contrast these views with those of five cases selected because of their close identification and warm relations with their fathers. One says flatly that "I don't think we're far from it." Another points out that the population increase will bring about troubles, but he is hopeful because of the parallel increase of the proportion of good people. A third declares that every mistake we make teaches us something, hence the world is getting better. A fourth believes that a Socialist society is developing, which he thinks is probably a "good thing," although Socialism is not an "ideal" society. Only one of these five holds that such progress is unlikely, attributing this to the increase of governmental controls; but he adds, characteristically, "Maybe concurrently with such controls you're getting more of the things that most people seem to want made available to them."

D

FATHERS AND SONS—AND HISTORY

The state is "man writ large"; the family is a microcosm of society. The history of a nation may, in considerable measure, reflect the changes in the ways children and parents, sons and fathers, struggle to get along with one another. Some of the characteristics of a nation's politics may rest on the resolution of these struggles.[12] With this point in mind, we turn to certain aspects of American and foreign politics.

To recapitulate, in American society: (1) "good" father-son relations are the norm; (2) of those youth with rebellious feelings against their fathers there are few for whom the rebellion takes

12. Melancholy experience suggests that it is prudent to note that I am not denying the importance of a nation's history, or of its geography and economics or of its current leadership, in shaping its destiny. I do not imply, for example, that German Nazism arose because of an authoritarian family pattern rather than because of the Versailles Treaty, or Article 48 of the Weimar Constitution, or the weakness of von Hindenberg, or what not. Within Germany, however, those whose fathers forbade them from speaking at the dinner table were more likely to be Nazis than those whose fathers were more indulgent. (See Levy, *op. cit.*) German fathers were more likely to be repressive in this and other ways than fathers in certain other nations. The *combination* of defeat in World War I, the nature of German family life, and other factors, no doubt, helped to create a public responsive to Hitler's appeals.

political form; and (3) there is a tendency for moderately damaged father-son relations to be associated with relatively low levels of hope, interest, and capacity to criticize political leaders. These tendencies are revealed in what may be called the American political "style" in the following ways:

1. American politics is often said to embody a kind of consensualism in which both sides tend to come together, rather than a bipolarization or radicalism. At the same time, campaigns become quite heated with highly critical comments passed between the partisans of one candidate and those of another. This situation parallels the qualities we find associated with sons of strong but nurturant fathers: lack of alienation but a capacity for outspoken criticism.

2. Compared with the citizens of other nations, the American citizen is reported to be relatively well informed about current events and civic matters. On the other hand, his intensity of concern is relatively low. He can exchange blows during campaigns and then accept the victory of the opposition without much trouble. This pattern (a considerable cultural achievement) is difficult, as we have seen, for the poorly socialized, and again suggests an important family component in American democracy.

3. It is often noted that a strain of idealism exists in American international politics that distinguishes it from the hard-boiled realism of the Continent. Wilson's Fourteen Points, Roosevelt's Four Freedoms, and Truman's Point Four illustrate the character of this idealism, an idealism nourished by the hope that we can do away with war and establish a peaceful world order. Behind these beliefs and supporting them in their many expressions lies that quality of hope and trust that is forged in boyhood, when the son is apprenticed to a protective and loving father.

□ □ □ □ □ □ □ □ □ □ □ □ □ □ □

Cultural Premises

Metaphysics

18

The Day after Tomorrow: Of Time and Ideology

The great majority of men and women, in ordinary times, pass through life without ever contemplating or criticizing, as a whole, either their own conditions or those of the world at large. They find themselves born into a certain place in society, and they accept what each day brings forth, without any effort of thought beyond what the immediate present requires. Almost as instinctively as the beasts of the field, they seek the satisfaction of the needs of the moment, without much forethought, and without considering that by sufficient effort the whole condition of their lives could be changed.

—BERTRAND RUSSELL, *Proposed Roads to Freedom*, p. viii

Every culture has its special uses of time.[1] In the middle ages, says Huizinga, legislation "looks more towards an ideal past than towards an earthly future. For the true future is the Last Judgement, and that is near at hand." [2] Zimmer divides the philosophies of the East into two groups, "the philosophies of time," and the "philosophies of eternity." In the Mahayana tradition,

---

1. See, for example, A. I. Hallowell, "Temporal Orientation in Western Civilization and in Preliterate Society," *American Anthropologist*, 39 (1937), pp. 647–670; Pitirim A. Sorokin and Robert K. Merton, "Social Time," *American Journal of Sociology*, XLII (1937), pp. 615–629.

2. J. Huizinga, *The Waning of the Middle Ages* (Garden City, N.Y.: Doubleday, 1954), p. 35.

Buddha declined himself to enter the timeless void of Nirvana
so that he might remain as a savior to shepherd all earthly beings
into this state of timeless grace.[3] "In the beginning," said a chief
of the Digger Indians to Ruth Benedict, "God gave to every
people a cup, a cup of clay, and from this cup they drank their
life. They all dipped in the water, but their cups were different.
Our cup is broken now. It has passed away."[4] At the time when
Miss Benedict knew them, the Diggers, like almost all American
Indians, were living in the past. The ancient Jews lived in the
belief of a promised land; the ancient Cretans, by the time mytho-
logical history finds them, live in the memory of a golden age.

Every culture has a *rhythm,* marked by the organization of the
life cycle, with an emphasis upon youth, the working years, venerable age. It has a *pace* characterized by punctuality and pressure
to crowd achievement into limited time, or alternatively, by a
careless, spendthrift attitude toward time. It has a *historical focus,*
which may stress the past for its remembered glories, or the future
for its promise, or the present for the gratification of the senses.
It has *generational continuities* and discontinuities according to
the uses and unity of the family. And all these aspects of temporal
life are reflected in the political mind.

Rhythm

The rhythm of life, associated with education, marriage, career, parenthood in its several stages, retirement and death, is not
marked by great discontinuities as is the case in some cultures.
The Eastport common man passes, perhaps painfully but by
small degrees, from boyhood into adolescence, youth, adulthood,
and retirement. There are no great puberty rites—nothing even
as mild as the debutante's coming-out party; there is no entrance
to the warrior class marked by initiation; he is not sent away to
school as are the British upper-class boys; he grows up in his
family, goes to work in his hometown, marries a local girl, visits
his parents and brothers and cousins on weekends, rears his children until they can earn their own way, and then retires, living
not more than fifty miles from where he was born. Asked the
most important event in their lives, most say "getting married,"

3. Heinrich Zimmer, *Philosophies of India* (New York: Meridian, 1957), pp. 534–
535.
4. Ruth Benedict, *Patterns of Culture* (New York: Penguin Books, 1946; first
published 1934), p. 19.

a few mention buying a new car. Thus the rhythm of life is continuous, and there is some social preparation for each new stage. Within a society where social change is very great, marked by economic earthquakes such as the Great Depression of the thirties and the war of the forties, these men have experienced continuity. The Lynds say of the workingman of Middletown that in the thirties, "This man, with his feet on the ground, jerked about disconcertingly by 'good' and 'bad' times, lives in the South Side subculture of similarly placed working people, in which one learns to tolerate as normal, kinds of discontinuities that would upset his brothers north of the tracks. . . ." [5] But this is not true, or at least no longer true, in Eastport. The Eastportian does not "tolerate as normal" discontinuities of this kind; he is worried and upset by them, for he has not been prepared for this treatment. Most of his life has had a predictable pattern, and he values continuity. We should expect, therefore, a more general attitude toward social change that emphasizes and values incremental steps and continuous adjustment. And there is evidence that this is the case.

Pace

The pace of life is urgent. Rising at five-thirty or six, the white-collar men shave (the others may not), dress, breakfast, and either wait for the car pool or drive or take a bus to work on a tight schedule where a few minutes either way may make a big difference. Many of them punch time clocks; they lunch on a half-hour schedule, meet their appointments promptly, are constantly aware of time. None was more than a few minutes late for an appointment with me. The "mañana" attitudes of those who live for the moment have no opportunity to get started in a regimen such as this. And this is true of the Eastportian's social outlook; he is impatient of "promises" that are not punctually fulfilled (he expects the politician to make a down payment); he is scornful of relievers who cannot maintain the pace of work estalished by industry; his attitude toward the civil service is often marked by the sense that they "waste time." But his attitude toward time has the result that he does not "take time" to reflect. The punctuality and crowded-hours motifs seem inhospitable to leisurely contemplation that encourages speculation on the purposes of life and the aims of society.

Historical Focus: The Day after Tomorrow

What shall we say of the evaluation of past and present and future of the American workingman? Within what time frame does he operate? On the one hand, the American is said to be future-oriented. Santayana says of him, at the turn of the century, "What has existed in the past, especially in the remote past, seems to him not only not authoritative, but irrelevant, inferior, and outworn. He finds it rather a sorry waste of time to think about the past at all. But his enthusiasm about the future is profound." [6] On the other hand the workingman is everywhere known to have a very limited horizon. At the head of this chapter Russell is quoted as saying that the common men of the world live "without much forethought," without a picture of how things might be different in the future. Studies of the British working classes stress their lack of a sense of history, their inability to see themselves and their times in perspective, and their living for the moment.[7] During the great depression, the Lynds said of the workmen of Middletown, "Many of these people struck one as having pulled in their personal future to the point where it has little existence beyond the drab struggle just to keep alive." [8]

Men who anticipate the future use these kinds of phrases: "when we save up enough money, we will . . . ," "when I finish my training, I will . . . ," "we are sending John to parochial school to prepare him for . . . ," "when I retire we will move to . . .". Those who dread the future may not refer to it at all, or, if they do, scatter such phrases as "unless something happens," or "who knows where we'll all be by that time?" or "don't borrow trouble." Among the common men of Eastport these phrases are infrequent; they neither live in happy anticipation of a future they are preparing for nor do they dread it. Rather, their view is something else; it is an intense focus upon *the day after tomorrow*. Something of the source and nature of this focus is revealed in their early concepts of a career, their use of money, their ideas of happiness.

6. George Santayana, *Character and Opinion in the United States* (Garden City, N.Y.: Doubleday, 1956), p. 104.

7. Richard Hoggart, *The Uses of Literacy* (Boston: Beacon Press, 1961); B. M. Spinley, *The Deprived and the Privileged* (London: Routledge & Kegan Paul, 1953).

8. R. and H. Lynd, *op. cit.*, p. 475.

One might say that a future orientation would begin young in a society where the future held so much appeal. A boy's future lies in what he wants to be when he grows up—at the earliest stage a fantasy of cowboys and naval pilots, later some more sober reflections. There is a success story here among the Eastport fifteen: Woodside, the conscientious railroad guard and auxiliary policeman, says: "As far back as I can remember I always wanted to be a policeman. I played gangbusters or I played, you know, guns with my brothers and neighbors—I had to be the policeman." Now, at last, he is one, or almost one. But too often there is a blank, not a fantasy, but a hollow shell: "I don't think I really tried to figure out what I wanted to do." "That's what's wrong with me, I never had any ambitions." "That's a funny thing. Right through the war I had no idea which way I was going to go after the war." "That's the trouble with me, I didn't have any ambitions at all, but when I got married I wanted to try to get ahead." "I never did have an idea of what I wanted to be. I used to think about that a lot. Nothing seemed to be attractive." "I always had a problem like that, even at school. They ask me what you intended to be. I never had anything; nothing ever set my mind." Almost all are like that. Here the future orientation seems stillborn—not their father's trade, not running away to sea, not lawyer or President, only a vague emptiness. A boy's life is inevitably future-oriented—yet here the future lacks not only definition but luster.

The nature of his life gives to the common man a temporal orientation closely associated with money. He is usually paid an hourly rate; he calculates his overtime carefully, for this is time especially well invested at premium rates; when the plant shuts down he goes on "short time." In this sense, *time is money,* but it is also true that *money is time.* Asked about planning for the future, most of the men immediately thought in terms of saving: "When you're barely able to save a few bucks a week, why you can't plan nothing." "We were going to put by so much money for this, and we would have the money put away for it, and boom, all of a sudden something comes up." The control over their lives is tied to the inflow of money, the saving of money; control over money is, to them, control over the future. Men much poorer than these men can save to give them this control. Woodside is among the least well paid—yet he saves, when Johnson and Rapuano and other more prosperous men cannot. A future orientation would encourage it and make it possible.

Close attention to the future brings disappointment, and, perhaps even worse, provokes a fear of failure and illuminates the problem of ambition with a light too strong to bear. The fear of disappointment comes quickly to mind, as these men think of the control of their own futures. "You never plan ahead because it never works out." "I think people really should plan, but not put so much hope in their plans that they'll be really disappointed if they don't pan out." "I wouldn't plan ahead and figure that it's really going to happen. . . . I would *hope* that things were really going to work out." But beyond that, as McNamara, a bookkeeper, says: "If you're ambitious I think you can plan and set a goal. I'm not much for goal-setting. I don't know why—probably just inability to be aggressive." "If you were wealthy," says Rapuano, an inventory clerk, "you could plan things, but when you are a workingman, you can't plan nothing." Flynn, from his place in the civil service, says, "I'd like to think that it's possible to shoot for long-range goals, but in my present situation I think I have to accept the latter view, 'whatever will be, will be.'" Certainly one could not say that the future holds much terror for them, but it is uncertain, somewhat beyond their control. It does not have that bright fascination that observers, remarking on American future orientation, seem to believe. Yet, about half expect their incomes to be better in five years and, except for temporary layoffs, most believe their jobs are relatively secure. And all but two believe that society is so thoroughly stable that democracy will be here in its present form for as far as one can think ahead. Their dominant view is a kind of worried trust in their own future situations and a concentration on the problems of the moment.

Happiness could be regarded as a future good, something that will come with waiting, with effort, with luck. As they talk about happiness some of the men reflect this attitude; they think of happiness as something that will come as a condition of some prior situation; for Rapuano it is education, and since this is the case he cannot expect much happiness in his lifetime; for Johnson it is a kind of security for his family that he has been unable to provide; for Sokolsky it is more money so that you can "buy happiness" without worrying where the money will come from. But for others, somewhat more than half, happiness is a present good they enjoy now: "I'm satisfied with my job, being healthy, being able to do things that I want." "I myself am happy the way I am, perfectly contented." Or happiness may be here but unrecognized, as when Woodside, the railroad guard, says, "Lots of times your thoughts will get the better of you—you want more, and you don't realize that you're—that you should be a happy man." There is a kind of future orientation here, more marked for some; but the main overt theme, one might say, is that happiness is where you find it—enjoy what you've got. This is the overt theme—but one senses that this is the voice of men preaching to themselves a little homespun philosophy; few of them take their own advice and enjoy the moment without worrying about the morrow. And their discussion of their worries proves it; happiness would be a net reduction of tomorrow's quota of demands and irritations.

Within that span of time measured by the birth and death of a man, the center of attention is not the present—these men scorn the hedonism of the reliefers and alcoholics. And it is not the distant future, for they do not believe it is possible to plan far ahead, and indeed they have no distant plans for and little apparent interest in the later terms of their lives. The pathos of this position, and its existential basis, is reflected in Costa's predicament—Costa, an assembly-line operator who in his forties faces a world of uncertainty and the shadow of unemployment. Asked about planning his life, he says: "Well, I'll have to put—I'll have to answer you by personal experience—that every time we have set a long-range goal in the last fifteen years, something has happened to smash it. We planned on buying a house, fifteen years ago, and we have planned an awful lot of things, but something has always happened. I've had a lot of sickness in the family. My wife has been sick a dozen times—she's been in the hospital a half a dozen times, and there's nothing that will drain a limited treasury as fast as hospitals and doctors will. So it's been my experience that we can't do any long-range planning. *We don't just plan for tomorrow—we try to get somewhere halfway in between.*" And Costa is more sanguine than many of the others. As we have seen, for all of them there is a sensitive nerve here, perhaps a guilty nerve that touches some hidden fear of failure.

The Single Generation

The life span of a man is the measure of time for the men of Eastport. They hardly glance beyond their family circle into a future where they would not be; indeed, the whole notion of a coherent and relatively timeless society was exotic to their individualistic views. Perhaps such a view is hard to come by in the *Gesellschaft* society of our time, with its loose personal ties (and tight economic interdependence). Perhaps it is because, as Margaret Mead says, "We are all Third Generation" and have no individual, deep, gripping American past—and because there is no sense of the future without a sense of the past. This would imply that continuity is essential, or perhaps that a sense of history and participation in history must give the future its personal importance. Perhaps it is because our ties to society are often self-made, voluntaristic, severable at will, and hence what the world does when we are gone has only a loose connection with what we are and were. Perhaps it is because in an era of change as rapid as ours, when the familiar outline of a downtown neighborhood crumbles daily under the iron ball and the fields of suburbia disappear beneath a fungus of model homes, the image of the future becomes an alien, perhaps an unfriendly, thing.

Is it curious that a nation that has so emphasized progress should have no sense of the future? I do not think so. Progress is a rather thin and emotionally unsatisfactory variety of continuity. It is the continuity of differences, the regularity of a rate of change, almost a rate of estrangement. The men of Eastport believe with all their heart and soul in progress; over and over again they take satisfaction in the technical things they have that their parents didn't have, and, with less certainty, the things their children have that they did not have when they were children. (To some this seems soft and wasteful.) They were bitterly disappointed by Sputnik because it implied that the one thing they thought we had—a progressive technology and science—was at least shared with the hitherto despised Russian Communists, who perhaps even excelled in it. They are ready for more science in school, more technological miracles, more change in their daily lives—but this does not give them any resonance with a future they will not see. Progress seems not to speak to the heart as sameness does, particularly a sameness remembered from childhood.

We are talking about men, of course, not women, and men—particularly young men—are unlikely to live in their children's future. For one thing, they do not know what these futures will be—relatively few Eastportians had definite plans mapped for them; few had crystallized ideas on how to bring children up for the times we live in; few talked with the enthusiasm of an Emma

Lazarus or a Carl Schurz that one might expect from sons of immigrants about how their children would make their way in American society. Perhaps it is the permissiveness of the age, the idea that their future is their own responsibility, that takes the emotional force out of the parental dream. O'Hara, a mechanic aged thirty, with four boys and a girl, says: "I'd like to have them grow up and be pretty much what they—what I—get along with people. But what they decide to be is up to them. What they want to take up is up to them. I don't want to go and say, 'Well, you do this—you're going to do this,' or 'You're going to do that.' I want them to do something they're going to enjoy doing." He is certain of one thing: he won't let them quit school; but aside from that, O'Hara and the others will not push their children. And so, because it is so vague, so lacking in moral purpose, so cut off from a man's own life career, the son's future is not one in which the father can live.

The disembarrassment by an immigrant, or the son of an immigrant, of his family past is a story told many times—nowhere more beautifully than by Oscar Handlin.[9] The commonplaces of American historical reference have a pathos here that we shall do well to remember: "Fourscore and seven years ago *our* forefathers brought forth upon this continent . . ."; "*Our* frontier tradition"; "*Our* Anglo-Saxon heritage"; "*Our* Puritan background. . . ." But the lack of a sense of the past does not divide the sons of immigrants from the native sons, for neither sees the past as a guide and comfort in the present. Compared with the Osage, whose youth can all tell the legends of their ancestral beginnings,[10] or the Greek boy who daily fights again the battles of the Peloponnesian wars, the youth of Eastport, whether they are descended from the sons of the American Revolution or from the sons of Mazzini's Carabinieri, are historyless.

Temporal Framework and Ideological Bent

Within this framework of time, built upon the temporal experiences the culture provides, an ideology assumes a characteristic rhythm, pace, and historical perspective. The ideology of these men that emerges, which has been explicated in detail above, has four characteristics that seem, more than others, to be shaped by the temporal outlook of these men. But before examining these,

9. Oscar Handlin, *The Uprooted* (New York: Grosset and Dunlap, 1951).
10. Ruth Benedict, *op. cit.*, p. 26.

we may turn briefly to a question raised by Mannheim and Scheler.[11] Does the fact that these men are members of a "rising class" encourage a greater historical perspective or a tendency to look forward, a "prospectivism"? Mannheim says only members of a social class who "expect something" from history view it in perspective as a process; others see it in terms of unrelated, isolated events.[12] Certainly there is no evidence of such a view in Eastport; indeed, it is probable that here, as in Jonesville, the middle and upper middle classes think about and assume responsibility for the future of the city in a way that is completely beyond the working class, the unions, and their spokesmen.[13] (Nor, so far as we can tell, is it true generally that intellectual spokesmen of working-class interests place their demands in a historical perspective more than do the spokesmen of conservative interests.) The Marxian framework that this assumes is a bad fit here—and may be a bad fit in Europe, as well.

What is true is that the continuity of life in Eastport, marked by external disruption in the case of depression and war, but otherwise gradual and organized so that each phase has preparation and follows expected patterns, encourages a demand for continuity in political and social life. Departures from accepted policy, as in federal aid to education, social security, assumption of international responsibilities, are to start small and change incrementally. There are many reasons for this, among which the fact that policy is hammered out through processes of compromise is most important, but the framework of expectations of the public and the style of thinking of legislators draw nourishment from the regular phased rhythm of their lives.

The language of American politics is often vague, often deals with generalities, more often speaks of goals than means.[14] Yet at its most typical it seems more precise, and seems to deal more with means than the romantic politics, say, of Mexico or Greece or even · of France. Tocqueville said that every day he is awakened in France with a great new universal principle; [15] André Siegfried

11. See the report of Scheler's views in Werner Stark, *The Sociology of Knowledge* (New York: The Free Press of Glencoe, 1958), p. 77.

12. Karl Mannheim, *Ideology and Utopia* (New York: Harcourt, Brace, 1949), pp. 129–130.

13. W. Lloyd Warner and associates, *Democracy in Jonesville* (New York: Harper, 1949), pp. 137–143.

14. See Paul F. Lazarsfeld, Bernard Berelson, and Hazel Gaudet, *The People's Choice* (New York: Columbia University Press, 1948), pp. 115–119.

15. Alexis de Tocqueville, *Democracy in America*, ed. by Phillips Bradley (New York: Knopf, 1945), II, 14.

says, "Principles and ideals are the very heart and soul of our politics, but their eventual application often remains a matter of quasi-indifference." [16] Is it not probable that the daily habit of punctuality, temporal awareness, and temporal discipline so characteristic of the lives of these men leads them to ask of politics, as of other matters: When? The indefinite future has no resonance with their own thinking; it is not real to them. Moreover, their experience with precise units of time and precise units of money leads them in their own terms to prefer concepts with more or less precise boundaries, pragmatic terms with clear referents. A language of politics that speaks of "human destiny" and "the soul of the people" and "the altar of humanity" sounds strained not only because it is embarrassingly "sentimental" but also because the referents are unfamiliar, rarely used in discourse, and have no associations that give emotional appeal. The pressures of money and time are pragmatic; political discourse, however it may deviate from the norm, is leashed by this preference for clear referents, defined boundaries.

But the temporal framework of the Eastport common man bends his ideology in two other directions of even greater importance. In the first place, the day-after-tomorrow focus eliminates a bread-and-circuses orientation, for that is too contemporary, and a chiliastic orientation, for that is too distant. The utopianism of the Communists who promise a glorious but distant future has no appeal for many reasons, but one of them is that it refers to a point in time out of focus for these men. They are not thinking about or planning for such a period; nothing that means much to them will happen in such a period; it is like a foreign land they have never heard of.

And in the second place, the failure to extend their private range of interests and attention beyond their own generation tends to limit the social goals that have much appeal to them. It erodes their nationalism and patriotism, for with this abbreviated time perspective there can be no "eternal nation" to carry on some significant interpretation of life; there is no Eternal America as there was an Eternal Rome. Moreover, there is no sense in Eastport, as there is said to be in Moscow, that one generation is building something for the next. Their discussion of Utopia, the perfect society, is emaciated in part because they have not given

16. André Siegfried, *France: A Study in Nationality* (New Haven: Yale University Press, 1930), p. 25.

a thought to the world they would like their children to live in. Their concept of "building a better world," to the extent that they have one, is to "brighten the corner where they are," that is, individualistic and short term. Intergenerational goals require cooperative efforts; but because their lives are lived in the generation of which they are a part, they are not forced to seek cooperative efforts. Ideology, under these circumstances, tends to remain individual and short term.

19

Place and Community:
The Geography of Ideology

Life [in America] has ceased to be expressed in static, spatial terms
as it was in Europe, where generation after generation tied their
security to the same plot of ground, or if they moved to a city,
acted as if the house there, with its window plants, was still anchored by fruit trees.
—MARGARET MEAD, *And Keep Your Powder Dry*, pp. 29–30

Like the sense of time, the sense of place and community
helps to shape a person's social outlook. The way he is attached
to his community, the way he thinks of foreign places, the image
he has of the unknown "out there," or of strangeness in people
and places, all give direction to his thoughts. Here we examine
two aspects of this problem, the sense of place and the conflict
between national and community loyalties and interests.

A
THE SENSE OF PLACE

For each individual, one might trace upon a map an outline
of places where he has been and that therefore have some personal
associations for him, places his relatives and close friends have told

him about, places he has read about in the papers or heard about
on radio and television. These places have associated with them
some differentiated characteristics, perhaps caricatured as on a
child's map. Outside these designated places is *terra incognita,*
which has blank spaces for the names of countries, cities, harbors,
and rivers or is known for some single trait: "Amelia Earhart
flew here"; "Here natives use poisoned darts"; "The Panama
Canal is someplace around here." For Dempsey this *terra incognita*
commences a few miles outside Eastport; for Flynn and Farrel it
shrinks somewhat, but still covers most of the world. In general,
the evidence of the Hollywood caricatures (the Fu Manchu China,
the Cuba of the conga line) is minimal. The world is a more serious place; natives are not "funny" any longer.

All the Eastport common men, with perhaps two exceptions,
have been outside their state; some of them a thousand miles or
more either in the armed services or visiting a relative's hometown in search of work. Four had been abroad when they were in
the armed service—but, of course, none as tourists. Our interest
is in how they thought about geographical space and place, how
they used it in their social philosophies. By means of a measure
of local (Eastport) versus cosmopolitan (national and international) interests, a measure to be explained below, I have isolated
two men who have very different kinds of orientations toward the
geography of the world, different senses of place: Sullivan, a truck
driver with a local orientation, and Costa, an assembly-line operative with cosmopolitan interests. A content analysis of all (136)
references to places in the interviews with these two men provides
the basis for several tentative conclusions.[1]

These men, Sullivan and Costa, cited places (countries, states,
cities) in the following ways:

1. The sites of things they themselves did: shop, work, reside,
visit.

2. The sites of things relatives and, more rarely, friends, did:
travel, go to school, reside, work.

1. All proper names of continents, regions, nations, states, and cities were included in the count. All specific references to places, even if the name had been
forgotten, were also included. The distribution and the relative length of the interviews are as follows:

	REFERENCES TO PLACE			*Total Pages of*
Name	*Foreign*	*American*	*Total*	*Interview Material*
Sullivan	19	9	28	184
Costa	57	51	108	243

3. The places where public men came from: Dewey and New York, Knowland and California.

4. The sites of public events of great and little importance, of which the sites of wars (Korea, Ethiopia) form an important part, but which also include the sites of conferences (Yalta), strikes (Racine, Wisconsin), spying activities (Brooklyn), bombing (Hiroshima), and so forth.

5. Geographical names to indicate the actors in public events. ("Russia is not so much ahead in missiles as people say"; "Washington will not go to the summit.")

6. The location of certain general attributes (Arkansas and Missouri as characteristic of agricultural states, New York and Pennsylvania as characteristic of states with large electoral votes, Arabia as characteristic or symbolic of the "poverty-stricken East").

First, Sullivan, the "local" truck-driver, employed place names more as the labels of actors than as the sites of events. For him place was an aid in dramatizing world events, not a setting for events that had a drama of their own.

Second, Costa, the "cosmopolitan" machine operator, not only associated place names with events in his personal life; he also used these personally known places to give meaning to public events. He uses his trip to the South and his brother-in-law's information about the South to bolster his discussion of desegregation. Some events in World War II are given special meaning because his uncle fought in France, Germany, and Italy in World War I.

Third, the use of place names is a feature of a more general specificity orientation. Costa is not more intelligent than Sullivan, but with respect to people and events, as well as place, he is more specific.

Fourth, familiarity with the geography of America or the world seems to have little bearing on fear of "strangeness" or xenophobic feelings. Sullivan is more ready to move than Costa; both men support the United Nations; both support local desegregation.

While these inferences have a general bearing on the world view of the Eastport common man, there are two other inferences that affect ideology formation with greater force. One of these (the fifth point) is the redefinition of a sense of place based upon an examination of the central quality, which makes Costa's discussion more fruitful and informative than Sullivan's. This is not his knowledge of place names. Rather it is the association of some one event with another event through the use of geographic place. It is this, and only this, that makes events in distant places more meaningful. It is through this device that a common-man geographer becomes a cosmopolitan.

And, finally (sixth), the sense of place defined in this way tends to pluralize the world; it reduces the "we-they" polarization apparent in Sullivan's thinking. Sullivan is not more xenophobic than Costa, but his interest in foreign places has to do with their relation to the United States. He is preoccupied with the question of whether or not Americans are liked abroad, what foreigners think of us. He sees reasons for their not liking us—the drunken behavior of American soldiers and sailors, our greater strength and very recent accession to power. But the focus is a "we-they" focus; his interest in foreign affairs revolves around a single axis. With Costa it is different; he mentions conflicts and wars in which the United States did not enter (Japan and China, Italy and Ethiopia) —something Sullivan did not do. He compares Germany with Russia; he includes more nonconflict references; he uses places to locate events with no partisan significance (Israel and anti-Semitism, Norway and Quisling). Neither of these men tends more than the other (relative to their own total references) to use the cold war as the major axis of perception. But it is certainly true that Costa's broadened familiarity with the world makes a more interesting, more complicated drama, a multidimensional plot.

B
COMMUNITY

If, like their personal geographies, their ideologies were somehow mapped, some men would have large sections devoted to the local community events, and some would embrace greater national and international areas. Rapuano, on the margin between blue and white collars, says "I'm not interested in local politics at all . . . [but] I can tell you probably the leaders, practically, of all the countries of Europe." Ferrera, a taxi driver turned shoe salesman, says "I'm more interested in local affairs. . . . The United Nations—that's something that has never interested me." Behind this lies a more general attention frame into which political interests may be fitted, a relatively stable map of interests and perspectives.

It has long been thought desirable that psychic space and political space be congruent; it is the crux of the idea of self-determination. This is said to make representation meaningful because the representative represents more than a loose aggregate of people with little in common; but there are also occasions when it is just as well for a larger comity that some groups should find their political space fractioned, or shared with others, as might be true of an urban ghetto or of the southern region of the United States. In Eastport, as in most cities, the political space marked off into words and precincts has almost no congruence with any meaningful classification of space in the minds of Eastportians—not neighborhoods, which are themselves of declining importance, not ethnic boundaries, with perhaps three or four exceptions. (It is true that Hilltop is something of an exception, a housing development with coterminous political boundaries, and hence common interests, a common organ of expression [The Hilltop Council], common facilities.) The county, the state senatorial district, the congressional district have no trace lines in psychic space such as those we suggested. Even the state has little meaning, loyalty, community. There are, in the minds of Eastport, two areas of importance: *local,* which includes an area larger than the city of Eastport, and *national,* coterminous with national boundaries. What is international becomes interesting because the United States and perhaps the "Old Country" is a participant, a competitor in international affairs.

Local Direct Experience versus Mediated National Influence

It is the rival claims of local and national interests in the minds of the Eastport common man that attract our attention. Twelve of the fifteen men were born and brought up in the Eastport area, and although most have been outside the area for visits and about half have been in the service, their friends are all local, and most of the relatives they speak of are within a visiting range. But it is the quality of experience, as well as its duration, that seems likely to affect their private geographical map, particularly the quality of childhood experiences. Kuchinsky, a roofer, speaks of swimming in the Eastport River; Costa, a factory operative, hates to see buildings he knew as a boy torn down in the redevelopment; De-Angelo, a machine tender, remembers the fields where they used to play ball until chased away by the older children. Eastport is *home* to them in a sense that has a remote and nostalgic meaning to the wandering professional man, tied to occupation but not to place. Some of the officials are known, as names familiar for many years, as high-school chums. This, it seems plausible to believe, *should* give to their thinking and discussion of local events a special personal quality, rich in association and references. I can illustrate this kind of experiential basis of discussion of local affairs with a few phrases from Johnson's discussion of "what the local government is doing these days." Johnson, a mechanic, says, "Well, one thing, we all know they're certainly been making some awful poor excuses about this snow removal. . . . They did make an awful job on the snow removal. . . . And that statement that Duffy [the police chief] made—he rode around for four hours and found the streets were passable. Oh, my God! . . . He lives up your way, there, you know; sure, he lives over on Fuller Avenue. It isn't far from you, you know. Laudano [the former mayor] lives over there on Roosevelt Avenue. . . . I know him to say 'hello' to." Ruggiero, the university maintenance clerk, takes a special interest in a jewelry store involved in a redevelopment conflict; Costa speaks with affection of a solid old building about to be torn down. The gossipy, hometown mention of names and places, common references, the "placing" of people by some personal association (one hears the villager say, "Oh, yes, that's Zeke's boy"); the locating of an event by anecdote and personal experience ("That's on my old paper route"); the special attention to snow removal (as above), traffic, lighting, street repair, garbage collection—these represent the signs of localism in the allocation of psychic space. Because they are immediate, close, emotionally linked to personal experience, they should be influential.

Competing with this is another set of influences centered on the media. The television often brings national figures even closer to home than local figures whom one may see in person; their presence is staged, dramatic. National affairs are set in the context of rivalry and competition in which Eastport is often on one side, whereas local affairs are often between factions one does not identify with, often merely matters of "competence" or "bungling." Magazines, with their color and special appeal, are national; the Eastport daily press, less local than Boston or San Francisco papers, for example, gives emphasis to national news. The features, the sports, the comics are national. Where once economic well-being seemed to hinge on local decisions made in the local mill or store, or on the local weather, now the men talk about United States Government contracts, national unemployment insurance, federal public works. Leadership, human-interest stories, the relevant economic decisions, the relevant partisanship in conflict have been nationalized. All this is reflected in the talk of the Eastport men. Local attention versus national attention: it is a fair contest for a man's limited attention and fund of public concern.

Local Space on a Psychic Map

In assessing the outcome of this contest, or, really, how this contest affects Eastport's outlook on local affairs, I use four terms: (1) *localism,* referring to the kind of thing mentioned above, an attention frame where the events of the city and its environs assume a special importance marked by personal association; (2) *rootedness,* the emotional hold the area has on a person's loyalties—the feeling that other places are "strange"; (3) *leverage,* the feeling that one can affect the direction of affairs, help to control one's destiny; and (4) *community identity,* a belief that one shares the place with like-minded others who are, so to speak, psychologically embraced as "we" and "us."

LOCALISM   As for the localism of the Eastport common man, it is an anemic thing, or so it appears in the record. About half of the men say that they are more interested in local affairs than in national affairs, but this interest seems not to be supported by the variety of rich associations and personal references one expects. Johnson's gossipy attack on "what the local government has been doing lately" is one of the very few that moves off onto these personal tangents. Local political leaders are known and talked about, but reference is mostly limited to their official roles, their official duties. There is hardly any difference in the style of answering the question "What has Congress been doing lately?" and the similar question on local government. Even the local irritants that can absorb a man and that government is supposed to do something about were diminuendo: snow removal was mentioned three times; parking, lighting, schools were mentioned once each. Perhaps Eastport is too large for localism to flourish; perhaps it has an ethnic base for which I was a foreigner; but even more important, perhaps the media have nationalized political gossip, along with diet and style.

ROOTEDNESS   Next to this general failure of localism, and at first somewhat inconsistent with it, is the sense of *rootedness* some of the men have, but most do not. In a discussion of how a man would feel if his job made it necessary for him and his family to leave Eastport, about a third of the men, the least educated, by and large, indicate that they would be very reluctant to go; about a third would go if necessary and if they could persuade their wives; and about a third would go wherever opportunity beckoned, with scarcely a backward glance. For the reluctant ones and the hesitating ones, the things that they would miss are illuminating for the question of local versus national interests. Costa illustrates this mood: "Well, of course, you must understand that I was born and brought up in Eastport. I did it [moved out of town] once, in 1947, and the thing I missed most—I was away for a year —and the thing I disliked most was, oh—walking down the street and not knowing anybody, and walking down the street and not being sure what the street was at the next corner. . . . It was difficult for the first few months. . . . With me, it was all strangers." But, he adds later: "In fact, I was reasonably happy out there. I would have stayed if things would have turned out the way we had hoped they would." Costa says he missed his nieces and nephews most of all. Ruggiero, who says he "would feel very badly" if he had to move, also stresses his family. DeAngelo says he would miss the people he knows, his family and friends. Kuchinsky says, "I think I'd be a little lost in another city or town— I mean, to make friends, and, uh, it's hard enough here." These words have feeling; Eastport *is* a place where they are not strangers, where they have family; they have to this degree a sense of place, a sense of home community. But it is personal and familistic. To a very considerable extent it is the closeness of an extended family that the immigrants brought here and continued among their sons and, in a weakening tradition, their grandsons, that makes Eastport home for these men. And this was more true of the wives (according to the husbands' reports) than of the men. As for the unrooted ones: Sokolsky says about leaving Eastport, "I think I would like it very much"; Johnson says leaving Eastport wouldn't bother him much, and under questioning says, "I don't think I'd miss anything too much." Rapuano says, "As of right now, I wouldn't miss anything in Eastport. Oh, no." Ferrera is footloose and ready to go, and so is Flynn, though with a slight hesitation about his wife.

The conflicting motives in these two kinds of cases are different. For the rooted, they center about a fear of strangeness, loneliness, and the unfamiliar; for some of the unrooted, they embrace in part a desire to run away from troubles, to chuck it all, to be someone else and act like someone else in a setting that would support this different self-image. Neither of these seems likely to lead to a greater interest in local public affairs. The desire to run away, held in check by some prudential calculation or more rooted wife, is not going to lead back into the community. But it is also true that for the rooted, the fear of strangeness and love of family and circumscribed family-visiting pattern has only a limited power to awaken a wider interest in local affairs. It is exactly the rooted person who is most likely to confine his interest and emotion to the daily round of work and home, television and church, family and relatives, with nothing left over for community, government, and politics. After all, downtown Eastport may be more "strange" than the familiar set of a television Western, and much more dangerous.

There are a few, however, who show a much greater interest in local affairs than in national affairs. If we look at the range of information they possess, naturally we find that the more intelligent and better-educated men tend to rank higher in both local and nonlocal information. If we look at those with much higher information scores in one area than in the other, we have a way of locating a group of "locals" and another group that, after Merton, we shall call "cosmopolitans." [2] (As it turns out, the two groups are remarkably close in average years of education.) Five men showed a discrepancy of over six rank differences in this comparison, two being markedly better informed about local matters than about national and foreign affairs, and three reversing this. Two of the three "cosmopolitans" (Farrel and Rapuano) were among the three born and brought up outside the Eastport area, while the third cosmopolitan, Costa, collects information about world affairs the way many people (Costa included) collect information on baseball statistics; the data become counters in conversational gamesmanship. Sullivan, the trucker with a pugilistic past, and Ferrera, the shoe salesman, are the "locals" of Eastport —Ferrera has been a minor Republican politician, and Sullivan

2. Robert K. Merton, "Patterns of Influence: A Study of Interpersonal Influence and Communications Behavior in a Local Community," in Paul F. Lazarsfeld and Frank N. Stanton, eds., *Communications Research, 1948–49* (New York: Harper, 1949), pp. 180–219.

has been on the Hilltop Community Council; they have lived their interest in local matters and they are infinitely cynical about the nature of man, events, and people beyond the immediate low horizon that hems them in.

In a crude way, one might say that local politics deals with people face to face, and national and foreign politics deals with events, or perhaps images of people—at least, the mixtures of these categories are quite different in these two areas. It is suggestive, therefore, that Sullivan and Ferrera, the locals, rank 3 and 5 on an "Information on Political People" scale, while the cosmopolitans, Farrel, Costa, and Rapuano, rank, respectively, 14.5, 8, and 12—this in spite of the generally superior level of information of the cosmopolitan group. The contour lines of the individual's political map are shaped by his interest in, need for, doubts about, fear of—other people.

LEVERAGE   While localism is minimal, and only a third of the men seem "rooted" in Eastport, there is no doubt that the sense of political leverage has a local focus. This comes about in several ways, one of which is the multiple contacts these common men have with authoritative persons: Costa has cousins relatively high in both parties and has witnessed the framing of a local party platform; Ferrera has forced the Department of Public Works to patch a street, or thinks he has. (Of course, there are disappointments, too: Hilltop rents were raised in spite of an organized protest, and the schoolyard was denied to a citizen group seeking to put up a skating rink.) Another local source of this sense of political leverage comes from the feeling that elections provide a better control over known candidates, for, as Flynn, a reflective railroad supply man, said: "The vagueness increases with the level of the election. In local elections they discuss issues which people can readily understand, because they're close to the situation." Except for Ruggiero, who is close to the congressman from the district, those who participate in elections participate in local elections. Much of the feeling that government is responsive to the needs of the common man comes from such experiences as this; much of the belief that "authorities listen to me" is a generalization from experiences with local authorities who did.

COMMUNITY IDENTITY   But is there anywhere, then, that broader sense of community identity, " a belief that one shares a place with like-minded others who are psychologically embraced as 'we'?" As we noted above in Chapter 14, the conditions are not present for such a feeling. It is the product of generations of common living; it is hard to create in one or two disoriented generations. It must be surrounded with a known and discussed history, a folklore and mythology, which only a few American cities seem able to record and keep alive. Rivalries and outside challenges help, but Eastport has no such historic rivalries. There must be a social vehicle to keep it alive, a continuing group where memories are reinforced by telling stories. Community identity is a product of an immobile society, a static society; the cost of labor mobility, equality of opportunity, and technical change is a lost community identity—and it is a real price to pay. Perhaps soon we shall find, to our mixed sorrow and relief, that national identity is going the same way.

Community and Ideology

How do these findings help to account for the political ideology of the common men of Eastport? The anemic quality of the personal references to Eastport places and people, the special familistic basis for rootedness where it exists, and the almost complete absence of community identity reveal again the weakness of the social bonds that bind the Eastport men to one another and to their community. This means, first, that local tradition has no real force; it neither develops into something different from the "traditions" of other communities nor does it offer any resistance to the nationalization of culture, convention, and ideology. The apparent lack of personal references to people and places, the apparent community detachment of some, and largely familistic attachment of others, the small sense of identification with Eastportians as such all impose obstacles to the development of ideas of how "we" in Eastport do things, the development of special strengths and characteristics associated with Eastport men, special beliefs and moral values. In this way the situation opens up a freedom of behavior and role interpretation that causes men, in their anxiety, to invoke another standard: Americanism. Some greater localism, such as local standards and customs and sentimentalized codes, would offer an alternative. But these local standards and loyalties fail, and Americanism and the "American way" must carry the load in their place.

A second inference to be drawn from this failure of localism deals with what we have termed "homelessness." Because of the nature of their experiences in the local community, those suffering this homelessness do not adopt a return to "community" as part of their half-conscious program of reform. Had they experienced real village life, or been embraced in some solidary homogeneous traditional society (perhaps a ghetto or a Little Italy or other ethnic enclave of long standing) they would have a standard of life that would fit their needs. Not having known this, their homelessness does not point in this direction; it is more destructive, more anomic.

In view of the fact that some current criticism of what is called "mass society" rests upon the loss of organizations and loyalties intermediary between the individual and the state, loyalties such as those involved in strong community identification, localism, and rootedness, it is worthwhile to look again at those who come closest to having these attitudes. They are, in our sample, those who would be most reluctant to leave Eastport (the rooted) and those who are relatively most interested in local affairs (the locals). The rooted, we said, were not more interested in local affairs than were the others; their source of interest in and adherence to the community was, in fact, their families and their fear of a strange world outside their familiar orbit. The locals, we found, were those who, among other things, seemed to know and to interest themselves in political people, as contrasted to political issues. I argued that it was the face-to-face quality of local politics and affairs, its gossipy nature, that reinforced other tendencies to keep them looking homeward. Although the evidence is slim, it does not reinforce the argument of men like William Kornhauser who fear that the decline of community attachment and loyalty weakens democracy—making leaders too accessible to masses, masses too labile and available for manipulation.[3] On the contrary, it seems that those who best serve democracy today are neither those who wish to leave home nor those who could not be moved, but those who hold community and local friends as valued ties in a world of plural values, some of which are served by mobility. Democracy's friends are those who can extract meaning from the less-personalized conflicts that, more than is the case in local politics, become involved in *national* political situations.

3. William Kornhauser, *The Politics of Mass Society* (New York: The Free Press of Glencoe, 1959).

20

The Explanation of Political Events

To be versed in the ways of nature means that a man has observed outside facts and reasoned about them. He has used his powers not to escape from the world but to think himself more deeply into it. To the Greeks the outside world was real and something more, it was interesting. . . . The Greeks were the first scientists and all science goes back to them.
—EDITH HAMILTON, *The Greek Way*, p. 22

In this chapter I want briefly to focus upon three aspects of explanatory style: (1) the relative emphasis placed upon personal and impersonal agents of change, (2) the way in which men draw upon culture, group, and self for material in accounting for political phenomena, and (3) the use of the self as an instrument for judging reality. All three of these issues, it seems to me, have crucial importance for the effective functioning of public opinion in a democracy.

A

THE "WHO" AND THE "WHAT" IN IDEOLOGY

If you ask men about the causes of war and poverty, as I did, or about race conflict, juvenile delinquency, traffic jams, or other

307

public issues, you will get answers that attribute the cause either to certain people or to certain circumstances. An adequate answer usually includes both: certain people who deal more or less adequately with certain situations in certain circumstances. But some respondents will tend to ignore the circumstances and focus almost exclusively on the men they think have the power to alter a situation, usually the political leaders, but sometimes a group of men thought to be behind the leaders. My argument here is that such an exclusive focus upon the causal role of leaders of a society is dysfunctional for a democracy, for the following reasons. In the first place it focuses attention upon men almost to the exclusion of issues, encourages the personalization of politics, and lends credibility to the evasive formula "I vote for the best man regardless of party." In the second place, it leads to a kind of passivity that is best exemplified by Dempsey's view of freedom as the area where "*they* let us do what we want." It weakens men's effort to think about the problem that faces them, corrupts their inclinations toward self-help. In the third place it makes the object of all reform (and antireform) the elimination of "bad" men from office and their replacement by "good" men, a style we have seen in municipal reform and then seen challenged by Lincoln Steffens' argument that the difficulty lay in a system of temptations and opportunities and power that trapped good and bad men alike. Fourth, and in a closely related way, it implies that under all circumstances a great-enough leader can relieve his followers of their frustrations, a point of view that under unfavorable circumstances leads to a search for a savior, a *caudillo*. And sixth, because the focus upon the main actors in an event to the exclusion of an understanding of their circumstantial conditions and limits can never offer a fully satisfactory explanation, it is a poor guide to political experience. It is unrealistic.

In the next chapter I shall show how rarely these men explain events by emphasizing *who* is to blame. Nevertheless, particularly in the discussion of the causes of war, there was some tendency to explain these ills as due, rather simply, to the greed of political leaders. Four men avoid this theme and turn to the economic, demographic, or other causes of war—or, in some cases, to what they interpret to be the "needs" (motives?) of the people. Here is Woodside, the railroad guard, representing those who mention "greedy leaders":

> When I think of war, I always think of a person that's greedy—so speaking, it would be a nation, not as the people themselves, but as the people running the nation. We'll say, for instance, Germany in the last war; it was just through greediness that they wanted to be the masters, so to speak. . . . It's because the government head itself, not the people, gets greedy and wants to be the aggressor.

And here is how McNamara, the bookkeeper, representing those who employ impersonal arguments, starts his answer to the question on the origin of wars:

> That's a good one. [pause] Well, I guess history points up that it's economic troubles—people living in spots where they can't provide for their own—their own living. The land is poor, or they have poor access to ports, the sea. And then, it may be just a natural urge to grow.

The three others who answer in this vein are Farrel, O'Hara, and Flynn.

Is this ability to deal with impersonal causes "topic bound," related only to war and not to other issues? As we shall see, in the discussion of the causes of poverty in the United States there were two emphases in that discussion: (1) poverty is primarily the fault of the individual poor, and (2) it is, at least partially, the fault of the society that fails to provide work or opportunity. Flynn balances his answers so carefully between these views that he cannot be assigned to one or the other. The other three (Farrel, O'Hara, and McNamara) are among the seven who stress, again, the circumstantial, social causes.

It is not hard to see what these men have in common that distinguishes them from the others. As a group they are somewhat better educated, they have occupations that (except for O'Hara) require of them somewhat more abstract thinking, and they are relatively more self-controlled and less impulsive, ranking 2, 3, 4, and 6 in ego strength. They are, as expected because of their education, low on authoritarianism. They are also low on "neurotic anxiety." But, unexpectedly, they are only about average on "faith in people." Except for this last measure, one might say they are the more intelligent, the more integrated members of the sample, and the men with the best social adjustments. (Farrel's presence in this group introduces an uncertain factor in the last judgment.) In talking about their own personal affairs, they are the most realistic.

As supporting evidence of my contention that the capacity to deal with impersonal causes is important for democractic man (and with due recognition of the intervening influence of education), I would draw attention to the fact that none of these men is among the cabalist group, none is an undemocrat, none is among those we said feared an extension of freedom, and none is alienated or homeless.

Two ideas follow with some insistence from these observations and evidence. One is that a central civic function of education is to release men from reliance upon personalistic explanations, to enrich their explanatory repertory to include social and impersonal causes. Ignorance personalizes! More than that, it causes people to think of men as autonomous of their environment, permitting explanations of why they act as they do solely in terms of a series of motives—rage, greed, ambition. Another way to put this is to say that one of the functions of education is to limit the range of explanations for which "free will" offers any kind of satisfaction.

The second idea follows from the first. A public opinion is only as "good" as its underlying explanatory premises; for a democracy, we have said, these must include a capacity to employ impersonal causes. Now we are engaged in a great international enterprise to encourage the gradual development of democratic forms in the developing areas of the world. Can these democratic forms be sustained without a public opinion some part of which is capable of using impersonal causes in their explanatory systems? Unless a public has learned in school or on the radio, or, less likely, in church, how to explain events in this way, unless leadership is given to this explanatory system, the support that public can give to democratic forms, I believe, is too fragile for the occasion.

B
THE SOURCES OF EXPLANATORY MATERIAL:
CULTURE, GROUP, AND SELF

The materials for a man's explanations may be said to lie in two places: in that part of the culture to which he is exposed, and in himself. Some aspects of culture are special to his position in society; some are more widely shared. A man weaves the suggestions he gets from these sources into something that serves his temporary needs with hardly a thought of their origins.

From his culture he may get didactic answers. Asked about the causes of poverty in China and India, everybody in Eastport answers "ignorance" or "lack of education." On the other hand, "we" are advanced because we are educated—it is a cultural axiom.

But sometimes the culture offers choices, and if these are linked to group identities, men are guided by this social identification. An interesting example of this is evident in the division between those who thought that poverty in America was due to individual failure and those who thought it was due to social causes—the issue mentioned above. Seven of the Eastport men explained poverty in individual terms. Sokolsky says, for example: "Well, if a person's in poverty, there's something wrong with the person themselves. Because there's a lot of opportunities in this country, and if a person really wants to go out and work, they'll find work." On the other hand another seven (we must eliminate Flynn from this count, as noted above) place the responsibility upon the system. Rapuano, the supply clerk, says: "It's not hard to say: poverty is caused by recession in business. Depression—people not working—that causes poverty."

I have mentioned one of the factors that account for the difference in these explanations, the capacity to deal with impersonal causes. But there is another. One might think that the stress on the individual causes of poverty might be a product of a conservative ideology, but the men who answer this way are no more conservative (on a liberalism-conservatism scale) than the others. They have something else in common, however; they identify with the middle and the upper classes. One of them (Woodside) thinks of the upper classes as "being in the knowledge of it all the time"; another one (Johnson) says the upper-class man "will help you out more than the middle-class man"; a third (Sullivan) prefers a businessman to represent his union (which he supports) rather than a workingman. Of the five men (out of fifteen) who classified themselves as middle class, all are in this group giving individualist explanations of poverty. Apparently people arrive at a *social* explanation of poverty by two very different routes—one is through education; the other is through working-class identification: the "egghead" and the workingman united again.

If a person relies too heavily upon cultural axioms, he has

nothing new to say, no leverage for criticism of anything except deviation; he is conventional, traditional, conformist. If he relies upon his group identity for explanatory material and guidance, he is limited to those views for which this has a bearing; within this area he is conventional; outside it, he is partisan. If he relies upon his interpretation of his own individual experience, he loses the increased reliability proved by the testing experiences of others, turns his private fantasy world into social argument, limits the range of evidence available to him. He runs the risk of unreality, rationalization, incommunicable ideas. Such is the dilemma of social explanation by the common man without experience in accounting for distant complex events, without interest in, access to, or time for study of the relevant information, yet with the responsibility for selecting leaders who advocate different policies that can be effective only if they deal with the real causes of a problem.

C
THE SELF AS A MEASURE OF MAN

Those who in their social interpretation rely heavily upon their own idiosyncratic experience, without checking it against the experience of others, assume that *others are like me.* They believe that for much of society there is a single model of man, and "I am it." Alternatively they may believe that there is only one good kind of man (people like me), matched against others who are defective in a variety of ways. From the exclusive use of the self as a model of man, there emerge factually inaccurate and misleading explanations, or judgments and policies that have at their core an egocentric view of the universe. Here I am arguing, therefore, that underlying a healthy public opinion, one best suited for a democratic system, a perspective on the self as one of several useful models of mankind is necessary.

This argument must be put alongside an apparently conflicting point of view expressed elsewhere: the view that men who think of others as like themselves tend to empathize with them and extend to them a share of moral credit. Both positions, I think, are true. What is required for a democratic public is that a substantial number of persons believe that there are many useful models of man, some quite unlike themselves, but that all of these models must be accorded treatment consonant with human dignity. (By homogenizing mankind, Eastport tends to go further toward the empathic moral goal than the scientific explanatory one.)

O'Hara—The Varieties of Man

Something of the pluralist view is glimpsed in O'Hara's interpretation of the social scene. He seems not to read men's needs or motives within a framework limited by his own qualities or judged against a background of his own characterization of himself. For example, most Eastport men polarize on the question of bureaucrats, but O'Hara neither regards all bureaucrats as lazy nor wishes he had a secure post-office job himself (even though he is in danger of being laid off at the time of the interview). On Negroes, he sees their variety: "Take the Negro—what could they do? Right now they put them on a farm and they stick them in a shack. Then you get a few of them out, and they get to school, and they learn . . . and some of your better doctors and dentists are Negroes." In his explanation of the causes of war, O'Hara lists more different causes than anyone else, regardless of education. In addition to his use of impersonal causes, as mentioned above, he finds five motives or goals pursued by people who go to war: First, "you get people who aren't educated, you can talk them into almost anything"—a contributing situation, if not an active cause. Second: "People want to better themselves; there's no doubt about it. The Chinese Communists want to better themselves . . . people are trying to bring themselves up . . . in Africa they want to better themselves." Third, there is the question of freedom: "When they tell some of these countries they should have their freedom, in a lot of them I think they're right. Of course, a lot of them, as I say, I don't think are ready for it." Fourth, there are problems of economic exploitation: "A country like Britain taking all the good out of your country, and what have they got in return? You take your oil over there is one of your biggest items." And, fifth, a different kind of situation and motive: "In some of your countries they get afraid—fear has a lot to do with it, fear about what somebody might do." A secure, vivacious, happy man, a man who loves sports and loves his work with the "Little

League," O'Hara lives in a pluralistic world where there are many legitimate motives, many varieties of mankind of which he represents only one.

The problem of the self as *the* measure of man, and its damaging consequences for social explanation and judgment, is best seen in case material where the background of the individual is paired with his social interpretation. Consider how, in the following cases, Ruggiero assumes that men who cause wars are built in his own entrepreneurial image; Kuchinsky assumes that politicians and statesmen are exhibitionists, as he secretly longs to be; and Dempsey believes that most people are, like himself, passive objects for an elite to direct and nurture.

Ruggiero—The Foraging Syndrome

The combined university job and post-office work, together with whatever else he can pick up, give Ruggiero the greatest return of any of the Eastport men—so much that he not only had just been forced to leave Hilltop because he earned too much but had also been able to make a substantial down payment on a new house. Diminutive, intelligent, nervous, and considered aggressive or forward by his family, he has scorn for the lazy or the sluggish person. His attitude toward the world is that of a confident forager in a well-stocked land, or of a boom-town workman where the demand for his services is high. His concept of effort and reward is reflected in his religion; he says: "I think God put us here for the reason to more or less leave you on your own, to see whether you could earn your keep in Heaven. [It's] supposed to be a reward. Just like workin': work if you want—if your work is considered very good, then you get good pay for it. . . . You're supposed to live out the life of God, and, if you succeed in that, then we have our salvation." You are being tested; reward is for initiative and work well done; rewards are justly meted out.

Now consider how the problem of the origin of wars fits into this framework. He says: "I think a country that can get so depressed could cause wars. I mean, for instance, that we have nothing. Uh, we're begging for food and stuff like that—we seen it during the war a little bit, in Europe. Uh, if I didn't have anything and my children were starving, I'd do anything. I'd be a professional soldier, to make money." And there is much the same theme in his analysis of poverty: "Well, I think ambition, too, is—you take a lot of people are satisfied. [Such a person] says 'fine with me'; he figures if his wife can't make ends meet on what he makes, that's it." Ruggiero's "causes" are brought very close to home; indeed, in his imagination, he himself becomes the citizen of a depressed country, and poverty is as close as the ambitionless brother-in-law—with the implied contrast to his own affluence giving the image a special piquancy. His explanations reveal the themes apparent in his life history and his religious faith: war, poverty, and damnation are for the lazy; peace, prosperity, and riches are for the enterprising. And, of course, he means the enterprising like himself.

Kuchinsky—The Voyeur as Social Interpreter

Kuchinsky's "drift" is harder to catch; the ideological symptom is clear, but the etiology is partially obscure. The "clue" that sets in motion a train of inquiry is the special motive Kuchinsky, and no one else in the group, ascribed to the leaders of warlike nations. He says: "I think they're trying to make themselves known to the world. . . . They want people to look upon them as a God. . . . I think that it's all for the public. I believe they want to be well known. They want to be in the limelight, all of them, always in the pictures." By itself this is of interest, curious, but it also recalls his description of a politician. He describes him as a man with a big flower in his lapel, and says, "They're very easy for spotting." I ask him if there is anything else that would describe a politician, and he says not and continues with this theme: "Of course, they make it so obvious, I mean, it's very noticeable, I mean [pause] not unless they want to be noticed." Both these descriptions are unique to Kuchinsky; both come to this idiosyncratic focus on watching and being watched, looking and being looked at, attracting attention. And both regard these forms of behavior as fascinating and reprehensible.

There are other clues that point in the same direction. In his discussion of freedom, Kuchinsky hardly turns to the usual discussion of freedom of movement, religion, and occupation; his first comments are instead about privacy: speaking of people in America, he says: "Nobody's jumping at 'em or knocking on the door. . . . I think you've really got freedom from somebody rapping on your door and pulling you out of the house from a family." He is fascinated by the then recent incident where Lana

Turner's daughter discovered her mother with an "unwanted" lover, and stabbed him. Some aspect of the daughter's position as a *witness* to this love affair seems involved. He is one of the most isolated of the men; he is the only one (except for Farrel) who belongs to *no* voluntary groups in Eastport—although he does go to church. He and Dempsey were the only ones unwilling to have me take them down to my office for the interviews. His wife's pathological fear of crowds seems, in this context, to suggest a mild *folie à deux*.

Something about privacy and being looked at, some fear of attention, fear of being public, seems to be working its way out in his ideological positions. His explanations of the motives of war leaders, their desire to "be always in the limelight, always in the pictures," is certainly of a piece with this syndrome, as is his definition of a politician as a man who "makes himself obvious." The origins of this pathology are lost in the mysteries of Kuchinsky's troubled childhood. Usually, of course, they would have a sexual origin, either in the early peeping or exhibitionistic acts of a curious child. Here, perhaps, there was a special reason for either wanting, or not wanting, to be seen. When he was twelve, Kuchinsky says, his nipples used to get "hard" at night, but during the day they were all right, and no doctor could ever find anything wrong with him. His mother tried to explain it with Old World lore: "Like my mother says, it has something to do—they have an old saying about an old witch at the time. They would claim they would suck your breast at a certain period of time." He is doubtful about the witch story now, somewhat uncertain about its reliability, but as a child he was frightened. The curtain, barely parted on this childhood drama of thirty years ago, permits only a glimpse of something that, oddly and inconsistently, colors the ideology of a hard-working Eastport roofer.

Dempsey—Traditional Man in Western Society

Here is a man who reveals in shadowy outline the traditionalist in modern dress. Dempsey is fifty-five years old, finished only six years of schooling, and comes from a mixed Irish-German family, choosing the Protestant religion of his mother rather than his father's Roman Catholic faith. He is one of the four men with damaged father relations described elsewhere. Reluctant to be interviewed, he insisted upon the interviews taking place in his kitchen, partly on the grounds of his health, partly because of some concern for strange surroundings and experiences. He lived with his mother until she died; finally he married, at about the age of forty. Round-faced, phlegmatic, slightly pompous of bearing, and un-flustered by anything that happens, he sat erect in his neat kitchen, almost emotionless throughout the interviews. With a regular job, two girls, a boy, and a solicitous wife, yet with a limited intelligence, he has made a modest success of his life.

Some flavor of the social outlook of a traditional man is offered in his reports on his emotional responses to the news. I ask him a question that stirs all the others (as it stirred Riesman's respondents): "Have you seen anything in the news recently—say, in the last year or so, that really made you mad?" Dempsey says, "No, as I say, I don't indulge so much in—as my wife tells me, I don't read enough." He is asked about TV. "TV? No. I go for Westerns, or something like that. I want to enjoy it—I don't want to have something to worry about. . . . I want to be relaxed." He is asked if there was anything in the news that made him feel good. He pauses a long time: "No, I can't say that either. I couldn't say that." He is asked about the American launching of a missile, the event that gave most satisfaction to most men during the period of the interviews. He answers, "Well, that's interesting," and goes on to say, "I get a big kick out of the one there in the funny paper there—Captain Easy, I think it is, with his Sputnik spinning around with a man inside it." I ask him about the Russian Sputnik, a common source of indignation and irritation among these men. He answers that he was "irked" that the Russians got there first, but "downright mad" that they had imprisoned a helpless little dog in the satellite. The events of the world are best assimilated through comic strips and human-interest stories; the trivial, pathetic, comic, capture his attention because his perspective on the world has no means of discriminating the important from the unimportant.

He is dependent; consequently he thinks of the world as managed by "the higher ups." For him, this takes the special quality of a childlike imagery, as might, perhaps, be expected of a man who lived as a bachelor with his mother until he was about forty. Of the Bill of Rights and the freedoms of our society, he says: "I don't think they could give us much more [freedom] than they're giving us. They allow us these things [reference obscure]—they don't stop us in any way—as, let's say, unless we get too noisy and boisterous." The image is of little children who, if they are naughty, will be punished. The same theme creeps into his description of the causes of war: some [unidentified] warmakers say, " 'well, he's got so-and-so and I haven't got it. Let's go get it,' the same as, probably, children fighting over a ball." He accepts the situation that comes his way—thus, aside from cutting taxes, his solution to the problem of recession and unemployment is for the nation to learn to get along on less.

But most important for our purposes, Dempsey shows in many ways his imperturbable sense that yesterday, today, and tomorrow are welded together in a destiny fixed beyond our control; moreover, as the present is generally similar to yesterday, so tomorrow will be like today. Asked whether we are moving toward a better society, he says, as we have quoted elsewhere: "No, I don't think so. I don't think so. I think that we're going to stay on the same lines we are right now." Asked about the future of democracy, he says: "That's hard to say. I hope the future generation, and democracy, has it just as good as we're having it." To this he adds, "and probably a little bit better," but covers himself a minute later: "I hope I'm not wrong." Asked what changes he would like to see in this country, he blinks and stares at the ventilator fan in his kitchen. "Nothing in particular," he says. "I think the country on the whole is all right." As for the future of poverty: "There probably are a certain element that will live that way." He agrees with the view, as noted above, "The Bible says there will always be wars until the end of the earth." It is a timeless, changeless world for Dempsey—a world he never made, and beyond his control, and to a large extent beyond the control of even the "higher-ups." Basically, the "explanation" of events is that this is the nature of things; this is the way it has always been.

The roots of traditionalism in this case cannot be said to draw nourishment from an Old World peasant mentality of recent origin. His parents (Irish and German) were born in America; he was protected at least by a generation from the peasant's heritage. It is not so much cultural as personal. Although of multiple origins, such a traditional mentality seems particularly closely derived in Dempsey's case from his prolonged dependent relationship with his mother—as well as the lack of education, which is supportive of such a view of the world. This dependent relationship is at the crux of Dempsey's story; it not only evolved a character structure in which a feeling of responsibility for events—a sense that they could or should be changed by assertive action—is missing; it also deprived him of experience in making decisions for himself or for others. Intervention in the continuity of things so that one can actually experience the effect of creating change, altering the course of events—first in the small, private world of the child and then in a social world—is a necessary training for an understanding that the social order itself is not fixed. Brandeis says that responsibility is the breeder of men; in the same way we may say that command over some class of events is the source of the idea that events can be commanded.

D
EXPLANATION AND IDEOLOGY

At the roots of every ideology there are premises about the nature of causation, the agents of causation, the appropriate ways for explaining complex events. In the discussion on freedom reported above, there is an assumption that legal restraints cause many people not to engage in wild, aggressive behavior. In the discussion on equality, it is assumed that differential incomes cause people to work harder and more usefully. The discussion on government reveals an assumption about the way in which popular elections cause political leaders to modify their behavior. One could hardly find a policy, a belief, an attitude that does not rest upon a host of causal assumptions. And these assumptions, of course, are at the core of every explanation.

In the discussion on explanatory styles and sources, I have said that for the purposes of democracy, as well as for accuracy, a substantial part of the public must be able to employ impersonal causes; otherwise they are led by a series of implicit tendencies to a search for a great leader who can deal with problems inevitably mystifying to them. Second, I have suggested that the reliance upon any *one* source, culture, group beliefs, or self, leads a person into grave risks and hampers his capacity for reasonable explanations. And third, I have suggested that, inasmuch as all men employ their own image of themselves as a measure of man, it is necessary for accuracy and fairness to use the self in a pluralistic world where there are many suitable models of man. It is necessary, I mean, to keep the self in perspective. But now, fourth, I would add that inasmuch as we all do use ourselves as the model by which we judge the world and as the prism through which we look at the world and interpret it, there is an additional reason for interest in social character. The prevailing elements of social character in any society represent a roster of the prevailing measures of man to be employed. Thus the explanations of events offered by the bourgeoisified Eastport working-class men bear traces of their personal qualities: they are less hostile toward others, less frustrated, less anomic, less authoritarian, less prejudiced and ethnocentric, less distrustful of people than the proletarianized working classes of Europe or the day laborers and lower working classes of Eastport. In this sense, when they use themselves as models of man, when they think projectively, they do not people the planet with alienated and hostile men.

Ethics

21

The Lost Sense of Evil:
Low-Tension Morality
and Low-Tension Politics

> In the moral world everything is classified, systematized, fore-
> seen, and decided beforehand; in the political world everything
> is agitated, disputed, and uncertain. . . . These two tendencies,
> apparently so discrepant, are far from conflicting; they advance
> together and support each other.
> —ALEXIS DE TOCQUEVILLE, *Democracy in America*, I, 43–44

"As concerning justice, what is it?" asked Socrates, "to
speak the truth and to pay your debts—no more than this?" The
men of Eastport no less than the men of Athens; Rapuano, an
inventory clerk; Johnson, a mechanic; Dempsey, a drill-press
operator, no less than Glaucon had conceptions of what is just,
what is right, what is moral. And in Eastport, as in ancient Greece,
the relevance of the moral code to political belief is not to be
doubted.

A

THE UNMORALISTIC AMERICAN

Much has been made of American Puritanical traditions, of
the Victorian mortality in the nineteenth-century America, of
"inner-directedness" in earlier American life, of American con-

cepts of sin and redemption in the evangelical churches, of the blue laws and Prohibition, of the gospel of hard work, even of the so-called Puritanical strain in the American (Irish) Catholic church. Compared with Latin cultures, perhaps these moral stresses are stronger in the United States than elsewhere. But the unraveling of the many moral themes is incomplete; the nature and direction of change are unclear. Tocqueville observes that "travellers who have visited North America . . . agree in remarking that morals are far more strict there than elsewhere,"[1] but he also says, "In the United States hardly anybody talks of the beauty of virtue." Rather, he says, they speak of moral life as enlightened self-interest.[2] A little after the turn of the century, Santayana suggests that Americans do not detect vanity and wickedness in people, do not blame others, for they think "life splendid and blameless," and hence are not looking for such evils.[3] In the 1950's Commager says that Americans practiced a double standard— retaining the ethical ideals of the nineteenth century but modifying certain ethical practices in a marked degree; political morality improves, he says, while personal morality declines. Instead of learning morality from the church, we learn it from the movies and the press.[4] Certainly in what he says there is little suggestion of a *moralistic* people, and none whatsoever of the old Puritanism. In the guise of an impartial analyst, David Riesman scolds America for its loss of an inner-directed conscience, its substitute morality of shame and conformity.[5] Yet Brogan says Americans "like absolutes in ethics. They believe that good is good."[6] In Plainville, "morals is given much local lip service";[7] in Middletown, morality is stressed;[8] and everywhere, according to Warner, it is the "level of the common man" where "the moral code is more rigid and strict, . . . than at the top and bottom social levels."[9]

1. Alexis de Tocqueville, *Democracy in America,* Phillips Bradley, ed. (New York: Knopf, 1945), II, 204.

2. *Ibid.*, pp. 121–122.

3. George Santayana, *Character and Opinion in the United States* (Garden City, N.Y.: Doubleday, 1956), p. 131.

4. Henry Steele Commager, *The American Mind* (New Haven: Yale University Press, 1950), pp. 425–428.

5. David Riesman, *The Lonely Crowd* (New Haven: Yale University Press, 1950), *passim.*

6. Dennis W. Brogan, *The American Character* (New York: Knopf, 1956), p. 158.

7. James West, *Plainville, U.S.A.* (New York: Columbia University Press, 1945), p. 122.

8. Robert S. and Helen M. Lynd, *Middletown* (New York: Harcourt, 1929), p. 315.

9. W. Lloyd Warner, *American Life: Dream and Reality* (Chicago: University of Chicago Press, 1953), p. 231.

In Eastport it is as Tocqueville described it; the moral decent life is central—and assumed, but there is little talk of morality. The world is not seen through moral glasses; the criteria of "right" and "wrong," "good" and "bad" are not usually the first to be applied to a man, a program, a party. This is easy to say, hard to prove, difficult to make specific and convincing. The criteria on which I base this judgment form a kind of operational test—suggestive more than precise. In the first place, then, Eastport judges public officials (except justices of the court) on instrumental grounds: Is he doing what he was sent to do? Is he looking out for the interests of his constituency, his nation? The common man of Eastport does not ask right away, Is he a "good" man? Is he a moral man? Second, with only a few exceptions, the "major problems facing America today," or Eastport or Eastern State, are not moral problems, and are not couched in moral terms. Third, men do not list among their worries the problems of moral transgression; they are not wrestling with problems of right and wrong—not, in an acute sense, with drink, sex, delinquency, laziness, dual loyalties. Of course, fundamentally, most problems of maladaptive behavior are created or modified by conflict between what a person feels he ought to do and what he wants to do; but they do not emerge in a moralized way. In any event anger, not sex, is the more important issue here. Fourth, in their descriptions of themselves they do not set their pictures in a moral frame; they do not talk about their virtues more than about their skills and competences. Thus they report that they are "not too hard to get along with" rather than that they are loyal to their friends; they admit that they sometimes "blow their top" rather than admitting that they are unfair, make wild accusation, or swear at people without cause. Fifth, Utopia, a more perfect society, is characterized by its freedom from worry, and its opportunity, not by its freedom from evil and its morality. Measured by these five standards, one can only say that the moral dimensions of argument and analysis become subordinated to others of a more pragmatic nature, with consequences of great importance for the creation and management of a political ideology.

B

THE PREMISES OF LOW–TENSION MORALITY

The Substitution of Error for Evil

Just as it is true, as Neibuhr has said, that there is no longer a moving and searching sense of sin in the American conscience,[10] so it is also true that there is no sense of evil. This is a feature of the moral portrait painted above, but it has implications of its own. At first one might suppose that a sense of evil in the old-fashioned manner, willful wrongdoing, a desire and capacity to violate moral standards springing from a free, uncoerced choice, must have a theological base. Yet reflection on the nature of evil in the vulgarized Marxism that is rife in the metropolitan streets of the West and the rice paddies of the East shows very simply that the exploiting capitalist is an evil man, just as Simon Legree was an evil man. But in Eastport there are almost no evil men; there are none who are willfully hurtful, sadistic, immoral. In the place of evil, there is error, people who make mistakes in judgment, who are more selfish than they should be, less kind than they should be, chiefly *because they haven't been properly educated.* Thus, not moral regeneration or moral rearmament, but better education is the answer to many moral problems, among which is the morally difficult problem of desegregation.

Education is a kind of magic, in this process; there is almost no real understanding of how education does what it is supposed to do, or why; but it is seen as a potent charm that conjures virtue as well as truth, or rather, since being right *is* being good, it is a charm with many benefits. It works on the varieties of mankind. About the Negro, Woodside, the railroad guard, says: "I think that education is the biggest factor behind all this [race conflict], because I think if you have a person that's—that's ignorant, regardless of what you try to show him, or do, he doesn't get the true value of it. All he's thinking about is what he wants, and what he can do." And McNamara, a bookkeeper, who finds that he and his family get along well with their Negro neighbor next door, says, "In the South it's a little different. . . . Sometimes you've got to

10. See Reinhold Niebuhr, *The Nature and Destiny of Man* (New York: Scribner, 1951).

take it easy—maybe try to educate people a little more"—this rather than a Court order or the sending of troops to Little Rock. T. W. Adorno and his colleagues interpret the emphasis on education as a means for avoiding institutional or effective reform— perhaps there is some of that in these answers too.[11] But there is also a grounding of this faith in education in a broad philosophy of a beneficient world, populated by people who would do good if they could see clearly, and whose interests do not fundamentally conflict—a set of circumstances that would naturally make a person look to education before setting about the serious business of reform. Reinhold Niebuhr blames the educators, the social scientists, and the ministry for such a failure to understand the individual—not collective—role of conscience and their consequent misguided faith in education.[12] Here we find that they have communicated their misinterpretation to the public.

Faith in education is a secular faith; it is part of the humanistic "religion" of the West, but in moral dilemmas it might have been supposed that men would turn to the teachings of their own church for guidance. Perhaps they do, but in dealing with the problem of race relations neither of the two Protestants mentioned God's version of the equality of men, and ten of the twelve Catholics were silent on this matter, even though their church has a fine, clear record, an unembarrassed and outspoken record. One of the two Jews said: "Their skin is black. Well, God wanted their skin black, so he made it black. It's not their fault." But he is hardly relying on theology here.

The substitution of "error" for "evil" is apparent in many moral dilemmas. In discussing corruption in government, many of the men seem to follow Johnson's lead in supposing that although many practice it, they don't "mean any harm." Big business may have too much power, but the abuses that come from this are accidental, not purposeful or the product of evil intentions. In the end, perhaps only Communists are evil, the heretics of the age; but their besetting sin is that they have been "duped"; they believe Russia is a better place than the United States and the solution is somehow appropriate, in this moral framework— send them there; they'll find out.

11. T. W. Adorno and associates, *The Authoritarian Personality* (New York: Harper, 1950), p. 700.
12. Reinhold Niebuhr, *Moral Man and Immoral Society* (New York: Scribner, 1936), *passim*.

The Natural Moral Order

The moral reformer, eager to adjust men's moral codes so as to correspond to his vision of the world, is sustained by his confidence that his attention and intervention are necessary for a proper moral order. It would be unwise to let things go. In Eastport the underlying moral premise is just the opposite, at least in its main tendency. Since people are basically decent, though often all too "human," the presumption is that by themselves they will find a moral answer to their problems. This means, in general, that neighbors should not intervene, social workers should mind their own business, and government should follow a policy of non-coercion wherever possible, but it may alter the rules and the calculations of self-interest; it may provide services and "bring people together" when necessary. A belief in this natural moral order, stronger that the belief in a natural economic order, finds expression in a number of situations among which are those embodying race relations, political corruption, and sexual perversion.

The problem of desegregation in the South, something almost all the men "believe in," posed a difficult choice after Little Rock, as we have seen. Perhaps they are only wishing the problem would be taken out of their field of vision, but at least for a number of men faith in the conciliatory and natural processes of mutual goodwill seemed paramount. Rapuano, for example, makes this position easy by observing "the progress they were making before the Court stepped in." He then goes on to say: "In time they would have cleaned their own house—swept their own house out, and apparently they would have had Negroes in the white schools, too. It might have taken maybe three, four, maybe ten years, but in time it would have come about, by themselves . . . in due time it would have come about down South—the same as it did up here." Sullivan, a truck driver, who has not hesitated to use force in his time, says: "The problem was working itself out slowly, but it was working itself out, anyway [pause] except for a few die-hards down South, and as time went on, as these die-hard leaders die or are put out of office, as generations are going on, it would have been working itself out more and more." And Flynn, not unsympathetic to the problems of the colored man but eager to get out from under his moral responsibility, says: "I think it's a problem for each individual. . . . The tension [between the races] is something that's created, generally, because people call it such. My own feeling on it is that if there wasn't so much attention paid to the problem . . . they may get along well." This is not the idea of natural law, which is difficult to find and must be interpreted and obeyed; it is the idea of natural harmony, which will uncover itself if you don't meddle with the sweet order of things, if you allow Rapuano's governmental abstinence and Flynn's therapeutic personal inattention to open the doors for this work of natural progress (and kindness) to move of its own momentum. As with Herbert Spencer, to attempt to do good is really to do evil.

The laissez-faire morality of Eastport, and America in general in the twentieth century, has a special application to the matter of corruption in politics. As we have seen, most people believe it is there, and not on a petty scale either, although mostly confined to the local and subordinate ranges of politics. But most of the men also believe that the use of governmental power to give your friends jobs, or to get contracts for firms you're interested in, is simply another method of payment, like a medical-fee system or a church tithing system. They do not see how it affects the quality of service in any serious way. And, since they think the level of temptation very high, they do not believe the degree of wickedness implied is very great. It does not affect their confidence in a responsive government; it is not, indeed, a source of great concern for them.

In the same way, homosexuality is dealt with in an unemotional tone of voice, no somatic symptoms, no indignation, no alarm. It is taken out of the moral theater by calling it a sickness; it is a health problem. It is not to be punished, but treated. And there is no need for any great effort to stamp it out.

Thus, the natural moral order, self-adjusting and hopeful, is preserved by a faith in the goodness of man, by minimizing men's moral defects, by treating what seem to be the immoralities of man as naturally caused deficiencies—succumbing to temptation, and following a wayward impulse. There are some indignant men here, some moralizing men, but they are few, representing a minor, not a dominant, urban American theme.

Blamelessness

In Salem, Massachusetts, in the late seventeenth century, in Torquemada's Spain, among the Dobu of New Guinea, if something went wrong, the first question was, "Who did it?" or "Who is to blame?" Partly this is the product of a metaphysics that makes room for magic and sorcery; partly it arises from a projection of some guilty feelings within the individuals of the time and place; partly it is merely the effort to assign responsibility and hence develop control of a situation. It seems to be a rare question in Eastport. At least, it is less frequent among these men of modest education than might have been supposed.

In the matter of desegregation, the attempt to *understand* the Southern white as well as the Negro by those who believed in desegregation was very strong. Similarly, the easiest and primitively most appealing rationalization of our dropping the bomb on Hiroshima is the old one: "They started it," or "They brought it on themselves," or "They are to blame for their own destruction." Surely a blame-oriented culture would have said this. Instead, overwhelmingly the men used a functional argument—the bomb saved lives. Nor is the situation different in the moral discourse on corruption. There was little effort to blame the low moral standard on the bad men in office; instead there was an accounting of the causes, the temptation, the opportunities, the fallibility of mankind.

But the evidence is stronger than this; indeed, it came first to light in the routine questioning on "who is to blame" or "who is at fault" for the development of the "major problems" facing America, Eastport, and Eastern State as these emerged in the discussion. We shall let O'Hara speak on this. He is a man for whom assertion, conflict, authority hold no terror; he is not afraid of criticism or reprisals. He works on the maintenance crew in a large factory and is explaining his situation in the recession: "I know up in the shop right now, they cut the help on the maintenance; . . . they're going to have trouble because you can't get the machinery fixed now, and I thought that—when I got pushed back, here about a month and a half ago, I had to go on nights steady. Of course, then they started rotating since then; but I had to go on 11 to 7, after about eleven years, because they laid off. And your maintenance force up there right now is smaller than it's ever been, and you've got twice as much work as they ever had; . . . they're cutting so darn low they're cutting their own throats." Here we are sure to be close to an issue that is pivotal in a man's life; he is speaking rapidly, leaning forward, emphasizing his words. He goes over it several times, explaining how the machines are "down" because of maintenance problems, and then he continues: "Of course, *you can't blame the company for all of it.* Unions are all right too, if they're run right." In the course of his discussion he comes to the government's responsibility for the decline in defense contracts; he understands the government's position on inflation, discounts it, but allows it some merit. He does not blame the government. O'Hara is a strong Democrat—I asked him later who is to blame for the problem of the defense lag he has outlined. He says: "Well, they [both parties] all holler that they want to cut down armament and everything," and seems about to evade the question, but goes on to say, "The Republicans are in power, so who do you blame?" It is not merely a rhetorical question, for he believes both parties are responsible. The emotion that went into describing the situation dwindles to a thin trickle when it comes time to assign blame for the recession. I asked him whether he has in mind any particular man. "No, I wouldn't say definitely who's who. . . ."

Sullivan, a truck driver, is similar in many ways; he illustrates another facet of this high blame threshold. Of all the "problems," the spy and subversive problem is usually most likely to evoke charges and countercharges of laxity, disloyalty, softness toward Communism. "Things that have bothered me?" asked Sullivan in response to a general question, and he proceeds in a contemplative fashion, "How easy it seemed to be for [pause] a foreign country, mainly Russia, to just walk off with atomic secrets, missiles, and so on—just walk off with them." I asked him, "Are you thinking of any particular case now, or what?" This was his chance. He says: "No, not one in particular—any one of them—[pause] Goldenberg, Greenglass—[pause] it just seemed to be that—[pause] I think it was just too easy. But it couldn't have been them alone. There must have been someone higher up that was making it easy for them." I am ready now for a blast at subversion in the "highest places," and, because he has stopped talking, try to prod him along. "Have you any idea who it might be, or where?" Sullivan pauses thoughtfully, "No," he says, "it probably isn't one person or one department—[pause] the government on the whole, there, was—like I say—the program was probably rigid enough on security, but not on individuals." This comment, by a former pugilist and Marine, is cryptic enough in one sense, but for our purposes it is admirably clear: the problem lies with the system of screening civil servants; this, rather than placing the blame on certain weak, soft, disloyal men in government.

Often it is hard to distinguish between an analytical attribution of cause, an assignment of responsibility, and a fixing of blame. But in instance after instance, it appeared that the least fruitful questions were ones of "Whose fault was it?" "Who is to blame?" and within the body of the free-flowing discussion the level of indignation about the failures of men and groups to perform as the Eastportians thought they should was at a very low level indeed.

It has been said of the American nativist agitator in the midst of his tales of woe that if you asked him "What?" he will answer "Who?" We are here recounting this story in reverse. Often asked "Who is to blame?" the men of Eastport, to a surprising degree, answered in terms of "what." Queried on the missile lag, their most frequent answer was an anonymous American failure to support science and education; on the decline of business in downtown Eastport, they said the fault was the growth of the suburbs; only in the Little Rock crisis of desegregation (1957) did many men find a person to blame, in this case Governor Faubus.

C
SOME USES OF LOW–TENSION MORALITY

If the Eastport common man is unmoralistic, he is not amoral; if he thinks more easily in terms of error than of evil, he does not forget about good and bad; if he is slow to blame, yet he knows what blame is. He has a moral code that he follows—and applies to the situations confronting him.

In a lower-middle stratum of the population one can reach upward and engage the behavior of the ruling classes in a moral grip, or downward and prick out the violations of the moral code of the unrespectable, the *outré*, the failures. There is gratification to be had either way, but Eastport's common man chooses to moralize downward, not upward. He spends more time condemning the failures of the poor than in condemning the extravagance, the sinful living, the exploitative behavior of the rich. The poor are under his nose, while the rich are not; but the activities of the rich are reported, while those of the poor receive less public notice. (Yet it is true that the misbehavior of the stars of the entertainment world attracts a kind of lip-licking moralistic attention.)

It is the *economic* failure of the poor that occasions comment, not their loose living or indulgence or self-gratification. This economic criticism cannot be made of the rich, for they are successes. On the other hand the rich might be criticized for their shady practices, their exploitation, their monopolistic controls, their conspiracies against the people, their withholding from labor the fruits of its effort, and their deliberate organization of recessions. These things are said, but they are said infrequently—more as explanations than as moral judgments. No, the relief chiseler is morally worse than the price fixer; the person unable to hold a steady job is worse than the landlord who does not fix his broken railings. In general the moral defections of the upper-status groups are more tolerable in Eastport than the moral defections of the poor and lowly.

The relation between morality and success may assume many shapes in men's minds; one of them, greatly feared by Tocqueville, is that men will, upon seeing a successful man, "impute his success mainly to some of his vices." This has the grave consequence that "an odious connection is thus formed between the ideas of turpitude and power, unworthiness and success, utility and dishonor." [13] In spite of the widespread recognition of corruption in government, Eastport does not make this "odious connection"—on the contrary, there is a tendency to believe that men in high places deserve the power and honor and responsibility; otherwise they wouldn't be there. They deserve it, it is true, because of talent, not virtue—but had they been notably unvirtuous they would have been found out. At the other end of the social scale, those who are notably unsuccessful are indeed thought to have failed, in considerable part, because of "playing the ponies," drink, laziness, or shiftlessness. The net consequences of this framework of relationships is a reinforcement of the moral idea: it pays to be good, a premise they follow out in their own lives. Of course, here we speak of the majority; three or four believe, in some degree, that it is otherwise, and have themselves sought to shade the moral code in business dealings where it was too restrictive.

One notable feature of the target area in moral discourse is the absence of a dichotomy between "good guy" and "bad guy." In

13. A. de Tocqueville, *op. cit.*, I, 226–227.

speaking of political leaders, as in speaking of their friends and neighbors, they are good dramatists, mixing the good and the bad. Even more significant there is no moral "we" and an immoral "they"—unless the line between the quasi-failures in the neighboring public housing project is considered important enough to merit this distinction. But these failures are weak, not evil, and certainly not threatening. Kuchinsky, the anti-Semite, comes close to creating a class of wholly bad people (but he supports the Jewish governor of a neighboring state); Ferrera, after a little superficial tolerance, finds "I have no respect for the Irish"—in general, we know the symptoms, but the moral outcast has no currency here, with, again, the single exception of the Communist.

Indeed, with respect to the Japanese and Pearl Harbor, the Negro and the Southern white in Little Rock, the corrupt politician, the chiseling businessman, there is a willingness to grant a wrongdoer a moral character, however eroded this may be through misguided advice, or modified by misinformation. Riesman calls this "tolerance," and finds it to be a substitute for moral judgment; in some ways it is. But if religion has had anything to do with it, it is a triumph of Christian ethics (in one of its several facets). What may be called the *moral incorporation of the opponent* is not quite the same as "Love thine enemy," but it is a first step and in the same direction. And it follows from, and contributes to, the more general blamelessness noted above.

The closing lines of the Declaration of Independence run as follows: "And for the support of this Declaration, with a firm reliance on the protection of Divine Providence, we mutually pledge to each other our Lives, our Fortunes, and our sacred Honor." It is "Honor" that is called sacred, not fortunes or lives, and around the world the concept of honor is today in many ways at the very core of the moral system. In the Bushido code of Japan, or in the modern Japanese concept of *"giri* to one's name" (roughly, the honor owed to one's name),[14] in the concept of *"lien,"* or moral face, of the Chinese,[15] in the *pihlotima,* or honorable pride, of the Greeks,[16] there are captured various concepts of a world view of honor. The central idea, I believe, is a moralization

14. See Ruth Benedict, *The Chrysanthemum and the Sword* (Boston: Houghton Mifflin, 1946), pp. 145–176.

15. Hu Hsien-chin, "The Chinese Concepts of 'Face,'" in Douglas G. Haring, ed., *Personal Character and Cultural Milieu* (Syracuse: Syracuse University Press, 3rd rev. ed., 1956), pp. 447–467.

16. Dorothy Lee, *Freedom and Culture* (Englewood Cliffs, N.J.: Prentice-Hall, 1959), pp. 141–153.

of reputation, a belief that a detracting remark or a slur on one's "good name" is an immoral act that infects the injured party unless he can in some way counteract it. He may do this by demanding retraction, or by retribution, or by receiving some form of "satisfaction," often by demonstrating bravery, as in the chivalric codes of Western Europe and early America.

The urbanization, commercialization, and modernization of a culture, its retreat from feudal forms and vices, have caused the concept of honor in this sense to atrophy; in any event, as Montesquieu says, it is more likely to be a central theme in an aristocracy than in a democracy. But while the concept of honor may change, the emphasis upon reputation and respect may remain. Even in a modern democracy this could well be the center of the moral world; but in Eastport it does not seem to be. Where honor and respectability *are* the center of a moral world, they are not debatable. But in Eastport a man's own economic success, his drinking habits, his performance on the job, his courtship, the vices of his parents, his ambition—in short, almost everything can be examined. He shares his life in a way not common among Europeans; he answers questions from both Gallup and Kinsey that are less easily answered in Europe or Asia or South America; he nods sadly over his own shortcomings but does not consider that his *philotima* has been hurt, his name dishonored, his pride cut to the quick. Although he does not know much about himself through introspection, he does not resent examination of himself through sensitivity and pride. He has not, to this extent, moralized his reputation.

D

MORAL CONFLICT IN PUBLIC AFFAIRS

What we have said about the unmoralistic American may suggest an anesthetized moral nerve. That is not the case. Without talking much about the good and the bad, the Eastport men yet deal sensitively with public issues that present them with moral conflict. Briefly we may look at three such issues: desegregation, the atomic bombing of Hiroshima, and corruption in government.

Johnson, an electric-utility mechanic, wrestles with his conscience on the desegregation problem (as was foreshadowed in his comments quoted in the opening pages of this book). He says: "I mean like I have five children and there's five colored kids running around—they have as much right in this world as my children have. . . . But," he continues, "it just isn't right for a colored boy to be dancing with a white girl." Flynn, a railroad supply clerk who is an officer of the Hilltop Community Council, was faced with the problem of what to do about teen-age dances at Hilltop. At first he opposed it; then, when he saw how much the teen-agers wanted it, he supported it, worrying all the time whether or not he was doing the right thing. Costa has a brother-in-law from North Carolina who, as he says, "can't stand the sight of colored people," and Costa himself feels that the Supreme Court desegregation decision was a mistake; things are going too fast in the South for the Southern whites to assimilate. But it is a moral problem for him—he seems free of conventional prejudice as he says: "The nicest people I know are colored people. I would go in their houses; I would eat with them; I would drink with them—that's the way I feel. I work with them."

The dropping of the atomic bomb on Hiroshima presents a moral dilemma of another order, more distant from their lives, more likely to be rationalized in terms of national defense and patriotic sentiment. Perhaps it is the case, as has been suggested, that moral superiority lies with those who condemn the American use of the bomb. If that is true, only two of the men earn these moral credits. But another estimate of moral strength may be made on the basis of the nature of the arguments employed, the effort to assess human costs involved either way (dropping or not dropping the bomb), the sensitivity to suffering and pain, the awareness of the calculations and responsibilities of those who had to decide. Looked at in this way, those who argue against dropping the bomb lose standing: their principle motive seems to be fear that the Japanese will some day retaliate against us. The ten who unequivocally justified our bombing did so largely on the ground that it was less costly in human lives than an invasion, and often they pointed out that it saved Japanese lives as well as American lives. Moreover the discussion was especially sensitive to the suffering involved: "I know it killed an awful lot of people—thousands of people, if I remember right, and people are dying from it today"; "I can't see [people] crippled or, uh, hurt that way"; "I think a lot of 'em [people in government] were well educated here and I think they could have found another solution for that"; "It meant saving a lot more than probably would have been maimed and injured, if they'd gone on fighting any other way."

But it was the arguments that they did not use that revealed their sensitivity to moral questions. Consider the possibilities for relying on the law of retaliation, an eye for an eye and a tooth for a tooth. This was not beyond them—"They didn't worry much about us when the time came for an attack on Pearl Harbor"; "The Japs had done everything inhuman to our men"—but it was rare. The symmetry of Pearl Harbor and Hiroshima was ignored. Nor did they ever, not even once, rely on General Sherman's "War is hell," which with a shrug of the shoulders might have dismissed moral questions as irrelevant to war. In short, they did not evade the need for a judgment, for a moral response.[17]

Almost exactly fifty years ago, Bryce was able to say: "No impression regarding American politics is more generally diffused in Europe than that contained in the question which the traveller who has returned from the United States becomes so weary of being asked, 'Isn't everybody corrupt there?'"[18] Even though today the decline of the bosses and corruption is a familiar theme in American discourse, Eastport, like Europe and the rest of America, is aware of a substantial amount of corruption in government, and sees clearly the discrepancy between the official code and the informal code of behavior. Their reaction is, generally speaking, a tolerant one, certainly not indignant, not moralistic, possibly insufficiently censorious. It is marked by the belief that *the system encourages corruption*, that somehow it is "natural" to politics: "It's true that corruption and politics seem to go hand in hand" (Flynn); "I guess it'll always be in the peoples' minds that a politician is receiving money other than his pay" (Ruggiero). This is true, not because bad people go into politics but because ordinary people do. "If I went out to make an extra dollar [in this way], they'd probably talk about me too" (Dempsey); "We are all subject [to temptation]" (Woodside). And since this is the case, and they are merely people like us, they surely won't do any harm to the country: "In fact you can't blame them. Look, they're out to make money, as long as they figure, as long as they're not hurting anybody" (Sokolsky); "If they can get it, good luck to them.

17. Helen Swick Perry argues that the combination of American "inattention" to the problems of atomic bombing and defense of the rightness of the decision to drop the bomb reveal a strong guilt feeling for this act. See her "Selective Inattention as an Explanatory Concept for U.S. Public Attitudes toward the Atomic Bomb," *Psychiatry*, 17 (1954), p. 236.

18. James Bryce, *The American Commonwealth* (New York: Macmillan, 1910), II, 156.

. . . I don't think they take bribes so much" (Dempsey); "I don't believe they're going to do anything to hurt the country" (Johnson). It is as though politics involved a set of fees and payments that, although disapproved of, were still accepted as a cost of doing business; not a high cost, and not one that interfered with the main business, which is the provision of services to the electorate, but still an underhanded business arrangement that exposed the "firm" to considerable criticism. Under these circumstances Eastport is *understanding* and somewhat sympathetic to men who are tempted and who follow the less honorable, but frequently applied, immoral rules. These men reserve their moral indignation for the transgressions of movie stars.

In these three situations there is a conflict between moral claims: the rights of the Negro versus the rights of white Southerners or white Northerners at Hilltop, the humanity of withholding the bomb versus the humanity of an expeditious ending of the war, the violation of honesty and approved practice in corruption versus the conventional "claims" of men to payment for services. In most of these situations there is some advantage to the men themselves in one solution compared to another: they would like to be relieved of "the Negro" problem by having it swept from sight; they had a stake in an earlier end of the war that they did not have in saving Japanese lives; they gain a little something from their own political ties, which become valuable only through informal and slightly disreputable claims for favors. How, then, shall we characterize their major responses to these moral conflicts?

In the first place there are several things that they are not. There is little *denial;* they do not maintain that the Negro problem is unimportant, that the Japanese were not "really" badly hurt, that corruption is negligible. With respect to corruption, Bryce felt that under the circumstances a frank admission, which he also observed, was better than "covering things up as the English do." [19] *Hypocrisy,* a form of deceitful denial, was not a feature of this discourse.

Nor is cynicism a feature, in the sense of a belief that the moral code is just for show, that Negroes and whites are out to get what advantage each can of the other, that war has no room for moral considerations, that all men are corrupt and it is only the opportunities that vary, and that, anyway, "Justice is the will of

19. *Ibid.,* p. 245.

the stronger." Of course, there is a broad conviction that men pursue self-interest, but not to the exclusion of other considerations. It is the difference between a belief in human frailty and a belief in human wickedness.

Bryce says that Americans respond to the question of corruption with a kind of fatalism; [20] Lerner refers to the "despair of ever getting any reform accomplished." [21] There is something to this. A few say, with respect to race prejudice, "You can't change human nature"; germane to the question of atomic bombing, most men believe that "there will always be wars"; on corruption in politics, McNamara speaks for many when he says, "I think it [corruption] goes along with politics like errors go along with baseball." But it is also true that Farrel, a social worker, speaks for many more when he says of corruption, "It's just a question of how you can keep it down to a minimum." And only a few men disapproved of governmental action to help the Negroes, while, those who thought there "will always be wars" believed that continued negotiation, the use of the United Nations, and some limited foreign aid might reduce the probability of imminent war. Fatalism about moral delinquency or an unsatisfactory outcome is not characteristic; rather the view is melioristic; things can be made better.

If the moral conflicts are marked by absence of denial, hypocrisy, cynicism, fatalism, what positive qualities do they have? Of course, they have the opposite of these—a certain candor, a certain hopefulness, some sense that evils can be brought increasingly under control. But beyond that, I think, there is a remarkable attempt to *understand* the situation, a willingness to see both sides of the conflict before judging. The pleasures of denunciation were postponed, not forever, but for long enough to grasp what it was the "other side" might claim. Moreover, I do not think these men have, in a marked sense, turned their consciences over to someone else. For example, it is sometimes said that Hitler's hold on the German people was made greater by their willingness to vest in him the definition of right and wrong. Or, in our own experience, David Riesman suggests that the American's sensitivity to group opinion has resulted in his abdicating responsibility for his decisions on right and wrong.[22] Of course, all morality is

20. *Ibid.*, pp. 347 ff.
21. Max Lerner, *America as a Civilization* (New York: Simon and Schuster, 1957), p. 385.
22. David Riesman, *op. cit.* (New Haven: Yale University Press, 1950).

anchored in convention and group opinion, but the clues to an abnormally atrophied *individual* conscience are not marked in the conversation of the men of Eastport. They do not, for example, support their moral judgments on segregation, Hiroshima, corruption, or other matters such as delinquency, foreign policy, subversion, with such comments as "All of the fellows say . . . ," "Around here we think . . . ," "He's got a bad reputation," "I was just talking to ———— the other day, and he said. . . ." They do not preface their judgments with a glance at me, a hesitation, and, "Maybe you won't agree with this, but . . ."—or with an apologetic gesture or diffidence, or waiver of some kind. Dempsey declines comment here and there ("That, I couldn't say"), but it is the product of a limited mentality, not an other-directed conscience. Costa is deferential; he would prefer to rely on another. Most men do not try to find out how I feel, do not publicly ground their views in the opinions of others, and do not embrace a group and speak for them; they are the custodians of their own consciences, at least in the limited sense described.

These are the major themes, but moral discourse offers many an obbligato with variations on these themes.

E

SOME SOURCES OF LOW–TENSION MORALITY

The circumstances of their lives do not put a heavy strain upon the consciences of Eastport's common men. For one thing, they do not suffer greatly from the conflict between competing moral codes. It can be shown that certain, but by no means all, business callings impose on a businessman a competitive ends-justify-the-means ethical code that runs contrary to the codes of behavior a man must live by to be accepted as a good man in family and community.[23] The politician's conflict between pursuit of what he conceived to be a broad and general (public) interest and the requirements of party and personal continuity in office often pose moral dilemmas. But for the most part there are few such situations for the working man. In the work area, perhaps he suffers from the cross-pressures established by a sense of workmanship as this clashes with his obligations to his brother workers not to excel in such a way as to break their rates or "show them

23. Compare Thorstein Veblen, *The Engineers and the Price System* (New York: Viking, 1921), and *Absentee Ownership* . . . (New York: Viking, 1923).

up." Or perhaps a conflict emerges between the advantages of the individual in a piecework situation where this runs counter to the advantage of others who suffer from an individual's neglect or careless work. Sometimes the demands of union membership conflict with workmanlike producer interests. Beyond these, in the home, the demands he may experience as breadwinner and status aspirant sometimes conflict with the demands imposed by his role as father or husband. How much time to spend on a second job? How much on overtime? But none of these kinds of conflict puts a man in a moral bind like that of the businessman or the politician (or the doctor or lawyer, for that matter). The great hue and cry about conflicting moral codes in our society emerges from the scrutiny of the lives of the entrepreneurial, managerial, and professional classes, not the working and lower-middle classes.

Although it is true that working-class men do not suffer certain of the moral conflicts of the entrepreneurial classes, they have, nevertheless, absorbed the content of the bourgeois moral code almost without exception. Where the proletariat of the Continent may develop concepts of working-class morality distinct from the morality of shopkeepers and clerks, here it is the same. Where in Europe the sins of drunkenness, adultery, fornication, and unthrifty behavior might be regarded with horror by the petty bourgeois and more leniently by the blue-collar workers, here the steady working class, the roofer, the machine operators, the building custodians, the mechanics, and maintenance men have middle-class standards. The social division comes at another place in the stratification of society; it comes at the place where "demoralization" has set in: among the reliefers, the part-time unemployed, the members of broken homes, the transients, those on the margin of delinquency. For this reason the upper-working-class man is not torn between a bourgeois code and a working-class code; the encapsulated bourgeois conscience is lodged firmly in his mind.

There were a number of these men, particularly among the Irish, who reported that their fathers, or perhaps uncles, had the gravest sort of difficulty with liquor—the drunken homecomings, the anguished mother, the colorful street-corner fights were outlined in tragicomic detail. In this generation the incidence of drunkenness is lower. Not quite facetiously it might be said that television is the moral equivalent of alcohol. Reading between the lines in some cases, and the direct account in another, one sees the fathers of these men having more "affairs" with women; certainly they were more likely to go out with "the boys." (Ferrera's father was a great card player; Sokolsky's father had to be picked up after his parties downtown; Flynn's uncle disappeared on weekends; Woodside's father brought his women home.) But the Eastport men stay home, or, if they go out at all, they go out as couples—except for the bowling and sports events. The summary picture is of men less tempted, less torn, less engaged in moral struggles of the conventional personal variety.

It is said that in the periods of history when moral codes are relaxed so that there is a conflict between the internalized parental conscience and the freer and looser contemporary styles—as in the Elizabethan age in England or the post-World War I period in Europe—the personal moral conflicts thus engendered quickly become social conflicts. They are projected outward onto others; there is scapegoating, witch hunting, public accusations of a wild nature. On the whole, in Eastport in the fifties, there seemed to be no such conflict between internalized parental codes and contemporary codes, hence no need to discover an outside representative of the "raging evil" within.

In terms of roles, of subcultures, of personal and familial situations, of discrepant "moral ages," Eastport men were not markedly caught up in conflict situations. Their attention is not thus turned to moral discourse; they are allowed to relax their moral guard, without in any sense becoming amoral or unmoral, they are permitted to become unmoralistic.

F
CONSCIENCE AND IDEOLOGY

Since these men have consciences, they must shape their social outlook, must provide direction and content to their more vaguely formulated, less articulate statements of belief. Several particulars are worth examining.

The Conservatism of a Conscience

A conscience may be conceived as a voice in an eternal debate with one's self—the other side of the argument. On the one hand, the voices of desire, ambition, self-interest are assertive, their arguments outspoken. On the other hand, the conscience will speak of the "public interest," "the other fellow's interest," or even one's own long-run or "better" interest. Where interests divide along class lines, along labor-management lines, the conscience of the rich or of the management group tends to argue the case for the others—the poorer groups, the employee groups. In the same way, among the common men of Eastport, conscience speaks of management needs and interests, the rights and privileges of the rich to the uses of their wealth. When one of the men says in a small group discussion (from which I was absent), "If you're the businessman and I'm the workingman, I don't care if you make a hundred million dollars a year, as long as I make a living; in other words, you got your money invested; you're supposed to make money," he is according to the owning classes —a group he attacks when they appear as the managers of the plant where he works—their "rights" and "privileges." Earlier we mentioned the tendency of the Eastport common man toward the moral incorporation of his opponent. Here this tendency is working across class lines.

In a later discussion we shall show how Eastport brings to bear its hearthside experience with budgeting upon the problems of the national budget. In the home the libido says, "spend, indulge"; the superego says, "Save; watch out for illness, for educational expenses, for a rainy day." In the national economy, particularly when it goes on short rations, the common man is eager for increased government expenditure, the letting out of new contracts, the development of public works. But his conscience whispers to him of the other side, the conservative side, of the argument. DeAngelo, a machine operative hears his conscience in this role:

> That seems to be the argument amongst the people in the shop, you know, that the Democrats will spend more money to keep the people going. People don't seem to care whether the government is going into the red deeper and deeper as long as they are working, y'know what I mean? The Republicans are a little bit different; they look for the government. I mean you gotta look for the government angle, too, y'know. You just can't let the government go into the red, y'know?

The trained nerve to hold back, not to give into what one clearly wants now, to save, comes to the rescue of the conservative forces

of society, so that we do not have only the external struggle between spenders and savers, working class and managerial class.
The fight is internalized, too; and the conscience is a conservative.

Conscience and Fair Play

The frame of mind that accords to "opponents" the status of
moral men, however they may be in error, softens and dissolves
in some places. As we observed elsewhere, the idea of a fair hearing and, to the extent that it is understood, "due process" seems
most appealing where there are property interests at stake. In
morality cases and "subversion" it is rather weak, particularly in
the latter. What happens to the Eastport conscience when it confronts the Communist problem?

Only a few, perhaps three, see that the legal impediments to
immediate official punitive action against American Communists
are part of a larger democratic order that they support. Most of
them would agree with O'Hara, certainly one of the least punitive men in the group, when he says, after contemplating why
any American would want to be a Communist: "If they want to
go with the Russians, get rid of them. . . . They say 'put them
in jail.' Sure, you put them in jail—what good are you? You still
got them, and when they get out they're probably worse than
before you put them in. Get rid of them, deport them, if you have
to. They're wrong—if they want to go, let them go over where
they've got that way."

What happened here to this moral incorporation of the opponent? Two things. In the first place, the person who commits
the crime of subversion is put outside the bounds of ordinary
decent people and hence outside the protection of the law that
normally applies. Rapuano, a packinghouse checker, is explicit on
this, and says he thinks the Constitution was made to protect
people like himself, not Communists. In the course of events in
Germany, the German people went through what Gilbert calls
"the selective constriction of affect"; [24] empathic feelings were
made to apply to a narrower and narrower group. Something like
that happens with the sense of fair play and due process; the idea
of fair play is not modified, only the people to whom it applies.

In the second place, the nature of the "crime" is thought to

24. See R. M. Gilbert, *The Psychology of Dictatorship* (New York: Ronald, 1950),
p. 278.

offer a uniquely appropriate solution, one quite in line with the idea of coercion for the individual's own good. His crime is that "he does not like it here; he is critical of our way of life and seeks to establish an alien system." The solution, offered with a delighted sense that in this way he will discover his error at the same time that he gets what he is asking for, is to send him to a Communist state, "and see how he likes it." "Why the hell don't they deport them all," says DeAngelo, "and get them out of here?"

Conscience and Group Interest

Marx and Engels have argued that capitalist policy and morality is but bourgeois self-interest "transformed into eternal laws of nature and reason," and capitalist jurisprudence is "but the will of your class made into a law for all." [25] If it is true that moral arguments are rationalizations of someone's more material interests, in whose interest does the conscience of Eastport's workingman make its appeal?

The appeal is not made consciously in the name of any social group—class, religious, ethnic, even the national appeal of the "American way." There are, of course, unconscious group ties that guide and prompt the moral sense and give a moral rationale to certain advantages sought for, say, the Italian-Americans, or to the workingman. But, as we must make clear, often these ties are really weak, in part because they are so rarely talked about. As a consequence, perhaps because there is almost no other group for it to moralize, the conscious moralizes *the public*. It reifies and then moralizes the public interest, the general welfare, in a way not dissimilar to the philosophy of those in 1789 who, creating a Constitution and fearing class and party interests, grounded their thinking in concepts of natural law.

Low-Tension Morality and Low-Tension Politics

The introduction to the Declaration of Independence states that "the Laws of Nature and of Nature's God entitle" the people of the United States to revolt and establish a separate nation. Communism has intellectual roots both in an interpretation of history and in a moral doctrine of equality. The arguments that

25. Karl Marx and Friedrich Engels, *Manifesto of the Communist Party* (New York: International Publishers, 1932), p. 26.

justified the French Revolution to its followers were stated as universal rights—"The Rights of Man." In the Granger Movement, the Populist Movements, the Nonpartisan League, the Progressive movements of 1912, 1924, and 1948, the language of politics was moral language; men sought to protect their rights and to redress wrongs done to them and others. Those who defend the *status quo* make other moral appeals; they call on tradition, a divine order, contractual arrangements implying individual and group integrity as moral sanction for the going order. The language of politics is moral language; it is moralized language. Without this, it must speak only in terms of self- and group-interest and as such loses its power to move men to sacrifice, to forego immediate personal gains for long-term group gains, to subordinate themselves to leadership and discipline. Although the play of "interests" is always significant, no movement, party, or issue endures without a moral justification.

Placing this consideration next to the discussion of the unmoralistic tendencies of the American common man at this stage in history—and, according to Tocqueville, in earlier stages, as well—we perceive one reason for the low political tension and the rather low level of political participation in the United States. Politics has not been moralized; the parties have not been invested with strong moral feeling; the issues are not seen as moral issues; the political leaders have not been made moral heroes and villains. This has the effect of reducing the stakes in elections and making the commitment to one political group a rather loose affair that can be dissolved as the situation may require. It permits ticket splitting, switching, and a rapid adjustment when the opposition party wins.

More than that, it deprives politics of the explicit ideological character that is so apparent in other parts of the world. This is so because a forensic ideology cannot survive without a strong moral component in which there are specified evils, villains, exploiters, usurpers, devils on the one hand, and somewhat vaguer restitutions, reforms, heroes, and salvation on the other. This morality, rather than logic, is what holds an ideology together, and without it the whole thing tends to disintegrate into a series of piecemeal and pragmatic adjustments to changing circumstances and demands. Pragmatism too has its moral foundation, but since it is so often inarticulate the morality of pragmatism will not serve as the cement for an ideological structure.

A tendency to moralize is, very often, a tendency to rationalize, that is, to convert real interests and operational motives into principles that embody the moral themes conventionally thought to be sacred in a given society. When this occurs, the grounds on which an opinion is held, the circumstances that would have to be affected before the opinion is "vulnerable," are concealed and protected, and discourse is less likely to be persuasive. Since government by discussion, at every level, is frustrated by this tendency to rationalization, it is dangerous and dysfunctional in the extreme. In this sense chronic moralization, a disposition toward indignation on the part of a broad public, is a disservice to democracy, just as are themes of cynical demoralization in a culture.

The unmoralistic nature of the common men of Eastport, their lack of a sense of sin and evil in the world and in themselves, their belief in a self-adjusting moral order, their tendency to seek to understand rather than to blame, all hold perils for the social order. Perhaps they protect the *status quo* a little too carefully; perhaps they imply too sanguine a view of the outcome of inaction; perhaps they lead not only to a pacific politics but also to a stagnant politics. But when they are supported by a personal moral code that guides men's lives in humane and decent ways, the lack of moralism is, on balance, an advantage in a functioning, changing, democratic society.

Epistemology

22

Conceptualizing in Political Discourse

> The typical citizen drops down to a lower level of mental per-
> formance as soon as he enters the political field. He argues and
> analyzes in a way he would readily recognize as infantile within
> the sphere of his real interests. He becomes a primitive again.
> —JOSEPH SCHUMPETER, *Capitalism, Socialism and Democracy*
> (1950), p. 262

At least three times in Western history a society has developed a brilliant civilization characterized by self-knowledge and
a groping comprehension of the forces ruling its destiny—indeed,
with something of a mastery of these forces—and then has fallen
back into a condition of irrationality and mystification. In each
of these societies, science as well as art was a flourishing branch
of knowledge; the spirit of rational inquiry was abroad, the desire
to perceive reality clearly, without the aid of myths and demons
and divine forces. "In the ancient world ruled by the irrational,
by dreadful unknown powers, where a man was utterly at the
mercy of what he must not try to understand, the Greeks arose
and the rule of reason began." [1] But the rationalism of the third-
and fourth-century Greeks began to run into stronger opposition

1. Edith Hamilton, *The Greek Way to Western Civilization* (New York: New
American Library, 1948), p. 19.

in the second century when men like Archimedes were confronted by the rising cult of astrology; and, says Dodds, by the first century "the tide of rationalism, which for the past hundred years had flowed ever more sluggishly, has finally expended its force and begins to retreat." [2] For whatever reason, the failure to develop an experimental method, the importation of new religious and mystical doctrines from the East, "the unconscious flight from the heavy burden of individual choice which an open society lays upon its members," [3] a turning away from science and reason in human affairs as well as in the study of nature, laid waste a great civilization.

Prompted by a revived humanistic interest in ancient Greece, the restless rise of trade, and the curious ancillary products of petty wars as well as great crusades, the Italian Renaissance once again lifted the spirit of rational inquiry into prominence. [4] Although it was under the influence of a capricious church and challenged by the pseudosciences of the stars, nevertheless Italy at the close of the fifteenth century offered the world a forum where Palo Toscanelli, Luca Pacioli, and Leonardo da Vinci might speak. Later, Galileo was to crown these Italian efforts. This spirit was not the exclusive possession of a narrow elite. Burckhardt says that it is "unquestionable" that in the Italy of the Renaissance, "a whole people takes a natural delight in the study and investigation of nature, at a time when other nations are indifferent, that is to say . . . the discoverer is not threatened or wholly ignored, but can count on the friendly support of congenial spirits." [5] But the Counter Reformation, the Inquisition, the astrologers sometimes working with the church, and "a stupid fatalism" in human affairs robbed this new beginning of its momentum. A second flowering of the rational spirit of inquiry, a capacity to look nature and man in the face, was lost, if only temporarily.

2. E. R. Dodds, *The Greeks and the Irrational* (Boston: Beacon, 1957), p. 247.

3. *Ibid.*, p. 252.

4. Etienne Gilson places "the primacy of reason," as opposed to revelation, earlier, linking it to the work of Averroës in the twelfth century. Averroës' work is a species of scholastic reasoning, however, which, as Gilson says, "is wholly unrelated to scientific discovery." This should caution us on the various meanings of the word; by "rational" and "reason" I mean Man's reason, not God's, a secular orientation with a penchant for evidence and a tropism toward verification procedures. See Etienne Gilson, *Reason and Revelation in the Middle Ages* (New York: Scribner, 1948), pp. 37–66.

5. Jacob Burckhardt, *The Civilization of the Renaissance in Italy* (London: Phaidon Press, 1944), p. 174.

A third—but much more modest—instance of the triumph of the irrational in human affairs, the escape from freedom of mind and, in this case, body too, is too recent to need citation. It is not, of course, that the Second Reich represents a flowering of the rational spirit, but the broader German culture, particularly when combined with the Austrian culture, nourished in the late nineteenth and early twentieth centuries a coterie of remarkable scientific talent, natural and social, including Weber, Simmel, Sombart, and Freud, with, in the last instance, many associates and disciples in Vienna and a few in Berlin. The destruction of this cultural effort by the myths of race and blood and the cult of nationalism impresses the modern mind with the power of the irrational and the capacity of the common man to borrow and use explanations for his plight that may easily set the world in flames. This is no more than a backdrop for an inquiry into the nature of the thinking the men of Eastport devote to public events, great and small, of the day—their day. But it will serve to remind us of the fragile thread of reason that has snapped in several other periods, one of them not so long ago.

A

PRINCIPLES AND PRAGMATISM

Tocqueville thought that "the Americans are much more addicted to the use of general ideas than the English and entertain a much greater relish for them." The English, he says, were concerned only with "particular facts" and "only generalize in spite of themselves." On the other hand "Among the French . . . the taste for general ideas would seem to grow to so ardent a passion that it must be satisfied on every occasion." [6] As we noted earlier, André Siegfried says of the French, "Principles and ideals are the very heart and soul of our politics." [7] But of the Americans no one has repeated Tocqueville's observation; on the contrary they are said to be as pragmatic and as addicted to facts as Tocqueville says the English were some 120 years ago.

The discussion of this issue is loose; it is complicated by the fact that every explanation of an event requires, implicitly or explicitly, a set of generalizations. Thus one interpretation of these

6. Alexis de Tocqueville, *Democracy in America*, Phillips Bradley, ed. (New York: Knopf, 1945), II, 14.

7. See above, page 293.

alleged differences is that some people tend to *describe* situations rather than to explain them. If this were the allegation with respect to the American pragmatism—that it is a discourse based on description—the evidence from Eastport would tend to refute it. In the discussion of "major problems," of the causes of war and poverty, of the functioning of government, and elsewhere, there is a marked tendency to explain, a focus on why things happen the way they do.

But a causal explanation has two main ingredients. Popper says, "To give a *causal explanation* of an event means to deduce a statement which describes it, using as premises of the deductions one or more *universal laws,* together with certain singular statements, the *initial conditions.*" [8] When the French, with their alleged emphasis upon principles, explain an event, they may elaborate the universal laws, generalizing about the nature of men and society, and they may slight the statement of particulars, the facts, or, in Popper's phrase, the initial conditions. When Americans explain an event—and certainly this is true in Eastport—they may assume the universal laws and focus upon the initial conditions, the facts that characterize the situation. It is, indeed, true, that the man of Eastport tends to explain matters in terms of latent principles and manifest facts, and when he argues the argument more often turns on the characteristics of the situation, not on the rules that govern the universe. But, of course, he has ideas about these rules, ideas that remain part of his somewhat inarticulate and often unconscious assumptions of the nature of things.

The latency of the principles employed in social explanations tends to be supported by two other features of the American ideology. In the first place there stands the belief that most men are more or less the same; thus the rules governing human behavior are intuitively known through introspection. They are assumed, not discussed. Second, the common unchallenged assumptions about government derive from the almost universal acceptance of the same Lockean model, as Louis Hartz has pointed out.[9] One consequence of this latency is that the American finds it difficult to argue about political principles, and there is little doubt that one reason why Americans become so furious over the arguments

8. Karl R. Popper, *The Logic of Scientific Discovery,* 2nd ed. (New York: Basic Books, 1958), p. 58, his emphasis.
9. Louis Hartz, *The Liberal Tradition in America* (New York: Harcourt, Brace, 1955).

of the Communists is that their own political principles are hard
to tear from their native bed in the unconscious.

B

MORSELIZING AND CONTEXTUALIZING

"Our way," said Edith Hamilton of contemporary civilization, "is to consider each separate thing alone by itself." On the
other hand, she says, "the Greeks always saw things as parts of a
whole, and this habit of mind is stamped upon everything they
did. It is the underlying cause of the difference between their art
and ours." [10] Others, too, have spoken of the fragmentation of the
world in modern times. Yet one of the features of what is sometimes called "understanding" is to grasp the context of an event,
that is, temporally to know what went before and what is likely to
follow, spatially to know the terrain, in human terms to see the
play of the many motives involved. To understand an event in this
way is to *contextualize* it; not to do this is to *morselize* it, to see it
isolated from the surrounding features that give it additional
"meanings." What education does for a man is to help him to
contextualize events, particularly public events, but the unusual
man, as we shall see, can capture some of this context without
formal education.

In Eastport, as elsewhere, some men morselize the political
world and some contextualize it. We can see how this works by
stripping their discourse bare of the "I don't knows," the repetition, the false starts, and giving a summary outline of the ideas
presented by three men as they discuss Soviet-American relationships. DeAngelo, who left school in the seventh grade but who is
now shop steward of his plant and a hard-working factory operative, sets forth the following ideas on this subject: "It doesn't
seem like you can negotiate with them [because] they've just got
their minds set." "We're trying to do things with 'em peacefully."
"We are keeping them surrounded with air bases, kind of keeping them in check." "They'll start trouble somewhere." "It's not
our fault." "It's just like Germany—they want to conquer the
world." "There's no religion . . . if a man doesn't believe in
anything, you can't bargain with him." "I don't know who's behind the Russians," "We must protect ourselves." "The whole

10. Edith Hamilton, *The Greek Way*, p. 169.

world today is all fouled up." There is no dearth of ideas here; DeAngelo, with his tongue getting in the way of his speech, is a rough, untrained observer, but not unintelligent.

McNamara finished high school and went to night school to learn bookkeeping. He says: "Inflation and defense policy are related." "Russia's come a long way in twenty years," "No one knows what the Russians have accomplished." "It appears they are ahead of us in the science field." "You've got to be careful." "They're probably now as powerful as Germany was, and Germany stirred up a lot of trouble." "Our policy is pretty well set: go along carefully and every once in a while pass out a few threats; a display of power here and there doesn't hurt." "We are now in a scientific race." "Barriers between nations don't help; perhaps we should open up more trade." "We're making the same mistakes with them we made with Germany." "War may not be inevitable."

Flynn, who did finish high school but never had any training beyond that, except what he picked up as a young assistant on a water-company survey, says: "The trade problem and the defense problem are related." "Mutual scaring of each other by us and the Russians is risky." "The philosophy of disarmament runs into the difficulty that the Russians won't compromise." "A firmer foreign policy ten years ago would have prevented some of this." "While we have been building up other countries, the Russians have been building up their military strength." "You will never get disarmament until each side is certain of armament parity." "Full-scale disarmament is too idealistic." "We believe that you can't trust the Russians, and they believe they can't trust us." "Agreement is difficult because of the many nations involved." "War is probably inevitable, but the horror of nuclear war may prevent it." "Agreements are worthless in preventing atomic warfare." "We set the precedent for dropping the bomb."

What do we learn from this? It is a pretty fair sampling of the way these men wrestle with a policy problem somewhat more remote from their experience than the problems they like to deal with. In the first place, there is a wonderful "off the cuff" quality to it; judgments are made with an abandon that terrifies and paralyzes the analytic mind. (How would you, the reader of this book, analyze and meet the proposition: "It's just like Germany —they want to conquer the world"?) There is not in any of the three a real argument, a building up of a case. Instead their statements represent a series of impressions. Third, there is a marked difference among them that reflects something we have said about the scope of the concepts involved; for DeAngelo, these are somewhat narrow and tied to the specific instances involved (a defense policy defined by bases, negotiation as a function of religious faith). McNamara seems to broaden out this straitened view somewhat so that the instances of the present case fall into a larger context. For one thing the idea of Russia is not limited to Russia *now;* it is a part of the larger notion of historical and developing Russia; then too, an important link between domestic and foreign policy is forged, and the concept of a broader fiscal-defense unit of thought is created. Still, the thinking is fairly instance-specific; the conceptual setting is rather meager. With Flynn, however, it broadens again. Like McNamara he links several problems together, for example, defense and trade, and our foreign aid and Russia's rapid advance. His conceptualization includes the Russian side—when he speaks of how we see them he adds how they must see us; it is a conceptualization that embraces one more step then, a feedback concept. He refers not simply to disarmament, but to "the philosophy of disarmament," including by reference, then, a much broader concept of an idea, one to which he is opposed at this time. Like McNamara, his conceptualization includes a time perspective—American foreign policy over the past ten years. He broadens the conceptualization to include other nations: negotiations, he understands, cannot be only bipartite anymore. His concept of a problem and a policy, then, is topically broader, spatially more inclusive, and has historical depth. But more of the men are like DeAngelo than like Flynn, or even McNamara.

If one does not see the instance in its context, the man in his setting, the event in a pattern of events, he misses the significance of what he sees, and missing this, he has no adequate means of dealing with the relevant social or political problems. Sokolsky tells of juvenile delinquency where the delicious details are the focus of his attention and the limit of his observation; Woodside, a railroad guard, sees it in a broader framework; he sees it as falling within a class of minor crimes likely to happen in two or three familar parts of the city and to be committed by youth with certain characteristics; Farrel, the educated man who slipped into our panel by the processes of randomization, sees it as a part of a social pattern with a broad metropolitan distribution, certain family and psychological correlates, and consequences affecting educational programs and school-leaving age requirements. This treatment of an instance in isolation happens time and again and on matters close to home: a union demand is a single incident, not part of a more general labor-management conflict; a purchase on the installment plan is a specific debt, not part of a budgetary pattern—either one's own or society's. The items and fragments of life remain itemized and fragmented—at least at the conscious level.

Contextual political thinking, then, is not just pigeonholing, not labeling, not in any necessary way associated with the "ismatic" terminology of today (Fascism, Communism, Federalism.) It reflects a configurative and relational turn of mind—in several ways. One way is to picture an event as part of a stream of events; that is, it is historical. Another is to compare and contrast events so as to group them in some way that sheds light on their common characteristics. Still another is to bring the event into contact with a conceptual framework such that it may be seen to illustrate or modify or rebut some part of that framework. Yet it is true that any one of these ways of placing "figure against ground," "contextualizing" an event or an idea, often reaches beyond the experience of the individual in time or place; they are not encouraged by a quality of thought that is characteristic of Eastport workingmen: the tendency to keep concepts narrow and close to personal experience. For while this intellectual sobriety may ensure that the men know the evidential basis for their observations, it deprives them of some of the sources of interpretation that make an event meaningful. And in a curious sense this itemization may then mean that they derive their interpretation of an event from a free associative fantasy process rather than through the social and historical context to which the isolated events may be said to "belong."

C
CONTEXTUALIZING AND IDEOLOGIZING

Now, the very morselizing tendency that prevents these men from discovering the pattern and significance of an event also prevents them from ideologizing. While they do not place events in the context of a pattern of history or policy, neither do they place them in the context of some more or less rigid and exclusive interpretation of world affairs, a forensic ideology. They do not make events illustrate a predetermined theory of the way the world lies for the simple reason that they do not have such a theory; rather, they have several conflicting theories with vague referents.

Only in one or two instances did it seem to me that these men of Eastport attempted consciously to increase their understanding of an event by explicitly placing it in the context of a forensic ideology, though of course the individual, private, latent ideology of each man served as a constant sentinel at the gate of his mind. Sokolsky, arriving in an angry mood because of his brush with the supervisor on his part-time janitorial job, argues against equal income for everyone regardless of occupation on several personal and pragmatic grounds ("I look with horror on everybody exactly the same"), but he finds room for one more argument of an ideological sort: "I think that would be swinging a little toward your Communists, wouldn't it?" This is more window dressing than anything else, but it illustrates what it is that, on a larger scale and with more emotional force, and with greater elaboration, might be the central characteristic of a political debate. (The fact that we must use this slender example for illustration is significant in itself.)

Consider the difficult case of Sullivan, an over-the-road truck driver, with a laconic but penetrating style of discourse. His argument must be read with the understanding that four out of five of the Eastportians hold that Communists should have no right to free speech in the United States. He does not suffer fools gladly, and while in the Army nearly beat a man to death because he talked after "all quiet" (and brought down punishment on the barracks). Turning to the question of whether or not Communists should be allowed to speak, he says: "Well, [pause] it's a hard thing to say 'no' to, because—I mean I'm not too happy about it, but [pause] you can't very well have a democracy, and freedom of speech, if you don't let them, even though it's [pause] it's not something you agree on or particularly like. There's not too much you can do without changing the policy or the foundation of the country. [pause] I wish there was, but I guess there just isn't something." The logic is clear. This son of a former Jesuitical student argues: freedom of speech for Communists is a necessary part of the general class of things included in the concept "democracy." Since democracy is established by law, and not subject to change, freedom of speech for Communists is not subject to change—and

probably shouldn't be. Substitute the right of an employer to contract individually with each of his employees for the rights of free
speech for Communists, and substitute "due process" for "democracy," and you have the reasoning of the Court in *Hammer* v.
Dagenhart and other child-labor cases.

When is a person contextualizing and when is he ideologizing?
In each case he adds to his understanding by bringing additional
material to bear upon a single event; in each case he must select
which material to use; in each case he is guided either explicitly
or implicitly by a theoretical construct. The difference centers on
the need to confirm the pattern of ideas employed in this process;
if the event is used and needed to support an emotionally involved
theory or interpretation, the tendency is toward ideologizing.
Moreover this frame of mind protects the sacred theory by admitting ideas only from approved sources. The ideologue takes his
cue on the interpretation of information from its source; the contextualist is more open to information from all sources. Furthermore, the ideologue keeps the things he believes quite separate
from those he doesn't believe so that their colors, their whiteness
and blackness, do not mingle; the contextualist permits a shading
in his pictures of the world. For the contextualist information is
a positively useful tool, an enjoyment; for the ideologue information is a threat, and therefore suspect, unless it can be made familiar by attaching it to a known system of ideas.[11]

Judged by these standards, Sullivan's wrestling with the problem of civil liberties for Communists by placing the problem in
the context of democratic principles could not be said to be ideologizing, for instead of forcing an event into a preferred interpretation he is reluctantly yielding a preferred position to the
logic of an over-all pattern of ideas. But Sullivan is exceptional
only in the explicitness of the conflict; the others not infrequently
confront an event with a cherished principle and tolerate the conflict. Those who believe that unions advance working-class interests accept evidence of their abuse; lifelong Democrats admit
that it is unfair to blame the recession on Republicans; 100 per
cent American "working-class capitalists" admit that the Russian
people are better off these days. Theories of the advantages of unions, Democratic administrations, capitalist economies make room
for contrary evidence. Thus in two senses we must say that East-

11. Some of these distinctions derive from the excellent discussion in Milton
Rokeach, *The Open and Closed Mind* (New York: Basic Books, 1960), pp. 54–82.

port tends not to ideologize: first, the use of forensic ideologies, of theoretical constructs with well-defined referents, is minimal; second, the smaller and vaguer theories, the segments of ideologies employed, are used more as guides to interpretation than as defenses against the real world.

D
RIGIDITY AND COMPROMISE

Closely allied to the concept of ideologizing is that of rigidity, the inflexible mind, whether because it is doctrinaire (ideologized) or merely stubborn, willful, unyielding. Perhaps these men are, in this sense, rigid; that is, they may tend to uncompromising assertion in the face of contrary evidence and argument. Uncertainty of the kind modern men face sometimes produces rigidity. There is good psychoanalytic evidence for this, and some further evidence that it is exactly when their faith seems most at odds with the evidence that religious sectarians become most assertive about their beliefs.[12] I cannot say that I found the men of Eastport rigid, for, of course, I did not argue with them, but rather supported and rewarded the views they brought out themselves to create the most permissive atmosphere possible. But, as mentioned earlier, my associate James D. Barber did arrange for some debate among them in a room where a recording apparatus had been set in motion (with the knowledge of the men) and where the men were then left alone to thrash out a problem by themselves. There were two groups of three; one group was selected because of the prickly personalities of the men, and another group for their rather more easygoing dispositions. They argued a half-hour each on four topics. I have taken the last topic discussed, on the grounds that by then the men were most heated and free; as it turns out this is also the most controversial topic: "Are unions doing a good job?" The angry, prickly group (whose members I shall not identify, since they have met each other) includes one who recently knocked down a man for a slighting remark, another who nearly beat a man to death in the Army, and a third, who not long ago punched someone in the face for an alleged slur on his mother. At the end of the fourth half-hour argument, Number One, a member of a strong trade union, has been defending the union; Number Two has just been telling of how unions

12. Leon Festinger, Henry Reicken, and Stanley Schacter, *When Prophecy Fails* (Minneapolis: University of Minnesota Press, 1956).

caused his brother-in-law to go bankrupt by "stalling along on the jobs." Number Three finds abuses everywhere but generally thinks unions are a good thing. Here are their summary statements:

NUMBER ONE: Well, I'd say that [pause] the unions are good. You have to have them—the workingman has to have them, and well, I think they're a little too strong, some of them, now. And some of them are a little bit too lax, too. But on the whole, they're good, and on the whole I think [pause] any man that's a union member is getting paid what he's worth. And every union man's got a right to make a little bit more than a nonunion man. . . . A nonunion man just sits back, and when the unions get raises for other members he just falls right in.

NUMBER TWO: Well, I think that unions are a necessity. We've got to have them. But then, again, I think they're getting out of hand. I think they should be controlled, for one thing. I think they're lax—the union itself is lax, as they do allow certain undesirable elements into the union that shouldn't be there, and as a whole I don't think they're doing a good job. I think they're taking advantage of this organization, and just running hog-wild, right now.

NUMBER THREE: [after some critical comments about unions and a statement of agreement with number one—"where they do need unions"]: Yes and no—I think it's just about fifty-fifty.

During the course of the prior discussion, which revealed some real differences of opinion and some strong feeling, there was a tendency to accept part of the opponent's argument, just as there is in the summing up just quoted.

The theme that these three men are working out in these passages, not quite rising above their passions, might be stated as "there is good and bad in unions." Indeed, this general theme could be emblazoned on Eastport's crest: "There is good and bad in everything." When a man speaks evil of something, he will retract it a little later on by saying something good. In Anna Freud's phrase, we are always "undoing" the evil that we do. On the other hand, there is little glorification, either. The exposed evaluative position is rarely rigidly defended—there is, instead, a search for neutral ground.

There are several routes to the "neutral ground" they seek.[13] One is to *deny that there are real differences* of interest among men, and this often follows from their position on the reality of a

13. For a discussion of basic roots as well as routes of this flexible nondoctrinaire theme in America, see Erik Erikson, *Childhood and Society* (New York: Norton, 1950), pp. 275–277.

true public interest. Another is to stress the reconciliation of apparent differences by *bringing the conflicting partisans together*. Johnson discloses this penchant in his belief that the "race problem" might be solved by bringing the parties together. Discrimination in certain areas is "not the American way of doing it," he says, and, in a pleading and rather desperate tone, he adds, "But I should think there should be some way of bringing it out between them." It is his vain hope that the Negroes could be persuaded to accept a segregated arrangement, and thus relieve him of what is really a rather bad conscience. DeAngelo gives the idea of bringing labor and management together a classic expression. He has just said that he believes union pressure is partly responsible for the high cost of living, and continues: "Well, I don't know; the union—they won't press for wages unless, y'know, things keep goin' up. I mean, [pause] I think the government, big business, unions—they gotta get together and straighten the thing out, as best they could. Y'know what I mean? Talk it over; see what the hell they can do about it. [pause] I mean, I don't know, it's gotta be settled some way—if—I think the only way they can settle it, they gotta get together and settle it."

But for these men in their difficult tasks of suggesting policy, the main device is to pursue a kind of *centralist* tendency, something like the one described by Alfred Jones in Akron, Ohio, some twenty-five years ago.[14] Given three policy choices the men will choose the "middle" one; given two choices they will yield a little on each, borrow something from the other, obscure the differences. You see this in the concluding statements of the three men on the unions; it is true of many other situations as well. This holds for "feeling strongly," too. On tests where they are given an option to state how strongly they agree or disagree with a proposition, they tend to squash their feelings down into a middle range. Inevitably this produces a certain uniformity of opinion, roughs off the edges and idiosyncrasies, factors that may have caused Bryce to remark how "Americans appear to vary less, in fundamentals, from what may be called the dominant American type, than Englishmen, Germans, Frenchmen, Spaniards, or Italians do from any types which could be taken as the dominant type in any of those nations." [15]

Something might be said here of how this search for neutral

14. Alfred W. Jones, *Life, Liberty, and Property* (Philadelphia: Lippincott, 1941).
15. James Bryce, *The American Commonwealth* (New York: Macmillan, 1910), II, 886.

ground, this tendency to try to adjust between apparently disparate positions, produces, in the end, that minimal speculation and originality characteristic of Eastport's common man. If everyone is trying to be a broker of opinion and to bring other people's opinions into harmony, none will range far in the pursuit of new ideas. In a way, this represents the substitution of "goodwill," a quality Laski says Americans believe will solve all problems,[16] for hard thinking. For the functioning of a political system, of course, both are required, but in Eastport, at least, the balance is in favor of goodwill; the common man there is likely to be only a middle man.

Perhaps this is a condition of any successful democracy; perhaps it is more specially American. A hundred and twenty years ago, Tocqueville argued that "the great privilege of the Americans does not consist in being more enlightened than other nations, but in being able to repair the faults they may commit." [17] We are able to acknowledge our mistakes and to correct our errors—something incompatible with rigid thinking. If, as Riesman says, there are penalties to the loss of inner direction and the conscientious knowledge of what is right, flexibility and the lack of rigidity are the contrasting benefits.

E

DIFFERENTIATION

There is an economy in stereotypes, says Walter Lippmann. "For the attempt to see things freshly and in detail, rather than as types and generalities, is exhausting, and among busy affairs practically out of the question." [18] Stereotypes are the mind's shorthand for dealing with complexities. They have two aspects: they are much blunter than reality; they are shaped to fit a man's preferences and prejudgments. Thus two principles are involved: differentiation or its lack, and biased preferential perception. "An attitude toward Russia may be focused upon a highly amorphous subjective impression of that country or upon a highly differentiated one. . . . The object of an attitude varies in its differentiation. . . ." [19] This is our problem for the moment.

There are many reasons for a blunted differentiation, of which

16. Harold Laski, *The American Democracy* (New York: Viking, 1948), p. 708.
17. Alexis de Tocqueville, *op. cit.*, I, 231.
18. Walter Lippmann, *Public Opinion* (New York: Penguin, 1946), p. 66.
19. M. Brewster Smith, Jerome S. Bruner, and Robert W. White, *Opinions and Personality* (New York: Wiley, 1956), pp. 34–35.

we distinguish three: insufficient information (cognitive bluntness), blockage by strong emotion, especially anger (emotional
bluntness), and remoteness from one's own beliefs and values
(ideological bluntness). Dempsey, who never advanced beyond the
sixth grade, illustrates the first of these. He says the word "government" suggests to him, "Well, someone to govern, to rule over,
probably [pause] to guide people in the right way." While interesting for many reasons, not the least of which is the passive
and dependent tone of this response, it is certainly a blunt and
undifferentiated idea of government. The next "witness," a week
later, said: "To me it means organization. [pause] It brings to
mind, at least, a society which is regulated, that is, it's governed
by a set of rules and a governing body." This is our friend Flynn
speaking, a white-collar worker who has completed high school.
Dempsey's comment has the bluntness of tautology, with the
"guidance" feature added; Flynn breaks down the idea into three,
still large but more explicit ideas: organization, the rules of law,
an organ through which government acts. Flynn goes on later
to develop these ideas, while Dempsey has little more to say. (I
ask him what kinds of things the government ought to do, and he
responds, "That I couldn't say; I'm not up on that.") This is what
we call a cognitive difference in differentiation based upon information, but there are others.

Rapuano, a volcanic man with the burden of his Americanism
lying heavily across his broad but stooping shoulders, answers
the same question, after a pause and some heavy breathing, as
follows, "Government? What do I think of?" He pauses again.
"Politics, for one thing. Oh, yes, [pause] politics is about all I
could think of. [pause] There ain't anything that's unpolitical
that's not—that's government. Everything that seems to be government is politics." I ask him what kind of things the government
ought to do, and he answers after another short pause: "Well,
that's hard to say. I mean, I'm not that smart. Let's see what the
hell they should do." But he can find things for them to do; he
almost finished high school, has an active mind, and is interested
in political affairs. What accounts for the bluntness in this case,
of course, is the emotional reverberations that echo so loudly in
his mind that, so to speak, "he cannot hear himself think." This,
then, is a case of emotional bluntness.

This pattern is marked in the cases of four men (Rapuano,
Ferrera, Sokolsky, and Kuchinsky) and observable in others. But

as we said above, in Eastport the level of indignation is generally low; the flow of affect is moderate; the responses to "things in the news that made me mad" are not very "mad"; the tendency to avoid blaming keeps emotion at a modest level; the adjustive strategies make the nursing of anger dysfunctional, and all in all emotional bluntness is kept at a minimum. As a system, the American low-keyed political style keeps open the windows of perception and differentiation to a remarkable degree.

The third type of failure to differentiate, ideological bluntness, is based on the principle that the further away from a person's beliefs and values a group of objects lies, the less significant do the differences between those objects appear. Rokeach illustrates this with the difficulty a follower of Senator McCarthy had in distinguishing between Communists, Socialists, and advanced liberals.[20] In the same way, in 1961 liberals found the distinction between positions held by the *National Review,* the John Birch Society, and Barry Goldwater hard to discern, although conservatives saw important differences. Now, it is significant that a search through the discussion of "subversives in America," "big business," "Russia," "the causes of war and poverty," and other areas of discourse where rejected groups or conspiracies or evil systems have their abode does not discover much blunting of perception. The measure for blunted differentiation includes: (1) an increased use of derogatory labels instead of descriptive terms, such as "a crazy bunch," "madmen," "bloodsuckers," and so forth; (2) a substitute of programs of quick violent action prior to, or probably instead of, description and analysis; (3) dismissal of a problem or group with a phrase, refusal to treat it seriously, contemptuous withdrawal. Only in the case of the domestic Communists was there much evidence of undifferentiated perception and quick prescription—and not by any means in all such cases. Here, for example, is the way Costa begins his discussion of subversive elements in America. Costa is a frequent and militant defender of "the American way." He says:

> Well, I think there are too many. Too many leaks, too much of our secret information gets out. I don't know whether that's because we're a democracy or whether there's just people—I mean, I can think of several things, like the Rosenbergs, for one, like that Dr. Fuchs over in England. . . . Are you asking me does Russia have an organized [group]? I think they do.

20. Milton Rokeach, *op. cit.,* pp. 38–39.

In the context of Costa's usual level of differentiation there is no loss of differentiated thinking here, no ideological bluntness. Thus the over-all impression (the reactions of about half of the men to domestic Communism excepted) is one of continuity of perception, differentiation, conceptualization—each at his own level—as one moves from areas of belief and support to areas of disbelief and opposition.

Differentiation, as the anthropologists tell us with respect to language, is a measure of social focus, a clue to what the society cares about. Speaking loosely, and about this stratum of lower-middle- and upper-working-class men, I would say the American political mind is differentiated more in terms of rights than duties —almost all men mention and illustrate the various rights that Americans enjoy; they had more trouble in explaining the nature of citizenly or patriotic duties—here the terms were more global and more derivative. Secondly, their capacities to distinguish and deal intellectually with the problems of race relations were greater than those of interclass relations—they had thought more about the one than about the other. Third, their concepts of appropriate means of social adjustment, of how to behave in different situations, are elaborate and clear in their minds—much more elaborate and clear than their pictures of themselves. If one may be elliptical to make the point: each person knows more about *what* he should do than about *who* he is. The American tendency to objectify, rather than subjectify, the world is reflected here. They have differentiated and easily articulated concepts about work, money, and consumption, but their conceptualization of their religious beliefs, the duties of the church, and the purposes of life are blunt and unsophisticated. It is as though they put forth a special effort to homogenize all religious and moral thought. When it came to commentaries on the dogmatic beliefs of their churches, the products were indeed a meager gleaning; and, as we noted before, their time perspectives are differentiated by short-range matters, which may account, in a way, for the optimism of the American outlook. It is only in a perspective that encompasses the period of death that a profound sense of tragedy is likely to develop.

We have said that the political mind of Eastport tends to emphasize one of the ingredients of an explanation, the initial conditions, at the expense of the other, the universal laws. Eastportians tend to morselize their knowledge rather than to contextualize it, thus losing much of the significance or meaning of an event. On some intercultural ideologizing scale, I would guess that they would be "low"; they use events to confirm or defend a world view less frequently than others. They avoid exposed positions, yield quickly in an argument, seek middle ground, and compromise where they can. And while they often use stereotypes and blunted perceptions of events, these tend to flow from lack of information rather than from disagreement or anger.

There are other characteristics of their thought with consequences for the political system: they rarely *organize* their views. Kuchinsky begins his interview as follows: "We have a lot of problems today, and, um, in this country concerning the other side, [Europe] uh, which I think, uh, this country's really gone overboard on a lot of things—I mean throwing a lot of money away." About four sentences later he is speaking of the rent increase in Hilltop—it is a kind of stream of consciousness. On the other hand Flynn begins his interview: "The major problems? Of course that means defining, Number One, what the major problems are. They're in two areas, I guess, foreign and domestic." He turns to the domestic first and discusses this before he moves on for a fuller treatment of the foreign problems. The group mode is closer to Kuchinsky than it is to Flynn; there is an almost complete lack of an effort to think through a question before attempting to answer it; it is a rare moment when a man speaks of the "areas," "levels," "stages," or "phases" of a problem, or uses the apparatus of analysis of component elements of a complex affair, treating them one by one.

These men rarely acknowledge a difference between the speculative and the known, making a point of the *differences in certainty* or familiarity. One blends into the other without a break. There is no *strategy* to their discourse, no attempt to persuade through such a logical development that if one admits one point, the next must follow. In short, their discussion is not self-conscious, not planned; it has a kind of "free form" associative quality. In this sense they are open to new information, open to experience. Without the blockages of strong emotion, or the walls of ideological defensiveness, their minds, like the society itself, seem pluralistic, with both liberal and conservative roots to which new ideas can attach themselves and grow.

23

The Uses of Political Knowledge

We may say that if the political education of the average American voter be compared with that of the average voter in Europe, it stands high; but if it be compared with the functions which the theory of the American government lays on him, which its spirit implies, which the methods of its party organization assume, its inadequacy is manifest. . . .
——JAMES BRYCE, *The American Commonwealth*, II, 288

It is a dangerous situation for . . . without accurate information it is difficult to be an effective citizen; and most people have neither the time nor the means to explore for truth in the news.
——HAROLD LASKI, *The American Democracy*, p. 648

The American political system places a heavy burden upon its citizens, treating them, as Bryce says, not merely as electors but sometimes as governors as well.[1] Under these circumstances the substance and boundaries of their knowledge are important, and beyond this, so is their attitude toward knowledge and learning, particularly political knowledge. It has sometimes been assumed that men seek knowledge as they seek food and that Americans, guided by the high value placed upon education in their

1. James Bryce, *The American Commonwealth* (New York: Macmillan, 1910), I, 289.

culture, are especially hungry in this respect. Elsewhere we have argued the other side of this case—the positive value to some men under some circumstances of such ignorance as helps them to avoid conflict or preserves useful illusions or protects the legitimacy of their angry outbursts (needed for other reasons) or keeps their social relations smoother.[2] Here we examine only a small area of a large problem, and ask, not "What do the men know?" but "What is their attitude toward political knowledge?" How do they handle it and its opposite, political ignorance?

A
SOURCES OF AMBIVALENCE

In my examination of the scope of their knowledge of civic matters, current events, political figures in the news, and how to get things done politically; in the discussion of political conversations and whether it is better to "have a person who jokes and keeps things from getting too serious, or to have a person who knows a lot about a subject and can give people the answers"; and in the comparative evaluation of "the mayor of a big city, the president of a university, and the chairman of the board of a big corporation," there emerged a series of latent attitudes toward political knowledge that often cast it into shadow, and took off the luster one might have thought was there.

Civics Is School Knowledge

Woodside hears the voice of a schoolteacher in the questions about certain civic matters. I ask him if he happens to remember how long the term in Washington is for a senator. He muses for a moment with somewhat embarrassed manner and then speaks of himself: "Eleven years out of school—let's see now. I used to know all of them." Later, apologetically, he says, "It's been so long; I know it was one of things you had to learn in school, you know." Rapuano, turning his face aside, says, "I should know that because I learned it in school, years ago." Flynn merely suggests that knowledge of government is rooted in his past; he says slowly, "Well [pause] I—you're taking me back now." How dramatically this contrasts with knowledge of whom to see if you want to get a

---

2. Robert E. Lane, *Political Life: Why People Get Involved in Politics* (New York: The Free Press of Glencoe, 1959), pp. 113–114.

street repaired—that is adult knowledge, useful knowledge. Certain knowledge about government (as contrasted to politics) is burdened with lingering resentments associated with school; for the duller children the humiliation of ignorance in school, for the brighter child the satisfaction of "knowing" along with the tedium of learning often found in the large public-school classroom. Along with this, moreover, is the guilt most men feel for having stopped their education before they finished high school. Insofar as "civics" reminds them of this, it is a painful subject.

People Who Know a Lot Are Often Unpleasant

In the discussion of the relative values of keeping a small political discussion lighthearted or keeping it informed, about two-thirds of the men preferred the lighthearted, joking approach. This was for several reasons, of which one was their image of the knowledgeable person. "I like a fellow that, uh, is jokable," says Kuchinsky. "I mean, I like his ways about him if he don't get too smart." "A person that's too serious and dry—you soon lose interest in the subject," says Woodside. And Farrel recalls a well-informed person: "He's often very witty and sharply biting . . . he tends to be a little too pedantic."

Knowledge Taken Seriously Leads to Controversy

The most frequent reason for steering clear of the well-informed and serious man is his tendency to lead a group into bitter controversy. "It's better to have someone who jokes around and keeps them happy, you know? I mean, sometimes guys start to worry a little bit too quick" (DeAngelo). "Well, if one of them had to leave, I think the best one to leave would be the one who knew so much because the remaining people then, I think, would be less likely to argue amongst themselves" (Flynn). "First thing you know, some people will really get hot. . . . Joking about it doesn't hurt anything" (O'Hara).

The Man of Knowledge Is Not Associated with Power and Wealth

In its favor, it is said that knowledge is something a person must achieve for himself; he cannot get it by being someone's son, or by "politics." These are some reasons for evaluating a university president higher than a mayor or board chairman of a corporation. But on the whole, if the choice must be made in terms of the position a person would choose for himself or for his son, those who choose the position of the man of knowledge (and this is how the university president is seen) are fewer than those who choose the wealth and power of big business; while relatively few choose mayor. Honor is a fine thing, but wealth and power are better.

Yet we have chosen the word "ambivalence," not "rejection," to describe these attitudes toward knowledge. These men are ambivalent about school, recognizing it to be the road to achievement, wealth, power, even understanding. They are ambivalent about the serious, informed discussant; most of them want such a man present, though they want him less than the "jokable" man. They do indeed honor the university president; there is something "purer" about him than about the men who have fought their way up in economic and political life. For these men, knowledge and learning not related to the immediate, the practical, the useful skill has two faces, two values—it, and they, are ambivalent.

B
CIVIC INFORMATION:
THE HANDLING OF UNCERTAINTY

It would certainly be of interest to discover how it is that college professors handle situations where they are asked questions they feel they should be able to answer—and cannot. The working class has its evasive, self-excusing, aggressive ways, too. In discussions with the Eastport men of questions dealing with the nature of government and the public affairs of the times, everything was done to make it easy to say "I don't know." Moreover, the information and comment requested are not highly prized in the working- and lower-middle-class culture of these men; they can admit to one another that they don't know the answers, and receive little status loss thereby. But inevitably there is a sense of achievement in answering a question, a sense of defeat in failing to answer. It is the working out of this tension centering on civic knowledge, uncertainty, and ignorance that attracts our attention.

Some devices for the handling of civic uncertainty keep the men within the field of inquiry and, while protecting them against the bruising effects of having their ignorance revealed, orient them toward learning more. Some, on the other hand, direct their attention elsewhere and attract them, like a wandering child, toward some more colorful or safer territory. They all give balm to the irritations of an exposed ignorance, but some do this by accounting for the failure in terms of some quality, experience, or defect of the self. These we have called "excuses." Other devices tend to account for one's imperfect knowledge by attributing to the environment some failure of reporting—we term this a "blame." There are several ways of dealing with the questioning situation itself so as to relieve the pain of embarrassment; those that are denigrative of the questions or questioners we have termed "gambits"; those that try to substitute something else for the required information we have called "trading offers." Finally there are the tendencies to drift into irrelevancies—tendencies we label "escapes."

Tending To Keep the Focus within the Field of Discourse

EXCUSES   One of the most common devices men hit upon in their moments of embarrassment is to say that this failure of knowledge is part of a broader but specified weakness. Woodside, a railroad guard, cannot remember the name of the alderman in his ward. He explains that he has a poor memory for names. De-Angelo, after a series of increasingly embarrassing (for him) exposures of doubt and error, says, in apologetic tones, "I have a bad memory anyhow, you noticed that?" This device, which might be termed a *generalizing excuse,* does two things: it disarms the interrogator, possibly extracting from him (and often it did from me) some placating or soothing statement; and it also limits the area of failure or defect by saying, in effect: "I am not stupid. I simply have a bad memory," or, as in Woodside's case, "I have a bad memory for names—but I never forget a face."

A second variety of such self-referential treatment is in the more specific *circumstantial excuse:* Kuchinsky says he doesn't know the name of the state senator because "I wasn't around"; Woodside and Flynn suggest that their lack of information is due to the long time they have been out of school—not a matter for blame.

Then, in the third place, there are the *high-standards excuses,* which cast a favorable light on the individual's inability to respond. Dempsey, a drill-press operator, illustrates this and at the same time reveals how morality and "principle" often are screens that hide ignorance. Asked whether Eastport has a city manager, he implies that he answers questions only when he has the evidence well in hand. He says: "That I don't know. I think they did at one time, but whether they still do or not, I couldn't say, because I'm not positive on it."

Then, again, there is a fourth variety of excusing comment, which implies how close one is to the desired knowledge, the *almost-knowing excuse*. It may be that this is simply intended to make the degree of ignorance seem smaller; perhaps, too, it is an expressive act, releasing the tension that builds up when recall of things once known fails. The first of these elements is seen in Johnson's comment on his failure to have any idea what the United Nations is doing: "I haven't read too much about it; I used to follow those boys fairly closely." And the second, I think, is seen in Costa's remark when he can't think of the name of the prime minister of Great Britain: "I know his name; all I've got to do is to think of it. Well, like they say on quiz programs, could we come back to it?"

ENVIRONMENTAL DEFECTS   It is a matter for some surprise that so few of the men employed *media-blaming*, attributing their failure to know to the poor reporting of news. There were a number of men who took a fine moral tone about the crime and sex in the press, but they did not excuse their ignorance of "higher things" in this manner. Sokolsky suggests the way this might have gone for others, but didn't. He has been asked about the United Nations: "You don't hear about the United Nations much in the paper. I don't know why, but you don't." A far larger number of attributions of fault have to do with the failure of the individual than with the failure of the reporting services—a matter that reinforces what we have said earlier about the lack of a tendency to blame others or society for what goes wrong.

EXPRESSIVE IMPUNITIVE BEHAVIOR   Just as the somatic symptoms of tension do not seek excuse and do not distribute blame, so some verbal postures also had their neutral quality. (The somatic symptoms of tension were not so great when the men expressed civic ignorance as when they sought to express the meaning of their religion and national origins.) Some of the men reacted to uncertainty by trying to find the answer, that is, by asking me. When I said I would not tell them until we were through this section, they looked for cues. Partly this was anxiety, partly curiosity. O'Hara ends four of the first five answers with a glance in my direction and the phrases "Isn't it?" "Doesn't he?"

Tending to Shift the Focus outside the Field of Discourse

These we said kept the focus within the field; they are centripetal, they do not distract attention, and they make it possible to go on and learn. But, of course, one of the most usual ways of dealing with uncertainty is to point to something else and talk about that.

Some excuses similar to those mentioned earlier seem to prohibit further discussion; in the guise of *avoiding conflict* these moves are, in effect, inquiry stoppers. This was true in Dempsey's principled and self-righteous statement that he never discusses politics and religion because they tend to create hard feelings—a comment that withered my hopes for the interview but proved to be a fragile barrier, easily overcome. Then, too, a practice more common in sophisticated circles is to explain ignorance in terms of what interests a person—*the boredom excuses*. On the United Nations, Ferrera says, as observed above: "That's something that has never interested me. . . . I never pay much attention to it." Unable to answer some questions on Eastport, Rapuano says, "I'm not interested in local politics at all." These, of course, convey the message "If I were interested I would know," and "It is lack of interest, not stupidity, that accounts for my poor showing." More than that, however, they say, "Don't bore me; let's talk about something else."

When asked what Congress has been doing recently, Rapuano said, "Sitting on their fannies"; asked what the Mayor of Eastport had been doing recently, Costa said, "He lit the Christmas tree"; asked about Congress, Flynn said, "They're getting ready for recess again." There is something in common in these responses, something I find less astringent than the frequent comment about Eisenhower's activities at the time. ("Playing golf.") They are all facetious; they make a little joke out of the institution or person they purport to describe; they have the effect of making light of the question and, in some mild form, of the questioner. The *facetious gambit,* then, has the result of expressing frustration and mild hostility, and discouraging this particular line of inquiry. It seems to come to mind in situations where knowledge is slight or, and this may be important, where conversational fatigue has set in.

A more direct attack upon the question and the questioner may take the form of Ferrera's comment, "Professor, you sure think of beauts"; or it may be more subtle, as in Farrel's repetition of every question in a quizzical tone, suggesting that it has been badly phrased or is a little foolish. The gamesmen here, to use Stephen Potter's term, can rely upon tone and manner exclusively and to good effect. Turning the focus, then, upon the questioner or the questions, the *inversion gambit,* finds its advocates in the white-collar group. I've commented elsewhere on how golden was the opportunity in these interviews, for the men so inclined, to employ this gambit—and how rarely it was used.

There is a moment in many conversations when a conversationalist seeks to show not only what he knows but also elaborates on what he doesn't know, showing the depths of an ignorance that at other times he must prefer to conceal. Under certain circumstances it is not, I think, so much a baring of the breast, an appeal for forgiveness, as it is an aggressive forensic device, much like crossing the line a boy has dared you to cross, or knocking the chip off the old-fashioned schoolmate's shoulder. Dempsey has a certain versatility in his defensive footwork; here I think he has taken the offensive, employing a *depth-of-ignorance gambit,* which he could sustain in many areas. He has just told me he does not know the names of the senator from his state, the congressman from the district, or his alderman (who happens to live a block away). He says: "No, I wouldn't know any of them. Even if he [the alderman] was to come up on the street to me and say, 'I'm So-and-So,' I wouldn't even know." I cannot see that he has moralized this position, in his usual manner; rather it seems to me he is saying, "I not only do not know the things you have asked me; I do not know much more than that." Implied, I believe, is the question "What will you do about it?" And, too, there is an echo of "So what?" in the words and tone employed in this instance.

The *anecdotal escape* surely is familiar to the parlor conversationalist as well as to the scholar. Johnson, a mechanic, is a master of this practice:

LANE: Could you describe what the Electoral College is?
JOHNSON: No, I dont think so. [pause]
LANE: Yes, that's a hard—
JOHNSON: By the way, not to change the subject, but I was in the Supreme Court, you mentioned, this summer. Out of this world! Have you been there?

LANE: Yes.

JOHNSON: Out of this world, isn't it? You know what surprised me? [And so forth]

Johnson sometimes surprises himself, forgets the question, and finds himself talking about things he had no intention of discussing.

The *opinion conversion escape* is a variation wherein a question calling for a factual response is understood as a question of opinion, and is answered as such—with the added bonus of emotional catharsis thrown in. As David Riesman has pointed out, it is always easier to say whether you like or do not like a play, book, or building than to display a knowledge of the work. Kuchinsky, whose words flow with a greater turbulence and in a more unruly stream than those of the others, employs this method. Asked if he has any idea what the city government has been doing recently, he says: "Well, building schools, which is a wonderful thing for the years to come for the kids. I think it's a good thing, especially this one- or two-floor business; it's wonderful, I think. Three or four stories high is no deal for these kids. I think they should have 'em all on one floor. I think they're doing a wonderful job." On many occasions, asked for a comment on a public policy, he reveals at the same time an absence of information and a flood of indignation or enthusiasm.

Sometimes it seems that there is a trading propensity among the men, a tendency to negotiate the terms of the conversation so that what they can offer will be acceptable as a substitute for what they cannot supply. In one variation of this approach the individual who cannot provide the information required offers something he would like you to accept as almost as good. This *substitution offer,* which has the added advantage of taking the conversation away from the embarrassing topic, is seen in its most naked form when Rapuano, unable to think of a state legislator's name, says, "I could give you some senators' names, and I might know some senators from different other states." Kuchinsky cannot think of the alderman's name but offers, instead, information on the number of children the alderman has. In a confused world, where the purpose of the information gathering is lost from sight, and where its value has never been very clear, it must appear that one counter in the information-exchange process is very like another.

But there are other occasions where even the objects being negotiated change, or rather some of the latent terms of negotiation are made more manifest. At bottom the inquiry situation is one where the men give the questioner information, and he gives or allows them some sense of pride or achievement, some increment of self-esteem, in return. When, as it develops, the individual cannot offer information, he may, by making a virtue of his candor in owning up to his ignorance, pluck some small reward from a situation that is not in the least rewarding in any other way. He seeks psychic payment for his conduct, since he cannot earn it by offering information. Johnson, on several occasions, uses the disarming device of prefacing his report on his lack of knowledge with the words "to be truthful with you"; others say, "I'll be honest with you," or "The truth of the matter is . . ." The *frank admission offer* is surely one of the more civilized of these little devices for salving wounds.

Now, it is notable that by far the most prevalent of these devices were the excuses, and of these, the kinds of excuses that kept the topic within the field of vision and did not block further inquiry. The blaming of the media, of the government, of the schools for their failure to prepare the men for their civic tasks, including answering such questions as I put to them, was rare indeed. Even at a relatively subtle level of inspection, I found the use of denigrative gambits minimal; the process of inquiry between the men and me was accepted, and they did not fight back against the uncomfortable pricks that might occur along the way. There is, then, a certain maturity here—more maturity and psychic strength than sophisticated knowledge; but in any political calculation that is a fair trade.

C
THE PARTHENOGENESIS OF KNOWLEDGE

To evade the bondage of system and habit, of family maxims, class opinions, and, in some degree, of national prejudices; to accept tradition only as a means of information, and existing facts only as a lesson to be used in doing otherwise and doing better; *to seek the reason of things for oneself, and in oneself alone;* to tend to results without being bound by means, and to strike through the form to the substance—such are the principal characteristics of what I shall call the philosophical method of the Americans.
—ALEXIS DE TOCQUEVILLE, *Democracy in America*, II, 3.
My emphasis.

We are all bondsmen to habit, in some degree; but the habit may embody a search for alternatives, a spirit of inquiry. Such was the Greek way; it was also, as De Tocqueville points out, the American way, though in a more limited form. There is, among the men of Eastport, a modest spirit of inquiry about many things, including political matters; but, as we shall point out, even as implied in the above quotation, there is a paradox at the heart of the inquiry, a frustration that impedes it and denies it fruit.

"To seek the reason of things for oneself, and in oneself alone," as Tocqueville says we do—or did—presents a problem right at the start. If this is so, where do men get their knowledge of politics? In campaign periods, it is all around them, and in Eastport there is a local, state, or national election every year. At other times the events of history, the comments of partisans of one policy or another, the implications of a given policy upon their own lives give cues that, if they cared and could, they might quickly take up and convert to a policy stance. Asked where he would go for advice in a local election when he "didn't happen to know much about the candidates or issues," Sullivan, the truck driver, thinks a long time. Then he says, "Well," and thinks another long time. He says he would go to "our organization, our union." But he reconsiders that point: "That would be kind of silly, I guess, because I know how they'd vote, how they'd want to vote. [pause] If [pause] There's no one. That's a hard question. There's no one, really, that I'd go to. [pause] I wouldn't just go to a friend, or something like that. . . . That's not something we talk about as a rule." I ask him if he can remember ever actually getting advice on how to vote. He says: "No. I think if I was told to vote one way, I'd be tempted to vote another way. I think I would." And in this comment is reflected the pathology of individualism, the individualist's morbid fear of being "influenced."

Sullivan is not alone; rather, he speaks for most of the men. Sokolsky, a factory machine operator, thinks he might ask his alderman, but is doubtful about this source. "If I couldn't get anything out of him, I would go around to different people and I would ask—ask about the man, what did he do, how long he has been in politics, what are his qualifications. . . . ["By 'different people' do you mean—?"] Anybody, anybody, any John Doe on the street, any of your friends." I ask him if he can ever remember getting such advice. He does; he remembers asking a friend at the shop who was a special friend of Laudano's when he was running for mayor. Sokolsky received information and orientation: "He told me he was a good man, that he knew the score around"—but Sokolsky voted for Donovan, Laudano's opponent. McNamara, a clerk, feels this way, too. He waits a long time before answering, then says: "That's tough. I probably wouldn't go to anyone. I'd probably just vote the same way," by which he means he would vote Democratic. Did he ever seek advice? "No. No. [pause] I've talked to people—but not exactly looking for advice." Harold Laski may be right that the Americans, bedeviled with too many political choices, "take on trust, for the most part, the advice of a person or an organization in which they have confidence," [3] but they certainly deny this and resist it where they can without too much effort.[4]

This fear of appearing to be influenced, and denial of any relationship that might make it appear that the individual was not independent, might lead men to avoid political discussion altogether. It is true that more than a third of the men say there isn't much point to having political discussion with one's friends. As Flynn, the railroad supply clerk, puts it: "I'm not able to see any value to it, myself. I really don't. . . . If you're talking about our own local politics [pause] I don't know how much good you would gain from it. . . . I don't recall getting involved, myself, to a point where it would have any effect on my own thinking, and I'm sure I haven't done a great deal to influence anybody else's thinking, so [pause] what's the use?" Again, as may be seen, it is the matter of influence (spontaneously brought out, here), and not enlightenment or entertainment, that comes to the fore. Even those who argue for the value of political discussion ("Gives guys different ideas and different, you know, outlook on things." "A few gatherings in the field of politics would enlighten the [poorly informed] person") usually suggest that its value is to give the better informed person (themselves) an opportunity to enlighten the poorly informed person (others). If there is any influencing going on, they wish it to be clear who is influencing whom. Yet, of course, they all (except Dempsey) do talk politics with their friends and at the shop; the point is not that they withdraw but

3. Harold Laski, *The American Democracy* (New York: Viking, 1948), p. 145.
4. Compare: "However strong the group identification, and however firm the association between group and political objects, the member may resist the intrusion of 'nonpolitical' groups upon the political scene." Angus Campbell, Philip E. Converse, Warren E. Miller, and Donald E. Stokes, *The American Voter* (New York: Wiley, 1960), p. 321.

that their capacity to learn must overcome this parthenogenetic pathology.

The claim to be spontaneously generated political men appears in a larger context. Asked about historical events happening in their lifetimes, such as the Spanish Civil War or the Nazi-Soviet pact, or the Korean War, which had an impact on their thinking, their response is a kind of numbed and fumbling unresponsiveness. History is a flow of events (as the news is a flow of words) that erodes a predisposition or strengthens it, or offers a rationale for it, but does not offer, without special assistance and more effort than most men can make, memorable changes in orientation. As they talk about school and favored teachers, one sees that education, too, has this same characteristic. Influence is *glacial,* not climactic. This, along with the fear of being influenced, is another reason why, no matter how indirect the questioning, men cannot recall and can hardly talk about the sources of their political orientation, or even where they go to learn.

One more thing may be said on behalf of the men who claim that if they want to know something about politics, they don't go to any learned sources; they fail to contact insiders; they have not the slightest inclination to approach the League of Women Voters; they distrust their unions' advice; they do not, by and large, read the news magazines; the libraries are beyond their trade routes; in short, they look to themselves. What must be said is that they have, taking only our sample and excluding the overeducated Farrel (who doesn't know much about politics anyway), a variety of kinds of knowledge and skills and sources of influence. Costa has some of what we called "school knowledge" —here is the way he starts his answer to the question "What is the electoral college?": "There's 531 electoral votes, and each state has one electoral vote for each elected representative and senator." Flynn, respected by all, has a self-taught background knowledge that is considerable (he read Kennedy's *Profiles in Courage,* for example), and he has the judgment to interpret this material as well—but he is more conservative than most of the men; O'Hara, who ranks highest (except for Farrel) on information about current events, easily mentions four things that the UN is working on; Ruggiero knows the names of all the public figures asked about, including the British prime minister; he and Ferrera and Flynn know their way around town and can get things done in the city that they want done—all three have demonstrated this.

Moreover, Ruggiero and Ferrera have close connections with Morelli, the congressman, and Flynn and O'Hara have connections with Mayor Donovan. In short, somehow, when these reaches of "the masses" fall back upon their own resources, they find that these are very considerable. There is weight to what Henry Commager says, with a touch of asperity, "For in defiance of the conclusions of European students of the masses, Americans revealed themselves susceptible not so much to propaganda as to political instruction, or *at least to political experience.*" [5]

D

THE KNOWN AND THE UNKNOWN

Mannheim makes the point that the logic of men's "interests" and the perspectives of their social position prevent them from knowing many features of the world they live in. The failure of the liberal bourgeois democrat to see the irrational and brutal forces in the world is a product of his need to believe that everything can be subordinated to reason. "This bourgeois intellectualism expressly demanded a scientific politics, and actually proceeded to found such a discipline." [6] It is a common understanding among anthropologists that cultures selectively borrow and include culture traits as these traits are congenial with other elements in their system. By the same token they are constantly rejecting beliefs, knowledge, techniques. In asking what the working classes know, we are asking what do they not know, and we are asking why.

In this arena, perhaps the most interesting aspect of social ignorance is the failure of these men to see the broader costs and wastes and inefficiency of a social situation which each must face and interpret for himself. A recession had hit Eastport at the time of the interviews; most of the men were hurt, not for the first time, and each of them was facing the situation bravely, sometimes resourcefully—and totally alone. Kuchinsky's private on-the-side roofing business had fallen off so that he had to cut back his standard of living. Ferrera had just emerged from bankruptcy and was trying to start a new career as shoe salesman. Sullivan's highly ir-

5. Henry Steele Commager, *The American Mind* (New Haven: Yale University Press, 1950), p. 336. Emphasis mine.
6. Karl Mannheim, *Ideology and Utopia* (New York: Harcourt, Brace, 1949), p. 108.

regular employment in over-the-road trucking was less regular than ever. Costa had been cut back to a minimal work week and had been drawing unemployment insurance—the firm that employs him is partially dependent on government contracts, and these had not been forthcoming in the recession period. O'Hara had been fighting against the maintenance reduction in his plant; Sokolsky had taken a part-time janitorial job to piece out his income during the recession in his bicycle firm. All this entails a degree of woe and worry that the mere recital of the facts does not convey, but because of the rationales they have adopted to explain their social situation, these men and their observers accept things as they are without the search for alternatives that, rightly or wrongly, would extend some basis for hope of change. What is excluded, then, from their range of knowledge is Socialism—and this, not because they have escaped the pricks and goads of the present system (as well as receiving its providence) but because the philosophic basis for explaining their modes of existence is one of individual responsibility and self-help. As over the past two centuries the bourgeoisie have needed to believe in the power of reason, and have explained their own situations in these terms, so these men, not proletarians but rather individual climbers from the lower-status tenements of their fathers, need to believe in the power of the individual to survive and to achieve. There are many causes for their not knowing Socialism; but the fact is that they do not know it, and this enduring and officially approved individualistic theory to account for each man's life situation is one of the causes. In a striking passage, Adorno and his associates say, essentially of Socialist thinking and the penetration of the current social order: "Once again, as in the era of the transition from feudalism to middle-class society, knowing too much has assumed a subversive touch, as it were. This tendency is met halfway by the 'authoritarian' frame of mind of large sections of the population. The transformation of our social system from something dynamic into something conservative, a *status quo,* struggling for its perpetuation, is reflected by the attitudes and opinions of all those who, for reasons of vested interests or psychological conditions, identify themselves with the existing setup." [7]

They are ignorant of religion; they are churchgoers but they are ignorant. They have no important knowledge of how the

7. T. W. Adorno, Else Frenkel-Brunswik, Daniel J. Levinson, and R. Nevitt Sanford, *The Authoritarian Personality* (New York: Harper, 1950), p. 662.

dogma of the Catholic Church differs from other dogmatic beliefs —and twelve of them are Catholics. They pray, but their prayers are only the expressions of a wish for help, an expression of a need for consolation, a cry cast in the vague direction of a vague God. Asked what his religion meant to him, Kuchinsky coughs and tilts back in his kitchen chair: "Well, ah, ahem, [pause] yah, it means a lot. I mean, ah, it's just like, ah, anybody that has a faith their own religion. I mean, ah, [pause] I believe, ah, [pause] it helps out quite a bit. I mean, when I do go to church, and when they go to church, I think it [pause] makes me feel a lot better to know my two kids are being well brought up and well mannered. . . . They got quite a lot of respect for us and their grandparents, and I think it's [pause] through the church that they get all that respect and love and things like that." Only Flynn and DeAngelo bite into this question—such is the state of religious education today. Tolerance, the assimilationist doctrine that is winning the clergy as well as the laity, the separation of church and state, the superior explanatory power of science on many matters once held theological—all these ideas and forces create a social situation where ignorance of religion is not just the residue of neglect but is a positively useful value.

They are ignorant of history—beyond what might be expected of their lower level of education; they are ignorant of system, and do not organize their concepts; and while it is true, as Max Weber says, that system is the product of juristic and scientific schools of thought and education, they narrow their conceptualization beyond this point, too. These are, as we have noted above, products of social situations, immigration and mobility, on the one hand, and a life style that includes a constant readiness for change, on the other. But, in many ways, the most striking feature of the political mind of lower middle Eastport is the capacity to embrace knowledge and thought of a variety of kinds, the low utility of forensic ignorance. These men have absorbed the standard values of democracy; they believe in the rule of the many, government by the people; they believe that in the last analysis—they, not the elite, run things. At the same time they hold that representatives in government may be venal, are often fallible, and usually vulnerable to a variety of influences. And these are not compartmented beliefs, but are held in full knowledge of each other. I am reminded of Edith Hamilton's description of the Greeks, whom she termed "pre-eminently realists. The temper of mind that . . .

kept their poetry within the sober limits of the possible, made them hard-headed men in the world of every-day affairs. They were not tempted to evade facts. It is we ourselves who are the sentimentalists. . . . The Greeks looked straight at [the world]. . . . They had no vital lies." [8] The men of Eastport, too, are realists, at least in this sense. Their views of democracy are not greatly sentimentalized; they see it whole and take it pretty much for what it is. Here, then, is a segment of a belief system held together by the adhesions of reality; it is not necessary to dissolve politics into cynicism and then to rebuild it again with a myth of state, folk, race, class, or chiliastic future or golden age gone by.

The heroes of Eastport are life size, neither more nor less. In the discussion on the nature of leadership and the idea of a politician, there is never any suggestion by those who admired Roosevelt that he was other than a fallible man who liked power and used it for the ends which they approved; and those who are most disappointed in Eisenhower attribute to him what they call "sincerity" in the midst of his negligence toward them and theirs. There is no need here, as in hero cultures, to be ignorant of the warts on the hero's face, the less noble of his motives, the errors of judgment he made in office. And there are no villains whose humanity must be disguised to preserve their villainy.

They know the here and now. They know human behavior and how to make their own behavior fit into the scheme of things they have inherited; that is, they know and rarely fumble their social codes. They know the postponement of gratification, the scheduling of desires. They know, if somewhat distantly, how to work the institutions of law, democracy, justice. They know the meaning of ideals modified by reality. They have foraging skills in an industrial urban jungle. They know how to work hard, but they do not know many uses for their leisure. They can, within limits, use print and spoken word to grapple with distant problems, often bringing their own experiences to bear upon them; their judgment on foreign and national affairs, while frequently wrong, is rarely divorced from reality. There are no Poujadists, Ham-and-Eggers, Trotskyites, Millerites, National Socialists, Coughlinites, and such ilk here. And, while cautious, they are timorously brave in the face of the unfamiliar, the untried, the unknown.

8. Edith Hamilton, *The Greek Way to Western Civilization* (New York: New American Library, 1948), pp. 58–59.

□ □ □ □ □ □ □ □ □ □ □ □ □ □ □

Personal Qualities

24

Identity Diffusion and Ideological Caution

> The process of American identity formation seems to support an individual's ego identity as long as he can preserve a certain element of deliberate tentativeness of autonomous choice. The individual must be able to convince himself that the next step is up to him and that no matter where he is staying or going he always has the choice of leaving or turning in the opposite direction if he chooses to do so.
> —ERIK H. ERIKSON, *Childhood and Society*, p. 245

As a thought machine, the mind has one characteristic it shares with relatively few other machines: it thinks about itself. These thoughts, then, inevitably affect the production of new ideas, fantasies, beliefs and, of course, ideologies. We shall call the image of himself that a man constructs from these self-referential thoughts a man's "identity." [1] It includes (1) his self-awareness, that is, the degree to which he is attentive to and aware of the wide range of phenomena that take place in his own mind; (2) his self-description, that is, the characteristics he thinks

---

1. See Erik H. Erikson, *Childhood and Society* (New York: Norton, 1950). "This sense of identity provides the ability to experience oneself as something that has continuity and sameness, and to act accordingly" (p. 38). See also "The Problem of Ego Identity," *Journal of the American Psychoanalytic Association,* IV (1956), pp. 56–121.

describe him and are important features of his person; and (3) his
self-esteem, that is, the value he places upon himself and his ideas.
A person has a clear sense of identity if he is relatively aware of
his desires and fantasies, if he has a reasonably accurate picture
of himself; he has a clear and *positive* identity if he generally
approves of what he knows about himself.

Our argument in this chapter is that the personal, individual
identity of the Eastport common man is relatively strong, though
curiously objectified, while the social identity, the sense of self
deriving from group memberships, is pitifully weak. The weak,
diffuse social identity of these men, we shall say, contributes to
a diffuse, unstructured political ideology.

A

A PROFILE OF PERSONAL IDENTITY IN EASTPORT

In Eastport, as elsewhere, there are considerable differences
in the nature and strength of men's identities. One clue to their
strength is the way in which men enter upon the task of describing themselves.[2] Compare, for example, how Rapuano, a packinghouse checker, approaches this matter with the approach of Johnson, a mechanic. After a brief comment about his friendliness,
Rapuano goes on trying to describe himself: "Geez, I don't know.
That's hard to say. I mean, I don't know anything about myself,
really." I ask him about his "good points," and he answers: "I
don't think I have any good points, really, or bad points. I'm just
another guy, and I mean, really, I don't know what the heck my
good points are. I mean it would take somebody else to show me
my good points." Johnson, however, suffers no such doubt. He
says, leaning forward with only a touch of embarrassment: "Well,
I would think of myself as possibly [pause] a great imagination,
for one thing. [pause] A great thinking about the future of things
that may be. . . . [Here he expands on things he would like to
do.] I think of myself as a fellow who isn't afraid to make a move."
He is talking about real qualities, for he has this adventurous
spirit. He has a sturdy and a positive identity. Judged by these
and other criteria, most of Eastport falls somewhere between
the two, but it is the special nature of these identities and their

2. See Gerald Gurin, Joseph Veroff, and Sheila Feld, *Americans View Their Mental Health* (New York: Basic Books, 1960), pp. 52–83.

social support that interest us, for they mold their ideologies in a direct and crucial way.

Objectifying

When an Eastportian tells his life story, he tells about events, not feelings or settings. He is Hemingway, not Tolstoy or Proust, and, being a Northerner, he is not Wolfe or Faulkner. His autobiography is not in terms of states of mind, the moods of adolescence, and the quandaries of the young adult. Ruggiero, an Eastern State University maintenance clerk, in his rapid-fire way, is typical of the narrative style of these men. Asked to tell me the story of his life, he says: "Let's see, my father—I think was fourteen when he came over and I think my mother was around ten or eleven. Something like that. They came over and, of course, they, uh—my father settled in the, uh, Philadelphia. And, uh, some Jewish family took him over and taught him the tailoring business; that's why he's a tailor today. And, uh, he always made a good living for us. Uh, he met my mother when he came to Eastport to work, [pause] and I think she was working in the same place. I think my mother was fifteen and my father about seventeen when they were married, yeah. So, of course, then they had their family; five children; there's five of us in the family. And, uh, I was the first boy. My schooling—just attended the grammar school, of course, I went from one school to another in Eastport, then I settled in Middleport, and graduated from Middleport High School." It is breathtaking; in about ten sentences and twenty seconds he has told me the story of his parents' immigration, their marriage, his family, and the first seventeen years of his life. Nor is he an insensitive man, or an unreflective man—but, like the others, he defines the story of his life, not as it seemed to him while he lived it, but as an observer might describe "what happened."

This tendency to deal with the events of their lives and not the feelings accompanying these events seems to arise from a want of reflection, not from want of candor. They tell their life stories "objectively"; they speak of their failures as breadwinners or their concern for their parental roles or their personal faults with such pain as they feel—but they speak of them. Johnson hardly wanted to say that he had been cheating a little with his outside mechanic's work; Ferrera did not find it easy to speak of his past introversion and timidity, but telling it was a pain he could bear; Costa, Woodside, Rapuano, and Johnson spoke of their physical defects and ailments with difficulty and embarrassment—yet they spoke of them. They can look at themselves with strength—but not with sensitivity because they have not been led to reflect upon the nature of man; their minds are not tuned by their reading, and certainly not by television and films, to subtle variations and interpretations of mood, desire, pathos, and tragedy.

Self-Acceptance

While Rapuano struggled with deep ego-alien (sexual) impulses and Sullivan strove constantly to prove something he doubted (his toughness) and others, like most of us, concealed their "baser" natures and hid their fears, for the most part (on a level nearer consciousness), these men did not pretend to be something they were not. For the most part, then, they accepted themselves and their views with consistency, giving continuity to their opinions and minimizing the false front and the role-playing that might have seemed attractive in talking to a professor. This judgment involves an interpretation of the "transference" situation, the way the man responded to me; it involves an attempt to match what is said in one area of our conversations with what is said in another; it involves an interpretation of the way in which a man's emotions match his words. This honesty resting on a self-acceptance is best illustrated by examples of its opposite, the false front, the impression management, the concealment of the rejected self.

Costa, an assembly-line operative, alone of all the men, dressed up for the interviews; he employed a vocabulary a trifle beyond his grasp, was often and visibly worried about the impression he was making. His eulogies about "this wonderful country we live in" were somewhat out of phase with his grave concern over his job and the fact that he was drawing unemployment insurance at the time. His smile, while broad, was confined to his mouth; his eyes at the same time that he smiled were often sober and wore a worried expression.

Farrel is an underpaid social worker; his frequent failure to "understand" the questions put to him, his eagerness to question the questioner, and his persistently low speech (making the tape a horror to transcribe) suggest a foot-dragging operation dissonant with his professed interest in the study. His espousal, until recently, of Henry George's single tax suggests—but rather tenuously—a desire to find a political philosophy that served more to differentiate him from others than to solve the social problems of the day. He is a professional man from a working-class background, and maintains that it does not make much difference to him whether or not his children go to college because he prizes the working-class way of life.

Johnson, a mechanic, has the most engaging, friendly manner imaginable; he bubbles over with an overt enthusiasm, tells stories well; but he says he doesn't "really" trust anyone, rates lowest on the "Faith in People" scale, and at every point seems cynical of human motives.

Kuchinsky, a roofer, was the most suspicious of all the men, put me off several times on the telephone, used improbable excuses for several months, and finally agreed to the interview only if it could be in his own kitchen and then only—I think—because it would permit him to say some things about labor unions he has been wanting to say for a long time. He belongs to no outside groups other than his church, yet he affected a merry "social" style in the interviews, and claimed that "I made a lot of friends in the last twelve years, an awful lot of friends. . . . I have 'em call me up casually and ask me how I am."

I mention these cases because they illustrate the clues I was looking for, the "measures" of self-rejection I employed; they are important not for their occurrence but for their paucity. On the whole, I think, the men of Eastport did not "put on an act" for me, do not masquerade for their friends. Whatever self-rejection they may experience, whatever disappointments they may have in themselves (and they have many), they do not pretend to be very different from what they feel themselves to be. Fromm says of modern man that he has a marketing personality, seeking to sell himself, using the self as an instrument for gain.[3] The Eastport common man does not work so hard pushing this merchandise.

3. Erich Fromm, *Man for Himself: An Inquiry into the Psychology of Ethics* (New York: Holt, 1947).

Striving

They see themselves as striving, these Eastport men, eager to achieve some goal, overcoming handicaps; they are in movement toward some end, an end, however, that is dim and obscure when confronted directly. For most this is not at all an ascent up the status ladder; it is more likely to be the purchase of a new machine or the payment of debts for an old one. Their dreams turn on the ownership of a house, but they are discouraged about this possibility. They work to save for nameless contingencies or to achieve greater seniority at the plant and so to protect themselves against layoffs or to get their children to self-supporting stages of life. For each, the image of the self is teleological, purposeful; the purposes are individual or for the family, not social or communal.

Self-Confidence

Their feeling about their jobs, for most of them, is that they are, indeed, "cut out" for their work; they are less confident about their roles as parents. Their self-confidence in another sphere is put to a test in the interviews. It is a difficult test, as I learn by watching a few lick their lips, adopt truculent poses, or seek to avoid the interview entirely. As with self-acceptance, self-confidence is appreciated best in contrast with its opposite. Consider Ferrera's unconfident state of mind revealed in the following comments (Ferrera, with an athletic scholarship, has had two years of college). Asked about the main problems facing America, he says: "I've never really given this much thought, or at least have never been aware that I have. Perhaps during my day-to-day experiences I have thought of the subject, but not realized it. . . ." Then he speaks generally of the moral decline of the nation. Asked if there is anything we can do about it, he says, "I'm unprepared for this," and goes on to elaborate further on the degeneracy of the times, concluding, "I hope I'm making sense here." He is reassured again and asked about problems facing the national government, to which he responds: "Well, once again, I must refer to the fact that I don't dig into the political aspect of things; I just skim through it very quickly," but he launches into a discussion of the recession that is, in fact, better informed than most of the others. Lack of education does not give men this sense of inadequacy—and, of course, the better educated everywhere are usually more articulate. Ferrera shows us what lack of self-confidence and lack of a sense of personal worth and competence do, under certain circumstances, to the readiness of a man to formulate his ideas of public policy.

It is the absence of this kind of hesitation that is remarkable in this group. Even Ferrera accepted the view that he should have opinions on Russia, taxes, urban redevelopment, juvenile delinquency, and much more. In this acceptance and willingness to be tested, there is for each of these men an implied belief that he is worthy to have opinions and that his opinions are worthy of attention. Society encourages this view. Nor are they, in their own eyes, merely storage vessels into which other people's opinions are poured to be held until called for. This is a horrid thought to them. Each accepts himself as worthy of opinion-making on his own, with his own modest talents bent to the task. Although oblique, this is a real test not only of confidence in the self but also of self-esteem.

Shared

Although worthy, the common man of Eastport believes that, in one sense of the word, he is, in fact, common. He believes, that is, that his interests, beliefs, needs, and aversions are widely shared among men of all classes and occupations, that he is a fair sample of mankind, that he is, in a statistical sense, typical and normal. Asked about himself, he emphasizes what he has in common with others and what it is about himself that permits him to get along with others, not what is different, unique, individual. Asked if he is a leader or follower, in his embarrassment he says he "goes along"; asked about intelligence, he says he is "average"; picturing himself among his friends, he draws a portrait of a man who stands out in no special way. But it is this very sense that he is like others and that others are like him that provides the basis for an easy confidence in the social order, an empathic identification with the hard-working rich (this, more than the lazy poor), and a genuine shock when the political deviant comes into view. He had thought his self was like all other selves.

Unaffiliated

It is only an apparent paradox that this sense of a shared or universal self coexists with a sense of an ungrouped, self-sufficient, unaffiliated self. It is as though the common man of Eastport said, "Basically, everyone, rich and poor, Catholic, Protestant, and Jew, is like me; but there is no particular group that is like me and with whom I share something special." This picture of the individuality of the self emerges in part from the infrequent use of the collective pronoun "we." It is a striking thing how rare is the reference to collective experience, collective emotion, collective action. When it occurs, moreover, it seems to be an *ad hoc* group, such as a group gathered together to protest the rent increase, or a car pool. Speaking of the problems facing America, or Eastport, the problems are often referred to personal experience, but not to group experience; the incidence of trouble is individual, not collective.

If the individual's self-image is his identity, the portion that "places him" in society and relates him to others is his *social identity*. And this individualization of a social identity has so much influence on social outlook, it must be examined more closely.

B

THE DIFFUSION OF SOCIAL IDENTITY

> The tendency to gloss over differences and construct a kind of generalized American religion, and the tendency to talk a great deal about what we believe without feeling any obligation to sharpen our definitions—both of these express a unity in American life. . . . Starting from the view that different creeds can live peaceably together, we gradually come to the notion that, if creeds can live together, they must be fundamentally similar.
> —DANIEL J. BOORSTIN, *The Genius of American Politics*,
> pp. 157–158

This story of social-identity diffusion has been a long time in the making. Men living in tribes have much provided for them; they have a role assigned by custom, a set of human relationships decided by their birth, a ready-made code of behavior, an established religion, and an established secure place in the social order. All these together give a man a sense of social identity: he can infer from his social situation cues regarding his appropriate characteristics. The sharply defined categories of family, birth-order, lineage, rank, totem, kin, stranger, alien, help in this placement; he knows which apply to him and what the rights and duties pertaining to his position are. There are always marginal men; but here they are few, hence the conflicts (and innovations) that arise from men in these positions are also few.

Erich Fromm has recorded and interpreted part of the long process of detribalization, the part that has taken place in the four hundred years called the modern period.[4] It is a record of increasing individuation, the weakening of custom, the substitution of systematic evidence for revelation, the thrust of new choices on the individual, and, above all, the atrophy of established social bonds providing a clear social identity. Where once a person had a social identity made for him, now he must interpret one from much more ambiguous materials.

The problem is illuminated by a closer examination of the meaning of social identity and its empirical base in Eastport. The concept is to be distinguished from those dealing with good social relations, the way a man deals generally with people, concepts of isolation from or integration in a general social framework. Those who have the best and warmest social relations may have the most diffuse social identity. Rather, it refers to *the use of attributes derived from a man's identification with social groups to describe and define himself.* It is the contribution made to his answer to "Who am I?" by his sense of belonging to some specified part of human society, a community, a professional society, a church, a nationality group, a kinship group, even sometimes a neighborhood ("the Tenderloin," "the West End"). From these identifications a man acquires ideas about what values, codes of behavior, opinions, traits are appropriate for him. Without these, the working out of a self-image is much more difficult.

Our argument here is that in Eastport, as in American society more generally, the development of a social identity is made more difficult by three social doctrines and practices: social mobility, religious tolerance, and ethnic assimilation. These institutionalized doctrines deprive men of the kind of enduring and legitimate group identifications that would give them clear social identities. Social mobility, the opportunity to find a place in

4. See the first half of Erich Fromm, *Escape from Freedom* (New York: Rinehart, 1941).

society according to individual merits (and the belief in this opportunity), inhibits men from using social class as a reference for values, opinions, behavior. Religious tolerance, as Boorstin suggests at the head of this section, tends to homogenize religious dogma, to depreciate religious differences, and to weaken the power of a church to create a solidary group with a culture and code of its own. Ethnic assimilation enjoins men to shed their national cultures with their identifiable ways of life and become indistinguishable from other Americans.

Often, of course, there is a dissonance between the approved doctrine and day-to-day practices, a matter that creates a strain among men seeking to achieve an unambiguous identity. For this reason these men often seem to take back what they have said, to deny the implications of their remarks, to repress feelings that might have led them to see themselves more clearly. Both the social doctrine and the strain are visible in the responses of the Eastport men to questions about their feelings on social class, religion, and nationality. Sullivan, a truck driver who likes his work, illustrates the ambiguity of feelings about social class membership. He is a strong supporter of his union and is one of only three who feel that they share something in common with other union members throughout the country. He says: "Well, every union member has something in common. . . . The fact that they belong to a union . . . makes them a little closer together." But this is a very limited identification. Asked about social classes, he says "class is another way of saying groups, that's all. . . . It isn't a good thing. It's all right as long as one don't look down on the other . . . I mean people being class conscious isn't too good." He says he belongs to the working class. How does he feel about his? "Well, it don't bother me. . . . If it wasn't for the uncertainty of the trucking business, I'd say my job is a lot better than most people's in the middle class or upper class. I'm satisfied." From such ambivalence and denial and defensive affirmation, little of value for the formation of a social identity is likely to emerge.

While Sullivan is more class-conscious than most, Ruggiero is more religious than most. What social identity can he derive from his religion, for him a powerful reference group? Asked about the meaning of religion to him, he says he is a better-than-average Catholic, and then goes on to say, "Well, I think it's a whole life, actually; I really do." He says prayers morning and evening, and "I usually whisper a little prayer when I'm having dinner." He hardly ever passes a church on foot, he says, without going in. But with this relatively intense identification, he must nevertheless adjust to a religiously mixed society. "I'd say in my personal friends, I have—they're equal as far as bein' Jewish—I have two very close Jewish friends, and, uh, a number of Protestant friends." He talks about religion with them, but, of course, never criticizes their religions—only their lax attitude toward their own religions. Asked about the things that make Catholicism unique, its dogma or special creed, he says he can't judge since he has never been anything else. From this situation he comes to the view that almost any intensely held faith is as good as any other: "I'm not gonna criticize any religion, because to me, all religions—if a man even believes in a typewriter, but if he actually believes in it, and prays to it and everything else, he'll be a good man. I think we would have a good world."

Ruggiero is extracting an identity from his religion; his religious work gives him an image of himself as a moral man, a socially useful man, a dutiful man. But when he must contrast this to others, it is less his Catholicism than the intensity and activity of his faith that form the (public) grounds for his special identity. The pressure to be tolerant dilutes and diffuses the message he can extract from this membership.

Ferrera, like the others, is conscious of nationality traits. He says: "I associate the Irish with people who like to indulge in a lot of drinking and, actually, without too much determination and push or ambition; I associate the Jewish people with a desire for monetary gains; I associate Italians with people who don't generally care about any particular thing other than, ah, gaiety, singing, music, ah, good foods; and the English I associate with the characteristic of insipidness." About three-quarters of his friends, he says, are Italian; he says he feels "very strongly about" the "faint undercurrent of prejudice" against the Italian people that he detects in Eastport; he is very antagonistic toward the snobbishness of those who feel that their English ancestry gives them superior status. But he feels that attention to national origins is declining: "The United States of course has just gone through the final stages of being a nation that's considered a melting pot. It is growing to this point where it is more or less of a uniform country. I think in the trying periods through the twenties the generations were instilled with certain prejudices

against other nationalities." He experiences a strong emotional
bond with a cultural group, which he nevertheless sees appropriately weakened over time. History is obliterating his social
identity along with prejudice.

These three comments on the counterclass, counterdogma
(religious), counterethnicity forces experienced in Eastport tell
us something about the circumstances of social identity. Here are
three social ties that are, at the same time, *experienced and denied*. The feelings associated with them are *ambivalent;* the ties
are thought to be somewhat *illegitimate;* history is thought to
be working against them so that, in some ways, they are thought
to be *transitory*. These are some reasons they contribute to a
diffuse social identity.

But let us return more specifically to the content that group
identification can give to a man's identity. What are these attributes a person acquires for himself when he identifies with a
social group?

Qualities of Personality and Life Style

Three of the Italian-Americans mention the fun-loving, food-
loving, musical nature of the Italians, but they respond to it in
different ways. Ferrera fights against it and speaks of the fact that
Italians are "instilled with ability" to succeed and "don't give up
easily." Ruggiero, asked if being an Italian-American helps a
person to succeed in Eastport, says "the Italian songs seem to get
Number One on the radio station. . . . I'm just taking that as a
point. So I guess it is an advantage here in Eastport." And
Rapuano uses the reputation of the Italians as fun-loving music-
loving people to counter an argument he has heard about the
cruelty of the Italian Fascists. Being Italian carries a specific
message on expected behavior, perhaps a stereotype or caricature,
but again it is ambivalently received.

The personal or stylistic qualities associated with class are less
clear. Asked what distinguishes one class from another, most say
money, but many speak of "ways of life." The ingredients of this
way of life include honesty, hard work and, sometimes as consolation, happy family living. These men may say to themselves
these are *my* characteristics, but because they are unclear, because
there is no proletarian culture different from the bourgeois culture, they derive few specific cues from this. The Lynds say of

the working-class members in Middletown that they pursue a way of life that is an imitation of the middle-class way, but without the means to give it reality.[5] These men of Eastport are closer to their bourgeois model; but there is little that is distinctive about it to give them satisfaction or security or a social identity they can use.

Values, Attitudes, or Opinions

A related kind of message a group reference can give to an individual in search of an identity is a set of values or attitudes or opinions. Having no opinion on a subject usually means that a person does not know what his reference-group memberships imply for that subject.[6] If, as in England, a workingman knows that the proper posture toward the authorities (in some cases) is to connive against them, or that certain attitudes toward adversity are expected from men in his station in life, he can create a self-image he knows has social support.[7] In speaking of the distinctive features of whatever class they said they belonged to or of the beliefs distinctive of their religion, the men's lack of specificity was notable, and the effort to obscure and homogenize was apparent.

Group Goals

The same thing is true of *group goals* that might serve as criteria for an individual's own evaluational procedure, indeed, as his very own goals. Asked whether people in different classes wanted different things so that there might occur some competition or conflict between classes, Ruggiero says, "Oh, yes, you have that with the postal rate [!] right now." It seems there is a wealthy manufacturer who wants a lower rate for his bulk mailing—a pale shadow of class conflict, indeed. DeAngelo considers taxes a bone of contention; his solution is to give everybody a little tax relief because "it's too high for *everybody*." Flynn says about class conflict, "I don't think so. . . . I don't think they're in conflict in any way." The very idea of men in one income

5. Robert and Helen Lynd, *Middletown in Transition* (New York: Harcourt, Brace, 1937).

6. Eugene L. Hartley, "The Social Psychology of Opinion Formation," *Public Opinion Quarterly,* 14 (1950–1951), p. 673.

7. Richard Hoggart, *The Uses of Literacy* (Boston: Beacon, 1961).

bracket as a group struggling for social objectives incompatible with the aims of those in another income group is obscure and, indeed, slightly offensive. There are no class goals. Nor are there incompatible goals for religious groups; at least, Eastport men see none until the matter of school buses is brought to their attention. The nationality, religious, and racial groups compete for place on a "balanced" ticket; they compete for "recognition" in political appointment; but because of the ambivalence these men have toward their ethnicity, they minimize (at least to me) the extent to which their groups are involved in the pursuit of collective goals. There is little here that can be used for a conscious formulation of identity, few individual goals that can be borrowed from a set of collective goals.

Status

Another element of group identification contributing to a person's identity is the status he acquires along with his group memberships. On social class, men accept, reluctantly, their class position as an act of fate. Of his working-class position, Dempsey, a drill-press operator, says, "There's nothing you can do about it—just try to get out of it, I mean, if you possibly can." Then he tells of his one great effort, an attempt to start a small restaurant in his home, and the ensuing bankruptcy. Asked what social class he belongs to, Ferrera, a shoe salesman, says poignantly: "It's hard for me to think there is anyone in the upper class and I'm not in the upper class because I know what's within me. . . . I like to think of myself as being in the upper class; of course, I realistically cannot do so. I know that I'm in the middle—in the working class, because I'm a workingman. . . . I imagine I'd have to be classified in the middle class." About two-thirds of the men say working class and about a third say middle class. For all of them the status they acquire by this classification is a significant feature of their self-images, yet the working-class identifiers do not readily take on a commensurable personal working-class status.

Asked whether in Eastport it helps or hurts to be a Catholic or a Jew or an Italian or an Irishman, there is again a divided opinion. Most of the men, being Catholics in a Catholic town, find that this is certainly not a disadvantage; but they worried about "why a Catholic can't be President" (something they need no longer worry about), and, as we report elsewhere, they are a little concerned about the influence of Masonic groups upon hiring policies. But status, if not so salient in religious matters (for Catholics and Protestants), is indeed salient for general ethnic reasons for the Pole, the Russian Jew, and the six Italians. Sokolsky says: "There's a lot of people that don't like a Jew. I know that," and he says, "I think that hurts a person." Kuchinsky isn't sure that a person with a Polish background is respected: "I believe a lot of them say something against my nationality"; but he adds: "I myself get mad once in a while, maybe at somebody who is, say, Italian. I'd say something against him, which I didn't mean. But you say it. You do come out with words once in a while, but I think they should forget it and you make out with 'em." He is struggling, but you know that he can be hurt. And although the Italians are more numerous, three of them worry about their status.

Of course, there is the reverse of this. The Irish derive a sense of higher status, as does the Yankee and even more markedly the half-Danish Johnson. Men, like Ruggiero, Ferrera, and Flynn, who are in the above-average income group in Hilltop have a status edge on the others. But the salient fact is not that these men derive high or low status from their group memberships but that they derive ambiguous status. From such a derivation they cannot easily assimilate to their own identities a clear image of an appropriate rank. To the extent that their self-esteem is dependent upon comparative ranking, this, too, must rest upon an ambiguous footing.

In other cultures, perhaps, a social identification provides a person with a social history, a set of meaningful symbols, even a special language. Subcultures thrive on such material as this; but the class and ethnic subcultures of Eastport do not provide it. The individual cannot take from a remembered general strike or a set of ethnic heroes or a saga in a special mother tongue anything that, because it belongs to his group, is therefore his own. These culture items simply are not there for these men.

Defining the Group

Finally, there is the question of defining the group he uses as his reference group, the social ground for his identity. The Eastport men were asked three questions: "Do you think it is easy or hard to go from one social class to another?" "Is it easy to change from one religion to another?" and "Do you think a person with a foreign-sounding name should change his name if he wants to, or not?" These questions were intended to see how fluid these men thought their class, religious, and nationality boundaries were. In the case of the social class almost all of the men thought that it was hard to change but that the unusual person (not themselves) could do it. Ruggiero, who is the richest of the group, says, "It's just the ambition of the fellow," but he feels there is an upper limit imposed by the qualifications of birth. DeAngelo says: "If a guy's got a good personality and enough education he could fit in with anybody. . . . Course the people got to accept him; that is another thing." The boundary is permeable and a little vague. Men classed "objectively" on Hollingshead's Scale as "middle" (III) may classify themselves as "working" (IV). McNamara, a bookkeeper, says he is working class; the utility mechanic Johnson says he is middle class. The creation of a social identity is confused by these vague and shifting boundaries.

For a person to change his religion he must overcome greater obstacles. By and large these are thought to be internal, conscientious obstacles; not obstacles due to problems of acceptance, as with class, although the members of the religion he departs from will certainly feel hurt and resentful. Many of the men know someone who had changed his religion, particularly men or women who changed because they married someone of a different faith. DeAngelo expresses a common view on the changing of a religion: "I guess it is how strong you are in your religion. Maybe certain events happen in your life when you have to change from a Protestant to a Catholic or from a Catholic to a Protestant. . . . But one that don't practice his religion, he wouldn't be good in which one he took, y'know what I mean?" For all but two of the men it is unthinkable in their own cases; their boundaries are fixed, their reference group (except for sectarian differences among Protestants and among Jews) is relatively stable.

As for nationality, there is divided opinion about those who attempt to "pass" from a minority group to the majority. For the Anglo-Saxon, the half-Dane (Johnson), and the half-German (Dempsey) it seems logical that people should want to do this and even desirable as part of the assimilation process. For the

Irish it doesn't seem to matter ("Oh, I think he can do what he likes about it"). For the Polish Kuchinsky it is mainly a problem of simplification of spelling—but more than that rouses resentment: "Definitely not. I don't see why it [the foreign name] should hurt him." The Jewish Sokolsky opposes it. The Italians think it is cowardice. ("If your forefathers used it, I can't see why you can't live with it. Why is a guy ashamed of his name?")

Of course, this taps only part of the issue of ethnic boundaries, but for those who may suffer from ethnicity these answers imply a sense of group inheritance. Men are not to think of assimilation by denying this group tie, but rather by reducing the height of the barrier imposed by it. In a way, it suggests that those of a special national origin must work as members of a group, to create the right impression, to reduce the barrier; not as individuals to escape from it. But this means that the group must work together to destroy their own group identification. Such an injunction is certain to create an ambivalent basis for social identity.

In the Middle Ages, says Burckhardt, "Man was conscious of himself only as a member of a race, people, party, family, or corporation—only through some general category." But in the Italian Renaissance, "man became a spiritual *individual*." [8] In twentieth century Eastport this individualism is thrust upon men whose group identifications have been eroded by social mobility, religious tolerance, and ethnic assimilation.

Social-Identity Diffusion and Ideology

The consequences of social-identity diffusion for the shaping of an ideology are important and multiple; let us look at four. In the first place, as we have said, an ideology is almost always a rationalization of group interest. Mannheim suggests that the liberal democratic ideology was in part a rationalization of the interests of the growing bourgeoisie and an outgrowth of their perspectives on man.[9] Marx and Engels say of the capitalist class that their spokesmen developed an elaborate law designed to form a rationale for their group interests.[10] In both instances it is

8. Jacob Burckhardt, *The Civilization of the Renaissance in Italy* (London: Phaidon, 1944), p. 81 (his emphasis).
9. Karl Mannheim, *Ideology and Utopia* (New York: Harcourt, Brace, 1949).
10. Karl Marx and Friedrich Engels, *The Manifesto of the Communist Party* (New York: International Publishers, 1932).

assumed that the spokesmen and followers of the owning classes had no doubts of their class membership; they had no social-identity diffusion. But the Eastport man has. In order for him or his spokesmen to develop a rationalized group interest, the group identification must be much more clear and salient than it is now. If ideology is a superstructure on a social base, it must have an identifiable social base. If it is to be nourished by a sense of social identity and group membership, this identity must be there in the first place.

The second consequence has to do with the development of opinions and attitudes, something less than an ideology. As noted above, opinions on taxes, labor legislation, civil rights, urban redevelopment, and foreign policy are usually shaped by reference-group opinions. Where reference groups have an uncertain status or uncertain boundaries, the policy opinions they usually guide are also uncertain. Under these circumstances men become more cautious and tentative in their expression of opinions.

A third consequence deals with the nature of social conflict and social change. To the extent that a social identity encourages explicit ideology formation and policy, it involves a person in conflict, the rejection of ideas, their designation as hostile, immoral, inimical to the "public interest." The very process of group definition, then, produces argument, dissent, conflict. Without this group definition, and following from the atomization of argument, men tend to seek the kind of consensus, uniformity, and adjustment that I found to be characteristic of Eastport men. For, without group support, conflict is painful; it is individualized and deprived of the moral justification that comes with a rationalized group position. Under these circumstances a person moves most cautiously to differentiate himself from others, for he must do it alone. Public opinion changes by incremental adjustive strategies, not by the clash of great arguments where each side represents some rationalized group interest.

A fourth consequence has to do with the nature of an individual's relation to political parties and elections; it deals with the basis of political participation. Where a man has achieved a clear and strong social identity, anything that affects a group he has embraced and incorporated in himself makes him a partisan. He enters politics as a group member, finds his rationale for activity in the (internalized) group goals, evaluates success and failure in terms of group (and therefore self-) advancement. Where the social identity is diffuse, as in Eastport, individual goals and purposes must serve as political motives, and since the relation of politics to these individual purposes is often obscure, the drive to participate in politics is often weak. Political participation unsupported by a strong social identity is difficult for the amateur to sustain.

□ □ □ □ □ □ □ □ □ □ □ □ □ □ □

Notes on a Theory of Democratic Personality

Anchoring political ideology and political practice in personality or national character has a long history and a substantial current literature. Perhaps the foregoing discussion of a single phase of this topic, problems of identity, will assume a more realistic perspective for certain interested readers if we offer a glance at some of the ideas currently being argued. Then, even more briefly, I shall suggest a synoptic concept of undemocratic man, the impoverished self.

A
THE PATHOLOGIES OF DEMOCRATIC MAN

We may conveniently look at those alleged pathologies said to inhibit a man's contribution to democratic society under three heads: those focusing primarily on the self, those primarily relating the self to others, and those relating the self to society.

Self-Referential Pathologies

LOSS OF IDENTITY   One broad category of personal problems comes under the heading of the concept we have just examined in Chapter 24, identity and the loss of identity. Erikson is the inventor and expositor of this concept; for him identity "connotes both a persistent sameness within oneself (self-sameness) and a persistent sharing of some kind of essential character with others." [1] The loss of this identity, in both personal and social senses, says Erikson, deprives the individual of his political balance, "for when established identities become outworn or unfinished ones threaten to remain incomplete, special crises compel men to wage holy wars, by the cruelest means, against those who seem to question or threaten their unsafe ideological bases." [2] Erikson notes how modern technological and economic developments have tended to weaken the old identities and thus to jeopardize established orders everywhere. Lucien Pye, influenced by this view, shows in persuasive detail how the loss of identity of the Westernizing elites of Burma makes them distrustful of themselves and others, destroys the basis of their certainty, creates frustrations that cast to the surface the high aggressive potentials in a developing, changing, once-traditional society.[3] But the problem is not limited to these areas; it exists in metropolitan centers as well, and loss of identity, of a clear answer to "Who am I?" tends also to inhibit democratic life in the West.

SELF-ALIENATION   A somewhat different approach is suggested by those employing the concept of alienation as their focus of concern. This is a broad term, with many meanings. The one we focus on here is self-alienation, expressed by Fromm in the following terms: "The alienated person is out of touch with himself as he is out of touch with any other person. He, like the others, are [*sic*] experienced as things are experienced; with the senses and common sense, but at the same time without being related to oneself and to the world outside productively." [4] According to Fromm this alienation leads a man into apathy and withdrawal and makes him an easy mark for manipulation. But the term may be employed in a somewhat different sense, one closer to Freudian usage. Franz Neumann, for example, uses it to mean "the alienation of the ego from the instinctual structure or the renunciation of instinctual gratification," [5] and believes that this has been en-

1. Erik Erikson, "The Problem of Ego Identity," *Journal of the American Psychoanalytic Association*, IV (1956), p. 59.
2. *Ibid.*, p. 114.
3. Lucien Pye, *Politics, Personality and Nation Building* (New Haven: Yale University Press, 1962).
4. Erich Fromm, *The Sane Society* (New York: Rinehart, 1955), pp. 120–121.
5. Franz Neumann, *The Democratic and the Authoritarian State* (New York: The Free Press of Glencoe, 1957).

couraged by modern industrial society. Its political implications become manifest as this alienation increases beyond a certain point and produces anxiety. Anxiety, in turn, tends to produce a demand for a new Caesar to relieve men of their worries and fears.

ANXIETY   Anxiety has a life of its own. According to Auden, this is the "age of Anxiety," and hence it comes to the focus of attention in several ways. Lasswell says, "The ideal conception of democratic character includes the specification that the self-system shall have at its disposal the energies of the unconscious part of the personality." [6] Anxiety not only reduces the energy available to the individual but also destroys his perspective on life, and releases destructive impulses that otherwise would be well under control. Since "hostile impulses of various kinds form the main sources from which neurotic anxiety springs," [7] it is natural that anxiety should be associated with destructiveness and, consequently, with hostile social acts generally unsupportive of democratic methods.

LACK OF SELF-CONTROL   Some have focused on the problem of lack of self-control. H. V. Dicks, Geoffrey Gorer, and Margaret Mead all speak of the Russians' great indulgences of their impulses, drinking orgies, and emotional abandonment of all kinds, followed by guilty feelings over this indulgence.[8] Knowing this about themselves, they are said to demand strong external authority to keep them in control of themselves.[9] Almond, in a somewhat similar but more modest way, argues that the mood swings of the American public, from optimism to pessimism, from involvement to isolation in foreign affairs, has been dysfunctional for the functioning of the nation's foreign policy.[10] I have argued elsewhere for the relation between ego strength and democratic participation; it seems to be a close one.[11]

6. Harold D. Lasswell, "Democratic Character," in *The Political Writings of Harold D. Lasswell* (New York: The Free Press of Glencoe, 1951), p. 503 (italics omitted).

7. Karen Horney, *The Neurotic Personality of Our Time* (New York: Norton, 1937), p. 62.

8. Henry V. Dicks, "Observations on Contemporary Russian Behavior," *Human Relations*, V (1952), pp. 111–176; Margaret Mead, *Soviet Attitudes toward Authority* (New York: McGraw-Hill, 1951); Geoffrey Gorer, *The People of Great Russia* (London, Cresset, 1949).

9. Margaret Mead, *op. cit.*, p. 26.

10. Gabriel A. Almond, *The American People and Foreign Policy* (New York: Harcourt, Brace, 1950), pp. 69–115.

11. Robert E. Lane, *Political Life: Why People Get Involved in Politics* (New York: The Free Press of Glencoe, 1959), pp. 147–155.

IRRATIONALITY   The capacity of man for rational thought and his tropism toward irrationality, misperception, illogicality, have long been a grave concern among those who doubted whether popular government could ever work.[12] It is reflected in the contemporary discussion as well. In his earlier work, Lasswell argued that the mind of political man was essentially furnished with rationalizations of his private and highly personal problems. Displacing these feelings of anger, shame, and hate onto political objects, political man wove a plausible story to legitimize these guilty feelings.[13] Broadening the term, Smith, Bruner, and White speak of political opinions as representing "externalizing" maneuvers. By this they mean more than projection and displacement: "Externalization occurs when an individual, often responding unconsciously, senses an analogy between a perceived environmental event and some unresolved inner problem. He adopts an attitude toward the event in question which is a transformed version of his way of dealing with his inner difficulty."[14] Obviously this is disruptive of a means-ends rationality in the real contemporary world in which the event takes place. Several perceptual, intellectual, and cognitive malfunctionings have been explored in political contexts: men rationalize the defects of their preferred parties and political leaders;[15] they learn and forget partisan material with speeds that favor their own partisan stands;[16] they misperceive the positions of political leaders when caught in conflicts between preferred positions and preferred candidates;[17] they employ stereotypes to save time and protect their illusions;[18] they repress frightening information[19] and information that makes them feel guilty;[20] there are certain kinds of men who are per-

12. See, among many others, Graham Wallas' discussion of "Impulse and Instinct in Politics," in his *Human Nature in Politics* (Boston: Houghton Mifflin, 1909), pp. 21–58.

13. Harold Lasswell, *Psychopathology and Politics* (Chicago: University of Chicago Press, 1930).

14. M. Brewster Smith, Jerome S. Bruner, and Robert W. White, *Opinions and Personality* (New York: Wiley, 1956), p. 43.

15. Allen L. Edwards, "Political Frames of Reference as a Factor Influencing Recognition," *Journal of Abnormal and Social Psychology*, 36 (1941), pp. 34–50.

16. Jerome M. Levine and Gardner Murphy, "The Learning and Forgetting of Controversial Material," *Journal of Abnormal and Social Psychology*, 38 (1943), pp. 507–517.

17. B. Berelson, P. Lazarsfeld, and W. McPhee, *Voting* (Chicago: University of Chicago Press, 1954), pp. 220–230.

18. Walter Lippmann, *Public Opinion* (New York: Macmillan, 1922).

19. Irving L. Janis and Seymour Feshbach, "Effects of Fear Arousing Communications," *Journal of Abnormal and Social Psychology*, 48 (1953), pp. 78–92.

20. Helen Swick Perry, "Selective Inattention as an Explanatory Concept for U.S. Public Attitudes toward the Atomic Bomb," *Psychiatry*, 17 (1953), pp. 78–92.

sistently dogmatic or rigid in their mental functioning, making them inhospitable to new information or making them pervert it to serve a preestablished doctrine; [21] and there are other men who are persistently "intolerant of ambiguity," making unresolved situations and unclear perceptions and postponed decisions hard to bear.[22] This latter quality is associated with authoritarianism, and is often incompatible with the democratic way of muddling through.

ANTI-INTRACEPTIVENESS   The authoritarian syndrome is a pattern that includes self-referential, as well as other-referential and societal-referential, elements.[23] Toward the self, the authoritarian is "anti-intraceptive," that is, he is unwilling to explore his own motives and personality—for fear of what he might find. This also makes him generally opposed to psychological inquiry, preferring to employ circumstantial explanations for events. Other qualities of authoritarianism, taken in isolation as well as together in the complete syndrome, seem to offer impediments to democratic functioning: the tendency to stereotype, the aggressiveness and toughness, the exaggerated concern with sex, and much more. Although the concept has been eroded by criticism, much of this criticism seems to have been made in the spirit that unless the research is methodologically correct the concept must fail,[24] and some of the criticism seems to have been on the basis of a very limited set of tests.[25]

Interpersonal Pathologies

Except for analytical purposes, it is almost impossible to separate qualities that refer primarily to the self and those that refer primarily to others, because the self is, as Rousseau remarked,

21. Milton Rokeach, *The Open and Closed Mind* (New York: Basic Books, 1960).

22. Else Frenkel-Brunswik, "A Study of Prejudice in Children," *Human Relations*, 1 (1949), pp. 295–306; and "Intolerance of Ambiguity, as an Emotional and Personality Variable," *Journal of Personality*, 18 (1949), pp. 108–143.

23. T. W. Adorno, Else Frenkel-Brunswik, Daniel J. Levinson, and R. Nevitt Sanford, *The Authoritarian Personality* (New York: Harper, 1950).

24. Herbert H. Hyman and Paul B. Sheatsley, "'The Authoritarian Personality,' A Methodological Critique," in Richard Christie and Marie Jahoda, eds., *Studies in the Scope and Method of "The Authoritarian Personality"* (New York: The Free Press of Glencoe, 1954), pp. 50–122.

25. Angus Campbell, Philip E. Converse, and Warren E. Miller, *The American Voter* (New York: Wiley, 1960), pp. 499–519.

socially created. Referring to the previous discussion, the reader will observe the alienated man as being "out of touch" with other persons; the loss of identity is partly a loss of a sense of whom I am like and whom I go with! the authoritarian's aggression and toughness may be free-floating, but it is often directed at other people. As is well known, a person learns about himself from what others think and say about him and from how they behave toward him.

MISANTHROPY   In spite of this interweaving of the personal with the interpersonal, there are certain qualities that are more distinctly related to others and that are said to be impediments to democratic attitudes. One of these is misanthropy, or a low estimate of human nature. Lasswell makes the point that a "confidence in human potentialities" is characteristic of democratic man; its reverse, of course, would be the lack of such confidence.[26] Pursuing this point with an attitudinal measure, Morris Rosenberg found that people who tended not to believe that "people can be trusted" also tended, logically enough, not to trust democratic officials or to believe that these officials cared much about the interests of the public.[27] In a forthcoming work, Gabriel Almond and Sidney Verba will show that this is, indeed, a cross-cultural phenomenon.[28]

CONSTRICTED EMPATHY   In a somewhat similar vein, Gilbert has shown how through "constricted empathy" the German people were able to endure the oppression of others without much guilt; they simply narrowed down the group for whom they had empathic feelings, retaining it for those whom they admitted to friendship.[29] Divorcing this concept from its ally, sympathy, it is possible to think of the more general quality of being able to put yourself in the place of another as an important ingredient of democratic man. Lerner shows how, in the Middle East, the capacity to think of oneself in another position, performing another role, was essential for the development of democratic institutions. Those who could not think of themselves, for example, as a news-

26. Harold Lasswell, "Democratic Character," pp. 502–503.
27. Morris Rosenberg, "Misanthropy and Political Ideology," *American Sociological Review*, 21 (1956), p. 691.
28. Gabriel Almond and Sidney Verba, *The Culture of Democracy* (forthcoming).
29. G. M. Gilbert, *The Psychology of Dictatorship* (New York: Ronald, 1950), pp. 278–280.

paper editor or as a governor of a district, turned out to be un-finished material for democracy.[30]

CLOSED EGO   Overlapping with these meanings is a term that Lasswell includes among his personal bases for democratic be-havior: the "open ego," by which he means that "the attitude to-ward other human beings is warm rather than frigid, inclusive and expanding rather than exclusive and constricting . . . an underlying personality structure which is capable of 'friend-ship.' " [31] The pathology, from the democratic standpoint, then, is the cold, constricted, closed ego. This is close to the "tenderness taboo," a fear of showing the soft, tender, or idealistic facet of personality, which Dicks found to be characteristic of the Nazis among a large group of German prisoners of war.[32]

"WE" AND "THEY"   Authoritarianism contains a strictly in-terpersonal component: the tendency to divide the world into "we" and "they," "in-groups" and "out-groups." This is a product of a more basic tendency to conceive of the world in somewhat hostile terms, in which case the most important question to ask of a person is, "Is he for me or is he against me?" Even relation-ships based on business or sport or strictly contractual matters are heavily loaded with this perspective. Along with this is the hier-archical view of relations with others: Does he submit to me or do I submit to him? [33]

CONFORMITY   Finally, there is the question of autonomy and conformity. David Riesman has argued that it is the conformists and the moralizers who appear to determine our political style and most influence our decisions; "the autonomous, insignificant in numbers, play a minor and scarcely discernible role in our politics." [34] Thus conventionality and unrealistic reform often seem to be the main alternatives available in such a political system. Moreover, the conformism of the masses makes of them so many cheerful robots, easily manipulated by a power elite.[35]

30. Daniel Lerner, *The Passing of Traditional Society* (New York: The Free Press of Glencoe, 1958), pp. 43–52.
31. Harold Lasswell, "Democratic Character," p. 495.
32. Henry V. Dicks, "Personality Traits and National Socialist Ideology," *Human Relations,* 3 (1950), pp. 111–154.
33. T. W. Adorno and others, *The Authoritarian Personality,* pp. 222–279.
34. David Riesman, *The Lonely Crowd* (New Haven: Yale University Press, 1950), p. 370.
35. C. Wright Mills, *The Sociological Imagination* (New York: Oxford Uni-versity Press, 1959), pp. 165–176.

Social and Cultural Pathologies

SOCIAL ALIENATION   What is interpersonal is social, but there is something more here. In the concept of alienation, there is a strong theme of something broader than simply a distance from the self and from others. In the Marxian version, and that of Fromm as well, there is emphasis upon the individual's alienation from an uncreative work life, a total alienation from society.[36] Kornhauser, whose main concern is the loss of community and pluralistic groups serving as strong links between men and the larger society, argues that these losses produce a mass society. "The central problem posed by the theory of mass society," he says, "is that of *social alienation*, or the distance between the individual and his society." [37] It is this combination of social alienation, atomistic relationships, and easy manipulability that make him fear for the future of democracy.

ANOMIE   Perhaps the term anomie has born the freight of more related ideas dealing with the sickness of modern urban industrial, and democratic, man than any other. From the original use by Durkheim, where he referred to the lack of rules to live by and loss of values to pursue,[38] through its extended modern usages there has been a common thread—confusion and loss of internalized values; but the source of this confusion has been variously interpreted. Merton, for example, attributes anomie, in part, to the discrepancies between the approved goals and the approved means for reaching those goals in the modern American culture. Some of the expression of this anomie produced in this way has political relevance: both apathy (retreatism) and rebellion fall in this category.[39] Sebastian De Grazia conceives of anomie as analogous to the separation-anxiety of the child; it comes with the loss of faith in the rulers and their codes of behavior. When the common belief system of society, including religion, is challenged and demoralized, when the rulers lose their closeness to the people and become merely decision-makers or employers,

36. See Erich Fromm, *The Sane Society*, pp. 120–151.
37. William Kornhauser, *The Politics of Mass Society* (New York: The Free Press of Glencoe, 1959), p. 237.
38. Emile Durkheim, *Suicide*, translated by John A. Spaulding and George Simpson (New York: The Free Press of Glencoe, 1951), pp. 246–254.
39. Robert K. Merton, "Social Structure and Anomie," in his *Social Theory and Social Structure* (New York: The Free Press of Glencoe, 1949), pp. 125–149.

the old panic strikes and people once again suffer this sense of abandonment, losing their own faith and their sense of security. They then may help themselves to synthetic ideologies and false political prophets.[40]

CYNICISM   The individual who finds neither in society nor in himself a source of values may take another road. It is described in a variety of ways by Nathan Leites as he portrays the political culture of the French: "the reign of the self," "the quest for privilege," "deceit, imposture, trickery," "I do as I like." There is an over-all theme here; covered by the word cynicism, a corrosive attitude that makes altrusistic and self-denying motives or behavior evaporate into thin air.[41]

CONSTRICTED UNIVALUE SYSTEM   A variation of this pathology turns, not on devaluation or on denial of values, but on a constricted univalue system. Lasswell says, "Let us speak of the democratic character as multi-valued, rather than single valued, and as disposed to share rather than to hoard or to monopolize." [42] The sharing of values is necessary in all political systems, but because the democratic system gives scope for the value miser in us all, this quality needs more internal restraint. And so, too, since democracy requires, more than other systems, a tolerance of others with different values, those who respect the pursuits of others for wealth or moral stature or fame, or whatever it may be, make a contribution in many discrete ways.

TRADITIONALISM   The traditionalism of the Middle East in Lerner's analysis, like the tradition-orientation in Riesman's typology, forms an impediment to democratic functioning.[43] The concept is one of a passive person on whom society acts but who does not believe that he himself has a right or a capacity to influence affairs. Public affairs are like the natural order of things— they just happen. For Lerner, the antidote lies in the development of psychological mobility; for Riesman in the development,

40. Sebastian De Grazia, *The Political Community: A Study of Anomie* (Chicago: University of Chicago Press, 1948).

41. Nathan Leites, *Images of Power in French Politics* (multilithed, 1961); see also his *On the Game of Politics in France* (Stanford: Stanford University Press, 1959).

42. Harold Lasswell, "Democratic Character," pp. 497–498.

43. Daniel Lerner, *The Passing of Traditional Society;* David Riesman, *The Lonely Crowd.*

perhaps after a period of inner-direction or other direction, of autonomy.

"THE WORLD IS A JUNGLE"   The authoritarian view is that the world is a jungle; hence, it is appropriate to claw and scratch in a struggle for survival. It is a world where power is the main good and where dominance and submission are the main human postures.[44]

B
THE IMPOVERISHED SELF

Most of the above concepts either are or may be framed negatively; that is, they suggest that the impediment to democratic support lies in a missing quality: loss of identity, "being out of touch with oneself," lack of self-control, absence of rationality, and so forth. This further suggests that a synoptic concept may best be framed in the same way, as an impoverishment. What is it that is missing? Are there some core deficiencies that summarize or, better still, cause these human failures?

I have attempted to achieve such a synoptic concept under the term *the impoverished self,* meaning, low self-acceptance, low self-esteem, and low ego strength. Let us examine these briefly.

Low Self-Acceptance

This concept was chosen only after some consideration was given to another related term, self-awareness. The reasons are important. One might easily argue that an awareness of one's personal and social identity is an essential ingredient in meeting the demands of a society in conflict, imposing one's demands upon it, resisting the incredibly insistent demands of others. One of the central explanations of politics relies upon the individual's pursuit of his own "interests," something he can grasp only as he understands "who" he is. But the evidence of Eastport spoke against this argument. There, one of the main personal themes was the objectification of the self, the treating of the self as a somewhat impersonal object with needs and qualities to be appraised from an outside perspective. One had to say, on balance, that the best

44. T. W. Adorno and associates, *The Authoritarian Personality,* pp. 222–241.

of the citizens were not intimately or sensitively self-aware, while some of the undemocrats and the alienated men were much more concerned with what was happening inside themselves. Moreover, interculturally, it is said that the ethos of the Latin countries, where democracy struggles to survive, leads to a focus on self-mastery, while the North American ethos, generally supportive of democracy, leads to a focus on mastery of the environment.[45]

Furthermore, in Eastport democracy is built upon a certain social-identity diffusion, a vagueness, not about the personal characteristics of the individual, but about his social membership, his reference groups, his political friends and enemies. When these crystallized, we found the individual politically "frozen" as, for example, an Italian-American or as a member of the working class or as a "lifelong Democrat." These social identities, then, became the touchstones by which almost all social policies, all judgments of politicians were transmuted into friendly or hostile objects. A clear social identity served as a substitute for penetrating observation and thought; the diffused social identity served the community somewhat better.

Upon reflection, then, it appeared that the concept that best expressed the quality we had in mind was not the self-awareness of the individual in the sense that he was in constant communication with his unconscious and clear about his social memberships, but the self-acceptance of the individual that implied that he was not in conflict with his unconscious and not rejecting his social memberships.

Thus clarified, it is easy to see how low self-acceptance, not, perhaps, *in toto,* but in part, creates a situation that fosters the pathologies we have discussed earlier. A person who rejects his impulse life and feels constantly guilty about it cannot have the low moral tension we argued was important for a democratic system. His struggle with himself impairs his capacity to see life "as it really is," because some parts of it are too dangerous to be seen this way; the individual in reliving old struggles and trying to master old situations will create an unreality, will have a faltering reality sense. Yet we said that a democracy requires a firm foundation in empirically verifiable and realistic metaphysics, and particularly in the acknowledgment of impersonal causes. For the

45. Patrick Romanell, *Making of the Mexican Mind: A Study in Recent Mexican Thought* (Lincoln, Neb.: University of Nebraska Press, 1952).

same reason his epistemology is distorted and his uses of knowledge are defensive, not instrumental.

In the same way, low self-acceptance is associated with anxiety that what he fears to know about himself—chiefly that he has hostile feelings—will become public knowledge. It is a feature in self-alienation; indeed, that is exactly what the failure to accept some feature of the self really is. It is partially embraced by the concept of anti-intraception, and includes that part of loss of identity that we regard as damaging to the democratic polity. Low self-acceptance, the rejection of some part of the self, rather than low self-awareness, is, it seems, an important source of democratic pathology, and one node in the complex called the impoverished self.

Low Self-Esteem

In a penetrating discussion of the psychology of the American Negro, Kardiner and Ovesey place low self-esteem at the center of a network of psychodynamic constellations. Created by the oppressive character of the social environment, low self-esteem encourages hedonism in some, rebellion in others, neurotic symptoms in still others.[46] In a somewhat analagous way it is relevant here: it produces in the citizen a sense that he is unworthy to hold opinions, to make demands upon the society, to be treated as an important individual. It is a feature of traditional man, who believes that important matters of state are not the proper concern of the "likes of him." To the extent that men use themselves as a template for others, "recreating" others in their own image, and who, at the same time, believe themselves to be weak or sinful or worthless, these men will adopt several of the pathologies noted above. They will be cynical and they will be misanthropic. They will reject the bad part of themselves, hence self-alienated. But, most important, they will have anomic feelings, for there can be little doubt that the core of devaluational feelings lies in the sense of a devalued self. That is one reason why, in the first and classic study of anomie, the resolution was the destruction of this thing without value, suicide. At the same time it is true that *some* doubt

46. Abram Kardiner and Lionel Ovesey, *The Mark of Oppression: A Psychosocial Study of the American Negro* (New York: Norton, 1951); see also Hadley Cantril, *The Psychology of Social Movements* (New York: Wiley, 1941); Robert E. Lane, *Political Life.*

about which values to pursue, some value confusion, and hence some aspects of anomie, are compatible with high self-esteem.

Low Ego Strength

There are many societies where men are self-accepting and self-respecting but where they are not capable of self-government because they are not self-governing. Without self-control, plus a sense of mastery over the environment (the ingredients of ego strength), it is possible neither to pursue a consistent long-term course of action nor to effect much social change. Equally important, without the inner experience of control, a man hardly understands how control processes can work; he projects anarchy or conspiracy upon the world. Political man is asked to become an ally of one group, to work with another, and to help defeat a third. Without a gyroscopic mechanism, a strong ego, he becomes putty; he has no "will" of his own. We have said that democracy works best when men view each other not exactly at arm's length but not fused in the warmth of an intense comradeship either. They must see each other as free-standing units; but this is impossible unless each has the ego strength that makes him free-standing.

Some of the pathologies flow directly from this concept—the lack of self-control, the lack of autonomy. Some emerge indirectly: anxiety troubles the mind when men are unsure of their impulse control. What we called irrationality is often a pursuit of immediate gratifications at the cost of long-run "deeper" and more enduring satisfactions. But ego strength implies just this capacity to schedule satisfactions. On balance, like self-acceptance and self-esteem, ego strength seems central to the democratic personality.

□ □ □ □ □ □ □ □ □ □ □ □ □ □ □

Ideological Stability and Change

25

Theory of Ideological Change

Does it require deep intuition to comprehend that man's ideas, views, and conceptions, in one word, man's consciousness, changes with every change in the conditions of his material existence, in his social relations and in his social life?

—KARL MARX AND FRIEDRICH ENGELS, *Manifesto of the Communist Party*, p. 28

Ideas can become powerful forces, but only to the extent to which they are answers to specific human needs prominent in a given social character.

—ERICH FROMM, *Escape from Freedom*, p. 281

The great strength of liberalism lies in the fact that it . . . is able to draw upon a dwindling but substantial capital of widely accepted ethical presuppositions. The ethics of humanitarian democracy are a continuation, in secular form, of the traditional doctrines of Christian charity.

—FREDERICK WATKINS, *The Political Tradition of the West*, p. 346

A

FOUR WAYS OF STUDYING IDEOLOGICAL CHANGE

The study of political ideologies has focused more often than not upon their merits as guides to reality and as ideals to strive for, but there have been at least four major approaches to the question How do they come about? One of these is grounded in the traditions of intellectual history, a tradition that might be illustrated by C. H. McIlwain's *The Growth of Political Thought in the West* or Frederick Watkins' *The Political Tradition of the West* or Edmund Wilson's *To the Finland Station*. This approach records, explicates, and interprets how the thought of one generation or one man influences another, how the circumstances of the times affect men's formulations and selections, and how these ideas serve to structure institutions and social life.

A second attempt to account for the development of political ideologies goes by the name of the sociology of knowledge, and may be illustrated by Karl Mannheim's *Ideology and Utopia*. In its modern form it arises from the Marxian doctrine that ideologies are merely the superstructure built upon the economic foundations of a society and designed to rationalize the pursuit of special interests. From there, Mannheim, Scheler, Merton and others have argued the case for a broader interpretation of the problem, emphasizing that not only rationalized interests are shaped by the social position of the observers but also attention, perspective, and truth itself have this relational property.[1] For example, Mannheim reports how the idea of "freedom" in the nineteenth century meant to the German aristocrat "the right of each estate to live according to its privileges," while to the liberal intellectual it meant the abolition of these privileges and the idea "that all men have the same fundamental rights at their disposal." [2] This conflict followed in part from the fact that the social position of each posed certain restraints that to the other were, in fact, conditions of freedom. It also followed from the "true" perceptions of the nature of man and society afforded by the particular angle of vision the aristocrat and the intellectual each enjoyed.

A third attempt to account for the development of an ideology argues that since ideologies are heavily laced with projective material arising from intrapsychic states, the modal personalities of the group selecting and using an ideology have a strong influence

1. In addition to Karl Mannheim's *Ideology and Utopia* (New York: Harcourt, Brace, 1949), see his *Man and Society in an Age of Reconstruction* (New York: Harcourt, Brace, 1948); Howard Becker and H. O. Dahlke, "Max Scheler's Sociology of Knowledge," *Philosophy and Phenomenological Research*, 2 (1942), pp. 310–322; Robert K. Merton, *Social Theory and Social Structure* (New York: The Free Press of Glencoe, 1949), pp. 199–264.

2. Karl Mannheim, *Ideology and Utopia*, p. 245.

on ideology formation. This line of argument is well represented by Kardiner and his associates in *The Psychological Frontiers of Society*. Social ideologies, says Kardiner, make use of the experience of a society, but they are "polarized in the direction of unconscious motivation." [3] As we shall see, Erich Fromm argues that social ideas acquire a certain "weight" only when they are congruent with the social character of a people. [4] The analysis of basic personality and the employment of psychoanalytic theory are central in this accounting scheme.

A fourth approach to the study of ideological development hardly employs the concept of "ideology" at all; rather, in a voluminous literature, it attacks attitudes and beliefs piecemeal. Studies of the correlates of liberalism, pacifism, unlabeled Fascism, internationalism, Machiavellianism, and so forth, make a joint and separate contribution to an understanding of the causes and conditions of social belief.

While they may isolate political ideologies or attitudes for special study, the best of the work in each of these traditions points to the contextual nature of political ideologies. The contexts they conceive to be relevant to ideology differ, of course: they may be the historical events of the times and the social conflicts in which the ideologies do service, or they may refer to broader belief systems or entire epistemologies, or they may place political man in the context of a man's "personality as a whole." From each of these contexts, each of these approaches abstracts some element for special study. With this cue perhaps we can take a more holistic view of ideological change than any one of these approaches has done so far.

B

A PARADIGM OF IDEOLOGICAL CHANGE

Gathering together what seem to me to be the main elements affecting the change of political ideology for a social group, I propose the following paradigm:

For any society: an *existential base* creating certain *common experiences* interpreted through certain *cultural premises* by men

3. Abram Kardiner and associates, *The Psychological Frontiers of Society* (New York: Columbia University Press, 1945), p. 46.
4. Erich Fromm, *Escape from Freedom* (New York: Rinehart, 1941), p. 280.

with certain *personal qualities* in the light of certain *social conflicts* produces certain *political ideologies.*[5]

This paradigm is designed to help account for ideological *change,*
not the origins of an ideology. By putting the matter this way, we
are confronted with the interaction of the old and the new, something a discussion of the origins of an ideology might more easily
overlook. It is a paradigm for a society or a group, not for an individual; hence the focus upon common experiences and cultural
premises rather than upon individual experience, exposure, and
belief. Both of these considerations also lead away from the focus
upon the individual innovator or theorist, the Bentham, Marx, or
Jefferson who first states the theory that later becomes, in vulgar
form, part of a social ideology. When these innovative ideas become part of the accepted beliefs of a group of men, they enter
our theme.

The terms for this paradigm are not self-explanatory. The
existential base embraces not only Marx's modes of production
but also the technological foundations of a society, the property
arrangements, the industrialization, urbanism, gross national product, the shape and content of social stratification, the pattern of
community life, the educational arrangements, the geographic
and demographic conditions of society—in short, the social and
physical patterns of life. The existential base to which the Eastport men must respond includes a pattern of urban industrial
living marked by rising per capita income, chronic but relatively
low levels of unemployment, private ownership of the means of
production, multiple employers, free public education for their
children, representative government, and ethnic heterogeneity in
the community. Two of these elements, "opportunity" and "community," are described in Chapter 14 above.

An economist or an anthropologist looking at a society reports
the patterns observed, but he does not *experience* them as the
members of a society do. In order to do that one must engage in a
life of work and love and hope and frustration in the ongoing
pattern; it must become "my" pattern, seen from the inside or as
close to the inside as possible. It is one thing to know that almost
6 per cent of the labor force is unemployed; it is quite another

5. I have borrowed here from a similar paradigm for the study of communication created by Bernard Berelson in his "Communication and Public Opinion,"
in Wilbur Schramm, ed., *Communications in Modern Society* (Urbana, Ill.: University of Illinois Press, 1948), pp. 168–185.

thing to be an unemployed man, rising in the morning with fading hope to a day committed to desultory inquiries, new deprivations, numbing frustration, humiliation, and growing apathy. The existential base must be translated into human experience before its meaning for the development of political ideology can be gauged.

Some life experiences in a community are wholly idiosyncratic to the person who has them; some are shared only by certain social groups; some are shared by everyone in that community. It is the shared experiences that contribute to social ideology, not the idiosyncratic ones. By being shared they create a basis for discussion; they are moralized by their group properties (see Chapter 21) and they attract the attention of educated interpreters; statements about them by one source have resonance in the experience of listeners or readers. Marxist interpreters believed that the common experiences of the proletariat would make the Communist interpretation of the social order meaningful by providing an explanation and a program resonant with these miserable experiences, while the capitalist ideology would appear plausible only to those who experienced the world as property owners. The salient economic experiences would thus be neither idiosyncratic nor communitywide—they would be shared exclusively within class lines. The experiences of the Eastport men include both holding jobs with "good" pay and the periodic threat to their income brought by each recession. They have experienced the kind of living possible in a clean, well-run, suburbanized housing development, located well away from the delinquency, flophouse, and tenement areas. They experience (at arm's length) interracial living. Income and debt, religious participation, the socialization of children—these social patterns are internalized and made "meaningful" through experience.

What is observed and what is experienced are interpreted through the use of *cultural premises;* these tell men (within limits) what they are to think of the experiences they have and how they are to cope with them. If they experience a period of unemployment, is it their own fault or is it fate or is it a conspiracy of others to punish them? If they earn more this year, do they save it for the expected disasters around the corner? Do they spend it, for who knows what tomorrow will bring, or invest it in savings bonds for their children? President Eisenhower disappoints them in the recession—how shall they account for this defection? Ideas of time and place, of cause, of purpose, of expectation, of others and of self are in their broad outline socially given. There is a culturally given metaphysics, an ethics, an epistemology, and a value scheme. These are premises for the study of political ideology; but of course each is also an inference, a deduction, a culture product in its own right.

The *personal qualities* of the men who use these cultural premises to interpret their experience help to shape that interpretation. Anxious men interpret experience so as to relieve their anxiety; authoritarians see the hierarchical features of a social situation where equalitarians may not; the marginal psychopathic personality does not employ the code of ethics his society gives him. When these qualities are idiosyncratic, they are like idiosyncratic experiences or beliefs, contributing little to the shaping of community beliefs or ideologies; when they are shared, modal, or "basic" elements of social character, they not only affect the development of cultural premises but also affect the way these are used and what is done with social experience. For example, in Eastport we found that three men had such problems of impulse control that the idea of greater freedom was threatening to them. Had this been thirteen instead of three, I would expect Eastport to show ideological tendencies toward the support of a "closed" society. Similarly, the combination of a relatively secure personal identity with a diffuse social identity contributed to the individualized (unsocial) goals these men pursued so strenuously.

These interpretations take place within a context of the *social conflict* produced by rival groups seeking the power, wealth, and status to be had in a society. Each such group must invoke a moral justification for its part in the conflict in order to retain the loyalty of its supporters, to enlist new supporters, and to counter the moral appeal of its opponents. Spokesmen for the group elaborate political ideologies embracing theories of divine right, of natural rights, or equal rights, of popular sovereignty, of exploitation that give moral rationales for their proposals. They provide theories of cause and effect: cycle theories of democracy and tyranny, theories of concentration and separation of governmental power, of race and degeneracy, of the profit-seeking nature of man and economic development. These moral and empirical theories, then, are advanced by the various parties to social conflict and, so to speak, are constantly "tried out" by the public seeking to interpret its experience from day to day. This trial consists of a series of tests: The ideological features must fit with the personal qualities of the men to whom they are addressed or they lack appeal. They must be seen as congruent with the cultural premises of the society, or they will be seen as immoral or unrealistic or dissonant with what is known. And they must somehow make the interpretation of real-life experience both more gratifying and more realistic.

In Eastport, social conflict is muted. There is conflict between management and labor, but for the reasons we have mentioned it is screened through a thick cultural curtain that distorts and muffles the disagreement. The religious rivalry is carried on sotto voce, as is the rivalry for place among nationality and racial groups. The rural-urban conflict simply is not visible to most men; the regional conflict has had no vitality since 1896. It is under these circumstances that ideologies become nationalized and homogenized within the American society. But they may spring to life in a social conflict between the American nation and some other nation-state.

An outline of this paradigm as it applies to Eastport is provided in Table V.

The Initiation of Ideological Change

In a static society, one that has not been subject to technical or social change for many years, the several elements of this scheme may be assumed to be in a kind of equilibrium. Under these circumstances the experiences men have are in line with their expectations; they are easily interpreted and explained by a metaphysics, are adequately known by an epistemology, are in accord with an ethical scheme, and advance both individual and social goals in harmony with one another. Children are trained to have the qualities that conform to the cultural premises and that are instrumental for the roles they will be called upon to perform —although, as Kardiner points out, there may be lags of several hundred years in adjusting basic personality to a given social state of affairs.[6] Social conflicts are routinized; the friction is reduced; and the areas of disagreement are very small. The political ideology of the society provides a rationale for the form of government it has evolved.

A change in the existential base, say, a development in the technics of a civilization, or the redistribution of wealth following

6. Abram Kardiner and associates, *op. cit.*, pp. 417–418.

TABLE V

PARADIGM FOR THE STUDY OF IDEOLOGICAL CHANGE IN EASTPORT

Existential Base (Objective)	Common Experiences (Subjective)	Cultural Premises	Personal Qualities	Social Conflict	Political Ideologies
Economic abundance, advancement, escalation.	Family: strong nurturant mothers; ⅔ had supportive fathers. School-home conflict in 2nd-generation group. Education in democracy; quitting school to prove independence, etc.	Time focus on proximate future; lack of intergeneration plans; punctuality.	Generally high ego-strength, high self-acceptance; self-esteem strengthened by economic success; e.g., few men with impoverished selves.	Social conflicts muted through cultural emphasis on: classlessness, tolerance, assimilation, unity, *the* public interest, compromise. Thus conflicts are atomized, individual.	Emphasis on occupational and consumer freedom; religion as choice; freedom from stimulation; tolerance of confusion; [fear of freedom by 3 men].
Industrial complex: private ownership, collectivized work, some machine tending, alternative employment, industrial discipline.	Economic: discretion on the job; humane foremen	Geographical polarization; lack of localism, rootedness, community identity.	Personal identities strong but objectified; social indentities diffuse.		Approval of inequalitarian society, justification of status of rich and poor, belief in need for "advancement" to induce work.
Society stratified by income, occupation, ethnicity; partial mobility.		Acceptability of impersonal explanations; modest projectivity, low traditionalism.		Real conflict: Italian-Irish, Negro-white,	Lack of cynicism about democracy based on experience and self-control.
Religious division among Catholics,					

Protestants, Jews (muted); Catholic predominance, secular society.

Contractual urban society, external-ized relations, emphasis on functional roles, work orientation.

Democratic "strong mayor" government, ethnic coalitions, "machine" influence, responsive to community needs.

and lack of a sense of exploitation; periodic uncertainty due to business cycle.

Political: solicitude of politicians; sense of leverage from "knowing" somebody; sense of duty discharged in voting, etc.

Low moral tension, error-for-evil, natural moral order, blamelessness, conscience as conservative.

Minor premise orientation, morselizing tendencies, low ideologizing, compromise orientation.

Approach orientation to information, avoidance of advice.

High empathy, faith in people, open, multivalued personalities.

Low anomie, ethnocentrism; middle authoritarianism [3 men low impulse control: 2 men "homeless"].

labor-management, Protestant-Catholic; but abundance, fluidity, and lack of dramatic historical feuds diminishes intensity.

General refusal to adopt "cabalistic" interpretation of power; belief that economic power is under control; power enough for all.

Faith in government and particularly in Congress.

"Allegiance" toward government and society; alienation of homeless men.

Collectivist tendencies in faith in government.

Lack of Utopian goals.

new trade patterns, can disequilibrate the system. Most attempts to account for political ideas tend to anchor their explanations in this existential base: Montesquieu's emphasis on geography and climate,[7] Wittfogel's theory of the hydraulic (irrigation and flood-control) basis of centralized authoritarian regimes in Egypt and China,[8] Watkin's emphasis on the mountainous protections of the early Greek city-states,[9] the emphasis in Burckhardt and others on the source of the Renaissance in the revival of trade,[10] and, of course, the Marxian doctrine linking ideology to the modes of production. Yet, I am not satisfied to say that in the model outlined above the only point of entry for fundamental change is in the existential base. In a pluralistic world culture diffusion not only of technics but equally of religious or philosophical ideas offers room for entry through the portal we have labeled "cultural premises." The very history of Marxism itself argues this point with convincing force. In his *Religion and the Rise of Capitalism*, Tawney gives due weight to changes in trade, but goes on to say that "side by side with the expansion of trade and the rise of new classes to political power, there was a further cause, which, if not the most conspicuous, was not the least fundamental. It was the contraction of the territory within which the spirit of religion was conceived to run. . . . The secularization of political thought . . . had profound reactions on social speculation, and by the Restoration the whole perspective, at least in England, had been revolutionized." [11] This is, in Tawney's view, not just a consequence of a change in the existential base; it is a concomitant phenomenon with an autonomy of its own.

Nor would I limit the role of the personal qualities of a group to that of "dependent variable" in this general scheme. Of course, new theories of child rearing, new requirements for mothers to leave the home and work in factories, and, more recently, new leisure both for mothers and for fathers reveal social personality as effect rather than as cause. But the very Eastport situation we have studied shows a kind of autonomous change developing to

7. Thus, Books XIV–XVII of *The Spirit of the Laws* deal with the effect on the laws of "the nature of the climate," Book XVIII deals with the effect of "the nature of the soil," etc.

8. Karl A. Wittfogel, *Oriental Despotism: A Comparative Study of Total Power* (New Haven: Yale University Press, 1957).

9. Frederick Watkins, *The Political Tradition of the West* (Cambridge, Mass.: Harvard University Press, 1948), pp. 4–10.

10. Jacob Burckhardt, *The Civilization of the Renaissance in Italy* (London: Phaidon, 1944).

11. R. H. Tawney, *Religion and the Rise of Capitalism* (New York: Penguin, 1947), p. 228.

differentiate the personalities of the immigrant generation from the second (native) generation and again from the third generation. This would be true even if there were no great changes in the environment, for there is an autonomy to this assimilation process once it is set in motion that is analagous to the idea of momentum in physics.

Social conflicts change with changing conditions, but, like other ingredients of the system, they have an autonomous development. Perhaps it is true, as the Beards argue, that the American Civil War was the product of a growing disproportion between economic and political power in the North and in the South.[12] But there were other contributing causes for that conflict, and once it had occurred the continuing social conflict between North and South affected the industrial development, the nostalgic backward-looking culture, the political ideals of the defeated South in a chain reaction that has not yet ended.

And, of course, the thing we are trying to explain, the political ideology of a group is, for other purposes, the starting point, the point of entry for change, not its product.

What I should like to stress, then, is that nature does not hold all other elements of this system constant, leaving them free to respond only to changes in the existential base. The paradigm sketches a system where change can come from many sources simultaneously, with many points of entry and many separate interactive patterns developing between one element and another.

Criteria for Selection: Functions

"Of what use to a man are his opinions?" Answering their own question, Smith, Bruner, and White reply that a man uses his opinions for three broad kinds of functions:

1. They help him to orient himself in a real world environment and to pursue his (largely economic) goals in life.

2. They help him adjust to others.

3. They help him to express his psychic needs and tensions.[13]

12. Charles and Mary Beard, *The Rise of American Civilization* (New York: Macmillan, 1933), Chap. xvii.

13. M. Brewster Smith, Jerome S. Bruner, and Robert W. White, *Opinions and Personality* (New York: Wiley, 1956), pp. 1, 39–44. Compare Milton Rokeach: "belief . . . systems are seen to serve two opposing sets of functions. On the one hand, they represent Everyman's theory for understanding the world he lives in. On the other hand, they represent Everyman's defense network through which information is filtered, in order to render harmless that which threatens the ego." *The Open and Closed Mind* (New York: Basic Books, 1960), p. 400.

Elsewhere we have argued that opinions and active participation in politics have an independent "cognitive" function (they satisfy curiosity), and an independent function in enhancing a man's self-esteem.[14] To these one might add the function of opinions in justifying a man's acts to himself, that is, a rationalizing and moralizing function. When we turn from individual opinions to more complex ideologies, a new emphasis appears.[15] Ideologies can more easily provide purposes and goals to life; they occupy a larger segment of attention; they inform and give direction to subordinate ideas and opinions and keep them consistent one with another; that is, they have an organizing and a consistency function.[16] They do all this as they help a man to interpret what he observes and what he experiences and what he is told about the world. Thus Sokolsky adopts a conspiracy theory of the recession because it helps him account for it in terms familiar to him; it helps him project his hostility upon an Establishment that tends to treat him, a Jew, as slightly less valuable than his gentile neighbors; it helps him to explain his own status and the status of some of his friends; it offers counters in conversational gambits that are sustaining for his ego; it has a certain plausibility that (while wrong) does not lead *him* astray; in short, it is as useful to him as any alternative ideological fragments he is likely to come across.

Ideologies have social as well as individual functions; that is, they contribute to the effectiveness or the pleasure or the morality of group life. In some ways these functions are the same as the individual functions, seen from a different angle. First, a political ideology helps to *protect group boundaries* by helping men to adjust to one another through a common bond; or, alternatively, it may protect these boundaries by designating enemy groups. The common democratic ideology of Eastport certainly minimized friction within the group, even when it was only a sugared-over ver-

14. Robert E. Lane, *Political Life* (New York: The Free Press of Glencoe, 1959), pp. 101–132.

15. "It is somewhat inefficient to ask separately for each and every belief, or opinion, or attitude, or act: 'What function does this serve in the total economy of the person?' . . . It is more economical to see what structural interrelations first exist and then ask a single question at the end about the functions served by all the variables that turn out to go together within a belief system." Rokeach, *op. cit.*, p. 401.

16. See M. Brewster Smith, "Personal Values as Determinants of a Political Attitude," *Journal of Psychology,* 28 (1949), pp. 477–486.

sion of an underlying authoritarianism, as with Ferrera. Second, the ideology justifies group goals as it does individual goals, and thus *coordinates common effort*. Social character, Fromm says, "internalizes external necessities and thus harnesses human energy for the task of a given economic and social system." [17] The same might be said for a political ideology; thus, third, by moralizing and rationalizing certain goals and codes of behavior it *enlists men for the group tasks to be done*. Flynn, without political ambitions, serves as an officer of a Hilltop Council partly in service to an ideology that tells him this is the thing to do. Fourth, a common political ideology may provide the *legitimation of political authority,* and in this way makes its sanctions and duties congruent with conscience, that is, internally enforced. The sanctity of the law in Eastport was hardly open to question. But, of course, an ideology can desanctify law and delegitimize authority just as well. And fifth, as Sebastian De Grazia has argued so well, without a creed in which to believe and rulers who are seen as solicitous and strong, men suffer from pangs of anxiety and anomie that has as its parallel the early separation anxiety of the growing child.[18] A political ideology fills this void; *it reduces anxiety and anomie*. In his loss of identity, Rapuano had helped himself to a super-patriotic creed to help to support and guide him in his disorientation.

Criteria for Selection: Congruence

The individual does not select an ideology as a person selects a new car; the processes, criteria, alternatives, expectations are largely, but not wholly, unconscious. Nor does a society frame an ideology as it might, through certain leaders, frame a constitution or a five-year plan. The ideology is a slow emergent product rooted in social character, culture, and history, as we have shown. The purely functional theories imply more explicit decisions than is the case. But, more inportant, they insufficiently account for the enormous brain-filling, painfully learned store of principles, doctrine, dogma, premises, values, theories, prejudices, habits, codes, defenses, and the like, with which the mind is furnished. The new

17. Fromm, *op. cit.,* p. 284.
18. Sebastian De Grazia, *The Political Community* (Chicago: University of Chicago Press, 1948).

ideological item is not the first piece in a barren hall, but the last piece in a crowded, familiar room. It must fit. It must be congruent.

The meaning of "congruence" in this usage is somewhat broader than that which has been given to it in other connections. Recently Rokeach said this about belief systems: "We organize the world of ideas, people, and authority basically along lines of belief congruence. What is not congruent is further organized in terms of similarity to what is congruent." [19] His argument is that a man accepts other people and ideas according to whether or not they are similar to himself or his beliefs. By congruence I mean: (1) the relationship between ideas and experience that prevails when a person finds the ideas correctly describe and predict what is happening to him, (2) the relation between ideas and other ideas that prevails when a person feels that he can hold both of them and not experience a sense of illogicality, incompatibility, cognitive dissonance, (3) the relationship between conscious ideas and the unconscious such that a person does not feel anxious on those occasions when they threaten to confront each other, and (4) the relationship between ideas and a "cause" or "movement" or group program such that the ideas seem to the group's adherents to justify their efforts.

The criterion of congruence, then, will apply first to the way in which a political ideology fits a man's experience. Even the most abstract ideology, the most utopian scheme, has an empirical content that must be squared with the small world of experience of the individual confronted with the problem of finding meaning in his world. And even the most facile devices for squaring particular experiences with incompatible interpretations—such as a "long run" inconsistent with any observable short run, the idea that whatever happens is "willed" by some vaguely outlined authority, the view that there is an inscrutable reality beyond all appearances, paranoid interpretations of the world, selective perception and memory, good-bad dichotomies, and so forth—even these must eventually fail to protect men from the abrasions of reality. Know-Nothingism, social Darwinism, the anarchism of the Western Wobblies are eroded, each in turn, by experience with Catholics, with governmental regulation, with the welfare departments of modern cities, Incongruence between ideology and experience extinguishes a social movement.

19. Rokeach, *op. cit.*, p. 295.

In the same way, an ideology will fail if it assumes an idealism in a material culture, a prophetic role where prophecy is incongruent with other ways of knowing, a code of honor appropriate to a courage culture transferred to an "ingenuity culture." [20] For social character, Erich Fromm has put the matter well:

> Ideas often are consciously accepted by certain groups, which, on account of the peculiarities of their social character, are not really touched by them; such ideas remain a stock of conscious convictions, but people fail to act according to them in a critical hour. An example of this is shown in the German labor movement at the time of the victory of Nazism. The vast majority of German workers before Hitler's coming into power voted for the Socialist or Communist Parties and believed in the ideas of those parties; that is, the *range* of these ideas among the working class was extremely wide. The *weight* of these ideas, however, was in no proportion to their range.[21]

And many a political ideology has languished because the social conflict that might have used it was still unborn, or perhaps, already waning. In many Latin-American countries the ideology of democracy, which presumes a stable and relatively large middle class, was only an adornment on the main structure of oligarchy in the predominantly peasant states. The ideology of political democracy was an inappropriate instrument, by itself, for the struggle of illiterate men for land reform.

C

THE CONGRUENCE THEORY APPLIED: EASTPORT AND OLD BALGAT

In a general way the propagandist recognizes the importance of fitting an idea to the culture of a target audience. In reverse, the shaping of an idea to fit a culture by those who borrow it is equally familiar. Thus Marxism became absolutistic in Russia, was absorbed into a pluralistic guild Socialism and a pacific parliamentarian Fabian Socialism in Great Britain, was employed as an element of ethnic protest, and absorbed into a diffuse concept of welfare statism in the United States, and in Asia and Africa was most serviceable as a vehicle against colonialism. Thus, also,

---

20. These are Lord Macaulay's terms. I borrowed them from Daniel Lerner's reference in his *The Passing of Traditional Society* (New York: The Free Press of Glencoe, 1958), p. 152.

21. Fromm, *op. cit.*, p. 280.

in the adaptation of Western political liberalism to the cultures of the East, where status becomes "face," a merit system is confronted with a kinship system, the doctrine of representation is merged with a doctrine of paternal custodianship, and majority rule may emerge as a search for an undivided consensus. Here we seek to explicate and illuminate this problem by confronting Marxism with the demands of the Eastport mind. In order to see this in a larger perspective, with some license we place this next to the problems of Western liberalism in Old Balgat, a Turkish village symbolizing the "passing of traditional society."

Eastport

Eastport has had a small indigenous Socialist party for many years; there is an even smaller Workmen's Circle with vague Trotskyite leanings. In addition there are the remnants of a popular-front group left over from the thirties, a group coming to life in Wallace's Progressive party campaign in 1948, active on behalf of the Rosenbergs and petitioning against their execution in 1951. These Socialist groups are miniscule, unimportant, invisible to the fifteen men we interviewed. For a worldwide movement with marked success in industrial cities outside America, the failure of Marxism (either as Socialism or as Communism) in Eastport and in America requires explanation.

Most obviously, the empirical world described by the Marxists seems dissonant with the world experienced by the Eastport workingmen. Instead of immiseration, they find themselves markedly better off than their parents, their real incomes rising each year in conformity with a 58 per cent increase in median income in Eastport between 1949 and 1960. Instead of a sense of being exploited by a ruthless capitalist class, they find their relations with their employers, as mediated through foremen, marked by a kind of humanity they can understand—and return. Instead of a government operated as the executive committee of the ruling class, they find a local government responsive to their housing, educational, and civic needs. It is a government to which they have access and over which they have a little leverage through relatives and friends in politics.

Yet for some there are available enough ingredients for interpreting their world in a Marxist framework: there are very marked inequalities of income in Eastport; there are prejudicial barriers against Jews and Poles and Italians of which they are often aware; there is a chronic pool of unemployed into which they might fall; the recession at the time of the interviews threatened their sources of income, status, purpose; three of the four machine tenders hated their work, and one saw his employer as hard, cruel, and grasping; both local newspapers are owned by a single wealthy family and reflect that family's extremely conservative views; the tax system in Eastern State and Eastport is somewhat regressive. From such material one could construct a Marxist world. But there are other inhibitions.

The metaphysical premises of Marxism (in its classic form) are incompatible with the Eastport mind. The time dimension embraces a period that includes a long era of struggle, followed by a dictatorship of the proletariat, followed by a society working through a rather vaguely defined Socialism toward an ultimate and even vaguer Communism. But the mind of Eastport has little room for intergenerational plans or even for projects involving the distant future of a man's own lifetime. The focus is on the day after tomorrow. The spatial focus of classical Marxism is international; the reference group is an international brotherhood of workers. Eastport men are not community-centered; but, as we saw with Sullivan, their interest in the international world is likely to be a polarized one, where other countries become interesting only when they are dealing with their own country. This is something that destroys the diffuse internationalism of the Marxist; it is a highly nationalistic point of view.

The causal explanations in Marxism have no resonance with the Eastport style of explanation. The dialectic employs a time sweep outside his ken or interest; it is abstract beyond his pragmatic inclinations; it employs a conspiratorial style of thinking that is congenial to only a limited number of Eastportians. Eastport discovers the materials for explanation in the common culture, not in a working-class subculture, and not so much, relatively speaking, in private fantasy worlds projected on the environment. The common culture, naturally enough, provides conservative, individualistic materials for explanations of poverty, crime, war, and so forth. These materials are inimical to the Marxist explanations.

Eastport attributes "problems" to error, not evil; while Marx-

ism attributes evil to capitalists, bosses, plutocrats, political puppets. Eastport tends to incorporate opponents in a moral scheme;
Marxism ostracizes them from the moral world. Eastport is slow
to blame; Marxism is quick. Eastport, believing in an underlying
moral order, relies on education to adjust problems; Marxism
believes the moral order is incompatible with an exploitative
class system, and rejects the possibility of educating the exploiters.
The conscience of Eastport says "compromise," "meet a man part-
way"; the Marxist conscience argues for tactical adjustments only
within the framework of a rigidly fixed goal.

Marxism employs a conceptual framework embracing an ex-
ceptionally wide range of life, including the arts, religion, the
family, as well as politics, law, and property. But Eastport morsel-
izes its problems, prefers them piecemeal, *ad hoc,* specific. Marxism is a major-premise idea structure; Eastport prefers to assume
or elide major premises and to go instead to the "facts," the minor
premises of an argument. Marxism protects itself from challenge
by assuming the rightness of the world view it implies and by
using facts and evidence defensively, if necessary. Eastport employs
a looser ideological structure where the relationship between facts
and over-all ideologies is obscured and the challenge of facts to
ideas is muted.

Eastport has an approach orientation toward information and
an avoidance orientation toward "advice." The Marxist literature
and argument are often couched more in terms of advice than of
new information.

We did not adequately explore the values of Eastport, but
among them, implied by much that we have said, is the achievement of individual security and the relief of anxiety, won by the
individual for himself and his family. He is being tested by the system; one of the great satisfactions in life is that *he has met the tests
so far.* For this reason, as we reported in the chapter on "The Fear
of Equality," he does not want a system where this satisfaction
would be available to everyone in a way that would deprecate his
own achievement. If the Marxist goal is a world where everyone
can have freely what he has precariously earned, he is not drawn to
it.

Marxism may be thought to offer special appeals to those,
among others, who have either of two qualities: hostilities looking for legitimate targets or dependency needs served either by
absorption in the party or by attraction to the idea of a society

marked by secure jobs and a nurturant state.[22] (Of course it has other appeals as well: it promises a more "orderly" managed system; it has strong underdog appeals; it suggests a way of imposing a higher culture on "the masses"; it promises to reorder the status system to correspond to "social contribution"; it suggests an elimination of competitive wastes, and so on.) But most of the men of Eastport do not harbor strong unattached hostile feelings, and those who do either find personal targets or choose social pariahs (Communists, gangsters) rather than established authorities. The men of Eastport with dependency needs either fought against them in a struggle for repression (Rapuano) or found a niche in the industrial system (Dempsey). The last thing Dempsey would have thought of would be a solution transcending the conventional order.

Marxism implies a strong social identity rooted in a working-class group. It anticipates, and helps to form, a proletarian subculture with values, morals, codes of behavior that a person acquires by virtue of his social identification. The strong personal identity combined with the diffuse social identity of the Eastport common man is exactly the reverse of this. The Eastport man gets almost no guidance from his class membership, no sense of brotherhood, no common goals or shared purposes. Marxist appeals to him as a member of a working class fall on deaf ears.

The inevitability of social conflict is central to Marxism. At the very core of the ideology is the notion of class conflict; indeed, this is the mechanism through which the promised perfect society is to be gained. But Eastport believes there is a general public interest that, once understood, will be grasped and agreed to by everyone. Social conflict, then, is a product of misunderstanding. Moreover, as a personal style as well as a social goal, compromise, adjustment, obscuring of differences are much preferred to open conflict. Eastport is busy concealing such sources of conflict as religion, class, and national origin, for the comity of day-to-day community life is dependent upon this patchwork. Eastport would need to reverse this busy half-conscious daily effort to accommodate a scheme that placed social conflict at the center of things.

The "selection" of an ideology, or of bits and pieces of an ideology, or of an opinion, is, of course, dependent upon how useful it is to a man or group. But, as we have tried to show, this

---

22. See, for example, Herbert Krugman, "The Role of Hostility in the Appeal of Communism in the United States," *Psychiatry*, 16 (1953), pp. 253–261.

selection is a matter of matching and fitting and searching for congruences with the experience and premises and personal qualities and ongoing social conflicts of a society.

Notes on Old Balgat [23]

If there is a lack of congruence between Marxism and the Eastport mental set, the lack of congruence between Western liberal democratic ideology and the mental set of the Asian or African or Latin-American traditionalist is even greater. The difference between these situations is that Western liberalism offers an increasingly better fit for the experiences associated with an urban industrial system now nascent in some of these areas, whereas Marxism has a currently deteriorated capacity to interpret the American experience realistically. But the problems of ideological congruence and resistance have several parallels. To show the adaptability of the general model, we may list them briefly:

WESTERN LIBERALISM	TRADITIONALIST THOUGHT AND EXPERIENCE
Experience	
The government is interested in your opinions.	Since time immemorial "they" have been indifferent to my opinions. "They" are part of a natural order over which I have no control.
There are rewards for ambition, for participation, for assertion.	Rewards come from obedience, loyalty to the chief, acceptance.
Mild heterodoxy is tolerable; if proved "correct" it is rewarded.	Orthodoxy is rewarded; deviance is punished.
The world is characterized by potential abundance.	The world is characterized by degrees of scarcity.

23. The analysis below is loosely drawn from Lerner's brilliant portrait in *The Passing of Traditional Society*. I have interpolated, added something from the general literature on folk societies, and somewhat altered the focus to embrace items in my general scheme. Mr. Lerner should not be held responsible for what I say here.

| WESTERN LIBERALISM | TRADITIONALIST THOUGHT AND EXPERIENCE |

Cultural Premises

(a) Metaphysics

Time is specific, pressing; the present is to be exploited in the interest of the future.	Time is vague (no calendars or clocks—rather seasons and sun time); the present is of interest for what it offers now.
The primary focus of political attention is the nation-state; There are broad spatial horizons.	The primary focus of attention is the village; there are more limited spatial horizons.
Nature is manipulable by man, even by common men; specific causes can be discovered and changed.	Nature is an extension of God's will, which is inscrutable; it is blasphemy to challenge it or try to manipulate it.

(b) Ethics

Morality focuses upon controlling appetites in favor of others.	Morality focuses upon honor, chivalry, and other ways of protecting one's own reputation.
Moral behavior includes impersonal treatment of others as customers, competitors, employees; separating person from role.	Moral behavior is personalized, specific to the individual.

(c) Epistemology

Curiosity is encouraged; the critical appraisal of "authoritative" knowledge is sanctioned.	Curiosity is discouraged; "it was ever thus" is considered an answer to inquiry; critical appraisal of authoritative knowledge may be blasphemous.
The boundaries of knowledge are flexible and may be pushed back.	The boundaries of knowledge are fixed; what should be known is already known.

| | TRADITIONALIST THOUGHT |
| WESTERN LIBERALISM | AND EXPERIENCE |

(d) Life values

The goal of life is "success," that is, increased income or social rank.	The goal of life is virtue, that is, a reputation for conventional moral conduct in one's established place.
One should aim for mastery over nature and people.	One should aim for accommodation to nature and people.
The rewards of life may be material and enjoyed in themselves.	The rewards of life lie in following the will of God (Allah) and achieving favor in his eyes.

Personal Qualities

A strong ego capable of long, purposeful, independent activity.	Strong superego emphasizing caution and denial.
Empathic capacities to permit wide, vicarious living.	Constricted empathy, narrowly circumscribed imagination.
Expansive, open style of interpersonal relations.	Limited trust in outsiders; cautious defensive personal style.

Social Conflict

Conflicts based on struggle for material values.	Conflicts based on ideal or religious values.
Atomized conflict (competition).	Little atomized conflict.
Idealization of nonviolent (verbal) conflict adjustment.	Idealization of war and physical courage.

It is in such a matrix as this that the Western man tries to teach the world the ideology of liberal democracy. That it can be done is proved by some successes here and there (India, the Philippines, Japan), however precarious these may be. That it is difficult, more difficult than first imagined, is now known. The failure of Marxism in Eastport and the indecisive struggle between Marxism and liberal democracy around the world suggest a careful attention not only to the experiential fit but also to the general principle of congruence outlined above.

○ ○ ○ ○ ○ ○ ○ ○ ○ ○ ○ ○ ○ ○ ○

PART THREE

The Political Consequences of an Ideology

26

Stability and Responsiveness:
The Public's Contribution

Man can act despite the fact that he thinks.
—KARL MANNHEIM, *Ideology and Utopia*, p. 129

If one cannot act effectively—one cannot think productively either.

—ERICH FROMM, *The Sane Society*, p. 191

Ideologies have consequences. The ideologies of a society shape its social and political institutions; when ideologies and institutions are more than normally out of phase, one may expect trouble. When men act without beliefs to justify and give meaning to their acts, they are coerced, confused, or moving like automatons through social routines, and, like automatons, are easily led to do something else. Here we ask: How does the ideology, the experience, the culture reflected in this study of Eastport support or inhibit the operation of the American democracy?

At an early stage of the argument presented in this book, we said that the term "politics" refers to the selection of rulers for a society and the allocation of rewards and penalties by these rulers. The political system, then, refers to the systematic organized ways in which these are done. Certain features of this system have a persistent interest for mankind: they are the features freighted with consequences for public order, for free expression, for "justice" in any of its many meanings. These features, shaped and modified by the ideology of the common man of the Eastports of America are: (1) the stability of the political system, (2) its responsiveness both to expressed pressures and to social changes, (3) the openness of the system, that is, its capacity to tolerate and use heterogeneity, and (4) the justice of the system, the evaluation of who gets what.

A

DOES THE COMMON MAN OF EASTPORT SHAPE THE POLITICAL SYSTEM?

A reading of some current literature might lead one to question the premise on which this discussion is based: Is it true that the common men of Eastport, or all the common men of all the Eastports in America, have much effect on the nature of the political system? Several lines of argument have been developed to weaken one's faith that there is, indeed, such an influence. One of these has to do with the capacities of the common man to think independently, to arrive at some conclusion of his own self-interest, to have a will of any kind. Of the voter, Fromm says, "He does something, voting, and is under the illusion that he is the creator of decisions which he accepts as if they were his own, while in reality they are largely determined by forces beyond his control and knowledge." [1] Here the individual is conceived as a passive force in the operation of the system; he affects it as a billiard ball affects the cue and cushions in a billiard game.

A second argument has to do with the atrophy of the pluralistic organizations that once formed instruments for expressing and mediating the individual's political life. Through them, through his community, his work associations, his enduring family ties, he could formulate his demands and bring influence to bear upon political elites. On many occasions in our view of Eastport we have observed the relatively ungrouped character of the common man; the fact seems clearly established. The inference William Kornhauser draws from this is that the members of these masses may tend either to withdraw from politics or, alternatively, respond in ways unguided by their own experience, without an

---

1. Erich Fromm, *The Sane Society* (New York: Rinehart, 1955), p. 151.

appropriate social filtering, with unstable and "total" behavior.[2] Under the first of these options, withdrawal, the influence of the common man upon the political system would, as in the case Fromm presents, be passive—influence through default.

A third line of argument affecting the nature of the influence of the ordinary man upon the political system he inhabits turns not so much upon the strength of that influence as upon the ideologically "thin," *ad hoc,* narrowly self-interested character of electoral responses. Campbell and his associates, examining survey data based upon a five-item "social welfare" scale and a four-item foreign-policy scale, and labeling the results "ideology," find the relationships between liberal-conservatism and electoral choice to be only moderate, and, as they argue, misleading. From the fact that the lower-income groups tended to support *lower* taxes, even though a liberal ideology would prompt them to support higher taxes and higher welfare services, these authors argue that the public is not, in fact, using an ideological structure to guide its voting decision, but rather is voting according to an immediate and unsophisticated concept of self interest. The greater "liberalism" on domestic issues of lower-income groups is an artefact of a prior and controlling concept of short-term economic advantage. This view is supported in general by the discovery that the lower-status groups and the least educated, even though they have most to gain from social change, are least in favor of it.[3] Although one might protest the use of the term "ideology" to cover such a narrow range of opinions, the important implication for the argument here is the narrowing down of the intellectual structure a citizen is said to bring to bear upon political decisions: "The pattern of responses to our domestic issues is best understood," say Campbell and his associates, "if we discard our notions of ideology and think rather in terms of primitive self-interest."[4] Again the notion of an unstructured mind, responding, if at all, to a quick calculation on an immediate political issue.

There are other reasons for wondering if the citizen has much independent influence upon the political system. Schumpeter and Dahl have shown how the calculations individuals make with respect to the political choices that confront them may not at all

2. William Kornhauser, *The Politics of Mass Society* (New York: The Free Press of Glencoe, 1959), pp. 43–51.

3. Angus A. Campbell, Philip E. Converse, Warren E. Miller, Donald E. Stokes, *The American Voter* (New York: Wiley, 1960), pp. 188–215.

4. *Ibid.,* p. 205.

produce a social decision consonant with their desires. Whatever influence they may exercise through the electoral process may be, therefore, quite distorted.[5] Schattschneider is skeptical of the possibility of broad citizen influence within the parties; he says, "Democracy is not to be found in the parties but between the parties."[6] And these are recent authors familiar with the American scene. In another generation and on another continent Michels presents a case purporting to show the inevitability of oligarchy in political parties and social movements; Mosca argues against the possibility of sharing power in any broad sense; Pareto argues that elites may circulate but masses rarely influence them.

In short, there is reason to doubt whether the individual in Eastport or anywhere else has much influence on the political system, or, if he does, whether the influence works in the direction he intends, or, if it works in that direction, whether his intentions of the moment have anything to do with his long-run interests. Let us see. "Prior to politics," says Dahl, "beneath it, enveloping it, restricting it, conditioning it, is the underlying consensus on policy that usually exists in the society among a predominant portion of the politically active members."[7] But, if the metaphor of "levels" may be extended, beneath the consensus on policy lies the ideological structure we have explored; and beneath that the metaphysics, the moral premises, the capacities for rational explanation, the basic orientation toward self and society. (And "beneath" that, perhaps, is a characterological structure that shapes these and other matters, but we touch it gingerly, and only when necessary.)

But it is not quite self-evident how this ideological structure affects a political system, strengthening it here and weakening it there, permitting some aspects to erode from cynical comment, others to atrophy from disuse, others to explode from too great stress placed upon them. By a series of figures of speech, perhaps, it will be possible to suggest the process whereby this comes about.

As a *communications network*, the Eastport men transmit news, evaluations, demands from one to another and to the out-

5. Joseph A. Schumpeter, *Capitalism, Socialism and Democracy* (London: Allen & Unwin, 1950), pp. 252–256; Robert A. Dahl, *A Preface to Democratic Theory* (Chicago: University of Chicago Press, 1956).

6. Elmer E. Schattschneider, *Party Government* (New York: Rinehart, 1942), p. 60.

7. Dahl, *op. cit.*, p. 132.

side world in a highly selective way. O'Hara says that when something happens in the news, they start "hollering" about it down at the shop. But they "holler" within the framework we have explored: they complain that Eisenhower is out playing golf and not that Eisenhower is a tool of "the interests"; they say that Faubus should be put in jail and not that the "niggers" should be put in their place. (There are Negroes where O'Hara works.) As a communications network, among themselves they screen, filter, exaggerate; they level and sharpen—as rumors are leveled and sharpened.[8] And then, because O'Hara knows Croly, the Democratic boss, and because Flynn knows the mayor as an old school friend, and because Ruggiero works closely with Congressman Morelli's assistant in Eastport, their filtered and reinforced views find their ways into the political stream.

Think of Eastport as a *work community*. It is true enough that each man works upon his task more or less alone, not really aware of any synchronization between his tasks and those of his neighbors—the drill-press operator and the policeman, the bookkeeper in one plant and the maintenance man in another. But the fact is, as the 1957–1958 recession made clear, that economic tides tend to affect many of them in the same way at the same time. It is not at all the usual case for one part of this work community to be thriving while another is depressed. In suffering together, they reinforce one another's criticisms, they echo each other's solutions, and they share one another's sense of insecurity or of hope. In this they come to evolve common concepts of industrial and governmental responsibility, of what is appropriate for the individual to do, whether wives should work, whether taxes are driving industry from Eastern State, whether the Republicans should or should not be blamed. And these, arising from more basic views on the proper relationship between social classes, the proper role of government, the proper way to explain a social event of this damaging character, go into the communications network and filter into the political stream as we have indicated.

Eastport is a *neighborhood* as well as a work community; men have common interests in redevelopment, in police protection, in desegregation policies as these are applied where they live, in roads and schools and playgrounds. They do talk about these things and bring to bear their value schemes, their short-run time

8. See Gordon W. Allport and Leo Postman, "An Analysis of Rumor," *Public Opinion Quarterly*, 10 (1946–1947), pp. 501–517.

sense, their "rootedness," their faith or lack of faith in "politicians," upon the current issues. Sullivan tries to get the school parking lot made into an ice-skating rink in winter, and becomes embittered when he fails. He was not prepared for defeat, and, embittered, he speaks corrosively of politics and politicians. Ferrera gets a hole in the street fixed by photographing it and sending the picture to the Eastport *News;* Johnson organizes a protest about the poor heating in Hilltop. Is this only self-interest? Perhaps, but the term does not explain why they do not, as in Sicily or the smaller towns around Naples, shrug their shoulders over the needed street repair and pass by on the other side; or why they seek recreation facilities rather than a monument to a patron saint to guard their highway, as in Mexico; or why they do not merely talk endlessly about the situation in cafés and bars, as in prerevolutionary Russia; or why they do not frame their explanations in terms of the corruption of officials, the domination of the "interests," the leprechauns and gremlins on the highways; or why they do not wait quietly until the "headman" of Hilltop sees fit to take action.

Eastport is an *audience* and, like every other audience, has a balloting function. When Kuchinsky buys *Confidential* he votes for the continuation and extension of this jaundiced interpretation of the world. Rapuano's muttered comments about the loss of "Cheyenne" on television in favor of some political broadcast gets into a Hooper rating or a Crosley rating or an advertising survey in one way or another. Dempsey interprets the Russian missile achievements through the portrayal in "Captain Easy," a comic feature of the Eastport *Star;* his devotion to this comic increases the circulation of the morning paper, which is more liberal than the *News,* an evening paper. Informing and guiding this balloting is a set of predispositions, capacities, interests shared by these men. If they had a blame orientation they would subscribe more often to *Confidential;* if they had a *Weltanschuaung* in which political decisions played a more prominent role they would prefer political feeder material rather than "Cheyenne" on television; if they read the papers for their news instead of their features, the circulation of the *Star* and the *News* might show marginal changes.

Eastport is a *nominating committee* and a *canvassing organization.* On the Hilltop Council, Flynn, as its secretary, emerges to prominence, becomes the spokesman in a rent-rise protest, finds the mayor easy to see, has the stature where a political career waits only upon his decision. So far he has resisted it; the new Hilltop secretary may not. O'Hara and others see "Boss" Croly in church almost every Sunday; they stop and talk to him on the steps, mentioning names, grievances, suggestions. Croly has for years controlled nominations in Eastport. On the steps of the church he is forming an opinion on who shall rule (under him) in Eastport. Joseph Laudano is a former mayor of Eastport. He asked Rapuano, whose aunt was buried by Laudano's funeral home, if he would canvass for him in a municipal election. Rapuano did it, although he disliked it. Into this work, on the doorsteps, he poured some of the corrosive skepticism, self-doubt, intense patriotism, ethnic-Italian repudiation, and bitterness toward doctors that illuminate his social outlook. It all came out as he spoke to men and women on behalf of Laudano, his candidate half forgotten in the churning ideological world Rapuano inhabits. Ferrera, too, has done canvassing for the Republican party. In a bitter mood he broke with them because they failed to recognize his importance, treated him, as he says, like a "peon." The two canvassers, then, both Republicans at the time, were, in fact, the politically alienated men; they are cabalists, they are undemocrats. They are lower-middle-class Republicans in a Democratic milieu. And they carry with them, as they go from door to door, their world view of anxiety and doom.

As an *electorate* Eastport common men make their ideologies felt, modifying the political system more directly. Ruggiero is one of the most active political men; he represents the post office to Congressman Morelli; he drives voters to the polls for Morelli; they are "very close friends." He has just moved from Hilltop to a suburb where the Republicans usually win; if he had moved to a more industrial suburb, he says he would have become a Democrat. He is balloting this way for a political system reflecting a most fluid partisanship. Move him back to Naples: would he then vote Communist in one neighborhood, Christian Democrat in another? It is not likely. He is a product of a political culture, but because he is extreme in both his participation and his fluid loyalties, he moves the system marginally in this nonpartisan direction. Most of the men admired McCarthy; they could not vote for him, but they could vote for one of his Senate supporters and against a man who made an issue of McCarthyism. The undertone of resistance to extended foreign aid in a recession period exercised a restraint on the enthusiasm of the local congressman for foreign aid, something he believed in. In the mayoralty elections the Italians tended to vote for Laudano, the Irish for Donovan— but the Italians were drifting over into Donovan's camp. Their assimilationist doctrines associated with their social-identity diffusion, their capacity to "hear" and use arguments from opponents, their low ideological bluntness, their pragmatic "minor premise" style of thought, their incorporation of their opponents in a moral order all made this shift possible.

In the sense used in the biology laboratories, Eastport is a *culture medium* in which the organism, "politician," is nurtured and matured. Just as it is not a unanimous electorate or nominating committee, so it is a nonhomogeneous culture medium; it grows many varieties, but they have much in common. Sullivan could get elected to the Hilltop Council because he has qualities of leadership among men, but he probably can not go much further because he could not tolerate the frustration of initial defeats in his negotiation with the School Board for school recreation facilities; he earned the reputation for being a "sorehead." Ferrera has his eye on the main chance, but his wounded narcissism led him to repudiate the Republican party, and to switch, perhaps temporarily, to the Democrats, something the Republicans may not easily forgive. Moreover, his "lack of respect" for the Irish may easily find expression in some unfortunate quotable statement, and his political future would then be somber indeed. Flynn and Ruggiero might easily move into political positions. With their positions in the plexuses of communication, they hear the common views about the rich and poor, the corrupt and honest, the national and local, the thrifty and spendthrift, the individual and the group, the present and the future, the possible and the impossible, the customary and the curious, the morality, the metaphysics, the epistemology of the common men whose world we have sought here to explicate. That is why they can be called representative, and through them Eastport shapes the political system.

There is something, I think, to learn from this examination of the micropolitical data that does not emerge from the review of mass behavior or the study of electorates. For one thing, influence is not limited to elites: the common man generates types of influence peculiarly his own. Moreover, the electoral moment is but a brief span in the long political day; much takes place at other times and in other ways. Again, the processes of shaping a system and sharing in decisions are often so casual, so linked with other events, so much a part of nonpolitical life that they can be captured only in a view that embraces almost all social life. Finally, they are so small, these individual political acts of common men, that they can be seen only in a microscope trained upon the areas where they occur.

As we turn to the influence of ideology, and its premises, on the system, two things are apparent. First, while the ideology is at the focus of attention, the experience that "taught" the ideology, out of which it is learned, stands looming slightly out of focus in the background. We shall advert to it from time to time. And, second, it would be a rare ideological component that affected only one part of the system; but to avoid repetition we speak chiefly of the areas where each component is conceived to have its dominant effect.

B

THE STABILITY OF A POLITICAL SYSTEM

In a general way everyone knows what an unstable political system is like: the Central American governments are unstable, the new governments of the Near East are unstable, and in a somewhat different sense the Third Republic in France was unstable. The term seems to refer to political systems characterized by changes of regimes unauthorized by the Constitution, or by such rapid changes in the executive power, the "government," that continuity of policy is difficult if not impossible. To this we might add (as Lipset has done) [9] the chronic threat by some important social group to the constitutional order. The history of the United States reveals very few situations, only one serious one, that might lead one to conclude we had an unstable political system, but at various times and places municipal and even state political systems have shown signs of such instability, and in many other places the dispositions of the public that produce such instability have become apparent. But, in the main, our problem faces in the other direction. The United States has the oldest written constitution, and it could be argued that it has the record in modern times for the greatest longevity of any regime. Why should this be?

9. Seymour M. Lipset, *Political Man* (Garden City, N.Y.: Doubleday, 1960), pp. 48–49.

There are a number of ways a public may become politically organized, or at least disposed, that encourage political instability. One of them is *polarization,* a situation where the public divides its support between two partisan groups, widely separated in purpose and program, viewing each other with fear and hostility. A second public disposition is, in a sense, the reverse of this, the *fragmentation* of public support, the creation of many mutually irreconcilable groups unable to coalesce into a governing majority. The third is *withdrawal of support,* where some group retires into apathy generated by a frustrated sense that nothing can be done about a government they believe to be illegitimate. And, finally, the fourth disposition of the public producing an unstable government is a *discontinuity of support,* a mood swing, as Almond says,[10] that offers ephemeral support now for one group, now another.

Polarization

It has been said that the American public does not polarize, as the Italian public tends to do, because at the nation's founding it had already arrived at a consensus based on John Locke and his philosophy, because class conflict was discouraged by the availability of free land, because it had no remnant of a feudal aristocracy to produce an intransigent left, and for other reasons.[11] Whatever the social structure and history contributing to this result, there are present in Eastport today strong ideological themes that discourage polarization. Some of these have to do with the unmoralistic character of the average American. Being slow to blame, he is not easily persuaded that differences with another group are irreconcilable. The low-tension moral code makes *rapprochement* possible, indeed, necessary, and such polarizing gap as there may be tends to close. It tends to close, moreover, because there is a positive search for neutral and central ground undertaken whenever differences appear. Riesman calls it "other-directedness";[12] "adjustment" was once a favorable term, but now it is soiled; we saw it at work in the argument three of the men were having over the worth of unions and we saw each of them try to

10. Gabriel Almond, *The American People and Foreign Policy* (New York: Harcourt, Brace, 1950), pp. 75–76.

11. See Daniel J. Boorstin, *The Genius of American Politics* (Chicago: University of Chicago Press, 1953); and Louis Hartz, *The Liberal Tradition in America* (New York: Harcourt, Brace, 1955).

12. David Riesman, *The Lonely Crowd* (New Haven: Yale University Press, 1950), pp. 17–25.

accommodate to the others' positions. And this, in turn, creates and is reinforced by a more general fear of partisanship.

Polarization in the United States might follow religious lines in some communities—a Catholic party and a Protestant party. It is inhibited from developing in this way because of the assimilationist, mobilist doctrines and their product: social-identity diffusion. In the same way class polarization is inhibited by the same ungrouped character of the public, the same diffuse sense of social identity. But the polarization of class groups is further discouraged by what we have called the fear of equality and by the acceptance by the common man of Eastport of his responsibility for his own destiny within the framework of law and support offered by a generous state. In short, the Eastport mental set is simply not conducive to a polarized political disposition.

Fragmentation

Splinter parties, unable to find a home in the great aggregating parties of normal American politics, have had short and miserable lives in this country. Why? Of course, the centripetal tendencies of the institution of the Presidency and the single-member constituencies make a contribution; the separation of church and state tends to remove one of the main grounds for intransigent small parties to develop; the nationalizing forces of the media tend to put a national stamp upon local politics; the flexible nature of the main parties, the wide distribution of property, also help to explain this phenomenon. But in Eastport, the mental set resists the fragmented parties for other reasons. Fragment parties are often anomic and destructive, on the one hand, or utopian and chiliastic on the other. But in Eastport neither of these dispositions has much support.

The anomic destructive party fails of support because, although there are a few cabalists in Eastport with a conspiratorial view of the world congenial to anomic parties, there are not many and they do not agree on the nature of the conspiracies they see. There are only three "undemocrats"; the faith in the democratic processes available to the common man is strong; the trust in the solicitude of government for the common man's welfare is potent and significant. The style of the anomic party is literally hateful; but these men are slow to blame and reluctant to hate—that is, most of them are.

The utopian parties—the Socialists, social crediters, the Communists (in their earlier days), the Prohibitionists, and others—strike no fire because there is no utopian mental set into which their pleas may fall. There is no distant future, no room for such a time as that in the crowded chronology of present and immediate tomorrow. Utopian parties are major-premise parties—they derive their strength from the generalizations they embody; aggregative parties are minor-premise parties—they derive their strength from their comprehension of immediate facts. As we said, the Eastport style is a minor-premise style. The morselization of problems defeats the fragmentation of parties.

Not all fragmentary parties are anomic or utopian; some are local, as were the Dixiecrats, the Wisconsin Progressives, the Farmer-Labor Party of Minnesota, or the Nonpartisan League of the Dakotas. But the nationalization of interests, the failure of localism, the weakness of rootedness work against these local interests. Moreover, the very social-identity diffusion remarked upon above weakens this local party. The White Southern Protestant may find a social identity for a time that makes the Dixiecrat Party congenial, but there are not many such cases. The Jewish metropolitan ghetto gave men a social identity that could sustain a cohesive Marxist party for a while, but then assimilationism, economic differences, intra-Jewish religious differences, and the movement to suburbs tended to dilute this identity and to destroy the Marxist parties. The Boston Irish for a time evolved a social identity based upon a homogeneous religious and ethnic community and supporting a special brand of Democratic party, but this too dissolved when the social identity became too diffuse for political purposes.

Withdrawal of Support

The apathetic man who withdraws his interest and emotional commitment from political life has been the source of much concern; he is central to Fromm's worried outlook, he haunts Kornhauser, and he is a feature of Mills' recent work; Kris and Leites speak of a tendency to "privatize" life under political pressure from dictatorship and democracy.[13] In Eastport there are those who feel that the burden of the "many tiny messages" and the

13. Erich Fromm, *op. cit.*; William Kornhauser, *op. cit.*; C. Wright Mills, *The Power Elite* (New York: Oxford, 1959); Ernst Kris and Nathan Leites, "Trends in Twentieth Century Propaganda," in Géza Róheim, ed., *Psychoanalysis and the Social Sciences* (New York: International Universities Press, 1947), pp. 393–410.

endless obligations is almost greater than they can bear. But there
are ideological forces working against this withdrawal solution.
For one thing, there is the very posture toward nature and society adopted by these men (with the exception of Dempsey); as
we said, being Western and being American, they seek to command nature, to make events do their bidding. Their language,
their moral codes, their role interpretations, their metaphysics
strengthen this posture. Only two men are political alienates, and
they do not embrace the portion of the alienated philosophy that
says that politics is all controlled or out of reach—they are or have
been active doorbell ringers. The source of their pathology is not
in personal alienation but in homelessness, which does not lead
men away from society; it makes them seek closer, more intimate,
more intense relationships.

Withdrawal tendencies have nowhere to go. They cannot escape into fantasy because that is a poor and unpromising region
for most of the men; certainly Utopia is ill furnished. They cannot escape in a projective cloud where they say, "It is not I; it is
you or him or the devil," because they have more or less committed themselves to accept responsibility for their own destinies,
at least until the pressure becomes too great to bear. Their cognitive styles, their ways of handling uncertainty in the face of a request for information, are not escapist; their little excusing devices tend to keep them in the field of discourse, not to encourage
a diversion. By and large they do not rely upon "vital lies" for
their faith in social processes—except, perhaps, for their exaggerated faith that great rewards are the fruit of great merit and their
confidence that "the people run things." And, not being dependent on many such vital lies, and aware of the defects of democratic
processes, they are not likely to be driven into withdrawal after
some disillusioning revelation.

I have found their realism generally impressive; they are positioned securely in the here and now; their discourse bore upon
the questions, and they could return to it after interruption—at
least most could. Asked to explain remote matters, they could
weave together a story embodying both personal and impersonal
agents of change.

And, of course, since they are experienced with democratic
processes, they know a little about how to make them work. They
have a tolerance for confusion and delay (most of them do, that
is), and, most important, they have a trust in government and

feel that, in the end, it is *their* welfare that is the criterion for policy. Why, then, withdraw?

Discontinuity of Support

In the phasing of their lives, these men experience a kind of continuity whereby each stage arises naturally from the one preceding it, each prepares for the next. Except for the war—a big exception for one or two—they have not been jerked about; the Great Depression of the thirties is a childhood memory for most. All but three were born and brought up in the Eastport vicinity; most of them have their families within visiting distance. As a consequence they have developed a habit of outlook that can only be called incrementalist, continuity-minded, phased. In the terms used earlier, we may say that although the pace of their lives is difficult, the rhythm of their lives is relatively smooth and synchronized, and their thoughts follow this pattern. Their political thoughts do not include the magical leap, the transformation, the touchstone policy that will transform the dross of recession into the gold of prosperity.

Most of these men have the kind of control over their impulse life that permits them to drink in moderation, to keep their debts within limits, to get angry but not *too* angry. These are the very things they worry about most (and a surprising number have given up liquor entirely), but while the internal evidence is one of uncertainty, the evidence from the pattern of their lives is one of sobriety and control. This is relevant to the continuity of political life, the assurance of relatively enduring support— enough to give a man or an administration a fair trial. It is a pattern of behavior that indicates generalized strength, control, direction—such a quality as is included in our measures of ego strength.

One of the most usual sources of discontinuity of political support is the personalization of politics. In discontinuous political behavior, men do not so much tire of a party, or become infatuated with a new policy or program, as they switch loyalties to a new hero on the scene. Those who really "vote for the man" (and most "really" find that the "man" is their party's candidate) are likely to contribute to the volatility of political life. It is therefore important to note that while these men of Eastport allege great independence, and some indeed say that they always vote for the best man regardless of party, they nevertheless have developed a metaphysics, an epistemology, and an ethics that undercut their position. Their religion has tended to become more theistic; tolerance has depersonalized God. Their explanatory system embodies a greater and greater reliance upon impersonal causes, the forces of natural agents. Their ethics is one that deemphasizes blame and seeks more to "understand" good and evil. They do not need heroes, and, not needing them, they look on political leaders as men, and not much more. Moreover, they are men with labels, and sometimes the labels are much more important than the men. By and large this labeling and lack of heroism is a stabilizing influence; it tends to encourage a continuity of support or opposition. In this way it makes more probable a pattern of political stability.

A Cloud No Bigger than a Man's Fist

The ideological support for political stability is strong; after all, what must be explained is a remarkable record of stability in the face of war, economic disaster, the expansion of the military, the following out of imperial destiny on a great continent, the industrial revolution, the tensions of race conflict breaking out into race war in some places, the assimilation of millions of men from a different tradition. It *is* a remarkable record. Nevertheless consider these facts: in Eastport the only effective, outspoken criticism to a fundamental order of things is anomic, cabalistic, destructive. *This* is the opposition prepared to "explain" matters and exercise leadership, if anything were to go wrong and crisis atmosphere to prevail. The politically alienated Rapuano and particularly the athletic Ferrera have a little political experience and some inner compulsions that might place them in the leadership of a little group of destructively idealistic men in an emergency. As against Flynn and Ruggiero, they are the counterelite.

Less remote, and more subtle, is the working out of the anxieties, the worries, the tensions with which these men must live. Will these tensions not create the kind of malaise that sustains the nihilistic patriot, the projective anti-Semite, the apostle of Armageddon now? How long can Costa continue to say of his disappointing situation, "I have only myself to blame"? How long can Johnson control his feeling that he is really cut out for something better? Can Kuchinsky believe that since McCarthy died "we have just been waiting for another fighter," and not leap up when some passing minstrel of hate strums the old tune that he loves? What keeps the anxieties and burdens of life from making service in some such cause seem to be a kind of freedom? What is the tensile strength of democracy in Eastport? Of course, no one knows; but at least it is the case that even with his ulcers Johnson finds work life and particularly home life a net gain, with a bonus of pleasure now and then. So also do the others— most of them—their work lives, their family lives, their lives in sports associations, their companionship in car pools, locker rooms, garages, ball parks, lodges, and unions, all make the pain and the worry worthwhile. And, by and large, they like themselves. Even in recession there was more than ideology; there was life satisfaction to sustain them.

C
THE RESPONSIVENESS OF A POLITICAL SYSTEM

Certainly there have been many political systems in the course of history that were stable yet unresponsive to the needs of the common man, and perhaps there have been responsive governments that proved unstable: Would the Weimar Republic so qualify? or the French Fourth Republic? or the Spanish Republic terminated by Mola and Franco and their allies? A political system is responsive, let us say, if it keeps open the channels for grievances to be heard (and permits their free expression), has effective working machinery for doing something about these grievances, and uses it to this end. Would it include the response to unexpressed grievances: public sanitation where the public did not know the source of disease? I think so. Here we shall use the term to embrace this custodial welfare function as well. In this sense responsive government is not the same as democratic government; it is effective government in the interests of the common man, such men as we talked to in Eastport.

Responsive systems require something from the public as well as from the elites, the government. Men must be able to translate their frustrations into articulate grievances and their grievances into effective demands. And they must see that their demands are placed before the right authorities in the right (most effective) way, and they must watch to see that something is done about it. Our task at the moment is to see what there is in the mind of the Eastport common man that contributes to this governmental responsiveness, or impedes it.

The Perception of a Grievance

People do not always "know" why they are unhappy and, if they really are, do not always admit it even to themselves. What is the meaning, for example, of the fact that 5 per cent of the British, 12 per cent of the Americans, and 33 per cent of the French say they are "not happy"? Is this a measure of personal alienation and anomy? If so, is it a measure of *political* alienation as well? Or is it merely a difference of national style, the alleged "hard cheerfulness" of the British underdog, the cynicism of the French? Is the American, the common man of Eastport, denying deeper feelings of incompleteness, loneliness, anxiety, depression when he insists that he is happy with himself the way things are? We cannot answer these questions other than to note that from the inner grievance to the expressed grievance can be a long way.

Yet assuming, as we have, that the men of Eastport accept themselves with more or less candor, and assuming, as we have again, that their grasp upon reality is reasonably secure, something more is needed in order for them to recognize a grievance worth mentioning. They must have a comparison, a standard; nothing is "wrong" unless there is a concept of how it might be right. And, by and large, this is exactly what Eastport does not have. It does not have a picture of a better organization of men and things in a better world, a Utopia. Nor does it have, what some nations have, a memory of a golden age, a sense of history, and a capacity to make historical comparisons. Perhaps, moreover, the European can more easily compare how his country deals with a problem with the way neighboring countries deal with similar problems. Occasionally the Eastportian manages something like this: he sees neighboring states permitting horse racing and he is seized with a sense of grievance. How different his grievance quotient might be if the neighboring states were of a different culture, competitive, and nationalistic!

Yet Eastport, like America, expects things to be better; the men expect their incomes to be better—even when they do not expect to have better jobs. They do believe in progress; and a belief in progress is a certain way to develop expectations that cannot be fulfilled, that is, grievances.

A political ideology, we said, includes a critique of the going order, a concept of a superior order, and a program for getting there. But it is in the articulated "forensic" ideology of a Marx, a Herbert Spencer or, segmentally, a Galbraith or a C. W. Mills, that these ingredients sharpen the sense of grievance, for they juxtapose what *is* with what *ought* to be. The latent ideologies of Eastport rarely bring together their inchoate goals with their diffuse dissatisfactions to make the contrast plain. Another way of saying this is that the major moral premises of a criticism, like the major premises of an explanation, are usually only implied, and the focus is upon the minor premises or the facts of the case embodied in the "current situation."

Where should this standard, this contrast come from, if not from some political ideology, or some utopian picture, or some knowledge of another period or place? Will it come from the press and television and radio? The media do not do this; they interpret their function as the reinforcement of faith in the present model and the spontaneous, *ad hoc,* informed but moderate criticism of each new situation when it becomes "critical." Nor will the Eastportian go far to look for an alternate view; his apparent belief in the parthenogenesis of his own ideas and unwillingness to seek political advice (as though being advised in such matters is like being violated in some way) will keep him close to orthodoxy. His very eagerness to belong and to believe, expressed in Costa's phrase, "It is a wonderful thing to believe, no matter what you believe—religion or politics," will keep him ignorant of an alternative standard. His trust in government and belief that legislators and governors and presidents are protecting his interests both have a quieting effect. He is not receptive to another view of life that might illuminate some aspect of his own. As noted in Russell's comment at the head of Chapter 18, "The great majority of men and women . . . seek the satisfaction of the needs of the moment, without much forethought, and without considering that by sufficient effort the whole condition of their lives could be changed." [14]

What this all adds up to is a pattern of "incremental" *ad hoc* responses to relieve the grievance experienced at the moment,

14. Bertrand Russell, *Proposed Roads to Freedom* (New York: Blue Ribbon, undated), p. vii.

and no planned effort to modify an underlying condition causing grief. The analogy with psychoneurosis comes to mind: the modification of behavior required to deal with the neurosis (the repression of the hated thoughts, the kindly act to "undo" the unkind intent) provides a kind of satisfaction, a secondary gain. To treat the underlying cause, the neurosis itself requires outside help.

From Private to Political: The Weak Bridging Functions

What is it that will translate some grievous experience into a *political* protest, a petition for the redress of grievances? One efficient translator is an ideology that relates daily events to political concepts, fitting them into a more comprehensive scheme. In Europe, the concept of the class conflict performed this service; everything that happened could be attributed to what "the capitalist bosses" wanted; every deprivation could be politicized by calling it "exploitation." In Asia and Africa, the concepts of colonialism and imperialism fulfill this function; they are so total in their embrace that every aspect of life can be politicized by the use of such magic powerful words. But Eastport has no such philosophers' stone to politicize the daily aspects of life. As we said, concepts are morselized, thought is itemized, and the political world shrinks in this conceptual style.

Any shared purpose moves men's affairs from the private toward the public; under its influence the impact of law is greater, the need for public facilities emerges, the partisan aspects become more visible to those of both parties seeking—as they should seek—for political implications. Living in a housing development partially supported with public funds, there were a few shared purposes and common causes (the elimination of a pack of dogs, the improvement of lighting across an isolated stretch, doing something about the poor heating arrangements in the first months, and most of all, protesting the high level of rental payments required); but these matters referred to so small a segment of life, engaged so modest a portion of a man's purposive capacity, and were such ephemeral stimulus responses, that they show only the gap where the common purpose might be.

Political space, we said, should be congruent with psychic space (the area of interest, friendship, knowledge) to enlist men's private motives for local political affairs. We considered this congruence to include a sense of localism, a feeling of being rooted, a genuine community identity, but then, in reviewing how things stand in Eastport, it appeared there was little localism, a rootedness arising from family ties, but nothing broader, and no genuine sense of community identity. Here, especially, a politicizing idea failed; this special kind of common purpose seems, thus, uncommon.

There are other bridges from the private to the political; they are broken bridges or only footpaths. High moral tension creates demand for something to be done about the many, very many, evils in the world. Government must act to repress, convict, censor, educate, remove the causes of evil. But Eastport has a low moral tension. The magic of a leader, his charisma, is the most potent of all attractions into politics, but Eastport appraises its leaders soberly. A hated enemy, a class enemy or a racial enemy or a nameless "enemy within the gates," will do it; but Eastport in its present mood has relatively few hatreds of this nature—none of them class hatreds. As we noted, each man in Eastport tends to accept responsibility for himself; he expects others to do the same. A wider sense that he bore some responsibility for others would make political life more nearly necessary—but this is probably never very strong, and in Eastport it is quite weak. In short, the bridges from the private to the political offered by great politicizing concepts, shared purposes, community identification, moral goals, ancient enmities, magic leaders are all fragile things, hardly used by the people of Eastport.

Government: A Ready and Familiar Instrument

If the motive is missing, the instrument is there and trusted. Eastport believes that political action is an appropriate and useful vehicle for getting something done. It believes that politicians are receptive to advice and counsel, give people friendly receptions and listen attentively to what they say, and respond as though their jobs depended upon keeping the petitioners happy. They have faith that their welfare is the criterion for most policy and that in this sense the people rule. Moreover, as we pointed out in a discussion of "the mind of the new collectivism," Eastport men vest in the government all powers necessary to achieve its ends; they assign it responsibility for seeing that things go right in America and the world; and, because they believe in the idea of a "public interest," they remove from sight any evidence of a long-continuing, sometimes bitter, chronic conflict of opinion about the proper ends to be pursued. If our political system is not responsive, it is not because men from Eastport and others like them repudiate the legitimacy, the effectiveness, the solicitude, or the appropriateness of working through government to relieve their grievances. Any cynicism that appears here in quick cliché form is denied by the premises of thought and action revealed in more extended discussion.

From Grievance to Proposal: A Modest Rationality

Is the thing asked for from the government relevant to the grievance? O'Hara thought that the reinstatement of the excess-profits tax would induce his firm to hire more people (their net cost in profit reduction would be less); many thought that government-run or -taxed horse racing would provide ample new funds for education and roads. Johnson thought that if the government would only bring the Negro and white together, they could persuade the Negroes not to demand so much integration. In each case there is a certain plausibility to the argument; they are not wildly irrational; they do not seem to embody a heavy proportion of projective thought. (Although Johnson's hopes would certainly be frustrated, as a delaying action his scheme might work.) Much has been written about politics as the area where the irrational is most vividly expressed, as though political demands were *only* thinly disguised and rationalized projections of private motives. They sometimes are that; we have seen how three men found explanations of war and poverty in the inner struggles of their own personalities, with only slight reference to the evidence of the outer world. But they are rarely only that in Eastport's political world. Eastport men use personal and impersonal explanatory material with discrimination; they do not scapegoat or seek a dependent status with a great leader; they keep their comments close to their own experience (sometimes too much so); they can manage to control their impulse life and even to sense some mastery over their environment. It is not that they are ready to be fitted into a rational model; they are not economic man in the political arena; but they have the equipment and the habits and the strengths to make grievance and remedy link together in a plausible causal chain.

27

Public Resources for
Liberty and Justice

They are, so to speak, driven by the combined force of their training and their environment towards the social average, and the
outstanding result is the difficulty with which they encounter
non-conformity or scepticism in any area where they meet it.
They go out into the world with a set of stereotypes which little
save an earthquake can persuade them to examine critically.
—HAROLD LASKI, *The American Democracy,* p. 341

If, in an interrelated way, the public resources for maintaining a stable political system are substantial, but the resources
for making it responsive to grievances much more modest, what can
we say of the public contribution to those other enduring goals,
liberty and justice? After all, we have been promised a nation
"with liberty and justice for all." What resources does the public
have to help fulfill this promise?

A

KEEPING THE SYSTEM OPEN

An open political system, like an open society, is one that
allows or even encourages heterodox views to be expressed. It
does not close at the source the critical opinions that go beyond

the conventional beliefs, challenge the moral norms, ridicule the established authorities, or suggest an organization of property, sex life, or religious practice different from that which prevails. Of course, it is a matter of degree; no political system tolerates unlimited expression, and in moments of crisis almost all will greatly narrow the range of challenges allowed. Authority is tempted to exaggerate the danger of criticism of itself and of the laws it must enforce; democracies ask of their leaders some self-restraint and organized protection of the individuals who present these challenges. But in addition to the self-restraint of authority and the organized protection of the courts, an open system requires popular support. It is the contribution that the public makes to the openness of the system that interests us here; and, the reverse of this, the sources of popular resistance to free and open expression.

Ideological Support for Civil Liberties

One might search in vain in the streets of Eastport for men familiar with the provisions of the Constitution protecting freedom of speech, freedom of assembly, freedom to petition for the redress of grievances. There is little knowledge of the rudiments of due process; the phrase "a government of laws and not of men" produces a blank stare; men willing to sacrifice for the rights of Communists for a fair trial, or atheists for a fair hearing, or those allied with them for a fair judgment, would be hard to find (though there are a very few). In short, the defense of any philosophical notion of freedom or of any abstract plan of freedom is, if present, an unreliable shelter for the open system; and when the implications of generalized advocacy for the Bill of Rights is shown to mean even a limited tolerance of Communists and atheists, this modest defense seems to fall away.

This does not mean the men fail to see the merits of wide latitude of expression and the tolerance of a diversity of views. As we observed in Chapter 4, most of the men valued having conflicting opinions from which to choose; they understand how one opinion can correct another; how self-interest can distort the truth, and how hard it is to judge expertise. But in this they were referring to relatively unmoralized topics; their defenses were, typically, based on the utility of diversity in achieving some commonly agreed-upon goal, not speculation on the foundations of our society. In this latter area, there is little support for the open society governed by an open political system.

The Defense of Preferred Styles of Expression

The most frequently defended freedom in Eastport is freedom of religion. ("I can go to any church I want to"; "I can bring up my children in any religion I want to.") As Catholics, for the most part, these men felt a slight jeopardy to their religious rights, not that they feared some government restriction here but that they feared a challenge to the respect and status associated with being a Catholic. Any challenge or even any criticism of their religious practices would raise a storm, for here is a kind of free expression that applies directly to something they want to do. If this is contrasted to their views on freedom of expression for political heretics, a vast difference is readily apparent. They have not the slightest inclination to say anything heretical, dangerous, subversive, or Communistic, or to challenge the Constitution, or show disrespect to the Founding Fathers. Defense of any right to do this, for such conventional men as these, must rely upon other motives, a more roundabout view of their interests, a cathected ideology of freedom. But this is exactly what they do not have.

Yet sometimes there is a kind of limited generalizing effect to be observed in the defense of any one right: its defenders protect other, similar rights. This seems to be limited to rights of a parallel nature: thus the Italian-Americans were sympathetic to the rights of Negroes because they knew what it was like to be called a "wop," but they have no interest in defending political deviants. Catholics protect the religious rights of Jews on the zoning of religious structures and similar matters; and the Republican who works in an almost all-Democratic shop (DeAngelo) strongly defends the general right of people to be respected for their independent views in a conversational group.

Anomic Release

War, revolution, social upheaval break the chains that bind men to their daily lives. One study in New England showed that men who did not like their jobs and were frustrated in their private lives were more likely than others to want war with

Russia now. The author called this the "Armageddon complex." [1] Hadley Cantril found that many of the people who believed that a broadcast of an adaptation of H. G. Wells' *The War of the Worlds* actually was the report of a Martian invasion wanted to believe this because such an invasion would relieve them of the intolerable pressures and irritations of their lives. [2] In the same way, in Eastport, it is the man (Rapuano) who says of his work, "I don't like my job, period; and it's a terrible thing to have to work at a job you don't like, believe me," who also believes that there is a major immediate menacing Communist conspiracy in this country. And it is the man who has spent a year of bankruptcy, unemployment, and depression (Ferrera) who sees the future of democracy in America as a very risky thing. These are the political alienates; one senses that a revolution (from the right), an embracing social movement (of a patriotic nature) ready to constrict popular freedom, would relieve them of the burdensome obligations of their lives, for then they could engage in a legitimate and somewhat destructive—as well as idealistic— diversion. Being unguided by a set of positive regulatory values, this behavior might be termed anomic release.

Yet in a summary of Eastport's resources for freedom, the obverse of this should be stressed: most of the men had no need for such anomic release because they found their lives generally satisfying.

The Need to Test Authority

Those who distrust authority and make scurrilous remarks about government tend to invoke this very authority and government to repress others. It is a kind of paradox. Among many causes for this behavior, one is the desire to test whether or not the distrusted authorities are really "on my side." They can prove it by being against "my enemies." It is a test that has a double satisfaction—if the government acts to repress the Communists, "pinkos," atheists, or alien agitators, the alienated citizen "wins" in participating in the desired repression. If the government tolerates the despised groups, the alienated citizen "wins" in having proved that his distrust was justified. For Rapuano, the despised

1. Maurice L. Farber, "The Armageddon Complex: Dynamics of Opinion," *Public Opinion Quarterly*, 15 (1951), 217-214.
2. Hadley Cantril, *The Invasion from Mars* (Princeton: Princeton University Press, 1940).

groups are the Communists and their fellow travelers; for Ferrera the despised groups are the moral degenerates, racketeers, and other undercover groups.

But Eastport generally trusts authority and government; it does not need to test the government to see whether or not it really is for people like themselves. That is assumed.

Ideological Density and Room for Deviance

If one thinks of psychic space much as Lewin thought of "life space," an enclosure occupied by a play of forces against ideas, one can conceive of a tightly organized, high-density, closely articulated structure filling this area—or of its opposite. A well thought-out "completed" ideology, with the connective links between one area of thought and another pushed through and bolted down, anchored to absolute values, would fill this psychic space with a rigid structure. The metaphor this figure describes would be illustrated by a Marxist philosophy, a Jesuit's outlook, a Benthamite–Adam Smith liberalism, or any other of the current world views. They have a "position" on most issues; in that sense the space is dense with ideas. They establish logical connections between one idea and the other making for coherence and consistency; in that sense they are closely articulated. They imply a set of moral premises; in that sense they are anchored to absolute values—or so it seems to their advocates. For all these reasons they exclude conflicting views; they make the recognition of deviance easier and its acceptance harder. It seems to challenge all that is beautiful, true, and holy.

But in the psychic space of the men of Eastport there is only a loosely articulated structure, with the interconnections between one area, say, the working of representative institutions, and another area, say, the power of big business, hardly ever pushed through to completion. In this space there are many positions "unoccupied." (Whom does the political boss represent? Is there a Christian stake in politics?) Consequently, one is not sure which positions are deviant, or, even being sure of this, one hardly knows what inference to draw from the challenge presented. In any event, because of the vague relationship of political positions to fundamental values, the challenge seems less destructive than would otherwise be the case. Although there are other reasons, this low-density, loosely articulated ideology helps to account for the tolerance of the confusion and delay of a legislature and for the low level of partisanship and the high blame threshold we have found in Eastport.

Congruence of Pathologies

One of the implications of the most impressive study of anti-democratic, anti-open-society strains in the American public, *The Authoritarian Personality,* was that there was only one important personality-attitude threat to democracy. The correspondence between such pathologies as ethnocentrism and authoritarianism was stressed in this formidable work. But, with a different kind of evidence at hand, we would stress both the congruence and the lack of congruence among a variety of social pathologies. Selecting the three "highs," we find them distributed among the various pathologies as shown in Table VI.

TABLE VI

Anomy	*Authoritarianism*	*Low Faith in People*
Johnson	DeAngelo	Ferrera
Sokolsky	Costa	O'Hara
Sullivan *	Ferrera	Kuchinsky

Political Ignorance	*Cabalists*	*Fear of Freedom*
Dempsey	Sokolsky	Sokolsky
Woodside	Rapuano	Rapuano
DeAngelo	Kuchinsky	Johnson
	Ferrera	

Undemocrats	*Political Alienates and "Homeless" Men*	*Sense of Political Futility*
Kuchinsky	Ferrera	Sullivan
Rapuano	Rapuano	tie { Costa, Kuchinsky, Dempsey
Ferrera		

* There is a large break between the second and third rank; hence, the third-ranking man, Sullivan, should be regarded as belonging to a different group.

The congruence is evident in the frequency with which Ferrera, Rapuano, Kuchinsky, and Sokolsky appear upon the list. But there are others who share one or two symptoms of tendencies that detract from the strong and effective working of an open political system but whose net contribution is positive.[3]

One of the reasons for the weakness of the challenge from the extreme right (or the extreme left), and particularly from the nativist agitators, has been their inability to combine their forces. Each must define his malaise and seek his support without compromise or sharing of audiences, funds, or media. One of the reasons for this is the nature of the extremists themselves; but another may be that the sources of malaise differ, one basing it upon anomic appeals, another upon his authoritarianism, a third upon his fear of free-impulse life, a fourth upon a sense of political futility. If it must have social pathologies, an open society profits from having these diversified in the needs that they feed upon and the ideologies that they find congenial.

Intensity of Interpersonal Relations

America is the land of cool friendships; they are often transient; many times they have "ulterior," that is, business, motives; they are multiple and changing.[4] They are the friendships of a *Gesellschaft* urban society; they are contractual, the product of a long history of movement from status to contract. This style of personal relationships has permitted the nation to absorb many immigrants, to pack up and move to the West or wherever opportunity beckoned, to find satisfaction in something less than complete intimacy. Many observers, including many European psychoanalysts, deplore this style and speak of the deterioration of the human community as, in their loneliness, they observe this situation.

But, on the whole, this style seems to support an open democratic system better than the many closed intimate, enduring circles of friendship produced by the folk, or *Gemeinschaft*, way of life. Out of this latter style comes the effort to duplicate the

3. Some of this noncongruence may be due to defective testing instruments. O'Hara, for example, behaves and thinks like a man who does trust others, although his two companions on this low-faith-in-people list do not.

4. Compare Santayana: "The milk of human kindness is less apt to turn sour if the vessel that holds it stands steady, cool, and separate, and is not too often uncorked. In his affections the American is seldom passionate, often deep, and always kindly. . . . His instinct is to think well of everybody, and to wish everybody well, but in a spirit of rough comradeship, expecting every man to stand on his own legs and to be helpful in his turn." George Santayana, *Character and Opinion in the United States* (Garden City, N.Y.: Doubleday, 1956), pp. 105–106.

intense interpersonal relationship on the political plane and to establish a more intense leader-follower linkage. This way leads to charismatic politics, personalization, submission. Eastport's "cool" style makes no headway in this direction. Moreover, the flexibility of political loyalties that permits adjustment to party performance and thus keeps the party in power responsible comes more easily from a set of less intense loyalties to other group members. Sometimes one must break with them. It is not just a parallel verbal construction to say that less intense and intimate personal relations provide less intense doctrinal and ideological commitments. In this way, Eastport's relatively "cool" group and interpersonal life produces the social relationships conducive to an open political system in an open society.

Constriction of Empathy (Moral and Affectual)

How does one "handle" the opponent? What rights does he have? The German people under the Nazis found it easier to accept the persecution of the "opponent" Jew or Pole or subversive not by changing their moral standards so much as by changing the range of people to whom it applied.[5] They could place their targets "beyond the pale" and so keep their standards for their friends. This pattern quickly closes down the number of people for whom a society remains open.

There is a strength in the Eastport style that works against this solution: it involves what we have called the moral incorporation of the opponent, the giving to him of the status of a man of moral character. This makes it hard for him to be made to appear contemptible, and so it becomes harder to adjust easily to his dismissal—hard, but not impossible. The low tendency to blame, the capacity for impersonal explanatory systems that do not ask "who" so much as "what," the tendencies to adjust one's own position in the direction of others' views, all make an opponent more human, more like one of "us," more difficult to cut off from group life.

Yet while this is true, it is also true that there are men now willing to do this to those labeled Communist, and to moral de-

---

5. G. M. Gilbert, *The Psychology of Dictatorship* (New York: Ronald, 1950), pp. 278–280.

linquents; and one can see some men, otherwise kind and gentle, struggling to cut off their sympathies with the advancing Negro. When we observe Flynn suggesting less attention to the race problem or Johnson pleading that they be made to understand how right it is for them to live a life exclusively among themselves, one sees the struggle for empathic constriction. But it is a struggle.

Self-Control and Self-Doubt

Three men, Sokolsky, Rapuano, and Johnson, thought that an increase in freedom would lead people to kill, rape, or steal. On examination it appeared that these were three of a small group of men who worried enormously about their own impulse life: sex, anger, consumption. Worrying about their own capacity to control themselves, they worry about others' capacities for self-control, for each of us is a model of man we use in our interpretation of others. But they were also frightened for what they themselves might do if the laws and rules and sanctions were eased a little bit. They needed the help of a strong external authority; they came close to panic at the thought that it might be removed.

At another point, much later in our analysis, we looked at the way the men coped with the interview situation, with me. We examined their feeling that it was right that they should be expected to have opinions on many public matters, that it was right for government to be concerned with what they thought, that it was right for their welfare to be a crucial concern for a welfare state. Taken all together, with other evidence, we conclude that, by and large, these men accept themselves and esteem thmselves, and take some satisfaction in themselves and their achievements.[6] The picture of the self is a complicated and sometimes contradictory affair, but self-acceptance forms a framework for self-control, not for doubts about self-control. What are accepted are, among other things, one's impulses and appetites. Most of the men in Eastport are reasonably sure that they have themselves under control; they do not need a closed society to bolster their shaky apparatus.

6. This satisfaction with their achievements was noticeably less marked among the three men who feared an increase of freedom. All disliked their work situations or, in Johnson's case, sought work elsewhere of a higher status and greater independence.

B

KEEPING THE SYSTEM JUST

A political system allocates rewards and penalties. The decisions made by politicians and bureaucrats and judges protect some and not others from the hazards of private life. Moral codes and legal codes often get out of phase with one another; time erodes morality, circumstances change it, but the law may not reflect these changes promptly. As the welfare state has grown to maturity, the distributive role of government has increased and the possibility of invidious comparison, jealousy, conflict, and a sense of injustice may have increased as well. It is for the elites, the governors, to keep the law within the community sense of what is just; they must themselves be sensitive to this; they must operate within a framework that is mobile and effective in responding this way. But the public has responsibilities as well; the many parts of this public must have social consciences, concepts of justice brought to bear on public affairs, and they must employ them in such shaping of policy and ordering of direction as they do along the lines outlined in the beginning of the previous chapter.

A sense of justice in public affairs includes (1) a belief that the rules of distribution in the system are "fair," (2) a belief that these rules are followed, and (3) a belief that the following of these rules produces a balance of rewards in society that gives to each person and group his "due." This third judgment involves both what is due to him in charity and what he has earned through merit. These are normative words, and we use them "relatively," that is, not in a natural-law sense, but in the way Eastport or any other place defines them and gives them content. A just society, then, is one where there is no class of men thought to be exploiting others, or plundering from the common wealth, or "living off the fat of the land," or unfairly rewarded for some special leverage they employ, or "getting away with murder," or exempted from the force of a law applied to others. And it is a place where none are thought to be unfairly used, "discriminated against," deprived of opportunities that ought to be enjoyed equally by all, punished for faults not their own, or in any way "given a rough deal." No one can doubt that these are concepts familiar to the public mind, whether it be the mind of the common man or a philosopher-king. And they inform and guide his public judgments. How shall we characterize the formation, nature, and employment of these ideas among the common men of Eastport?

The Cool Moral Climate

"It is better to know what is true than what is good or what is beautiful." Among the premises of the Eastport mind, this one operates to reduce the force of the judgmental evaluative faculties. The low moral tension tends to make room for a host of comments that take precedence over those dealing with the "fairness" of the distribution system or with the merits of a man's rewards. The amorality of these comments is illustrated by the typical phrase "If he can get it, more power to him." The fact of the matter is that there is very little thought devoted to the question posed here: Is the social system a just one? Is the political system just?

Part of this is due to some residue of the traditionalist mentality, highlighted in the case study of Dempsey, revealed in the discussion of the fear of equality, but rarely an important feature of these mobilist, contract-minded men. Partly it is due to the fact that those disposed to be critical are anomic, not systematic, striking out at targets of opportunity, not at systems. They fragment their criticism, as they morselize their concepts, so that it never rises to the level of the social system or the political system. But partly, also, it is due to a set of circumstances that inhibit evaluations of the system in these total terms. These circumstances and the social conscience and social judgments they produce are multiple. Among them is the prevailing view of the self.

An Objective Static Self as a Measure of Society

The self is an instrument, a measure, a model for judging society; what it does to the self becomes generalized and embodied in social judgment. We have said that the view of the self in Eastport is objectified; men tell their life stories with candor but with little introspection, little account of feelings, hardly any reference to good and bad behavior; there is not much on how they have been "badly used" or "given all the breaks" by society. What, in another culture, might have been an exercise in social judgment with the self as the criterion, here has no such theme.

Where in Greece men's concept of themselves involves a rather touchy sense of "honor," and in China moral reputation turns on the complex issue of "face," [7] in Eastport the nearest thing is "status"; this is an individual's reward for achievement. It is easier to provide objective criteria for status than for "honor" or "face." Like the men's account of themselves, the criteria by which status is measured are more objective, involve fewer calculations of a normative nature. And the struggle for status among the common men of Eastport is nothing like so strong as the struggle for honor or face in the villages of the world. Indeed, with a few exceptions, most of the men have given it up. They do not judge society against the standards set by high status aspirations.

This lack of status aspiration, acceptance of their own "station" in life, and satisfaction with the distances they have come is evident in several areas of thought. One is the discussion of freedom: freedom of opportunity occupies only a small portion of this discussion; it is nothing like as important here as it is in the works of interpreters of the American scene. They are more interested in freedom of religion, freedom to buy, and a modest relaxation of the industrial discipline than they are in freedom to get ahead. Their rationale for their own present status includes a heavy emphasis upon their lack of education, something attributable to their parents' lack of foresight and the carefree spirit of a young man hardly related to their own mature selves. But they do not blame society for this. Thus evaluation of the justice of the political system is not heated by embitterment over the failure of the American promise to make every man rich and famous. On the one hand, it is not the system's fault; on the other hand, "We're not doing too badly."

Hostility and anger must be legitimized; that is, for the angry man's sense of well-being he must find a moral reason to justify the way he feels. We have seen how these men feel guilty about their anger; but they tend to deny it ("I blow my top sometimes, but I don't stay angry long") before they rationalize it. In any event, their targets are not social targets; they are personal (Rapuano's apprentice, Sokolsky's brother, Sullivan's shop steward); hence, what rationalizations they use are specific to the personal or work situation, not broadly social. They have no ideological material quickly available to rationalize their anger in social

7. See, for example, Hu Hsien-chin, "The Chinese Concepts of 'Face,'" in Douglas G. Haring, ed., *Personal Character and Cultural Milieu* (Syracuse, N.Y.: Syracuse University Press, 1956), pp. 447–467.

terms. And, however one looks at them, they are not "angries" either in the sense made famous by Osborne in *Look Back in Anger*, and exemplified in what are called Britain's "angry young men," or in Riesman's sense of inner-directed, moralizing, indignant citizens.[8]

The Ungrouped Man and the Nonnormative Style

Groups, as contrasted to individuals, tend to moralize judgments. A deprivation for the individual is a disappointment, a frustration; a deprivation for a group becomes a moral issue, for the group develops norms about its rights, its destiny, its proper place in society, its glorious history. The group has a culture, and cultures are inevitably normative. For the individual to complain about how he is abused seems "selfish"; it sounds like special pleading, a rationalization. For someone to plead the cause of a group, say, the Italians in America, the laboring classes, the Veterans of Foreign Wars, has a generous aspect; it is for others that he is pleading; his words can achieve a noble ring.

Such being the case, the ungrouped aspect of American life, the identity diffusion upon which we have commented so often, tends to deprive men of their moral stance. They cannot easily develop a social conscience on their own, and they are not helped by group life to develop one they can use. By weakening group structures modern society tends to homogenize and to demoralize opinion. The clash of various groups forces each to invoke moral norms in its own defense; where this clash is lost in a broader consensus this pressure to moralize positions is weakened.

Partisanship in Eastport is weak; when attached to party labels men dread it; they fight shy of consciously taking up the part of coreligionists or of members of their own social class. But they also seek consensus on issues; in arguments, as we have seen, they seek some kind of central or neutral ground. This tendency is incompatible with a strong moral stand; once morality is invoked compromise becomes more difficult. The two tendencies are at war with each other and the compromising adjustive tendency is likely to win.

The decline of class feeling and class conflict has deprived these men of target groups; the assimilationist-tolerance-desegre-

8. See David Riesman, *The Lonely Crowd: A Study of the Changing American Character* (New Haven: Yale University Press, 1950), pp. 190–198.

gationist doctrine makes them feel guilty if they attack an ethnic group; the rise of fiscal liberalism to take the place of regulatory liberalism deprives them of the need for economic malefactors (trusts, grain elevators, cartels, "the interests"). The social structuring of group conflict is weakening, and the post-World War II prosperity has removed the crisis atmosphere in which moralized group conflict thrives.

Homogenized Man and the Loose Sense of Justice

In Eastport the emphasis upon education as a solution to so many problems is partly due to a desire to avoid moral judgments. It is a feature of a general view that man is good but sometimes is led astray. And this is consonant, and stems from a broader view that everyone is really basically the same and that everyone is basically "like me." This view of the similarity of mankind has given force to and perhaps arises from the "melting pot" doctrine, a phrase that in itself conveys the theme of complete homogeneity. It is a view that makes the rich and poor similar, not merely in some transcendental sense, but subject to roughly the same emotions and likes and dislikes. It creates a single standard of judgment; the common man must judge the rich by the same standard applied to his neighbors and himself. The rich are seen to be earning their own way just like the common man; the widow on relief is seen as having failed in her duty to be self-supporting just like the middle-class breadwinner. But to be realistic, the moral standards have to be rather loosely fitted, and the level of censure must be moderate—particularly, it seems, for the rich.

The conscience, we said, makes conservatives out of workingmen, liberals out of capitalists. Because it involves a moral incorporation of the opponent, an effort to see how he must feel about the situation, a strong conscience (in this limited sense) does not make men morally indignant, but paralyzes their indignation. They see the other fellow's side too clearly; they understand too much.

A Trusted Government Is Just

There have been times in American history when a substantial proportion of the population had reason to believe that the governments in office were, from their standpoints, untrust-worthy. The Greenback movement, the Populists, the Grangers, the Progressive movements, the Socialists and Communist parties and allied groups were able to muster significant support; their slogans and programs revealed that many men thought that the government was not operated in their interest and that it was not for them. On some occasions they sought greater control over the government through initiative and referendum, through the recall of judges and other officials; distrusting the parties, they voted for nonpartisan elections. And in the municipalities the reform movements were often motivated by a belief in the illegiti-macy of the men in power; they were usurpers. Under these cir-cumstances, the question of the kind of justice to be expected from the political system was a real question, an important one. And the social consciences of the public, no more humane than now but much more articulate, were central to their thinking about public affairs.

How different is the perspective from Eastport today! Elected officials are seen as responsive to the will of the people, that is, the common men of Eastport. Congress is a warm and friendly place for common people to visit; it is not just a rich men's club. The Executive, while occasionally delinquent, is rarely indifferent to the public needs—the needs of the great financial interests are not his principal concern. If there is corruption, it does not damage the interests of the public in any serious way. And even the city governments, viewed as rather mediocre affairs, are thought to be friendly and striving in the right direction. At least in Eastport, the number of cynics about municipal affairs is not large.

The major source of the change is an objective one: the rise of the welfare state. If they think of government as affecting their lives at all, these Eastport men think of it as giving benefits and protections (with the exception of the political alienates, of course). By the change in policy so dramatically effected in the thirties, the government became, with certain residual doubts, an ally, a friend. And even the city governments with their slum-clearing, redeveloping, relief-giving functions (mostly paid for from federal funds) have taken on a more trusted and a slightly more dignified public image.

It is in this framework that one must see the failure to ask the question "Is the political system just?" People do not ask if a benefactor is just. It is the sense of injustice that prompts the question, and in Eastport among the white common men this sense of injustice is, I believe, at an all-time low.

Trivialized Ideals and the Sense of Justice

The development of the concept of justice in Plato's *Republic* is prologue to the portrayal of a utopian communal society. This suggests that if Eastport had a well-developed sense of social justice, a picture of how things ought to be, they would have pieces of a Utopia to fit into place when we turned to that subject. But, of course, they did not. They had not thought about it. When we turn to certain specific ideals, freedom, equality, democracy, we find that the ideas are differentiated, that they are illustrated from life experiences, and that there is some emotional life in their discussion. Yet, somehow, the ideals are denatured, trivialized. Rather than freedom of expression, the common man of Eastport seems to value freedom of purchase. Rather than a view of equality of opportunity for all men, Eastport looks out upon a vista of small increments of income and status for "small people," and loses sight of the general principle in the process. The standards these ideals provide for estimating the justice of society and government are insufficient. But perhaps it is the century we live in: after all, the great revolution of the eighteenth century spoke of "liberty, equality, fraternity," while the great revolution of the twentieth century spoke of "peace, bread, and land."

More than this is missing, however; the shared purpose we spoke of earlier is notably not there. The man of Eastport has no cathedral building in his air space to raise his sense of importance and mission; he is not engaged anywhere in a struggle against want or fear or squalor in such a way as to engage his mind and take him out of himself; he is not, like the Italian Fascists who were his uncles, rebuilding a glorious Roman history; manifest destiny, the conquering of a continent, are parts of a history not quite his own, and anyway they refer to completed tasks. What shall he do that will call out the greatness in him? Against the background of a great purpose, he might measure the political system and say whether or not it is just. But he has no way to conjure up such a vision, and hence no way to take the measure of his society.

C
ENVOI

God made man to be torn between good and evil; Freud made him tensed between impulse and control; Marx made society in a dialectic mold, battling between the thesis of the past and the antithesis of the emerging present; Aristotle opposed being and becoming in fruitful union. It is as though every aspect of the world had two sexes. Or perhaps it is that the physical doctrine of a counterforce for every force, a reaction for every action, dictates this conflict of working opposites.

There is a lesson in this for the study of man in society. So much comment and criticism seem to forget that every position on every issue offers some good at the cost of giving up another. Man and society are in a state of tension by the very nature of things. There is no perfect solution, only an optimum one, a temporary compromise among the things we want. Consider the following tensions:

An ideological commitment gives men a sense of purpose and the criteria for appraising the justice of a society;

> but it poses a threat to the openness of society; it may make tolerance more difficult and adjustment to victory by the opposition harder to effect.

A developed moral code and salient moral sense help society to avoid a materialistic, antihuman culture; they give men a sense of purpose, a reason outside themselves for living;

> but they imply a clash of moralized goals by rigid men who care too much to invoke the canons of tolerant compromise.

Gemeinschaft society, mourned by many observers of mass culture, offers psychic security, warmth, shared purpose, individualized personal relationships;

> but it tends to be a closed society hostile to change; it is incompatible with labor mobility, rapid technological change, economic progress, rational and skeptical mentality.

Individualism, the responsibility of each man for his own fate, produces men with strong self-reliance, independence, capacities for growth in a changing culture;

but it deprives men of a sense of immersion in a purpose outside themselves, of mission, shared goals, community.

A strong equalitarianism levels up the poor, protects the weak, reduces subservience and dependency, encourages brotherhood;

but it inhibits the drive to excel, reduces the rewards for exceptional achievement, runs the risk of monotony and mediocrity.

Democracy and shared power make men feel respected, wanted, make society more stable, make grievances more likely to be heard and heeded;

but they run the risk of stasis, conventionality, lack of initiative, irrationality.

For each social form, a particular range of tensions is set up among the citizens of a society. There are better and worse combinations of stresses and strains, but there is no escape; there is no Utopia. Perhaps in another era, for another group of men, we may achieve a better balance, ease the pain a little. In the meantime, sleep well, you men of Eastport, for tomorrow it begins all over again.

○ ○ ○ ○ ○ ○ ○ ○ ○ ○ ○ ○ ○ ○ ○

Appendixes

APPENDIX A

The Interview Guide

The complete interview guide employed in studying the ideologies of fifteen Eastport men is too long (fifty double-spaced pages) for inclusion here. Instead of this, I have excerpted the most relevant portions, summarizing some of the questions, to help the reader appraise the nature of the interviews underlying the interpretations contained in this book. Questions on the causes of war and poverty and indignation over news events are gratefully borrowed from David Riesman's work; questions on electoral attitudes and participation (mostly omitted here) are adapted from the Survey Research Center 1952 and 1956 election-study questionnaires; many of the questions on work experience and experience with money, as well as on personal qualities, were generously made available for this study by M. Brewster Smith.

SUMMARY OF THE MOST RELEVANT PORTIONS
OF THE INTERVIEW GUIDE

Part One: Images of Politics

I. Policy Orientation
   A. General focus of attention
      1. What do you think are the major problems in America today?
         [For each problem mentioned] What should the government do about it? What should ordinary citizens like us do about it? Who or what is to blame for this situation?
      2. What about the problems facing Eastport?
         [Probes same as above.]
      3. What about the problems facing Eastern State?
         [Probes same as above.]
      4. Of all these problems which do you think are the most important? Why?
   B. Areas of emotional involvement
      1. Have you seen anything in the news in the last two years that has made you really mad?
         [For each event] Why did that make you mad? Was it anybody's fault? Whose? Did you do anything about it at the time? Do you think anything could have been done about it? Anything else?
      2. Have you seen anything in the news in the last two years that gave you great satisfaction?
         [For each event] Why is that? How did it happen? Who should get the credit? Anything else?
   C. Specific policy areas (if not covered in above discussion)
      [Here there followed a series of specific questions generally asking "How do you feel about" or "What do you think of" the following: labor unions, labor-management relations, international affairs, American foreign policy, Russia and Russian foreign policy, corruption in politics, big business, balancing the budget, taxes, the atomic bomb and dropping the bomb on Hiroshima, desegregation in the South and in Eastport, subversives, Senator McCarthy's investigations.]

D. Broad orientation and causal interpretation
1. What do you think causes wars? Will there always be wars?
2. What do you think causes poverty (people to be poor)? Will there always be poverty (poor people)?
3. Generally speaking, what would you like to see different in this country? Why?
4. Would you describe yourself as very liberal, somewhat liberal, somewhat conservative, or very conservative, or none of these? [Note: these terms often need interpretation.]
E. Flexibility
1. Do you often change your opinions on national or international political questions, or don't you change your opinions on political questions very easily?

II. Political Parties (omitted here)

III. Political Leaders (omitted here)

IV. Group Memberships and Identifications
A. Organizational memberships and activity (omitted here)
B. Identification with group and political implications (omitted here)
C. Organizations and political trust (omitted here)
D. The meaning of categoric group memberships
1. What does your religion mean to you?
   a. Is it important to you in your daily living? Do you think about it much? How about prayer?
   b. Does religion help a person to stay honest and keep on the right track, or doesn't it make much difference?
   c. How do you feel about people who belong to other religions? Do you feel that they are a little bit different in any way?
   d. Is it easy to change from one religion to another?
   e. Do you think it helps a man to get ahead to belong to your religion, or doesn't it make any difference?
   f. About the way men think of a person in this community: do you think they think more of him or less of him if he belongs to your religion?
   g. What about the special beliefs of your religion, the "dogma," as it's called, how important is that?

    h. Do you make many friends at church? Do you see them at other times?

    i. Are you active in your church?

    j. Do you think it is possible to have a religious (or Christian) approach to life without going to church?

2. [National origins] What would you say are your national origins? I mean, are you of Yankee, Italian, Irish, or mixed origins, or what?

    a. Do you think it sometimes helps to understand other people if you know what their national origins are?

    b. How do you feel about people with national origins different from yours?

    c. Do you think it helps a person to get ahead in Eastport to be (respondent's nationality group), or don't you think it makes any difference?

    d. How do you think people generally in Eastport feel about (respondent's nationality group)?

    e. Do most of your friends happen to be (respondent's nationality group) or not?

    f. Do you think a person with a foreign-sounding name should change his name if he wants to, or not?

3. [Social class] Sometimes one hears the term "social class" as in "middle class" or "working class." What do you think people mean by that term?
[Probes for income, education, style of life, friendships, "blood."]

    a. Would you say you were upper class, middle class, working class, or lower class? How is that?

    b. How important do you think social classes are in America today?

    c. Do you think it is easy or hard to go from one social class to another? For example?

    d. How would you describe the people who belong to your own social class? To other social classes?

    e. How do you feel about belonging to the (respondent's social class)?

    f. Some people say that the various social classes want different things and come into conflict with one another. How important do you think this class conflict is in America? Have you come across any evidence of class conflict of this kind?

4. Age groups and generations (omitted here).
5. Sex differences (omitted here).
6. Rural-urban differences (omitted here).

V. Political Roles
   A. Citizen
      1. Think for a minute about what an ideal "good citizen" in a democracy would be like. Regardless of whether there is such a person or not, what kinds of things would he do? What kinds of attitudes toward politics would he have? How close do most people come to this ideal? How close do you come to this ideal?
   B, C, D, E, F: Civic leader, Party man, Patriot, Union member, Church member, Congressman (omitted here)

VI. Political Ideology
   A. Democracy
      1. What is your understanding of democracy?
      2. What are the advantages of democracy compared to some other system?
      3. What would happen if we lost our democracy?
      4. What kinds of things would you consider undemocratic? Why?
      5. If there were another war with a threat of atomic bombing of this country, would you approve a temporary dictatorship in the hands of the President?
      6. Do you think democracy creates confusion and prevents important things from getting done? What things?
      7. About the organizations you belong to: are they democratically run? How do you mean?
      8. In general, do you think that the people or the elected leaders are more likely to know what is best for the country? Why?
      9. Democracy, according to some people, means that everyone, no matter how ignorant or careless, should have an equal vote. Do you agree with that?
      10. Some people say that in a democracy most people like to vote for the ordinary man rather than for a

person with greater ability than themselves. How do you feel about this?

11. Do you think it is right for the government to force people to do things against their will? Why?

12. You may have run across the phrase "a government of laws and not of men." What do you suppose that means?

13. What do you think the future of democracy will be in this country?

B. Equality

1. What is your understanding of the phrase "all men are created equal?"

2. In your own personal life, are there some people whom you regard as not equal to you? Who? In what ways?

3. How would you feel if everyone received the same income, whatever his job was?

4. Do you think people generally wouldn't work so hard under these conditions, or wouldn't it matter?

5. Are there any groups in America that you think have too much power? Too little power? [Probes on: minorities, labor, big business, politicians, bureaucrats, etc.]

6. Do you think all races and religions should mix socially in this country? Which ones? Why? Should any groups be kept out of important positions?

C. Freedom

1. What does the word "freedom" make you think of?

2. Some people think there should be more freedom than we have now; other people think there should be less. What do you think? What kinds of freedom?

3. What are the dangers of too much freedom in a country like ours? Too little? What happens when people feel too free?

4. Are there any groups in this country that will go a little bit too far if they have too much freedom? Who? How?

5. Do you sometimes feel that listening to all the different points of view on a subject is too confusing and that you would like to hear just one point of view from somebody who knows? For example?

6. Do you think there is any special way of bringing up

children in a democracy in which there is the kind of freedom we have here? How?

7. Are there any kinds of things you think might better be discussed privately instead of in the newspapers and on the air where anybody can see and hear them? What kinds of things?

8. Some people say that those who talk about "freedom of speech" usually turn out to be radicals of one sort or another. Do you think this is true or not?

9. A famous man once said, "Man is born free and everywhere he is in chains." Have you any idea what he might have meant by this?

D. Government

1. When you think of "government" what do you think of?

2. What kinds of things do you think the government ought to do? Ought *not* to do?

3. What part of the national government do you think is most important: President, Congress, Supreme Court? Why?

4. Would you say you were more interested in international affairs, national affairs, or local affairs? Why?

5. How does the government most affect your life? Work life? Community? What experiences have you had with the government? What experiences have your friends had with the government?

6. Who would you say runs the government?

7. How would you describe a congressman's job?

8. How would you describe a civil servant government worker's job?

9. Do you think there is any difference in the kind of people who work for the government compared to those who work for a large business organization? How is that?

10. How would you describe the President's job?

VII. Social Values: The Ideal Society

A. Utopia

1. What do you think the perfect (society, community, Utopia) would be like?

2. How would people behave there?

3. What would people do for a living? Would they have to work?
4. What kind of government, if any, would there be?
5. Who would run things?
6. What kinds of things that you do now, would you not have to do in an ideal society?
7. Are we getting closer to this ideal society?

Part Two: Participation in Politics

(This part deals with electoral participation, exposure to the media, pressure politics and activism, personal environment and political discussion, and political information. All except the last of these, Section V, are omitted here.)

I. Political Information
  A. Government
    1. Do you happen to know how long the term in Washington is for a senator? a congressman? a Supreme Court Justice?
    2. In your own words, could you describe what the Electoral College is?
    3. Have you any idea how a congressman gets to be chairman of a congressional committee?
    4. What is a presidential veto?
    5. Do you know whether the Supreme Court can declare a law unconstitutional even if the President approves the law?
    6. Does Eastport have a city manager or not?
    7. About how large would you say the city council is in Eastport?
    8. How often do we have elections for city offices in Eastport?
  B. Current events
    1. What has Congress been doing lately? How do you feel about this?
    2. What has the President been doing recently? How do you feel about this?
    3. Have you any ideas on what the United Nations has been doing recently? How do you feel about this?
    4. How about your city government? What has it been doing? How do you feel about this?

C. Persons

  1. Some people get to know the names of their elected officials, while others aren't interested in the names. Do you happen to know the names of the following:

    a. the senators in Washington from Eastern State?

    b. the congressman from your district?

    c. the members of the state legislature from your district?

    d. the councilman in the city council from your ward?

    e. the prime minister of Great Britain?

  2. Would you say that Eastport had a political boss? [If "yes"] What do you think of him?

D. Knowing "the ropes"

  1. If you wanted to get something done in Eastport, like having a traffic light put on a dangerous corner, or having a street paved, how would you go about it?

  2. Do you happen to know anybody with political influence who might help get such things done?

Part Three: Life History and Experience

I. Political History—Topics for Discussion

A. Politics in the parental family and school

  1. Early memories of political discussions in the home or parental politics.

  2. Early parapolitical feelings: "good guys" and "bad guys" in politics, patriotic feelings, fear of police, sense of being underprivileged.

  3. Crystallizing experiences: religious or ethnic conflict, unemployment of father, meeting a "radical," etc.

  4. As teen-ager: who were regarded as "our kind of people," any tendencies toward rebellion, "strange" ideas, etc.?

  5. Education: courses? extracurricular debating? special teachers? reading?

B. Adult life

  1. First vote: special meanings.

  2. Voting history and pattern.

  3. Responses to historical events: depression, New Deal, Spanish Civil War, rise of Nazis, Korean War, World War II, military service.

II. Personal History

A. Autobiography—request leisurely narrative starting with grandparents.

B. Return to salient features systematically:
   Childhood in the home, grammar school, high school, work history, social life, recreation, family life, military service.

C. Focused discussion on [summary of specific questions asked]
   1. Images of parents: good points and bad points, etc.
   2. Power relations of father and mother: who made decisions, etc.
   3. Siblings: nature of relationships, rivalry, etc.
   4. Image of self: pleasures, worries, ambitions, etc.
   5. Relations with parents: discipline, closeness to, etc.
   6. Major problems as child: how live childhood over.
   7. Health and sex: illnesses, sex worries, homosexuality, etc.

III. Areas of Experience

A. Work life
   1. Could you tell me a little more about your job? What kinds of things do you do at the shop?
   2. What kinds of problems come up that you have to handle?
   3. Whom do you work for? Who tells you what to do? How do you feel about him? How do you get along with the fellows you work with?
   4. What do you like about this job? What do you not like about it? Taking it all together, how do you feel about it?
   5. Do you like to "talk shop" when away from the job?
   6. What does the future look like on this job?
   7. Do you feel that you are "cut out" for this type of work?
   8. Have you ever thought seriously about changing to some other kind of job? Under what conditions might you change?
   9. How did you come to be interested in this kind of work?
   10. When you were a child, did your parents have any

special ideas about what you ought to be when you grew up?

11. What do your parents [if living] think of the job you have now?

12. What kinds of work would you like your children to do when they grow up?

13. Does your wife work? What does she do? How do you feel about this?

B. Income and money

1. About how much would you say your present income will be this year?

2. Is this better or worse or about the same as last year? Five years ago? Five years from now—just your best guess?

3. Do you get along all right on this, or do you feel it isn't quite enough to make ends meet? [If not enough] How much more would you need to get along the way you think you ought to?

4. What do you miss most that your present income doesn't permit you to buy? How important are these things to you?

5. What is the most important thing that money can give a person?

6. There's an old saying, "A penny saved is a penny earned," but then again, some people prefer "Easy come, easy go." How do you feel about that?

7. Some people like to take chances: "Win a lot, lose a lot"; other people are more cautious about money. What's your attitude on this?

8. Do you think people who are very rich are happier than people who are just average? Why is that?

9. What do you think is the best way to teach a child how to handle money?

Part Four: Personal Qualities

I. Self-Image

A. How would you describe yourself to someone who didn't know you at all, I mean the way you really are, both good points and bad points?

[Probes on: intelligence, skills, knowledge, temperament,

task orientation, leadership, whether or not he is "lucky," physical appearance, strength of character, anxiety, self-control, sympathy toward others, morality.]

II. Temperament in concrete situations

    A. When you go to a ball game or boxing match, do you get excited? Do you get right in there playing the game in your imagination, or do you stay pretty calm? Examples? [emotionality]

    B. Now, can you remember the last time you lost your temper? What happened? Impatience? Irritability? Tantrums as a child? Reactions to drink? [anger]

    C. Are there any recent events which have made you feel very unhappy and like crying? What was that? [Does he turn to other people, to action, or to solitude when unhappy?] [sorrow]

    D. What about your worries? What kinds of things do you worry most about? Examples? Do you lie awake at night worrying? Do you worry about things that aren't likely to happen? [anxiety]

    E. Some people think they can plan their lives and shoot for long-range goals—like what they will be doing ten years from now. Others, in the words of the song, say "Whatever will be, will be" and take things as they come. What do you think of this? Have you ever made any long-range plans for yourself or for a group of people? How did this work out? [ego strength, external dimension]

III. Social relations

    A. How important are friends in a person's life? How do you mean?

    B. What attracts you in a friend? For example?

    C. How do you choose (find) your friends? For example?

    D. What do you enjoy doing with your friends? For example? Anything else?

    E. Are you the sort of person who has a few close friends, or do you tend to have a lot of friends, or what? Which do you think is better?

    F. Think back to the last time you were out in the evening and had a good time. What was it that made it a good time for you?

    G. Think of the last time you had a bad time and didn't enjoy the evening. What made that evening a bad one for you?

H. If your job made it necessary for you (and your family) to pack up and move to some other city, how would you feel about leaving (your friends) here? Whom would you miss most? Why is that?

I. Think of yourself now in a group of friends. How would you describe yourself: the "life of the party," "a good listener," or what?

IV. Personal Values

A. Now, I should like to find out the things you have found important in life. Many people gradually develop some sort of philosophy of life, a general way of looking at things, though they may not know if they have one or may find it hard to talk about it. I wonder if you can tell me yours? Have you thought very much about such things?

1. What would you say the most important lessons of life have been for you?

2. What makes people happy?

3. What are the things you believe most in, or think most important?

4. What was the most important event in your life?

5. What is the point of living? Why are we here?

6. What kind of people would you like your children to be when they grow up?

APPENDIX B

List of Objective Measures Employed in *Political Ideology*

1. *Liberalism-Conservatism Scale:* A modified four-item version of Richard Centers' measure in his *The Psychology of Social Classes* (Princeton, N.J.: Princeton University, 1949).

2. *Political-Participation Scale:* Six-item scale from Julian L. Woodward and Elmo Roper, "Political Activity of American Citizens," *American Political Science Review*, 44 (1950), 872–855.

3. *Citizen-Duty Scale:* Four-item Guttman scale from Angus Campbell, Gerald Gurin, and Warren E. Miller, *The Voter Decides* (Evanston, Ill.: Row, Peterson, 1954).

4. *Political-Efficacy Scale:* Four-item Guttman scale from Angus Campbell, Gerald Gurin, and Warren E. Miller, *The Voter Decides* (Evanston, Ill.: Row, Peterson, 1954).

5. *Authoritarianism Scale:* Ten-item revised version of the original F-scale employed in Angus Campbell, Philip E. Converse, Warren E. Miller, and Donald E. Stokes, *The American Voter* (New York: Wiley, 1960). It has five reversed items to take account of response set. Unfortunately, it seems to be a less adequate measure of the concept "authoritarianism" than either the original thirty-item measure or a four-item Gutt-

man-scaled version I have employed elsewhere. See T. W. Adorno, Else Frenkel-Brunswik, Daniel J. Levinson, and R. Nevitt Sanford, *The Authoritarian Personality* (New York: Harper, 1950); Robert E. Lane, "Political Personality and Electoral Choice," *American Political Science Review,* 49 (1955), 173–190.

6. *Sex-Tension Scale:* Complete twenty-five item Likert-type scale devised by Harold D. Lasswell and Arnold Rogow (unpublished).

7. *Faith-in-People Scale:* Five-item Guttman scale complete from Morris Rosenberg, "Misanthropy and Political Ideology," *American Sociological Review,* 21 (1956), pp. 690–695.

8. *Dominance Scale:* Eleven items taken from sixty-item Dominance Scale in Harrison G. Gough, Herbert McClosky, and Paul E. Meehl, "A Personality Scale for Dominance," *Journal of Abnormal and Social Psychology,* 46 (1951), pp. 263–269.

9. *Anomy Scale:* Five-item scale taken complete from Leo Srole, "Social Integration and Certain Corollaries: An Exploratory Study," *American Sociological Review,* 21 (1956), 709–716.

10. *Anxiety Scale:* (*a*) Social anxiety, and (*b*) neurotic anxiety: Twenty-four items adapted by David Sears from unpublished scale developed by Seymour B. Sarason and Irving L. Janis.

11. *Ego Strength:* See Appendix C.

12. *Information Test:* See Part Two, Section V, in the Interview Guide. This was scored separately for correctness and certainty for each of the four parts (government, events, people, "ropes").

The following measures were developed through content analysis of the interview material:

13. *Fear of Freedom* (see Chapter 3)

14. *Undemocraticness* (see Chapter 6)

15. *Cabalism* (see Chapter 7)

16. *Political Alienation* (see Chapter 10)

17. *Homelessness* (see Chapter 11)

18. *Localism-Cosmopolitanism* (see Chapter 19)

19. *Moral Tension* (see Chapter 21)

20. *Ideological Bluntness* (see Chapter 22)

APPENDIX C

Ego Strength

The concept of ego strength has two basic elements: (1) ability to control one's own impulses, (2) ability to control (or at least deal realistically with) the environment. My assistant, David Sears, and I devised the following specific items to measure these qualities, judging each man independently on each item, and then providing summary scores for each person for each of the two basic elements:

1. Ability to control one's own impulses
   a. Not hypervolatile; can contain temper to a certain degree, though overcontrol is "suspicious." The point of ego strength is to maximize the use of one's own impulses for one's own good.
   b. Can curb spending impulses.
   c. Can drink in moderation; not tense about the liquor question.
   d. Rare fits of depression, melancholy, moodiness.
   e. Can accept temporary defeat without withdrawing; doesn't give up easily.
   f. In planning one's life, can give up immediate rewards for

long-term ones: can save, put into action long-range voca-
tional or avocational programs.

   g. Can set levels of aspiration to conform with realistic expectations.

2. Ability to control environment

   a. Interviewer estimate of "dominance in interpersonal situations."

   b. Score on "Dominance Scale."

   c. Can deal with authority figures in a realistic fashion; neither
   submissive nor rebellious.

   d. Feels in control of the larger impersonal forces of society;
   does not consider self a helpless victim of the economy but
   rather uses resources to advance own interests; doesn't feel
   unlucky; doesn't feel estranged and lonely; perceives job situation realistically.

Name Index

Subject Index